Modifying Our Policy Toward the People's Republic of China

A Critical Analysis of the United States Government's Policy Toward the People's Republic of China

editor

Scott Deatherage

Director, Northwestern Debate Society
Associate Professor, Communication Studies
   Northwestern University, Evanston, Illinois

327.73051
Mod

National Textbook Company
a division of *NTC Publishing Group* • Lincolnwood, Illinois USA

1946 7

China—Foreign Relations—U.S.

LC 96(1)06404

Published by National Textbook Company, a division of NTC Publishing Group
© 1995 by NTC Publishing Group, 4255 West Touhy Avenue,
Lincolnwood (Chicago), Illinois 60646–1975 U.S.A.
Manufactured in the United States of America.
5 6 7 8 9 ML 0 9 8 7 6 5 4 3 2 1

Contents

Introduction

The 1995–96 national high school debate topic encompasses a significant and clearly defined number of issues for competitors to discuss. The topic wording (*Resolved:* that the United States government should substantially change its foreign policy toward the People's Republic of China) leaves at least two important linguistic and definitional ambiguities to be considered. The whole notion of "foreign policy," for instance, is a complex one, encompassing economic, technical and development assistance, military and security policies, as well as diplomatic measures that can be considered policies. The term is a relatively broad one, easily leaving debaters with a whole season's worth of issues to unpack. Beyond "foreign policy," the boundaries of "China" are themselves at dispute, making the scope of the topic again difficult to determine. The People's Republic of China, established in what is now Beijing, formerly Peking, after Mao lead the 1949 Communist revolution, embodies the vast majority of Chinese people and resources. Mainland or Communist China, as the People's Republic of China (P.R.C.) is sometimes known, is the starting point for America's China policy. However, the P.R.C. ("China") claims the Republic of China—otherwise known as Taiwan, the Spratly Islands, Tibet, and Hong Kong, among other territorial and governmental claims. Taken together, the ambiguities surrounding the meaning of "foreign policy" and "China" should leave literally dozens of major issues to be addressed in this debate season.

SINO-AMERICAN RELATIONS SINCE 1972: AN OVERVIEW

It took the prerogative of a conservative United States President, Richard Nixon, to fundamentally reshape the American relationship with the People's Republic of China. Before Nixon's 1972 communiqué and subsequent visit to the Chinese mainland, official United States policy recognized the Taipei government of the Republic of China (Taiwan) as the only legitimate government for the Chinese people. In the years since Nixon's historic 1972 visit, Sino-American relations have ebbed and flowed. The relationship was initially a warm one; today, it seemingly turns hot and cold on a day-in, day-out basis. Still, despite strategic uncertainties, with responsibility for approximately one-quarter of the world's population, the Beijing government remains a focal point of United States foreign policy.

The near-term course of Sino-American relations is fraught with uncertainties. At 89, Communist Party Chair Deng Xiaoping is near death, and the process by which his successor shall be chosen is unclear at best. Hard-line communists compete with moderate democrats for influence inside the Chinese regime, and scholars of Chinese politics offer widely variant theories about the future of the government beyond Deng. At least four possibilities for post-Deng China have been offered by students of P.R.C. politics. First, the power struggle inside the Chinese government could produce a power vacuum leading to a Civil War among competing factions. Second, much like the post-Gorbachev Soviet Union, the Chinese state may break down, or devolve, into a host of smaller states, some attached to Beijing and others not. Third, some scholars speculate that liberals, like those who led the 1989 Tiananmen Square revolt, could backlash against the authoritarian control of the central government, leading moderate reformists to win the inevitable power struggle and take control of the state. Finally, some argue that traditional ethnic rivalries, represented by regional warlords, will take hold, causing post-cold war conflicts brewing globally.

In any case, the future of the coming succession crisis in the P.R.C. is full of both grave dangers and tremendous opportunities. The foreign policy moves that the United States makes in the years ahead will both influence and be influenced by the ill-defined Chinese government transition process. It is here, in the politics of the inevitable governmental transition, that both affirmative and negative positions must begin if their claims and assumptions are to have sufficient grounding for debate.

Policy changes in the future will occur against a backdrop of major issues. Future U.S. foreign policy objectives must address a wide range of these issues, such as the following: Government human rights abuses, the upcoming (1997) transition of rule for Hong Kong from Great Britain to the P.R.C., trade, patent, and copyright issues to be resolved between Chinese and American businesses, Most Favored Nation (M.F.N.) status for the People's Republic of China by the United States, Chinese economic development—including its transition to a market economy, the role of the P.R.C. in the ongoing renegotiation of the Non-proliferation Treaty, including Chinese arms transfers to the third world, American relations with the Republic of China (Taiwan), and Chinese power projection in Central and East Asia. These, among other issues, will define the scope of Sino-American relations for the foreseeable future.

HUMAN RIGHTS IN THE PEOPLE'S REPUBLIC OF CHINA

Human rights in the P.R.C. can be understood only in the context of the evolution of a dual-track planned and free market economy. After the 1976 death of Chairman Mao, the Chinese government began experimenting with free enterprise. For the first time since the 1949 revolution, local trade was permitted, in fact encouraged, in certain market sectors and in certain regions. In the early and mid-1980s, the government sold off inefficient state-owned enterprises so that today approximately 20 percent of the Chinese economy can be considered legitimately privatized.

Herein lie two crucial issues confronting the Beijing government and, subsequently, U.S. foreign policy with respect to China. With economic liberalization in the P.R.C., demands for political freedom have expanded significantly. Like the history of economic freedom in Eastern Europe and the former Soviet Union, the Chinese have discovered that economic and political freedom are inextricably intertwined. While privatization has led to substantial economic growth, an increase of nearly 15 percent in gross national product (G.N.P.) in 1994 alone, such growth has produced high expectations for prosperity for the nation's peasants. Such expectations sow the seeds of discontent as an overly centralized government faces the difficulties inherent in achieving equitable distribution of wealth and resources in a fast growing economy. Compounding this problem, along the way, new technologies have come to China and, owing to unprecedented rates of economic growth, younger generations of Chinese, particularly those in major urban areas, experience what is commonly known as a *demonstration effect*. That is, they see technology and growth as tied to democratic capitalism and, accordingly, they more intensely question the legitimacy of the central government.

Pressure for political freedom in communist China has been significant since the regime's inception. However, in recent times post-Mao economic reforms have correlated substantially with a rising tide of domestic unrest, which came to a head at Tiananmen Square in 1989. Initially, a small band of college students and young liberal elites began demonstrating for political freedoms on the occasion of the death of a long time activist, Hu Yaobang. When the government threatened a crackdown on the demonstrators, ordinary citizens of Beijing, followed by peasants from nearby villages, and eventually by people from nearly every Chinese province, flooded the Square in support of the demonstrators. By May 5, 1989, the height of the crisis, estimates of participants in the protest ranged from one to three million, far and away the largest populist threat ever faced by the Communist government. In the end, the government employed armed force to quell the rebellion. In the face of heavily armed army infantry, the unarmed protesters were forced to back down. A wave of political arrests followed the Tiananmen showdown.

The Tiananmen Square episode marked a major turning point in the state of human rights in China as well as in Sino-American relations.

China's Coming Constitutional Challenges

Arthur Waldron

As the years of Deng Xiaoping's paramountcy draw to a close, the most fundamental issues facing the People's Republic of China today—official pronouncements notwithstanding—are in essence the same that confronted the USSR a decade ago when Konstantin Chemenko died: namely, regime transition and constitutional structure. Moreover, the manner in which the Chinese solve, or fail to solve, these issues will affect far more than domestic governance alone. The influence of domestic change in China, as in the Soviet case, is bound to spill out, perhaps messily, into the international arena and bring with it either promise or threat to East Asia, all of Asia, perhaps the world.

These facts are worth stressing if only because so many China watchers today are necessarily preoccupied with the short term. When will Deng Xiaoping die? Can Jiang Zemin hold on as general secretary and Li Peng as prime minister? Or will palace politics make a turning, with perhaps Zhao Ziyang, the disgraced reformer, reappearing? But the short-term rearrangements of the current communist leadership—important as they are—can tell us little about the middle and longer term, dominated as it is by the questions: What is the future of the People's Republic as a regime? Does it have a future? And what are the implications of that future for the rest of the world?

China's striking economic progress, and the openness and pragmatism associated with it, are causes for substantial optimism. But the picture is by no means entirely positive. Domestically, none of the basic causes have been removed that produced the democracy movement and Tiananmen massacre of five years ago: neither the grievances of the people nor the inflexibility of the government. Internationally, China's neighbors are increasingly dissatisfied by Beijing's almost total lack of flexibility in dealing with territorial disputes in the South China Sea and Taiwan, and worried by its steady military buildup. It is no exaggeration to say that China's present situation, if it is

Arthur Waldron, Professor of Strategy at the Naval War College and Adjunct Professor of East Asian Studies at Brown University, "China's Coming Constitutional Challenges," *Orbis*, Winter 1995: 19–35.

projected *without change* into the future, must provoke some sort of crisis within a few years: domestically, a major strike, perhaps, in which the regime's survival will depend on the loyalty of this or that element of the People's Liberation Army, or a foreign adventure, such as a serious sea battle in the Spratly Islands, or a combination of domestic and external conflicts.

Yet despite such possibilities, U.S. policy makers can sometimes seem blandly optimistic about both the future of the People's Republic of China (PRC) and of Asia in general. Thus, the complex and potentially destabilizing linkages between economics and politics in the People's Republic of China are summed up by Winston Lord, an architect of policy in both Democratic and Republican administrations, as a matter of "restoring firm foundations for cooperation with China when political openness catches up with economic reform,"[1] as if that process were straightforward or simple. As for East Asia as a whole, another policy architect, Richard Solomon, describes it today as "a region that really is not burdened by major security threats."[2] True, we hear some talk about the need to adjust to China's incipient superpower status— in the next century. But the United States's Asia policy today seems implicitly to assume a stable PRC that will play a more or less positive role in Asia and the Pacific.

Why? The reason is perhaps the same that operated in the Soviet case. It is not that policy makers are unaware of, or underestimate, the difficulties facing China. Rather, they assume, as they did with Mikhail Gorbachev, that the new generation of Chinese leaders will be able to solve them, and do so more or less within the frameworks, domestic and international, with which we are familiar. In short, we assume that China *must* move in the "right" direction, because to assume otherwise would force us to call into question every other aspect of our military and economic strategy.

This optimistic assumption in turn informs our thinking about the whole range of China-related issues. As the Soviet Union did, the People's Republic of China promises to bequeath to its successors a list of difficult, and even explosive, problems in foreign relations. To name but a few: as these words are being written, the future resolution of the North Korean nuclear issue is not determined; the future of Hong Kong is in question; Vietnam and other Southeast Asian countries are drifting into collision with China over territorial claims in the South China sea; relations between Taiwan and mainland China are still threatening; problems with China's Tibetan and Muslim populations are unresolved. How these China-linked problems are resolved will affect other questions at least as important: Will ASEAN become a military bloc? Will India and China compete or collaborate? Will Japan undertake a larger security role in Asia? The common thread in all these questions is that none can be answered except in light of China's future course. More consideration ought perhaps be given to the less optimistic possibilities for that future, and their implications.

POLITICAL CHANGE IS INESCAPABLE

That China has wisely avoided the mistakes of the USSR is close to common wisdom today.[3] Support for the argument can seem very strong. Economics is the main piece of evidence: the USSR that Chemenko bequeathed to Gorbachev was an economic shambles, and Gorbachev has often been criticized for not reforming it before undertaking political changes. By contrast, the China that Deng Xiaoping leaves behind is economically vigorous. But what exactly are the implications for China of this contrast? Is it that China can avoid facing political and constitutional issues, or that doing so will be substantially easier in China than in Russia?

Let us assume that Gorbachev had done what his critics urged, put economics first, and achieved growth comparable to what China has enjoyed. At what point should he than have turned his attention to political questions? Specifically, would a decade of growth in Russia, comparable to what China has enjoyed, have brought him to that point? If the answer is yes (as it really must be), then one can ask how different the results of that political opening would have been? Would prosperity have smoothed the way for continued one-party Communist rule? Or would it—as it seems to do elsewhere—have undermined that possibility? And would resolution of the political issues whose consideration had been deferred—legitimacy, individual rights, and constitutional form, among others—have turned out to be significantly easier? The fact is that while economic development may make political change easier, it also intensifies and deepens demands for that change.

The real lesson of the USSR for China is that political change is both inescapable and bound to be difficult. In the USSR, perestroika was begun and failed; in China, not even economic changes are fully institutionalized, while political change has not only not begun, it has been resisted. For China, the hurdle where the USSR tumbled still lies ahead.

That is true even though what might be called the transition out of communism in the visual and rhetorical realms has already been largely achieved in China. The red flag with five gold stars still flies there, of course, and Mao Zedong's portrait still hangs at the Gate of Heavenly Peace. But the streets and shops of Beijing, not to mention those of the booming south and coast, Guangzhou for example, have lost the socialist character that was once so pronounced. The enterprises are commercial and many are effectively privately owned; the crowds of shoppers dress in fashion; even the style of signs has changed: traditional and modernistic calligraphy instead of the once uniform, red-painted simplified characters on a white background. The same is true of the intellectual landscape: communist ideas are barely visible, except in official publications, and ring false when expressed; they seem out of place in today's China, rather like the occasional poor, stranded statues of Mao Zedong that one still encounters.

But this hollowing out of communism cannot, as some observers seem to expect, itself create a new regime. A functional state requires institutional structures. Moreover, these are not spontaneously generated; they must be designed and built. Yet in China today, what we see is a growing gap between the codified institutional structures of government, and the needs, behavior, and realities of everyday life. Society and government are disentangling themselves and going their own ways, which is not good for either. Society cannot exist ungoverned nor can an economy grow without a legal system, nor, in the end, can a government survive without a social base. Talk of pragmatism, and the use of rhetorical resolutions, such as "one country, two systems," which are the staple both of Chinese officials and optimistic commentators, are simply not sufficient responses to the needs and challenges.

Nor is talk about Chinese nationalism. Some commentators believe that nationalism can function as the glue that will hold the People's Republic together after the last vestiges of communism wither away. This would seem to be at least part of the government's plan as well, for, since Mao Zedong's death in 1976, it has increasingly discarded the rhetoric and symbolism of communism (which was the avowed enemy of the inherited Chinese culture) and embraced instead the idea of China's traditional greatness and its five thousand years of history, most recently even Confucianism.

These expedients, however, are likely to prove inadequate. Like pure pragmatism in administration and economics, nationalism as a unifying ideology will not prove sufficient in politics. China's last hundred years are a story of creating nationalism, to be sure, but an especially conflictual form of nationalism. Far from unifying China, national pride and a shared awareness of the need for national strength have regularly intensified internal political conflict. The political contenders of twentieth-century China have all been avowed nationalists—Yuan Shikai, Chiang Kai-shek, Mao Zedong, even Wang Jingwei. But they have quarreled bitterly about the political expression of that nationalism, be it monarchy, militarism, communism, a constitutional republic, even collaboration or confrontation with the Japanese or Western imperialists. As for Confucianism, it has always served as the moral basis for a system of rule, and not that system itself.

For all its antiquity, greatness, and strength, China is like Italy or Germany in the sense that it is a civilization that has not easily found its modern political form. To be sure, cultural cohesion has repeatedly sustained China when politics failed. But culture or civilization are not substitutes for politics, and the economic and social changes not irreversibly under way in China pose political questions that require answers. As at earlier times in this century, culture provides the materials and sets the limits for the debate about those questions. Any attempt to understand China's future, and its implications for the rest of the world, cannot neglect these large questions of legitimacy and, above all, political form that are once again moving to the top of the Chinese agenda.

How will Chinese attempts to resolve these issues affect their foreign policy and the interests of other states? No question is more important in international relations, yet it is a question that has repeatedly caught the world by surprise, and may do so again. During the 1920s and 1930s, an anti-imperialist China, becoming stronger and more assertive than expected, began the disruption of the Asian order, and of Japan's position in particular, even-tuating in the Pacific War. During the 1950s and 1960s, Asia was again disrupted by a China that had unexpectedly chosen communism and, for a decade, aligned itself with the USSR. These examples may seem like ancient history today, for in its next international incarnation a strong China was cordially aligned with the United States against the USSR. But this association was the product of specific circumstances: first, a Soviet threat that China could not credibly meet alone, hence the imperative to find a great-power ally; secondly, a strong Chinese leadership able to enforce the policy. Today both those preconditions have disappeared, and China is already demonstrating that its foreign-policy agenda does not necessarily match that of its neighbors and the United States. But in making China policy, most states continue to talk and act as if the rather smooth relationship of the late cold war period could still be assumed, and as a result behave rather reactively and passively.

There are, of course, good reasons for that. The most important is the simple fact that because of its size and power, China is not easy to influence. The United States discovered this most recently in the Most Favored Nation (MFN) debacle, but the approach itself goes back much further. Arguably, it was born in the aftermath of the Sepoy Mutiny of 1857–58, when Britain took direct control of most of India and discovered just what a thankless and difficult task it was for a small European state to administer a large Asian society. The idea of dividing China among the powers largely perished at this time, to be replaced by an attempt to support the existing Chinese government while coordinating foreign policies so as to avoid the sorts of rivalries in China that regularly led to the threat of war in Africa and elsewhere. The Open Door notes were part of this general approach, as was the willingness of the powers, in the late 1920s, to accommodate the victory of Chiang Kai-shek's revolu-tionary party, even though doing so undermined treaties and international law.

Pragmatism might dictate such a policy. The MFN confrontation showed that an untargeted attempt to coerce China economically would hurt the United States at least as much. As for military coercion, the American forces that look impressive in the Caribbean or the Persian Gulf disappear in the Pacific; China, moreover, is a nuclear power. But an important assumption lies at the basis of such flexible and accommodating policy towards China, or at least of any belief that will succeed. This assumption is that China, freed of outside interference, will constitute itself into a relatively stable polity, and one that will cooperate with its neighbors, albeit perhaps for its own reasons. Problems have arisen, according to this line of argument, not so much because China had difficulty doing this, but rather because other powers interfered, and thus prevented it. The influence of this approach is still felt today.

WHAT "REVOLUTION" CONCEALS

The notion that China, once free of foreign pressures, will naturally constitute itself into a stable state and play a positive international role is, of course, a very major assumption, but one that, at least in the pragmatic version of the China-policy argument, is largely concealed. It is articulated directly, however, when analysis is linked to the concept of revolution. At least since the 1920s, revolution has been taken as the primary theme in China's internal development. How to respond to that revolution has, therefore, become the primary concern of those who think about foreign policy. Books with the word "revolution" in the title can be read, one after the other, to cover the whole extent of China's twentieth-century history, from *China's Revolution* by Harry Harding.[4] And in official historiography as taught in the PRC since 1949 (as well as, interestingly, in much of historiography as officially presented in Taiwan) the only events that receive sustained attention have been those that mark stages on the road to "revolution." And almost by definition, the concept of revolution posits a brief, perhaps violent, period of transition that ushers in a new regime that is solidly grounded and genuinely stable for the long term—far more so than the regime it displaces.

Until recently, such a concept of "revolution" has played a central role in thinking about China and its foreign policy. The approach has its origin in the 1920s, in the debate about whether or not to embrace the revolutionary Kuomintang, and it was easily translated in the 1940s when the communists became the revolutionaries.[5] In October 1950, John K. Fairbank lamented American weakness in "dealing with the Asian revolution," by which he meant, in effect, accepting and accommodating changes he believed drew on the deepest historical roots.[6] The writing of diplomatic history shared this approach, portraying China's revolution as conclusive, and American policy, therefore, as faced with the choice between accepting it and pretending it had not happened.[7] Policy makers finally embraced it in the 1970s: the diplomacy that began with Richard Nixon was suffused with a sense that, for better or for worse, the People's Republic was China's definitive modem form; the same conviction, perhaps not quite so firmly held, fundamentally orients the policies of the United States and most other countries today as well.

Yet the conviction can no longer seem as clear or obvious as it was twenty years ago, when to query the PRC was to invite not reasoned argument but ridicule or dismissal. The idea of revolution is not what it once was, even as recently as the bicentennial of the French Revolution. As a tool of historiography, the concept is exhausted. A few so-called revolutionary regimes still exist, but new ones are not being built, nor does revolutionary rhetoric retain much of its once powerful appeal. Fundamentally an artifact of nineteenth-century thought, the concept of revolution in fact seems unlikely to survive into the twenty-first century.

Certainly it has far less practical importance than at any time over the last two hundred years. The cultural and political reconstruction of the former communist states ranging from Germany eastward is being based not on revolutionary inheritances but on everything the revolutions sought to expunge. Civilizations like Russia and China are ransacking their cultural attics, looking for the furnishings the revolution drove out of sight, above all for the components from which to construct politics on something other than a revolutionary basis. Often only dimly remembered by the Russians or Chinese themselves, and almost completely unfamiliar to foreign experts, these objects, moved to the floors where previously decor had been strictly socialist, remind us of the possibilities that communism temporarily suppressed.

Students of foreign policy are discovering that this unfamiliar material is what they need to grasp if they are to understand the future of the world. The blissful sweeping simplifications that came with revolution are gone; in the service of foreign policy, as for other reasons, history is being rediscovered and recast. In China, the whole revolutionary tradition, from the 1920s of course, but particularly since the 1940s, is looking increasingly uninformative as a basis for understanding the present. Communism looks to have been a circuitous and ultimately wasteful detour; as it rediscovers the highroad, China is reviving and rebuilding its pre-1949 self.

That pre-1949 China (which is unfamiliar both to Chinese and foreigners) was preoccupied with the same search for a constitutional form that is beginning again today. That search will have important implications for foreign policy.

A TRANSITION TO CONSTITUTIONALISM?

Modern China has a long and well-developed tradition of debate about constitutional forms and attempts to put them into practice, although it is rarely recalled or studied. In fact, the events considered as revolutionary were generally aspects of that tradition. For example, China's revolution of 1911, to which today's Nationalist and Communist regimes look for legitimation (the first directly, the other collaterally), began over an issue of central versus local authority with respect to railway investment. That was fundamentally a constitutional issue, as was the grievance that prompted the unsuccessful so-called second revolution of 1913, which attempted to halt Yuan Shikai's flouting of the democratic constitution. The Nationalist revolution of the mid-1920s was different: it expounded social change and national strength through an avowedly dictatorial system (although one envisioned as transitional, and leading eventually to democracy, in accordance with Sun Yat-sen's ideology). But Chiang Kai-shek's victory did not put an end to agitation for constitutional rule: these demands were taken up by elements in the Kuomintang itself, as well as by the opposition parties, Communists included—demands that led to the democratic constitution of 1947 and China-wide elections the following year. Even the Communist victory did not expunge formal constitutionalism: elections were promised, and the first PRC cabinet had a Communist majority of only one.

Grasping this history puts China's present in a novel light. Not revolution but rather the search for a constitutional order to replace the dynasties has been the most important theme in twentieth-century China's history, and it remains so today. The long personal rule of Mao Zedong and Deng Xiaoping has only obscured this stubborn fact. But when Deng dies, the search for constitutional order is certain to resume, and although the quest may prove as abortive as it did before 1949, its implications for the rest of the world will nonetheless be very important.

In two parts of the Chinese world, Taiwan and Hong Kong, the explicit search for such an order is already well under way. Since the end, in 1987, of the state of emergency in the Republic of China on Taiwan (ROC), the 1947 Chinese constitution, substantially amended, has increasingly become the basis of government there in fact as well as in theory, a process that has raised key questions about Taiwan's future as a "China" or part of China. As for Hong Kong, although Governor Chris Patten's modest expansion of the democratic franchise there evoked bitter condemnation from the Chinese government, Beijing's ultimate response has, if anything, made its problem with democracy worse. PRC law now provides that the existing system of government in Hong Kong, including the elected legislative assemblies, will be dissolved when the PRC takes control on July 1, 1997, which means that, over the next three years, the PRC must draft an entirely new constitution for Hong Kong. What will it be? It is hard to see how Beijing can avoid facing, in one small but important corner of the Chinese world, the issues of legitimacy and governmental institutions that cast a shadow far beyond the returning British colony.

The basic resource in constitution making is usually some form of assembly. Twenty years ago, considering how to deal with the situation that world exist once Mao Zedong had died, the late prime minister Zhou Enlai planned to use the National People's Congress, China's nominal parliament, to consolidate the political succession and re-institutionalize, if not constitutionalize, the PRC government. China at that time lacked a full constituted government, and the Communist Party was so divided as to be incapable of acting in its place. To correct this condition, Zhou planned "to convene the National People's Congress—a body which, in spite of its sovereign status, had not met since the winter of 1964—and present to it a long list of candidates for government office and a twenty-year development program. He also planned a Central Committee meeting, so that those he had chosen for government office could be given the backing of high-party rank."[8]

Zhou died before Mao, so this precise scheme was never followed, and we cannot know how far Zhou intended to go in the direction of constitutional rule. What happened instead was that, although structures of government were reconstituted compared to what they had been after the Cultural Revolution, they were not made constitutional, for ultimate authority found its way, once again, into the hands of a single individual, Deng Xiaoping. But choosing Deng's own successor(s) is only one of the forces propelling constitutional questions to the fore.

Today's China is an immeasurably more complex society than was the one in which Zhou Enlai laid his plans; hence social and economic considerations, as well as those of elite politics, make constitutional questions inescapable. That is evident in the area of relations between the central government and the regions—the very issue that toppled the Qing dynasty. China is more prosperous now than it has ever been, but the central government's budgets are chronically in deficit. The reason is that Beijing draws its revenues above all from state enterprises, and these are mostly in the red. Supplementary revenues come from customs receipts and taxation of major centers such as Shanghai, but nothing like a comprehensive system of taxation exists. Now the central government is attempting to install such a system, but this attempt is eliciting local resistance that has perhaps broader implications.

Throughout history, taxation has repeatedly posed the issue of governmental legitimacy. No one would claim that the government of the People's Republic of China is truly legitimate, at least not by the standards generally applied today. It was created through a military victory a generation ago and has perpetuated itself since then through elite struggle and the laying on of hands: it has never faced any sort of election. So it taxes at its peril those who are not represented. Coexistence between center and regions up to now has rested on a sort of division of property, that is, a tacit agreement about which areas of the economy each will tap for revenue. The largely extra-legal status of the vigorous market economy, moreover, has kept its profits out of state revenue streams. Clearly, something has to be done to put finances in order, but forced recentralization by a weak government carries risks.

The obvious answer is a devolution of power, accompanied by general political relegitimation. Many of the pieces are now in place for such a development. The most important is probably the vigor of China's southern and coastal regions, now more than self-sufficient economically, and also increasingly autonomous administratively. Hong Kong and Taiwan, both outside the jurisdiction of the People's Republic, demonstrate, furthermore, what economic and political autonomy can do for a Chinese territory, while providing economic (and, in the case of Taiwan, potentially political and even military) resources for the coming recasting of China's political system.

One concept of such devolution, so-called *liansheng zizhi,* or federalism, has been present in the Chinese constitutional debate since the early years of this century. The 1924 Chinese constitution, for example, was explicitly federalist in character. Anathema to the centralizers, both Nationalist and Communist, the concept is now being advocated by a number of Chinese political thinkers as the most practical solution both to the domestic problems of center and province relations, as well as Tibet, Taiwan, and Hong Kong,[9]

But although economic development is forcing some devolution in fact today, the idea of genuine and legally sanctioned devolution remains out of the question for China's present leadership. Their defining crisis was the democracy movement and the Tiananmen massacre five years ago, an event that focused a whole series of constitutional issues.

The development of that crisis demonstrated just how ineffective and weak both government and party had become—ineffective because they had failed to prevent the high inflation that stoked the protests, weak because of the great difficulty they had in overcoming them. Although the foreign media focused on Beijing, the protests were nationwide, and they drew many government, army, and party people into their ranks, as well as ordinary citizens. The crackdown was driven as much by the need to reassert central political power over the country as by the immediate imperative of retaking control of the capital.

But like the other critical turning points of the post-Mao period, beginning with the coup against Mao's widow and her followers, the suppression of the democracy movement was conducted in an extra-constitutional manner. This fact was not lost even within the circles of government. During the period immediately before the Tiananmen massacre, a substantial number of the National People's Congress Standing Committee (NPCSC)—nearly a third—were involved in signing petitions calling for the convening of an emergency meeting of the NPCSC, an event known as the "Signature Incident." If it had succeeded, and the NPCSC had become involved in discussions of the grievances of the Democracy Movement and possible ways to resolve the conflict with the government, the dynamics of the confrontation would have changed completely, and it is quite likely that a solution would have been found without bloodshed.[10]

In the absence of such a resolution, of course, the military was the only resource, and it yielded an apparent short-term success: the government survived, the economy did not collapse, and, most important, foreign governments either maintained unbroken their support for Beijing or reaffirmed it after an interval of protest. But this was at best a stop-gap solution that only postponed inevitable change. Today it is becoming increasingly clear that, despite positive economic developments in China since 1989—indeed, to some extent because of them and the aspirations they feed—the massacre cannot be deleted from China's collective memory. There is both a demand, and, more important, the expectation, that before too long the official line will change, the protester's patriotic motives will be affirmed, and the massacre itself disowned.

Like its kindred demonstrations, also known universally by their dates in shorthand—*wusi,* or May 4, 1919, and *wusa,* or May 30, 1925—the Tiananmen massacre or *liusi* (June 4), marked a stage in regime delegitimation that it also accelerated. The *liusi* also demonstrated that even the security forces were not entirely reliable. In May 1989, as preparations for the movement of troops into Beijing were under way, one letter cautioning against the shedding of civilian blood was sent to the leadership by 150 active and retired senior officers of the PLA. A similar letter, from seven senior retired military leaders, is thought to have been sent at the same time. It was reliably reported after the massacre that 110 officers had seriously breached discipline, presumably by refusing to shoot, and 1,400 soldiers had dropped their weapons and left the scene. Twenty-one senior PLA officers were eventually court-martialed, including one general.[11]

THE PERILS OF POLITICAL FAILURE

The perils that a repetition of such an incident would bring to East Asia are hard to overstate. To begin with, no leadership succeeding Deng is likely to have the authority necessary to keep the whole military under control; recourse to force, therefore, may well lead to a split within the army, and perhaps usher in domestic conflict. And even if repression should succeed, it will have a chilling effect on trade and investment, which will further weaken a government that already confronts massive budget deficits.

Hence, many in the Chinese Communist Party and the current PRC government understand both the imperative for change and its inescapability. If a post-Deng leadership acts on that understanding and begins, for example, to enlarge the circle of rulers and systematically to apportion the power now theoretically held at the center, then China may be able to bridge the chasm between the governmental structures it now possesses and those that it needs. Such initiatives will require discarding much of Deng's legacy and will certainly not be unopposed. Their chances for success will be greatly increased if the economy can be kept growing steadily, with inflation brought under control.

But even under ideal circumstances, such a change will not be entirely smooth. There is a moment in any genuine process of reform when the system changes, when real authority passes from the strongman or ruling party into the hands of the people, including the opposition. Such moments can be risky and often highly conflictual—as the gridlock and fistfights in the ROC parliament amply demonstrate.

Furthermore, such transition may fail. The Chinese political situation today is, at root, a product of the collapse in the 1920s and 1930s of China's attempts at democratic and constitutional rule, and its pursuit instead of the largely illusory advantages of corporatism (in the case of the Kuomintang) and communism. What is more, the weaknesses and problems of Chinese society that led to democracy's failure earlier in this century are by and large still present today, which means that if the transition outlined above does not succeed, we could be in for a period of chronic political instability.

Even a China that puts communism behind it and embraces constitutionalism will face serious problems, and these will have important international implications. But they are as nothing when compared to the problems a regime will confront that resists political change, as the current Beijing government is doing.

Earlier in this century, Chinese analysts looking for the causes of so-called warlordism—the military and political struggle for power that smoldered and flamed in the 1920s—found it not in the ambitions of the military but in the failure of civilian politicians. In the 1930s and 1940s, the inability or unwillingness to find a Chinese political structure that could accommodate both Nationalists and Communists brought chronic internal problems, and eventually civil war.

Nor did the victory of the Communists end the danger. Indeed, the substitution of party, and then one-man rule, for any sort of constitutional politics did much to make China more unstable over the longer term, as Mao Zedong himself seems to have realized. The story is told of how, in fall 1973, Mao sent Deng Xiaoping and Wang Hongwen (then a rising young radical politician widely touted as a possible successor) out of Beijing on a joint tour of the country. "When the tour was over, Mao asked the two what they thought would happen in China after he had died. Wang replied that the country would continue to apply the chairman's 'revolutionary line' and would achieve unity on this basis. Deng, shrewder or more honest, said that warlords would emerge and the whole country would sink into chaos. Mao thought Deng's answer the better."[12]

Asked today about China's future, few observers would give Deng's answer of more than twenty years ago. Most are persuaded that the changes Deng has made in China will prove sufficient to spare it that fate, and they may well be correct. But as we have seen, Deng's changes have been almost entirely negative, in the sense that they have removed restrictions, rather than positive, in the sense of creating new institutions. On the political and constitutional side, Deng's decade and a half of one-man rule has to a considerable extent simply postponed the political problems created by Mao's three decades, while squandering the opportunity to make real institutional changes—like those instituted by Chiang Ching-kuo in the ROC—while the strongman can still preside over them. Such reflections come close to forcing an unwelcome conclusion about the future of Asia: that domestic problems in China may lead, not far down the road, to unpleasant international surprises.

SOME SCENARIOS

The most welcome shape for a future China would be one that was constitutional in form and commercial in ambitions. The second characteristic is already evident, particularly in the east and south, and the shift in the economic center of gravity towards the Yangzi Valley may yet draw political power there as well, as it did from the 1920s to the 1940s. Achieving domestic peace in such a China would require some compromise with Muslims and Tibetans, while peace abroad would require a genuine settlement with Taiwan (already advocated by some in the PRC) and a willingness to put aside claims to the South China Sea (this could be done by following the model of the 1959 Antarctic treaty, which simply does not discuss sovereignty). The benefits of such changes would be enormous, and a bold reformer may try to seize them, but opposition from entrenched interests would be massive.

If the next regime in China attempts to continue Deng's authoritarian ways, then some foreign-policy problems will almost certainly get worse. Remember that a small spark can ignite the train that eventually detonates a massive charge; history is full of examples. So suppose that the current disagreement between Vietnam and China over the Spratlys continues. At the moment, neither side shows any sign of compromising. Quite the opposite, each is acquiring the armaments necessary for a military contest. Vietnam, the weaker party, is also acquiring a potential allies through ASEAN. China's calculation seems to be that, in the end, her claims will not be effectively resisted. Vietnam, however, probably realizes that a small increment in military effectiveness will make it possible to interfere substantially with Chinese actions; anti-ship missiles, for example, could prove devastating. If Vietnam and China should come to blows, what will the rest of the world do? ASEAN, quite likely, would tilt towards Vietnam. And the United States? This is not a question to which our current policy provides an answer, because our current policy assumes the question will not be asked.

This scenario is a single example for a whole class, covering most of China's territorial disputes. They share three features. The first is a Chinese calculation that force can be used in a limited or controlled way to achieve an objective, or may not even prove necessary: Vietnam, Taiwan, or whoever, will ultimately prove pliant. The second is a Chinese misunderstanding of the amount of damage a threatened state can do. Vietnam cannot conquer China, nor can Taiwan, or any other power. But modern weapons make it possible for even a medium-rank power to inflict grievous damage on Chinese forces: to sink a naval task force, for example. Such a setback, moreover, might spell serious domestic trouble for the Chinese government at the time. The third is the near-inevitability that other powers will be drawn into such a dispute, through their treaty relations or calculations of national interest. The best way to avoid such dangers is to deter them clearly and early, both through unambiguous policy statements and through providing military counterweights to new Chinese military capabilities.

Deterrence can probably cope with the sorts of problems just outlined: nearly thirty years of peace in the Taiwan Strait, for example, are owed not to negotiations but to a sustained balance of power. Managing the last sort of problem China may present, however, is not even that easy.

The most worrying, and in many ways also the most likely, possibility for China in the years ahead is that power will be contested domestically. Tiananmen revealed the gulf between rulers and ruled in China; candidate and then president Clinton's responses revealed the policy dilemma. As a candidate, he called for support for the democracy movement; as president he has embraced the PRC government more warmly than any president since Jimmy Carter. And he has forcefully articulated the position of the United States that attributes legality and legitimacy exclusively to the Beijing government.

But suppose that government divides? Suppose that the conflict between liberalizers and hard-liners, already under way, polarizes Chinese politics again, and it is not clear who the winner is going to be? What then should the United States do? Do we simply stand aside, even though a liberal victory would be greatly in our interest, while the hard-liners might bring conflict? Do we intervene somehow? Again, these questions have no easy answers, but they should at least be asked.

Any conflict for power in China will see contenders seeking to mobilize foreign resources of all kinds. Some will be economic: Hong Kong and its wealth will come into play, as well as Shanghai and perhaps Taiwan. Some will be technical access to print media, to overseas transmitters, to intelligence—all of these could be provided by neighbors of China, and would play a part in a power struggle. Military supplies might play a role: although China is highly self-sufficient in most weapons, certain systems, such as state-of-the-art aircraft, are largely lacking, and could prove decisive. But the most important foreign resource will probably be recognition and diplomatic support. For most of this century, Chinese governments have vied with one another for international recognition, which they have then sought to parlay into domestic legitimation. Whom will Washington choose if the Chinese Communist Party splits, and democratizers in the south declare hard-liners in

Beijing to be illegitimate? Western powers have confronted such dilemmas in China repeatedly, ever since the first Opium War.

The point here, however, is not to predict China's future but rather to convey a sense of the sorts of questions that we may well encounter, and for which we are, at the moment, almost completely unprepared. Along every dimension, rapid and deep change is under way in China. That includes political change, although for the moment it has been halted. But the experience of the twentieth century suggests that it is irresistible, and, once under way, may be the most difficult to manage. China's neighbors, and the rest of the world, must consider now what sorts of outcomes they would like to see from the process of regime change in China, what tools they have to affect the process, and how those tools should be employed.

INTERNATIONAL IMPLICATIONS

Were China not such an important power, the linkage between its search for a new domestic political order and its foreign relations would not be a matter of such concern for the rest of the world. However, China is very important, not just by virtue of its size and power, but also because of the position it has been given by other powers in the Asian order. Both the pragmatic *laisser-faire* approach of the first part of this century, and the positive assessment of China's revolution in the second, have fed the attitude by which the rest of Asia waits on China, defers to China, and generally expects China to contribute to the solution of problems. Only slowly is the realization dawning that, not least because of its internal political situation, China may itself become a problem.

At the start of this essay, I pointed out that China's current policies, *if projected without change,* will lead to conflicts within a few years—if rapid improvements in military capacity continue, and if solemnly declared policies are enforced in the South China Sea against Taiwan and in other areas. Optimistic Western assumptions about the future are premised on political change that will make China more flexible; this fact should underline the critical importance of domestic developments in China for the peace and security of Asia.

Yet much of what we have said above should indicate just how difficult that domestic change will be. It is not simply a matter of "political openness catch[ing] up with economic reform." Rather it is a matter of recasting China, and giving it what so many thought communism had, namely, a modern form. The list of issues to be resolved is enormous: how to establish legitimacy; how to structure relations between provinces and the center; how to accommodate the rapid southward shift of the economic center of gravity; and how to find work for hundreds of millions of farmers who have left the land, and for tens of millions of highly educated and ambitious urban dwellers. Beyond China proper, the issues are: how to deal with Tibet, Sinkiang, and other areas of culturally distinct population now incorporated in the PRC; how to develop constitutional mechanisms for Hong Kong and Macao, allowing them to retain their present characters, and for Taiwan to associate itself (assuming anyone on Taiwan wants to).

Just to list these requirements is to suggest how unlikely it is that they all will be met. That means that China is almost certainly bound to pass through a period of instability, a possibility to which nowhere near enough attention has been given among policy makers. Even a smooth and peaceful exit from communism in China would require a good deal of foreign cooperation, patience, and delicate diplomacy if regional crises are to be avoided. Consider, then, the burden that a rough, or even violent transition in China would place on the world.

The problems the rest of the world are likely to face with respect to China in the years ahead, then, sound broadly similar to those we now face in connection with the former communist world and the USSR; they are a matter of managing not incremental change, as was expected, but regime transition. It is true that China today has advantages that the USSR lacked a decade ago, but the challenges it faces are substantial nevertheless. In magnitude, then, if not in detail, the forthcoming shifts in China will most likely be comparable to what we have seen in the USSR. And, if so, then China's diplomatic and international role is likely to be as nerve-wracking as Russia's is today. Change in China regularly draws in outside players. We can see that today in the economic sphere, where tens of billions of foreign dollars have spurred much of the recent growth, and where the relatively small number of Chinese companies that are wholly foreign-owned accounts for a disproportionate amount of foreign trade. Earlier in this century, we saw the process in politics as well. The British, and then the Soviets, were deeply involved in the affairs of the warring Chinese political parties from the 1920s to the late 1950s; the United States was actively involved in the Chinese civil war and was used by both sides.

Today, either a real contest for power in China, or a dispersal of power away from the center, would make it difficult for China to play the kind of leading role in Asia that both it and the world seem to expect. For at least a period of time, China's neighbors would of necessity become involved in trying to manage change there in directions they favored. At best they might help in the creation of a constitutional and legitimate Chinese state, willing to put into the past the issues that worry Asia today; at worst they might find themselves confronted with an anarchic China in which the "helpers" competed for influence and economic access—or with a China where hard-liners had won a tenuous victory. As we have seen, such speculations raise a myriad of possibilities. What they share, however, is that they would all be results of regime change. It is time we thought more about it.

MANAGING CHINA

The current situation puts China's neighbors and the rest of the world in a difficult double bind. For short-term stability, the easiest policy is to support the present regime; but for middle- and longer-term peace, it may be in the United States's interest to support regime change. If the post-Deng transition brings a strong liberalizing leadership to power, the difficulty may be avoided. But if that does not happen, then we face unpleasant prospects.

It is often suggested that economic imperatives will keep the temperature of Asian conflicts low. Thus, one can ask hard-line PRC officials when, exactly, the "liberation" of Taiwan would begin? On a day when merchant ships filled the Taiwan Strait, the coast was bustling with commerce, and tens of thousands of foreigners were in China, mostly doing business? The idea of starting a crisis out of the blue seems absurd. Yet history shows that crises do develop, even against the interests of all involved.

China has a great deal to lose economically in any confrontation in Asia. Not only would one series shock bring an anti-Chinese coalition of powers into being, it would also choke off the investment on which China's economic development depends. Were that to happen, a domestic financial crisis might follow from an international confrontation, but whether that would escalate or control the problem is difficult to say.

The conclusion would seem to be that the rest of the world ought to be doing now what it should have been doing in the 1980s for the Soviet Union: considering what course it wants unavoidable change there to take, and what concrete steps it ought to take to influence events. That will demand a cooperative and coordinated policy, for all the powers involved. We are far from having such cooperation today: among the major powers, China policy is fundamentally competitive, and although there is some coordination on weapons sales, economics is a free-for-all. No forum brings all the players together, from Russia to Europe to Japan, and some players (Taiwan most importantly, but also Hong Kong Chinese) are simply excluded from consultations, despite their potentially crucial roles.

Greater coordination of policy, and structures to articulate it, need to be created. The problems they face are enormous: not just the natural desire of states to ride free (as in the North Korean nuclear issue), but also issues of understanding where interests lie (with the current regime? with change?) and developing frameworks robust enough to express them.

Realistically speaking, the work of creating such a structure of consultation and a coordinated policy to deal with regime change in China is unlikely to take place until it is forced upon the world. Not far down the road, it most likely will be, perhaps by problems with the transfer of Hong Kong, or conflict in Inner Asia, or a revival of dissent within China. When that happens, we should be as ready as possible.

NOTES

1. Winston Lord, "U.S. Goals in the Asia-Pacific Region," in Michael D. Bellows, ed., *Asia in the 21st Century: Evolving Strategic Priorities* (Washington, D.C.: National Defense University Press, 1994), p. 9.
2. Richard Solomon, "Post-Cold War Security Structures," in Bellows, ed., *Asia in the 21st Century*, p. 245.
3. With some dissent, see, for example, "Where Russia and China Meet," *The Economist,* Sept. 3, 1994, pp. 20–21.
4. (New York: McBride, Nast & Co., 1912); (Washington, D.C.: Brookings Institute, 1987).
5. A good example is Dorothy Borg, *American Policy and the Chinese Revolution, 1925–1938* (New York: American Institute of Pacific Relations, 1947), which chronicles American dealings with the Kuomintang, while implying strongly that the same mistakes should not be made again; this time we should embrace the (Communist) revolution.
6. John K. Fairbank, "The Problem of Revolutionary Asia," *Foreign Affairs,* Oct. 1950, pp. 101–13.
7. The best statement is probably Warren I. Cohen, *America's Response to China: An Interpretative History of Sino-American Relations,* 2d ed. (New York: Alfred A. Knopf, 1980).
8. Richard Evans, *Deng Xiaoping and the Making of Modern China* (New York: Viking, 1993), p. 201.
9. See Arthur Waldron, "Warlordism versus Federalism: The Revival of a Debate?" *The China Quarterly,* Mar. 1990, pp. 116–28.
10. Hu Shikai, "Representation without Democratization: 'The Signature Incident' and China's National People's Congress," *The Journal of Contemporary China,* no. 2 (1993), pp. 3–34.
11. Michael D. Swaine, *The Military and Political Succession in China: Leadership, Institutions, Beliefs* (Santa Monica, Calif.: The RAND Corporation, 1993), p. 161.
12. Evans, *Deng Xiaoping and the Making of Modern China*, p. 197.

China in 1994

Marking Time, Making Money

David Bachman

Throughout 1994, the Chinese Communist Party (CCP) and the Chinese people waited for Deng Xiaoping to die. Succession and institutionalizing the economic reform process were very much on the agenda. But the repeated stories of Deng's imminent demise (always provoking a report from someone close to Deng saying he was "fine," and the more frequent and emphatic the denial the worse his condition was likely to be) led to a great deal of ideological rigidification and a sense of drift politically and bureaucratically. The sense of drift and ideological rigidity, however, misses a number of significant developments in the last months of *Gotterdammerung.* The tax reforms of late 1993 seem to have stemmed some of the hemorrhaging of central government revenues at the expense of some if not all provinces. The economic bureaucracy was preparing for Japanese style industrial policy. In the political sphere, a new "Shanghai Gang" was rising. And in the realm of foreign affairs, the People's Republic of China (PRC) had finally forced the United States to admit that it could not use trade as leverage against Chinese human rights policy in a year of very active diplomacy.

POLITICAL DEVELOPMENTS: THE NEW SHANGHAI CLIQUE

Deng made a brief appearance at Chinese New Year, and has not been seen since. Chen Yun was no more visible, though Bo Yibo and Yang Shangkun appeared fairly regularly. In a real sense, the successors to the revolutionary generation were finally running the country. While partially inhibited by Deng's declining health, President Jiang Zemin and Executive Vice-President Zhu Rongji undertook a number of steps that bespeak their attempt to ensure the succession around themselves. Two events were particularly striking.

David Bachman, Associate Professor, Henry M. Jackson School of International Studies, University of Washington, "China in 1994: Marking Time, Making Money," *Asian Survey,* January 1995: 37–47. © 1995 by The Regents of the University of California

First, Zhu made an inspection trip to the Northeast in April where he is reported to have fired the Heilongjiang Party Secretary Sun Weiben on the spot. But whether Zhu personally dismissed Sun in a face-to-face meeting or waited until after his return to Beijing and elicited Politburo approval, Sun's removal marks a fundamental change in the rules of the political game. The number three or four ranking leader has never before been in the position to remove Central Committee members from their duties, and provincial party secretaries in recent years have rarely been fired except in connection with factional conflict. Some combination of incompetence, power, and a willingness to try to intimidate other provincial leaders into being more responsive to central directives (kill the chicken to scare the monkeys) lies behind this extraordinary incident but the specifics remain obscure. It does illustrate great power on the part of Zhu—or flagrant incompetence and indiscipline on the part of Sun.

The second development of major note in the political sphere was the addition of Huang Ju, the mayor (and now party secretary) of Shanghai, to the Politburo at the fourth plenum of the Fourteenth Central Committee in September. This means that there are now four Politburo members who have served as party secretary and/or mayor of Shanghai (Jiang Zemin, Zhu Rongji, Wu Bangguo, and Huang Ju), a level of representation for that city not seen since the heyday of the Gang of Four. Moreover, other members of the Politburo are either Shanghai natives or have extensive experience there (Qiao Shi, Qian Qichen, and Zou Jiahua),[1] and former staff members of Jiang Zemin's administration in Shanghai now have important positions in Central Committee organs. While this shared path to the top does not guarantee close personal ties among the four, it does highlight the centrality of the Shanghai experience to the political and economic situation in the country. Wu Bangguo is likely to be named head of the Organization Department (other sources say the Propaganda Department) of the CCP, and he was added to the Central Secretariat along with Jiang Chunyun of Shandong. The addition of two more Politburo members to the Secretariat suggests that body will become at least as important as it was under Hu Yaobang in the early and mid-1980s.

Additionally, the CCP announced that the journal *Qiu Shi* (Seeking facts), which had replace *Hong Qi* (Red flag) as the chief ideological journal in 1988, was slated for termination by the end of 1994. At this time, it remains unclear what will become of its chief sponsor, Deng Liqun, the most outspoken and powerful advocate for using Marxist–Leninist ideological criteria to judge policies and behavior, or whether *Qiu Shi* will be replaced by a comparable, like-minded journal in 1995.

If these were the only major developments in 1994, we might conclude that China's succession looks increasingly technocratic, with coastal elites likely to dominate the political scene after the death of the few remaining members of the revolutionary generation. Shanghai would be powerfully represented as Jiang, Zhu, Wang, and Huang all see themselves playing a major role in Shanghai's economic revival, and are likely to continue to favor its economic interests (even when the Gang of Four were on the Politburo, it could be argued that their political and ideological positions were not supportive of the regional interests associated with that municipality). This prominence and power for Shanghai would appear to be a potential challenge to two groups: the central bureaucratic apparatus, with Li Peng as its champion, and the Guangdong-Hong Kong nexus.

But if this had been all, it could be argued that China's leadership had made some progress in moving away from the ideological concerns of Deng Liqun and the conservatism associated with Li Peng. These developments might not harken any fundamental change in attitudes toward political reform, but they did suggest greater pragmatism. Unfortunately, other developments cast doubt on this somewhat benevolent picture. In September the Central Committee promulgated a 13,000-character resolution on party building that upheld all aspects of one-party rule. While the document did play up internal party democracy more than might have been expected, its overwhelming message was no change from Communist Party dominance. The resolution came after an earlier Central Committee document on moral education in schools (failure to pay teachers their salaries and the increasing burden of school tuition and fees that cuts shorts or prevents rural education may have something to do with the problems of moral eduction). These official statements coupled with continuing human rights abuses and intolerance of societal political mobilization indicate a leadership with a bunker mentality as it prepares for the succession. No leader can afford to appear soft on political opposition or open to political reform that would challenge one-party rule. These ideological developments and the general uncertainty associated with the succession have immobilized many bureaucrats and organization staffs.

But one wonders whether, after the succession is completed, the trends identified in the more optimistic version of leadership developments are the fundamental ones, and the bunker mentality is more reflective of the great anxiety that grips the elite and the party generally as Deng's death approaches. If the leadership can survive Deng's death relatively unscathed, some of the organizational and other remaining elements of ideological rigidity may gradually be eased.

THE ECONOMY

The Chinese economy in 1994 continued its "half empty-half full" characteristics. The GNP continued to grow at double digit rates for at least the third consecutive year, with real growth of about 12% expected. Total trade was expected to reach about US$200 billion, and in recent months a slight trade surplus had appeared. Huge amounts of capital continued to flow into the country but at a somewhat lower rate than in 1993. China now produces 40% of the world's shoes and is the world's largest steel producer. The tax reform of late 1993 and early 1994 has allowed central tax revenues to increase as a percentage of all taxes, and revenues are up in general, but not by more than the rate of inflation. Much more negatively, inflation continues to run at more than 20% and seems unresponsive to the (limited) state measures to try to reduce it to single digit levels.

Up to two-thirds of state-owned enterprises continue to run in the red. Efforts to reform them appeared to have slowed down from a year ago when rapid and forceful measures to reform state enterprises were on the agenda. Again, the question of social stability after Deng's demise appears to be inhibiting decisive measures, along with the continued complexity of the issues involved in state sector reform. State banks continue to provide state enterprises with the bulk of their lending, at negative interest rates. A series of financial scandals, defaults, or just plain large losses have shaken foreign lender confidence in the China market. The Chinese stock markets in Shanghai and Shenzhen have seen a precipitous decline in their share values over the last two years briefly reversed by heavy government intervention (and speculation) and the suspension of new issues on the domestic exchanges. Nonetheless, by mid-October, the Shanghai exchange was falling markedly again.

The most significant economic policy developments of the past year were the tax reform and gradual elimination of foreign exchange certificates (FEC) at the end of 1993. The yuan was devalued by about 60%, and the official exchange rate was set at the swap market rate, about 8.2 yuan to the dollar down from 5.4. A number of reasons can be offered for this change, but the desire to get into the GATT (after January 1, 1995, the World Trade Organization or WTO) was one of them. There is also no doubt that China's trade deficit in 1993 and the existence of the differential between the official exchange rate and the swap market rate, indicating an overvalued yuan, also had something to do with the Chinese decision to devalue and eliminate the FEC.

The tax reforms were potentially the most important economic policy changes of this decade, though their effects are still hard to assess at this early stage of implementation. The most important changes concerned the extension of a value-added tax (VAT) throughout the economy of which the central government would receive 75% and the local level 25%. In addition to the VAT and the greatly increased central revenue resulting from the reform, rates on other taxes were simplified; for example, the income tax on state-owned industrial enterprises was reduced from 55% to 33%, the same rate as that for collective an foreign enterprises in China. In an effort to elicit acquiescence from provincial authorities, the center promised that provincial revenue would not decrease in 1994 from 1993 revenues. Since this deal was struck in the fourth quarter of 1993, there was an unprecedented increase in collections to provide provinces with the highest possible income floor for 1994. But how stable this tax system is and what transition problems it faces are still not clear, and provinces are less than pleased by the division of revenues. Nonetheless, the center has decisively moved to alter center-provincial fiscal relations in ways that run against notions of greatly enhanced provincial power.[2]

But while the tax system has undergone a major change, other promised actions from late 1993 have not been put in place. Though the Corporate Law went into effect on July 1, plans for extensive state enterprise reform have all but disappeared from the agenda over the course of 1994. Difficulties with the Chinese stock markets mean that no new offerings from the state sector will be made, limiting privatization. The fear of unemployment that would result from bankruptcies or layoffs from radical privatizations has also inhibited policy reform as the regime wants to minimize sources of social unrest in what are assumed to be Deng's last months. Inflation is undermining the stock markets, and again the regime is reluctant to tackle inflation seriously for fear of contributing to social unrest as credit is squeezed in the state sector. The money supply is growing rapidly, portending further inflationary pressures.

The state has been unsuccessful in using monetary and banking tools to guide the economy strategically. Instead, the emphasis has seemed to shift to Japanese-style industrial policy through elite bureaucratic organizations at the center. The first industrial policy was circulated in June for the automobile industry. Prior to this policy document, the PRC had suspended negotiations on new joint car ventures for three years and promised not to agree to any new ventures after that time unless the new venture immediately got 40% of its parts from Chinese suppliers.[3]

Industrial policy documents are not new in China, and there was a prior attempt to draft an industrial policy in 1989 that seems to have had no real influence.[4] This time, with the temporary ban on joint ventures and a more concrete document, it appears that the Chinese government is going to make a serious effort, at least in the automotive sector. Given the strains on the banking system and the "policy" loans that keep state enterprises marginally solvent along with the erosion of the job placement system for college graduates, it is hard to see how a truly expert, impartial, and effective industrial policy bureaucracy can be constructed. It is even harder to see what policy tools such an institution or set of institutions will have at its disposal to "guide" industry to seek its dynamic comparative advantage rapidly. Moreover, the more explicit the PRC's industrial policy proclamations and actions are, the more difficult it will be for the PRC to enter GATT/WTO.

There were many cases of industrial accidents, safety violations, and worker activism in Chinese industry, especially in foreign funded enterprises. In fact, the state was forced to insist that all such enterprises would have to have an official government-sanctioned union "to protect the interests of Chinese laborers." The bulk of the problems were with Hong Kong- or Taiwan-based foreign enterprises. With their purpose to utilize cheap Chinese labor, their hard delivery schedules, and small profit margins, these enterprises have heavy work loads and little time to spare on training. They must demand a great deal from their workers or lose business. Worker-management relations are therefore highly confrontational, and the state has stepped in. This may be a major disincentive for low technology, high labor content type ventures in China.

One other economic development is worthy of note. Since late 1992 many proposed foreign invested or funded power plants have been held up over the issues of how much control the foreign investor would be allowed to have and what rate of profit was acceptable. Over the last two years, the PRC has been holding to a tough line on profits in the 12%–15% range. Foreign contractors find this level unacceptable, and little progress has been made in formal, final contracts in what is perhaps the most crucial infrastructural category for China. In November, however, the PRC did sign a contract at a higher rate, but whether this was a fundamental change in the Chinese position or a one-time concession is not known at this time. The power sector is emblematic of problems in agreements on infrastructural construction, and while the issues have been argued most aggressively with power generation, it is feared that they will reappear with ports, roads, and telecommunications, among other sectors. Even as the largest recipient of World Bank loans, mostly for infrastructure, China needs perhaps 20 times more spending on infrastructure than the World Bank provides on a yearly basis to reach its stated modernization goals by the year 2000.[5]

The most common view of the Chinese economy by outside observers is that China faces serious economic problems, with perhaps disastrous consequences unless inflation and uncontrolled growth of the money supply are reined in immediately. If there is one lesson that China teaches the outside observer, it is that it is dangerous to adopt the consensus view. Contrarian strategies are sometimes best. The Chinese economy faces many problems but growth remains robust, and the outlines of what needs to be done are fairly clear in the minds of policy-makers. Fundamental prospects remain positive.

CHINA AND THE WORLD

China pursued an active role in international affairs in 1994, with substantial success. The highpoint, of course, was President Clinton's decision to "delink" China's most-favored-nation (MFN) trading status from human rights conditions. On that basis, there was substantial improvement in U.S.-China ties after a very unproductive start to the year. China was actively involved in affairs on the Korean Peninsula. There were frequent visits by heads of state, and with the exception of its admittance to the GATT/WTO, China's goals were largely achieved.

Prospects for U.S.-China relations appeared bleak early in the year. Clinton's linking of "overall, substantial" progress on human rights to a continuation of MFN status posed real problems in the relationship. After a deep trough in the summer of 1993, there were improvements later that year but positive momentum was not maintained in 1994. China made no major concessions at all on human rights, though in a meeting with U.S. Congressional leaders in early 1994, Jiang Zemin suggested these issues could be discussed. But such a discussion was brought to an abrupt end by several American actions that the Chinese state found provocative. The State Department's annual human rights report painted a grim picture of human rights in China and as always the PRC deemed the report interference in its internal affairs. Assistant Secretary of State for Human Rights John Shattuck visited Beijing in January, and met with a leading democrat, Wei Jingsheng, without informing Chinese officials. Again, this was interpreted as interference in China's internal affairs. When Secretary Christopher traveled to Beijing in March, he was upbraided by Chinese officials who made no concession at all to the U.S. position. U.S. businessmen in Beijing also let Christopher know that they were opposed to the trade-human rights linkage. The visit appeared to be totally unproductive. The Chinese government simply would not be pressured.

The failure of the Christopher trip forced a rethinking on China policy within the administration, leading to the president's formal delinking of MFN and human rights in late May. (Under the Jackson–Vanik amendment, the president is still required to seek a waiver, allowing MFN status for China, which is subject to congressional disapproval. Presumably, presidential determination in favor of continuing MFN will be nearly automatic.) Instead, Clinton suggested that U.S. strategy toward China would be multifaceted, and while human rights remained important, it was one of a number of goals the U.S. had in its relations with China. Engagement on a series of fronts was the rule of the day. In short order, Secretary of Commerce Ron Brown, Secretary of Defense William Perry, and the head of the Defense Intelligence Agency made visits to China; Vice-Premier Li Lanqing traveled to the U.S. in November, and President Clinton and Jiang met in November at the APEC meeting in Indonesia.

With human rights diminished in importance, trade issues and the situation on the Korean Peninsula dominated U.S.-China relations. Washington continued to press China to liberalize its trading practices, protect intellectual property, and do something to reduce the rapidly growing Chinese trade surplus with the U.S. It also headed the working group negotiating China's admission to GATT/WTO and held to a tough line, demanding fundamental institutional changes before China was allowed to join. Many had hoped that China would be a founding member of the WTO when it comes into existence on January 1, 1995, but negotiations broke down late in December.

On the Korea issue, China used its position as North Korea's only possible ally to achieve maximum diplomatic gains with all interested parties.

There were frequent diplomatic meetings among the major players in this confrontation. Beijing did not support U.S. pressure through the United Nations but may have contributed to the deal worked out between the U.S. and North Korea in the summer. South Korea President Kim Young Sam traveled to Beijing in march, and Premier Li Peng went to Seoul in October. Some Koreans were upset with Li being China's official visitor, as two South Korean presidents have visited China over the last two years while the Chinese have only reciprocated with one visit by the premier. In short, Li's visit can be seen as a diplomatic snub, though its results were generally positive.

Li Peng also traveled to Europe in the spring. While his presence elicited public protests on a number of occasions, he also signed more than $3 billion worth of contracts with European firms. In addition to the APEC summit, Jiang Zemin undertook a Southeast Asian tour, with stops in Vietnam, Malaysia, Indonesia, and Singapore, and in September he made a state visit to Russia. Thus, top Chinese leaders engaged in personal diplomacy with leaders of other major world powers and most of China's neighbors. Success generally followed. But diplomacy and threat were less successful on Greater China issues. Hong Kong, despite repeated threats, approved and implemented Governor Chris Patten's political reforms. China said it will undo them on July 1, 1997, but the results of the electoral process were not totally unpalatable to the Chinese government. There was a notable toning down of rhetoric on Hong Kong issues. In the fall, Beijing finally agreed to a deal on financing the new Hong Kong airport, suggesting that China could live with the situation in Hong Kong, at least until 1997.

Japan found itself in the middle of a China-Taiwan imbroglio, and it was perhaps no coincidence that Prime Minister Maruyama canceled a state visit to China scheduled for October. A Diet session also required his staying in Tokyo. Japan initially invited Republic of China President Lee Teng-hui to attend the Asian Games in Hiroshima, as Taiwan was to host the 2002 games. Beijing protested, and Lee was "encouraged" not to attend. However, Vice-Premier Hsu Li-teh, who also heads the Taiwan games organizing committee, did go to Hiroshima. Chinese reaction was predictable, accusing Japan of pursuing a one-China, one-Taiwan policy. In something of a surprise, Japan was not intimidated. Throughout the extended Japanese political crisis, the importance of China to Japan was an article of foreign policy (and economic) rhetoric. In recent months, however, a more assertive view of Japan-Taiwan relations has emerged in Japan.

PRC-Taiwan relations were strained by the robbery and murder of 24 Taiwanese tourists in China in the spring in Zhejiang, along with the deaths of the Chinese crew of the tour boat where the murders took place. The PRC's unwillingness to allow Taiwan officials to participate in the investigation of the crime, and the palpable sense that, at the very least, local officials were covering up some aspects of the case led to a strong reaction in Taiwan.

Tourism declined dramatically in April and May, with the ROC government discouraging tours, and direct investment from Taiwan also slowed down. The issue gradually dissipated but it contributed to the growing, overt Taiwanese nationalism that fundamentally threatens the PRC's hopes for reunification. In regard to that issue, the PRC continued to block ROC attempts to achieve greater international exposure and recognition, though the two sides continued to talk about functional issues.

STATE–SOCIETY RELATIONS

The Chinese state remained fundamentally opposed to autonomous political mobilization in 1994. Early in the year, Wei Jingsheng had been outspoken in his opposition to government policies, and these were widely reported in the international press. International scrutiny also pressured China into providing somewhat better treatment of some of its political prisoners. One of the so-called "black hands" of the 1989 Democracy Movement, Wang Juntao, was released from prison on the condition that he go into exile, and he is now in the U.S. The other supposed "ring leader" of the movement, Chen Ziming, chose to stay in prison rather than leave China. After Wei's meeting with John Shattuck, the government has effectively kept him under control. More people opposing the government's human rights policies were arrested during the summer. Other abuses, such as the removal of organs from executed prisoners for organ transplants, were also reported. In short, there was no change in the Chinese government's basic attitude toward formal opposition to CCP rule.

The state also refined and promulgated its eugenics law that will go into effect in 1995. Among its provisions, it bans marriage between people with "certain genetic diseases" unless they are sterilized.[6] The government has also banned the use of ultrasound examinations of fetuses to determine sex, with girls being aborted most of the time. The implementation of this measure will be problematic. But the reach and control of the government over popular activities continued to shrink, and the quest for wealth and prosperity, among other endeavors, continued unabated. Some estimates now suggest that the floating population is approaching 200 million as peasants seek to escape rural poverty and find the "good life" in the cities. The floating population and the peasantry in general were being blamed for increases in crime and social disorder, most spectacularly in a work called "The Third Eye" supposedly written by a German Sinologist, though his real identity was hard to determine—if indeed this was a genuine book by a non-Chinese.

Education, particularly in rural areas, continued to erode as tuition and fees became too expensive for many peasants. Teachers continued to leave the profession; either they could find more profitable lines of work or they were tired of not being paid for months at a time while local cadres used their salaries for entrepreneurial investments. Students, like the rest of society, pursued materialism with an unthinking zeal. And while it would have been foolish to say otherwise, college students interviewed around the time of the fifth anniversary of June 4, basically supported the government view, or at least suggested that the Democracy movement was ill-conceived. Superficially, and probably temporarily, post-materialist issues of freedom, liberty, equality, participation, and democracy were submerged in an unalloyed pursuit of personal gain.

Perhaps reversing much of recent history, the most politically active segment of society was the peasants. The number of serious disturbances reported in the countryside continued to mount. Despite official policies to the contrary, local cadres continued to impose ad hoc exactations. I.O.U.s continued to be given for grain sales, corruption remained rampant among officials, and the terms of urban-rural trade continued to worsen for the peasantry. All of these factors contributed to many serious outbreaks of rural violence, aimed at political figures or acts of the government. One hint at the extent of corruption was a report in early 1994 that the provincial procurate of Anhui had determined that 300,000 cadres in the province, or 20% of the entire cadre establishment, were involved in corruption.[7]

It is always difficult to assess the popular mood in China; nonetheless, society appears politically quiescent as the succession nears. Concerns are individualistic and materialistic in urban areas. In the countryside the situation is significantly more conflictual, though problems of overcoming the obstacles to collective action over a wide area appear insurmountable to the peasantry. Thus, as 1994 ends, the state is hunkering down, awaiting Deng's departure, while society pays minimal note to issues of succession. The pursuit of wealth continues to generate dynamism in society even if the state is increasingly rigid.

NOTES

1. See Wu An-chia, "Leadership Changes at the Fourth Plenum," *Issues and Studies,* 30:10 (October 1994), pp. 130–32.
2. Information on the tax reforms comes from *China News Analysis,* no. 1519 (October 1, 1994), p. 4; Tsang Shu-ki and Cheng Yuk-shing, "China's Tax Reforms of 1994: Breakthrough or Compromise?" *Asian Survey* (September 1994), pp. 769–88; and Christine Wong, presentation, University of Washington, November 17, 1994.
3. See Foreign Broadcast Information Service, *Daily Report, China* (hereafter FBIS, *DR/CHI*), June 16, 1994, pp. 48–50, and "Slow Car to China," *Economist,* April 16, 1994, pp. 71–72.
4. See FBIS, *DR/CHI,* March 31, 1989, pp. 40–51.
5. *New York Times,* November 7, 1994, C1, C7 (national edition); Asian Finance Survey (inset) in the *Economist,* November 12, 1994; and *Far Eastern Economic Review,* November 10, 1994, pp. 56–62.
6. *Newsweek,* November 28, 1994, pp. 36–37 (Canadian edition).
7. *Far Eastern Economic Review,* January 20, 1994, p. 15.

Hong Kong in 1994

Democracy, Human Rights, and the Post-Colonial Political Order

Suzanne Pepper

Long secure in its identity as an international trading center, Hong Kong seems uncertain in its emerging role as a political city moving ever closer into alignment with contemporary world trends. But for the brief interlude of Japan's occupation during World War Two, the British colony has been insulated throughout the twentieth century from the most unsettling political consequences of those trends. Everyone has also been very clear about the circumstances of its protection and the costs and benefits of life in this particular colonial backwater. Independence was never an option because the territory was never regarded as anything by Chinese. Yet, without Britain's presence, China's communist armies would not have halted their southward march at the Shenzhen River. Any sympathy Hong Kong may have felt for the revolution on the mainland was diluted over time by the generations of political and economic migrants who arrived after the Chinese Communist Party (CCP) won power in 1949. Thus, accommodation, apolitical pragmatism, and a thriving capitalist economy became the hallmarks of Hong Kong life.

Now, with the 1997 transfer to Chinese communist rule less than a thousand days distant, it is as if Hong Kong was rushing to make up for lost political time. A true independence movement is still not possible and self-determination is therefore out of the question, institutions of genuine self-government cannot now be built, social or human rights legislation is long overdue, and communism exists only as a remnant of its former self. Yet, all the major players seem intent on trying to fill these gaps in Hong Kong's political experience with the nearest possible equivalents in one grand end-of-century, end-of-empire finale.

Suzanne Pepper, Hong Kong-based American writer, "Hong Kong in 1994: Democracy, Human Rights, and the Post-Colonial Political Order," *Asian Survey,* January 1995: 48–60. © 1995 by The Regents of the University of California

The quickening pace of political change dominated events in 1994, propelled first and foremost by the culmination of Britain's two-year dispute with China over the structure of Hong Kong's future government. This episode ended not in agreement but with both sides drawing their respective lines in the sand. The British did not retreat and China conceded nothing, applying the same hard line strategy as that used in its concurrent stand-off with the United States over human rights and low-tariff trading status. Consequently, Sino-British relations remain tense, confrontation has overtaken cooperation as the dominant mode in all transitional work, and the prospects for turbulence on the final approach to 1997 appear greatly enhanced.

THE LOGIC OF THE 1992–94 SINO-BRITISH DISPUTE

As the final lines were being drawn between them in early 1994, Britain and China articulated their respective positions with unaccustomed clarity. However different their systems, both are equally adept in the arts of political presentation. Hence, even as their argument degenerated into acrimonious outbursts and sardonic retorts, each side continued to profess itself perplexed at the motivation of the other. Dark rumors were put about of a conspiracy by Britain and the West to use Hong Kong as a base for subverting the communist regime and dismembering China. British spokesmen, in turn, wondered how their "modest" proposals could be so grievously misconstrued. The spring 1994 statements aimed to minimize such gaps between public discourse and political realities.

London's fullest explanation appeared in the form of a parliamentary report issued by the House of Commons Foreign Affairs Committee (hereafter, FAC report) in March. Beijing's answer was presented to the public in statements by China's leading spokesmen on Hong Kong affairs. The dispute and the political reforms precipitating it have been described elsewhere.[1] To recapitulate, the so-called "Patten package" of reforms was introduced in October 1992 by Hong Kong's newly appointed British governor, Christopher Patten. This move represented a unilateral decision by the British government to manage more aggressively the final years of transition to Chinese rule.

Hong Kong's Legislative Council endorsed the overall package, as was customary in the colony, and some items were implemented immediately. Public attention then focused on the electoral reform portion that was to be submitted to legislation in the "new" fashion, for more scrutiny and possible amendment. This procedure was delayed for a year while seventeen rounds of talks were conducted between Britain and China in a futile effort to overcome the latter's opposition. Records of these talks, also published in early 1994, contribute further clarification.[2] Meanwhile, the British decided to proceed without Chinese approval. The electoral reform proposals were divided into two parts and passed into law by the Legislative Council in February and June 1994, respectively. Anticipating this end, China had already begun, earlier than planned, making its own unilateral preparations for the transfer of power. A Preliminary Working Committee (PWC) was created in mid-1993, ahead of the formal Preparatory Committee not scheduled to begin work until 1996. Composed of both Chinese and Hong Kong members, the PWC is a consultative body empowered to deliberate and advise the Chinese government on transitional matters.

The FAC report was issued at this critical juncture to explain how it had arisen and to assess the damage.[3] Considered as a whole, the Patten reforms are actually far from modest. They emerge instead as a concerted eleventh hour attempt to promote the cause of autonomous self-government and Western-style direct democracy for Hong Kong by introducing a comprehensive set of adjustments throughout the system.[4] As to why such concern for democracy was not manifested at some earlier and more opportune date, the report cited only the long-standing British defense, namely, fear of Chinese opposition and lack of popular demand by the Hong Kong people themselves. As to why such an effort is being attempted now, the answer quite simply was that the balance of world power and public opinion has shifted massively against China since the main agreements over Hong Kong's reversion were negotiated in the 1980s. The report cited the "end of the Cold War" and, in particular, the widespread "revulsion" over China's use of military force against unarmed civilians in June 1989 in Tiananmen Square.

The report, together with the records of the 1993 Sino-British talks shows that the British did keep to the letter of previous negotiated agreements and of the Basic Law. The latter was promulgated in 1990 to serve as Hong Kong's constitution from July 1, 1997. The Patten package, however, exploited loopholes and points of silence, especially those surrounding elections in 1994 and 1995, the results of which will straddle 1997. The package was also accompanied by an acknowledged "change of tone and style." The 1992 reforms can now be seen more fully in this context.

BRITAIN'S POLITICAL PROGRAM FOR HONG KONG

Following standard British colonial practice, Hong Kong's government is led by a governor, his cabinet or Executive Council, and the Legislative Council (Legco). By tradition, the latter was an advisory body and both councils were made up of appointed members only. During the past two decades, lower levels of government administration have been developed to the present territory-wide system of districts, led by eighteen district boards that are responsible for various public amenities at the neighborhood level. Two urban and suburban councils have similar responsibilities, which include public libraries, parks, recreation, sanitation, and so on. The first concerted effort to democratize this structure came in the 1980s, with China's sometimes qualified approval. The 1992 reforms accelerated that effort without China's approval. By 1994 all boards and councils (except the cabinet) contained a mix of appointed and elected members, and after 1994 all will become fully elected bodies. The district boards have also already been given greater responsibility and funding for local public works projects and other activities.

The sixty-member Legislative Council will be composed of twenty seats directly elected by geographic constituencies, thirty seats elected by functional or occupational constituencies, and ten seats indirectly elected by an electoral committee. This division was negotiated with China and written into the Basic Law, but the Patten reforms change quite drastically the arrangements for filing the latter two categories. These arrangements will now be used to form the 1995 Legislative Council, which was supposed to have a four-year term of office. The electoral committee responsible for filling the ten seats will be composed of all 346 district board members rather than a complicated mix of appointees, most of whom would not themselves ever have been directly elected under the plan envisaged by the Chinese.

The functional constituencies will be expanded and the indirect method of corporate voting will be replaced by individual voting, which will include virtually all working members of the population. Hence these thirty seats will *in effect* be filled directly, a neat maneuver designed to circumvent China's adamant refusal through lengthy negotiations to allow direct election for more than twenty members via the geographic constituency seats. This will produce a 1995 legislature as close to being fully and directly elected as possible while still remaining within the confines of Basic Law stipulations for the post-1997 government. Equally significant, the Chinese record of their 1993 talks with Britain indicates that the latter tried to win China's approval to use the 346-member electoral committee not only to fill the ten legislative seats but to choose future Hong Kong governors as well. The chief executive would then have become the nearest thing possible to a popularly elected official, given the Basic Law constraint. That law stipulates the same dual use of the electoral committee method but with a very different kind of appointed committee.[5]

Meanwhile, since 1992 the Legislative Council has been moved to center stage of Hong Kong's political life, with its greatly enhanced status and power paving the way for a shift from executive-led government to one with legislative checks and balances. The implication of the Patten program are clear. Its results, now routinely referred to as the "three tiers of government," have been adjusted to root autonomy, if not sovereignty, in the people of Hong Kong with a comprehensive set of popularly elected, self-governing institution from the grass-roots upwards. If the reforms could have been implemented entirely as conceived, they would have been modest only by the standards of those aspiring to direct election of both chief executive and legislature by all the people.

The FAC report cites in 1989 predecessor, which reflected the post-Tiananmen climate of that time. The 1989 report had recommended "full direct elections" for the 1995 Legislative Council, and that "Hong Kong people must be allowed to decide on their own system of government before 1997 as well as after 1997."[6] Clearly, the Patten package derives from a popular British mandate as reflected in the two parliamentary reports.

CHINA'S OPPOSITION

The main question hanging over Patten's program now, however, is whether long-term benefits will outweigh short-run costs. The Chinese "over-acted," say local Hong Kong pundits, and Britain is only worried about it "place in history." In fact, the assumptions underlying the latter claim serve to refute the former. The British are concerned about how history might judge them if they did not make the extra effort to prepare their last colony for self-rule, given the common assumption that Chinese communism is doomed and must soon go the way of its European counterparts. But the Chinese also know they are standing on the precipice, and they know better than anyone the seductive force of "world trends" bearing down upon them. This basic cause of their intransigence is rarely articulated. But then it does not need to be; the underlying argument is well understood.

For China, the action/reaction sequence has become a fact of twentieth century political life. Some dominant or rising foreign model is always being promoted as the key to national salvation. Yet, the consequences of actually attempting such a crash-course emulation of foreign ways and means have regularly been so destructive that the countervailing critique of "mechanical copying" can also be produced on demand. This sequence continues today with the dissident demand for "complete Westernization" and the "neo-conservative" response of the post-Tiananmen regime. China's leaders nevertheless know that the combined internal and external pressures are now overwhelming, and the most they can hope for is an orderly devolution on their own terms. For this, however, they need time, patience, a quiescent population, and a favorable international environment. They need, in other words, something like the combination of circumstances that allowed their old rival, the defeated Nationalist Party, to take refuge on Taiwan, preserve its remaining power undisturbed, revive its fortunes, and reform internally at its own pace.

Chinese leaders thought they had found such a solution in the 1980s, when they could assume they would be inheriting Hong Kong's economic prosperity and apolitical stability to serve as the flagship for China's twenty-first century development. Such was the plan until Governor Patten unveiled his reform program, clearly crafted to exploit the much-proclaimed goal of "convergence" between pre- and post-1997 arrangements by ingeniously slipping Western-style representative democracy into China via the 1997 divide. As one of China's Hong Kong spokesmen noted, the Hong Kong government in 1991 changed the Legislative Council's term of office from three to four years: "The obvious intention was that the Legco elected in 1995 would serve until 1999."[7] At the same time, the entire Western world seemed to be falling in behind the British effort.[8] A new international crusade was in the making and Hong Kong had become one of its causes. The Patten program was thus drawn into the controversy between "Eastern and Western values," which intensified as President Clinton's mid-1994 deadline for withdrawing China's low-tariff trading status loomed. Once the stakes were raised to so high a plane, pitting East against West, everyone had to choose, creating the classic modernization dilemma for those with loyalties on both sides.

Yet however melodramatic the controversy became, Beijing treated the 1992 reform program from the start as a genuine political crisis with all the attendant dangers and opportunities. The danger was twofold: (1) appear weak by conceding a measure of sovereignty to Britain and the people of Hong Kong; and (2) risk a directly elected anticommunist Hong Kong government, which could then set the precedent, serve as an example for other provinces, and risk in turn a chaotic end to Communist Party rule similar to that in the Soviet Union. On the other hand, a threatened government could build strength by standing firm against such provocation. For Chinese leaders, there was only one choice. The gravity of their predicament can be measured in their massive "over-reaction" as they block and counter literally every point on the British agenda.

Lu Ping, the senior Chinese official responsible for Hong Kong affairs, made his first trip to the territory since the Patten reforms were unveiled to deliver China's response personally—and in language as frank as the FAC report he was answering. The historical background giving force to his argument was as usual assumed, but the reasoning drawn from it was otherwise explicit. He acknowledged that some believed Hong Kong's capitalist system could only be guaranteed if China turned capitalist. Chinese leaders were dead set against such a course, he said, for fear of "chaos and disruption to the Chinese economy," which would mean disaster for Hong Kong as well. "Hence, any foreign government of Hong Kong people trying to exert pressure on the Chinese Government will not succeed. . . . I would like to stress that the value of Hong Kong to China has been and will be its economic value. Hong Kong has always been an economic city, never a political city." Declaring that 90% of Hong Kong's people would probably agree that their livelihood was more important than politics, Lu Ping said "there are always a handful who are so naïve as to think that they can turn Hong Kong into a political city in order to influence the mainland in the sense of politics. If that were the case, Hong Kong would be of negative value instead of positive value to China. This is disastrous for Hong Kong."[9]

Accordingly, everyone speaking for the Chinese side has reiterated that Patten's program will become null and void on July 1, 1997. Instead of completing their elected terms, all bodies elected under the new reformed rules will be disbanded and reconstituted along the lines laid down in the Basic Law.[10] The PWC meanwhile has stepped up its deliberations on the complex question of forming a completely new government from top to bottom "in accordance with the Basic Law," when the latter was actually drafted on the assumption of "through train" continuity between pre- and post-1997 arrangements. Increasingly, frequent meetings of the PWC's political sub-group have become occasions for publicizing Beijing's thinking as it enters these only partially charted waters.

Thus, group spokesmen now anticipate the early emergence of a "shadow government" including the selection of Hong Kong's new chief executive by the end of 1996. The Hong Kong Special Administrative Region (SAR) Preparatory Committee, to be formally established in early 1996, will then appoint a 400-member committee to select the first SAR governor or chief executive by year's end. The process will be one of Chinese-style consultation and consensus with the candidates most likely drawn from within the selection committee itself or those closely associated with it, according to PWC spokesmen. The PWC has also proposed that the same selection committee create a fully appointed sixty-member legislature to sit concurrently with the last Legislative Council (to be elected in 1995) during the final months of its tenure (until July 1, 1997). The hand-picked body will then continue in a provisional capacity for about a year, or however long it takes to approve legislation necessary to establish the new SAR government and hold fresh elections.[11]

The Chinese are also extracting a heavy price on nonpolitical matters where cooperation is essential for a smooth transition. Once the two sides agreed to go their separate ways, conciliatory statements from both suggested cooperation would resume to tackle the two-year backlog of work. So, too, did the prompt conclusion, within hours after Patten's reforms were passed into law on June 29–30, of a difficult agreement that had been pending for years on the transfer of military sites occupied by British forces in Hong Kong. But the timely deployment of People's Liberation Army units was probably the chief concern. The Chinese were evidently still hoping for some political concessions, and when none came they blasted British duplicity for trying to de-link political and nonpolitical cooperation.

As the 1994–95 legislative year began, the British sounded alarm bells over the list of unfinished business matters—funding for the new airport, allocation of contracts for a new container terminal, approval for a proposed pension plan, localization and adaptation of Hong Kong laws, extension of air services agreements, immigration, decisions on international rights and obligations, and so on. A breakthrough was announced on the airport financing deadlock in late October, but the Chinese otherwise belittled concern about unfinished business. Meanwhile, they had complaints of their own arising from their demands for sensitive data on Hong Kong's finances, economic forecasts, and civil servants. A dispute that added one more chapter to the historic contest between dictatorship and democracy has thus degenerated into tit-for-tat bickering, the merits of which are increasingly lost on those with most at stake in the outcome.

HONG KONG RESPONSES

To date, Hong Kong has responded to the political crisis with relative equanimity. One reason undoubtedly is that, despite China's fears, Hong Kong is still basically an economic city and the economy has continued to prosper. After the initial shock upon learning their fate in the early 1980s, Hong Kong's citizens took what precautions they could. During the ten years since the 1984 agreement was concluded on China's resumption of sovereignty, the economy has continued to grow an average of 5.5% a year, down from an annual average of 8.5% during the preceding decade, but respectable nonetheless.[12]

It is generally agreed, moreover, that the territory has been able to maintain this record because of the new opportunities for trade and investment in China, which have been reaffirmed since the political uncertainties of 1989. If the economy now seems undaunted at the approach of communist rule, then it is because the integration of the two economies is already well underway with each having become the other's biggest investor and trading partner. Ironically, the same prospect of integration with the mainland that has inspired so much political apprehension has also become a major source of confidence in Hong Kong's future! The balance cuts both ways, however. If Hong Kong benefits from growing links with the mainland, it is also more vulnerable to uncertainties originating there. At midyear Hong Kong's economy was still forecast to maintain its respectable growth rate in 1994 but several major sectors were losing their momentum, including trade where a significant cause was China's current austerity program.[13]

The backlog of transitional work also bodes ill, which is why the business community has persisted in its demands for improved relations with China. Nor did the community as a whole rush to embrace Patten's reforms. Such reserve followed, in turn, from a basic skepticism of democratic reform, apparent throughout its evolution during the 1980s, when business leaders became known for their fear of free lunches. The concept was regularly invoked to symbolize British-style welfare-state democracy or the inevitable economic hazards of too much citizen participation in politics. Hong Kong's experience in this respect might well give pause to those who have turned Marx on his head to proclaim the democratic inevitability of economic development. Nevertheless, fears about popular councils springing up throughout the territory may have been moderated somewhat by the district board elections in September, although no one has yet admitted as much. The firs to be held under Patten's new rules, these elections were billed as a popular referendum on the British reform initiative but moderation governed the exercise in all respects.

Perhaps because 1994 is almost equidistant from 1989 and 1997, the two key dates on Hong Kong's political calendar, the "effect" of each seemed muted. The "1989 effect" dominated formation of Hong Kong's political spectrum, which took shape around the issues of more or less democracy and closer or cooler ties with China. Accordingly, two dominant forces have now taken shape, identified in Hong Kong parlance as pro-democratic or liberal and pro-China or patriotic. Although current statistics are not available, the apparent facts of Hong Kong's political life suggest an unconventional lineup: capitalists have a tendency to ally with communists, middle class professionals are said to favor the democrats, and organized labor is clearly divided between the two.

Several small parties or political groups—another new feature of Hong Kong political life and previously forbidden—have taken their places along this spectrum, and most fielded candidates in the September polls. At one "extreme" is the new Democratic Party (DP) formed in 1994 from a merger of two groups (the United Democrats and Meeting Point with a combined membership of about 800); it maintains a confrontational stance toward China with a platform calling for repudiation of the 1989 antidemocracy crackdown and for amendment of the Basic Law before 1997 to allow full direct election of Hong Kong's governor and legislature, and the direct election after 1997 of Hong Kong's representatives to China's National People's Congress.[14] Standard bearer for pro-China forces is the Democratic Alliance for the Betterment of Hong Kong (DAB) with a membership of about 600. This group was formed after the 1991 rout, when liberals derived maximum benefit from the "1989 effect" ultimately winning seventeen of the eighteen seats contested in the first direct Legco elections. Despite China's opposition to the new rules under which the 1994 polls were held, it permitted supporters to contest with an energetic and well-funded campaign that called upon all patriots who "love China and Hong Kong" to get out the vote.[15]

The DP emerged as the most powerful group in the September polls, winning 75 of the 346 district board seats. But liberals overall captured only 32% of the seats and did not repeat their 1991 landslide victory. If there was a "1997 effect"—deriving from the maxim of "pragmatic" Chinese deference for authority whether or not those holding it are actually liked—this was registered in the improved fortunes of candidates running under the pro-China banner who won 14% of the seats. The real winners, however, were those who shunned party labels altogether. Independents captured 167 seats, 48% of the total.[16]

If these elections were a referendum of Patten's blueprint for democracy, then the results were inconclusive, which is perhaps just as well under the circumstances since it meant there was something for everyone. Voter turnout was acceptable for a low-level municipal election but not impressive. Just over two million registered to vote and 33% actually did.[17] A majority of the voting-age population seemed to justify Lu Ping's faith in Hong Kong as an apolitical city. The large number of victorious independents also seemed to underscore another maxim of Chinese political behavior, namely, the dislike of Western-style partisan politics that accentuates and legitimizes political differences.

Yet among the voting public, liberal democrats remain the strongest force. And if China were to change its mind about direct elections, the pro-China forces too might be able to hold their own in an open contest. This last possibility emerges from a closer look at the independents. District board constituencies are small, averaging about 17,000 people each, and their domain is the mundane world of neighborhood affairs where community ties dominate. Leftists have such ties of long standing in many older working-class neighborhoods, as they do among what remains of Hong Kong's rural population. Analysts calculate that between 110 and 120 of these grass-roots independents can be counted in the pro-China column. Its forces should therefore be able to capture at last three or four of the ten Legislative Council seats to be elected by district board members in 1995 under the new Patten rules.[18]

There is, however, another dimension to China's anger besides the issue of popular sovereignty and the legislative-led system it assumes. This concerns the specific ends to which enhanced legislative powers are being put. The Hong Kong government, after long years of procrastination, is now rushing to translate human rights safeguards into law—adding political insult to legislative injury in China's view. Hence the denunciation of Britain's "loyal members" in the Legislative Council for initiating a succession of such amendments.[19] Most prominent of these members in 1994 were Anna Wa and Christine Loh. From 1995, the custom of appointing legislators will be phased out entirely, but Governor patten has exercised his remaining prerogative to good partisan advantage. Activist lawyers both, Councillors Wu and Loh emerged quickly as leaders in sponsoring initiatives designed to put teeth into Hong Kong's Bill of Rights, which was belatedly promulgated in 1991 also over China's objection.

In fact, Patten also exercised his prerogative to block both councillors' "private member's" bills before they could even to put to a vote. Wu's bill contained provisions for a human rights commission and a tribunal to enforce comprehensive bans against discrimination on grounds of race, sex, disability, age, and sexual preference. Patten cited budgetary considerations but was evidently wary of further antagonizing China. Lu Ping had denounced the legal autonomy of the enforcement mechanism as a "monstrous product" and promised that China would dismantle the commission after 1997. As an alternative, the government announced its own less ambitious package of measures to protect women and the disabled. Loh's spirited defense of an equal inheritance bill was well received by almost everyone except Hong Kong's remnant rural males who lost their traditional right to exclusive inheritance of family land. But her Access to Information Bill ultimately went the way of Wu's effort, and the government similarly unveiled its own alternative, a "code of practice" that is to detail what government information can be made public. Predictably, freedom of information advocates called the new code inadequate for the cause of open accountable government, while Chinese spokesmen denounced it as another unilateral attempt to influence the internal workings of the executive branch that would not be allowed after 1997.

Activists, legislators, and concerned interest groups set the pace. Patten then tries to find a middle ground and China opposes all. The one area where Patten's administration has yet to hit its stride in this respect is the most dangerous, namely, the Hong Kong government's own restrictive legislation designed to maintain political law and order. Upon Patten's arrival in the territory, the Hong Kong Journalists Association presented him with a list of seventeen such colonial-era ordinances, including those dealing with official secrets, sedition, and film censorship; some date from the late 1940s when China's civil war heightened political tensions in the territory. These laws contain sweeping powers to limit freedom of expression and assembly with obvious potential for future abuse. Having seen fit to retain such powers even if they often lay dormant, the government now seems hesitant to amend or repeal them despite Patten's initial promises.[20]

Potential dangers were epitomized by the 12-year prison sentence given to journalist Xi Yang in China for "stealing state secrets." His crime: obtaining and publishing in Hong Kong's *Ming Pao Daily News* (April 4–10) confidential information on People's Bank of China gold transactions and interest rate adjustments. The case provoked another round of protest marches and petitions, but little else. Evidently given China's intransigence, Patten is having difficulty defining a middle course on this most sensitive of issues. Legislators considering the government's proposed amendments to one of the ordinances in June found them inadequate and sent them back for redrafting. By contrast, the PWC after considering the same amendments warned that they would be rescinded after 1997. The original law should not be relaxed because to do so would undermine the government's ability to control public gatherings. Indeed, all such laws amended before 1997 will be reinstated thereafter, according to all Chinese statements on the subject. The amendments, like the structures of elected self-government currently being built, will be treated as illegitimate interventions.

For colonial governors, the end is never easy. Patten presumably will not have to worry about barricades in the streets or guerrillas in the hills. but the chief players, including both patriots and democrats, are making certain that the burdens of his role as the last governor of Britain's last colony weigh heavily upon him. For pro-China forces, the lesson invoked constantly in 1994 was the end-of-empire syndrome, or Britain's alleged habit of leaving its colonies in disarray the better to fish in muddy waters and retain influence after independence.[21] For DP Chairman and Legco Councillor Martin Lee, campaigning to amend draconian colonial laws, the lesson was Britain's "track record" of leaving such laws on the books to be inherited by repressive successors. He cited Singapore's Internal Security Act as the most relevant cases in point. "It could yet be the ultimate irony," Lee wrote, "that after 1997, Governor Patten's fine speeches on press freedom are banned in Hong Kong under colonial laws he himself left in place."[22]

NOTES

1. John P. Burns, "Hong Kong in 1992: Struggle for Authority," and Burns, "Hong Kong in 1993: The Struggle for Authority Intensifies," *Asian Survey,* January 1993 and January 1994.
2. The two sides published their own separate versions of these talks, each blaming the other for failure to reach agreement. Full texts of the British and Chinese versions are in *South China Morning Post* (hereafter *SCMP*), Hong Kong, February 25, 1994 and March 1, 1994.
3. House of Commons, Session 1993–94, Foreign Affairs Committee, *Relations Between the United Kingdom and China in the Period up to and Beyond 1997* (London: Her Majesty's Stationery Office, March 23, 1994). The FAC is empowered only to examine government foreign policy and recommendations are not binding, but in this case, the report served as an authoritative reaffirmation of the British-sponsored Hong Kong political reforms.
4. Given its import, the reform package was of necessity presented in a piecemeal and elliptical fashion, which became a major handicap in garnering local support. A public opinion poll conducted by the University of Hong Kong's Social Science Research Center just before the Legislative Council vote in June found that 90% of 600 respondents did not understand the reforms, making it meaningless to gauge support for them. Respondents did not even know the significance of a fully elected as opposed to a half-appointed legislature (*SCMP,* June 25, 1994). The FAC report, although discussed in the Hong Kong press, was available only on an internal need-to-know basis or by mail order from London.
5. *SCMP,* March 1, 1994; and *Basic Law of the Hong Kong Special Administrative Region of the People's Republic of China* (April 4, 1990), esp. Annexes I, II, and the supplementary decision on forming the first Hong Kong SAR government in 1997.
6. FAC Report, p. xxxvi, para. 126.
7. Tsang Yok-sing, "Futile Efforts of the FAC," *SCMP,* April 19, 1994. Tsang is leader of Hong Kong's main pro-China political party.
8. Some important British voices remained in opposition throughout, however, including two former Hong Kong governors and three former ambassadors to China. Of the five, Sir Percy Cradock was most outspoken, serving as a tireless critic of the Patten reforms (e.g., FAC Report, paras. 160–69; *SCMP,* December 5 and 9, 1993; Percy Cradock, *Experiences of China* [London: John Murray, 1994], part 3).
9. Text of Lu Ping's Hong Kong speech is in *SCMP,* May 7, 1994. Lu Ping heads the Chinese State Council's Hong Kong and Macau Affairs Office and is also a deputy director of the PWC.
10. A decision to this effect was formally approved August 31, 1994, by the Standing Committee of China's National People's Congress (*Renmin ribao* [People's Daily], national edition, Beijing, September 1, 1994).
11. *SCMP,* July 18, September 2 and 8, 1994; October 7–11, 15, and 20, 1994. The Hong Kong government refuses to recognize the PWC's legitimacy and the Chinese have invited no supporters of Patten's reforms to participate in its deliberations.

12. Ian Perkin (chief economist, General Chamber of Commerce), "Economic Notebook," *SCMP,* October 9, 1994.

13. "The Hong Kong Economy in 1994: A Mid-year Review," *Hongkong Bank: Economic Report,* August 1994, p. 1.

14. *Ming Pao Daily News,* (Hong Kong), October 3, 1994.

15. For example, election day editorial, *Wen Wei Po,* (Hong Kong), September 18, 1994.

16. *SCMP,* September 20, 1994; *Ming Pao Daily News,* September 21, 1994. The business-oriented Liberal Party, Hong Kong's largest (1,500 members) has so far not been very successful in trying to define a centrist position for itself. It won only 5% of the district board seats.

17. This was the official tally (*SCMP,* September 19, 1994), which left some questions unanswered as to the actual number of registered voters. All persons over 18 years of age who have resided in Hong Kong for seven years are eligible to vote regardless of nationality. The actual turnout was 693,223.

18. *Ming Pao Daily News,* September 21, 1994.

19. Editorial, *Wen Wei Po,* July 20, 1994.

20. *Freedom of Expression in Hong Kong: 1994 Annual Report,* Joint Report of Article 19 and the Hong Kong Journalists Association, June 30, 1994.

21. A Chinese translation of British writer Brian Lapping's critical book, *The End of Empire,* was published to underscore this argument: *Diguo xieyang* (Hong Kong: Sanlian, 1994).

22. Martin Lee, "Dump This Colonial Baggage," *SCMP,* May 17, 1994.

Taiwan in 1994
Managing a Critical Relationship
Yu-Shan Wu

In 1994 the Republic of China (ROC) on Taiwan was preoccupied with its intractable relationship with mainland China. Economically, the island country was getting more and more dependent on the mainland market to maintain its overall trade surplus and fuel economic growth. This intensified dependence prompted the Kuomintang (KMT) government to seek a diplomatic breakthrough, which strained the already tense political relations between Taipei and Beijing. Related to the diplomatic situation, the most prominent issue in Taiwan's domestic politics was unification vs. independence *(t'ung-tu wen-t'i)*. On all fronts then—economic, diplomatic, and political—Taiwan found its relations with the People's Republic of China (PRC) the dominant issue. These relations were characterized by two conflicting tendencies: economic convergence and political/diplomatic divergence.[1]

INCREASING ECONOMIC DEPENDENCE ON THE MAINLAND

The 1990s were a period of medium economic growth for Taiwan. From 1980 to 1990, the annual growth rate averaged 8.25%, lower than the PRC (10.1%) and South Korea (9.9%) but higher than Hong Kong's 7.1% and Singapore's 6.3%. But in the 1990s Taiwan's economy slowed down to hover around 6% (6.2% in 1994).

At the root of Taiwan's economic problems are rising production costs brought about mainly by surging wage and land prices and increased environmentalism. The controversial fourth nuclear plant in Kungliao is a typical case. The government considered the plant necessary to provide electricity for Taiwan's industrial growth but it was vehemently opposed by antinuclear activists and the opposition Democratic Progressive Party (DPP). The nuclear

Yu-Shan Wu, Associate Professor, Department of Political Science, National Taiwan University, "Taiwan in 1994: Managing a Critical Relationship", *Asian Survey,* January 1995: 61–69. © 1995 by The Regents of the University of California plant's budget was forced through the Legislative Yuan in July 1994, with the usual scenes of legislators getting into fistfights and demonstrators clashing with the police outside the Parliament. Subsequently, the antinuclear coalition gathered enough signatures for a recall vote on prominent pronuclear KMT legislators. Besides the possibility of power shortages, there were concerns about the government's major infrastructural construction plan initiated under former Premier Hau Pei-tsun being scaled down by his successor, Premier Lien Chan. The plan was underfulfilled in 1994 because of land acquisition problems, scandals involving high officials, and financial constraints. The government's commitment to its election promise of installing national insurance in 1995 puts further pressure on the budget and makes public spending on infrastructure a less likely economic stimulator in the coming years.

Taiwan faced several major obstacles to export expansion in 1994. One was continuous pressure from Washington to cut down further Taiwan's trade surplus with the United States. Washington's move to redefine place-of-origin designation on textile products, for example, threatened to reduce Taiwan's textile exports to the American market.[2] In the first six months of the year, Taiwan's products constituted 4.07% of the U.S. market, compared with 4.35% in 1993 and 4.67% in 1992. Taiwan was also threatened by the Convention on International Trade in Endangered Species (CITES) for not coming up with necessary legislation, and not seriously enforcing existing laws to protect wildlife and crack down on trade in rhino horns, tiger penes, and elephant tusks. Last but not least, the prospects for Taiwan to join the GATT and become a founding member of the World Trade Organization grew dimmer toward the end of the year due to failure in successfully concluding trade negotiations with member states and the political obstacles posed by the PRC, which insisted on being admitted before Taiwan.[3]

With a deteriorating environment for investment on the island, and growing obstacles to export expansion, Taiwan saw a steady outflow of its capital toward mainland China. The actual amount of Taiwan's mainland investment is anyone's guess but it may have reached US$20 billion; the official figure is much lower: $10.4 billion from 1991 up to July 1994.[4] For the first seven months of 1994, according to official figures, Taiwan businessmen invested half a billion dollars on the mainland, 31.1% of Taiwan's total overseas investment for that period. If investment in Hong Kong is included (the bulk of which actually went to the mainland), 38.7% of Taiwan's overseas investment went across the Taiwan Strait. The PRC thus remained the major outlet for Taiwan's outflowing capital.

This tendency was undoubtedly reinforced by encouragement from mainland authorities. In March the Standing Commission of the PRC's National People's Congress passed the "Law on Protection of Investment made by Taiwan's Compatriots," upgrading the State Council's "22 articles" of 1988 on the legal status of rules protecting the interests of Taiwan investors. Then, an unprecedented National Economic Working Conference on Taiwan was held April 11–15, with the main purpose of encouraging large-scale investment on the mainland by Taiwan's major business conglomerates. The U.S. decision to continue the PRC's most-favored-nation status in June added to the attractiveness of mainland investment. Worrying about the high security risk involved in investing in Taiwan's arch political rival, the ROC government launched the "southward policy" *(nan-hsiang cheng-ts'e)* in an attempt to reorient Taiwan's outflowing capital toward Southeast Asia. However, few private enterprises followed the government's lead, and Taiwan's overseas investment in Southeast Asia for 1994 was negligible. Fearing that the "mainland fever" may dampen local investment, the cabinet-level Mainland Affairs Council asked the Economics Ministry to require Taiwan companies with mainland investments to make "counterinvestments" on the island. But that proposal was rejected as impractical by the Ministry, which had approved 4,444 product items (half of the total items produced in Taiwan) for mainland investment by the end of October.[5]

As a result, Taiwan exported large amounts of producer goods across the strait, mainly to meet the needs of Taiwan businessmen on the mainland, and by doing so accumulated huge trade surpluses. The first six months of 1994 saw a surge to U.S. $7.5 billion worth of exports to the mainland, 17.3% of Taiwan's total exports during this half-year period. It was further estimated that Hong Kong will soon surpass the U.S. as Taiwan's leading export market. In the cross-strait trade in the first half of the year, exports exceeded imports by a staggering $6.9 billion, or almost three times Taiwan's overall trade surplus in those six months, thanks to the restrictions Taipei put on imports from the mainland. With its trade surplus with the U.S. declining steadily ($2.1 billion for the first half of 1994) and its trade deficit with Japan on the rise (reaching $7.4 billion during the same period), Taiwan's cross-strait trade was the main reason why it did not develop an overall tarde deficit. The booming trade relations with the PRC has become the key to the medium growth of Taiwan's economy. Without the mainland factor, the annual growth rate will certainly dip below the 5% mark.

A vertical division of labor has gradually taken shape between the two Chinas, with the mainland providing cheap labor and land, and Taiwan offering capital, upstream producer goods, management know-how, and marketing. In this context, Taiwan's growth pattern has experienced a fundamental shift. In the past, Taiwan relied on the U.S. market as the major outlet for its labor-intensive manufactures; today it relies on mainland China as the major importer of its producer goods. Taiwan's traditional exports continue to lose competitiveness and market shares in the U.S. and Japan, but the island's trade-dependent economy has been compensated by its surging exports across the Taiwan Strait. This suggests the increasing economic dependence on the mainland market that has haunted Taiwan's political leaders since the late

1980s. In January Economics Minister P. K. Chiang made it clear that links with mainland China are the key to sustaining Taiwan's growth, and he publicly advocated direct transport and investment links.[6] Though Chiang was forced to retract his statement, the already existing cross-strait economic links obviously had created enough pressure to cause the government to rethink its mainland policy.

DETERIORATING CROSS-STRAIT RELATIONS AND DIPLOMATIC COMPETITION

Increasing economic integration between Taiwan and the PRC was a major factor behind Taiwan's "practical diplomacy." The more Taiwan is drawn into "greater China" economically, the stronger the ROC's effort to break its international isolation and seek security from recognition by foreign countries and international organizations. Ideological antagonism toward the PRC by the major opposition party, the DPP, provided an additional reason for the KMT government to distance itself from the Chinese communist regime, that is, it might be accused of betraying the interests of the Taiwan people.

Premier Lian Chan visited Singapore and Malaysia in January to "spend a vacation." This was followed by President Lee Tung-hui's trips to the Philippines, Indonesia, and Thailand during the Chinese New Year festival in February. Lee managed to meet Presidents Ramos and Suharto but failed to talk with the Thai prime minister because of pressure from Beijing. The "vacation diplomacy" was based on Taiwan's $15 billion investment in Southeast Asia, and signified Lee's attempt to reorient Taiwan's overseas investment away from mainland China. The president's venture to the United States did not fare as well, as he was denied entry for an overnight stay in Hawaii while enroute to Latin America. Also on the diplomatic front, French Prime Minister Edouard Balladur visited Beijing in January and, in an attempt to regain lost ground in the scramble for a piece of China's economic action, pledged to stop arms sales to Taiwan. In July Latvia broke its consular relations with the ROC, after receiving very little investment from Taiwan and conducting a much larger trade with the PRC.

The diplomatic competition was accompanied by deteriorating—except for trade—cross-strait relations. In March, 24 Taiwan tourists were robbed and murdered on board a cruise boat on Qiandao Lake, a popular resort in Zhejiang Province in eastern China. Because of the awkward coverup by local officials, the lack of transparency in the investigation and trial processes, and the summary execution of the three suspects, there was an eruption of public anger throughout the island. The DPP attacked the Taiwan government and Straits Exchange Foundation (SEF) officials for their incompetence, and whipped up anti-China feeling among the population. As a result, cross-strait educational and cultural exchanges were suspended, Taiwan officials stopped reviewing permissible import items from the mainland and investment projects there, and travel agencies organized a boycott on mainland tours.

However, these "sanctions" did not last long, as Taiwan was really not in a position to cut economic ties with the PRC, the tourist agencies could not afford to terminate the mainland tours that had been their most important source of profits, and suspending cultural exchanges did not make much sense once economic and tourist links were restored. But although the sanctions were lifted by the end of July, popular resentment was so strong that the support rate for unification dropped from 27.4% to 20.8% and those uncertain about the ultimate fate of the country rose from 32.2% to 43.1%.[7] According to the Taiwan Gallup, the pro-independence support rate jumped to an unprecedented 27% after the incident.

Cross-strait relations were further strained when the PRC conducted four military maneuvers from August to November on its southeastern coast near Taiwan.[8] During these months, the ROC made its second bid for United Nations' membership, a move easily thwarted by the PRC in the U.N. General Committee where Beijing's allies managed to exclude the issue from the General Assembly agenda. The Clinton administration failed to elevate relations with Taiwan except for some symbolic gestures, such as allowing Taiwan to change the name of its mission in Washington from the "Coordination Council for North American Affairs" to the "Taipei Economic and Cultural Representative Office" and allowing officials from the American Institute in Taiwan to visit the ROC's Foreign Ministry.

This was the first time that the U.S. had revamped its awkward rules governing its "unofficial relations" with Taiwan since Washington recognized Beijing in 1979. The expectation that Great Britain might take substantial measures toward normalizing its ties with Taiwan failed to materialize, despite all the recommendations in that direction by the British Parliament's select committees on foreign affairs. Neither did Taiwan fare well in its attempt at a breakthrough in relations with Japan. The Olympic Council of Asia originally invited President Lee to the opening ceremony of the Asian Games in Hiroshima in October. This incurred strong protest from Beijing, and Taiwan in the end was able to send only Vice-Premier Hsu-Li-teh to attend the games in an unofficial capacity. In November, the Asia Pacific Economic Cooperation (APEC) forum failed to invite Lee to the leadership summit in Indonesia, disappointing the president's advisors who had hoped to reap some political gains from Taiwan's southward policy. All these frustrations added to Taiwan's grievances against the mainland.

Negotiations between the SEF and its mainland counterpart, the Association for Relations Across the Taiwan Strait (ARATS), produced little in this poisoned political environment. The euphoria accompanying the historic Singapore meeting between the chairmen of the two organizations, Koo Cheng-fu and Wang Daohan, in April 1993 has evaporated. The talks between Chiao

Jen-ho, SEF's general secretary, and Tang Shubei, vice-chairman of ARATS, in August produced nothing more than a joint statement. On September 30, President Lee ventured an overture to the mainland, expressing his desire to meet his mainland counterpart on an international occasion, such as the Asian Games or the APEC summit. The purpose of such a meeting would clearly not be to reach substantial agreement, but for Taiwan to take part in international activities and demonstrate to the world that the two parties are equal, and that the ROC on Taiwan is a separate policy entity from the PRC. Beijing responded by welcoming the proposed meeting but rejected its international dimension, arguing that negotiation between the mainland and Taiwan is a domestic affair and should be held in Chinese territory. The cross-strait relations remained strained.

DOMESTIC POLITICS: THE KMT'S TWO-FRONT BATTLES

Taiwan saw President Lee consolidating his power in the KMT in 1994 but accompanying this development were mounting challenges to the ruling party from both the DPP and the New Party (NP) founded in 1993. Stimulated by the tense political relations between Taiwan and the mainland over the year and whipped up by politicians seeking political points, the unification vs. independence issue and other forms of subethnic politics reemerged in the year-end election, disillusioning optimists who had predicted that democratic reforms would defuse subethnic tension on the island.

The 1993 year-end election of city mayors and county magistrates were a big disappointment for the opposition DPP. Though garnering a larger share of popular vote than in 1989 (from 38.3% to 41%), the DPP seats dropped from seven to six, well short of the expected eleven. Party Chairman Hsu Hsin-liang resigned over his undelivered promise and was replaced by Shih Ming-teh. On the other hand, the KMT found itself emerging unscathed from dismal pre-election predictions, thanks to active campaigning by President Lee for the party's candidates. It was widely considered that Lee saved the KMT through his personal popularity, and this further strengthened his position in the party.

The KMT's mainstream faction that had supported the president then clamored for an expansion of his power. On December 30, 1993, just before three security and personnel agencies under the president's control saw their mandates expire, the KMT forced necessary organizational bills to retain the agencies through the Legislative Yuan. The ROC Constitution is unclear as to whether executive power ultimately resides in the premier or the president, but the retention of the three presidential agencies tilted the balance of power in the president's favor. Another important development along this line was the KMT-dominated National Assembly's approval of ten amendments to the Constitution in July after a three-month session filled with heated debate, filibusters, walkouts, and at times fistfights. One of the amendments provides for direct popular election of Taiwan's President; another stipulates the President's authority to appoint and dismiss officials without the prime minister's countersignatures. These were great expansions of the President's constitutional power, and created an unambiguous presidential system.[9]

Though Lee Teng-hui had consolidated his power in the KMT, the challenge from the DPP and the New Party became stronger. The NP splintered from the nonmainstream faction of the KMT early in 1993 after the fall of Premier Hau Pei-tsun, who was the last rallying point for the conservatives in the party. On Taiwan's political spectrum, the NP stood for the ideals of Chinese nationalism, the KMT took a Taiwan-first approach under the ROC constitutional structure, while the DPP advocated Taiwan independence and a new nation. With the NP gradually gaining strength and competing with the KMT for the latter's constituencies, the ruling party for the first time found itself facing a genuine two-front battle in the elections.

The emergence of the tri-party system, however, was not evident on the local level. On January 29, 1994, the KMT won an overwhelming victory in local elections for city and county councils, and mayors and executive chiefs of small cities, townships, and villages. In the councils, the ruling KMT secured 67.4% of the seats, compared with the DPP's 7.4% and the NP's 1%; for mayors and executive chiefs, the KMT won 82.2% vis-à-vis the DPP's 10.7%. Another round of local elections on July 16 saw the KMT garner 3,040 village and borough chiefs compared with the DPP's 64 and the NP's two, and 1,841 KMT representatives of townships and small cities, compared with the DPP's 140 and the NP's eight.

These huge victories brought about an unexpected political disaster for the ruling party. As the newly elected KMT councillors contested for leadership positions on city and county councils, many of them bribed their colleagues, and the irregularities were exposed after the councillors elected their speakers and deputy speakers on March 1. Pressured by mounting criticism from the society and the opposition, the Justice Ministry launched unprecedented investigations, targeting the council speakers and deputy speakers. Tu Teh-chi, head of the KMT's provincial party organization, was forced to resign. Indictments and stiff sentences followed the investigations, which amounted to a major reshuffling of the local political leadership throughout the island. The crackdown created great resentment among local KMT politicians, and it worried officials of the party's regional committees about the possible impact on the year-end elections.[10]

Corruption was but one issue raised in the December 3 elections for the governor of Taiwan, the mayors of Taipei and Kaohsiung, and provincial assemblymen and city councilors. As the candidates geared up for the elections, subethnic politics and *t'ung-tu wen-t'i* assumed increasing salience. This was the case particularly when there were strong mainlander competitors, as the KMT's gubernatorial candidate, James Soong, and the NP's nominee for the mayor of Taipei, Jaw Shau-kong. While Soong did his very best to make speeches in the Taiwanese dialect and showed his identification with the local culture, Jaw was fiercely nationalistic, accusing President Lee of harboring a hidden agenda to declare Taiwan independent by 1997. For his part, Chen Ding-nan, the DPP's gubernatorial candidate, ran a campaign focused on "Taiwanese voting for Taiwanese," attacking Soong for his mainland origins.

In the end, the voters rewarded candidates that supported harmonious subethnic relations. The mayoral race in Taipei was genuinely tri-party, as the KMT incumbent Huang Ta-chou faced strong challenges from Jaw Shau-kong and the DPP's Chen Shui-bian. Chen deliberately toned down the DPP's pro-independence platform, and emerged triumphant with 43.7% of the popular vote, compared with Huang's 26% and Jaw's 30.2%. The governor's race and the mayoral election in Kaohsiung were bi-party, though the NP did come up with candidates. The results showed Soong winning with 56.2% of the popular vote, compared with his DPP opponent Chen Ding-nan's 38.7%, relieving the danger of the "Yeltsin effect," that is, a popularly elected local chief subverting the authority of the national leader. In Kaohsiung, KMT incumbent Wu Den-yih won a landslide victory over the DPP's Chang Chun-hsiung (54.5% to 39.3% of the popular vote). In the Provincial Assembly the KMT maintained a two to one margin over the DPP, but a tri-party structure emerged in the Taipei City Council, with the KMT winning 20 seats, the DPP 18, and the NP 11. The NP proved a significant force in metropolitan Taipei but its expansion to other parts of Taiwan was stalled.

The ROC thus made another stride toward full democracy in 1994. Though losing the mayoral election in Taipei, the KMT managed to maintain its overall dominance in Taiwan's politics. The DPP captured the most important local administrative post but failed in its other challenges to the ruling party. The New Party made an impressive but circumscribed debut. The most encouraging sign for the country's democratic future was the confining of subethnic conflicts and the peaceful election process.

NOTES

1. Yu-Shan Wu, "Mainland China's Economic Policy Toward Taiwan: Economic Needs or Unification Scheme," *Issues and Studies* 30:9 (September 1994), pp. 29–49.
2. *Free China Journal*, October 28, 1994, p. 3.
3. *United Daily*, October 26, 1994, p. 19.
4. Mainland Affairs Council, *Liang-an ching-chi t'ung-chi yueh-pao* [Monthly report on cross-strait economic statistics], September 1994, p. 41; *Free China Journal*, September 2, 1994, p. 8.
5. *United Daily*, November 12, 1994, p. 19; the *Free China Journal*, September 2, 1994, p. 8.
6. *Far Eastern Economic Review*, February 17, 1994, p. 50.

7. "Survey of Public Opinion on Qian-dao Lake Incident and Cross-Strait Relations," Election Research Center, National Chengchi University, June 29, 1994.

8. Japan's *Sankei Shimbun* in October reported a mainland Chinese military plan to invade Taiwan. This report coincided with the scenario described in a Taiwan bestseller, *T Day: The Warning of Taiwan Strait War,* and aroused great concern.

9. *Far Eastern Economic Review,* August 5, 1994, p. 1.

10. *Free China Journal,* March 18, 1994, p. 2.

Hegemon on the Horizon?

China's Threat to East Asian Security

Denny Roy

Northeast Asia has been relatively peaceful for the past forty years. The post-Cold War era, however, will bring new security challenges to the Asia-Pacific region. Perhaps the most serious of these challenges involves China's expected emergence as a major economic power in the near future. While a developed, prosperous Chinese economy offers the region many potential benefits, it would also give China the capability to challenge Japan for domination of East Asia.

China's recent economic growth signals a change in East Asia's distribution of power and draws renewed attention to Chinese foreign policy. What are the consequences of Chinese economic growth for regional security?[1]

I argue that a burgeoning China poses a long-term danger to Asia-Pacific security for two reasons. First, despite Japan's present economic strength, a future Chinese hegemony in East Asia is a strong possibility. China is just beginning to realize its vast economic potential, while Japan's inherent weaknesses create doubts about the ability of the Japanese to increase or sustain their present level of economic power. China also faces less resistance than Japan to building a superpower-sized military. Second, a stronger China is likely to undermine peace in the region. Economic development will make China more assertive and less cooperative with its neighbors; China's domestic characteristics make it comparatively likely to use force to achieve its political goals; and an economically powerful China may provoke a military buildup by Japan, plunging Asia into a new cold war.

Denny Roy, Department of Political Science, National University of Singapore.
"Hegemon on the Horizon? China's Threat to East Asian Security," *International Security*, Vol. 19, No. 1 (Summer 1994): 149–168. © 1994 by the President and Fellows of Harvard College and the Massachusetts Institute of Technology.

ASIA'S FUTURE: CHINA OR JAPAN AS NUMBER ONE?

With the United States apparently committed to a drawdown of its global military forces, the Asia-Pacific region seems to have a vacancy for a successor hegemon. Many analysts expect Japan to inherit this mantle on the basis of its impressive economic strength and influence.[2] Nevertheless, two formidable obstacles stand between Japan and hegemony: the instability of Japanese economic strength and the weakness of Japan's armed forces.

Japan's inherent economic vulnerabilities amply justify Frank Gibney's term "fragile superpower."[3] The fragilities include Japan's lack of natural resources and consequent dependence on foreign supplies of raw materials; an aging workforce (Japanese now lead the world in life expectancy, which will result in a higher proportion of retirees to workers); a labor shortage (coupled with strong resistance to importing foreign labor); a declining savings rate; and a dangerously unfavorable corporate capital-to-debt ratio. Like the United States, Japan has begun to move production to developing countries with lower labor costs, which threatens to erode its economic base and to increase unemployment.[4] These characteristics and developments may undermine the long-term stability of Japanese economic power. Bill Emmott argues that the sun is now setting on Japan's economic heyday; the surplus of Japanese capital is declining and "may disappear altogether as early as 1995."[5] Economic growth will be impeded by claims for financial compensation from victims of Japanese aggression in the Pacific War, which may run into the hundreds of billions of dollars.[6] Finally, the political environment of the post-Cold War era, with its increased interest in trade blocs and "managed trade," is likely to prove less favorable to Japanese economic growth. The massive trade surplus that has become Japan's "staff of life"[7] is in jeopardy, and Japan's relatively small, stingy home market could not compensate for the opportunities lost due to protectionism that now looms in the bigger overseas markets. Since Japan's "bicycle economy" requires continuous forward movement to prevent collapse, even a slowdown could have serious ramifications.

Japan's military weakness is the other principal obstacle to Japanese hegemony. Rather than an "economic superpower," Japan is really an incomplete major power. As long as the Japanese choose not to expand their capacity to project military power, they will lack the abilities to protect their economic interests abroad and to exert decisive global political influence.

Tokyo also faces strong disincentives against attempting to deploy military forces commensurate with its economic strength. Consequently, the Japanese government is unlikely to undertake heavy rearmament in the absence of a serious new threat (such as a stronger China, discussed below). One problem with increased military spending is that it would erode some of Japan's economic strength. Japan would begin to suffer the financial drain that it largely avoided during the Cold War by relying on U.S. protection.

More serious are the political disincentives. The great majority of Japanese still oppose an increase in either the size or the role of their armed forces. Japanese also overwhelmingly support the "peace constitution" forbidding armed forces (now interpreted to mean forces capable of threatening neighboring countries), and are disinclined even to take up arms in defense of the Japanese home islands, let alone undertake campaigns of conquest overseas.[8]

Significantly, this pacifism appears to be based more on circumstances than on principle.[9] The Japanese know that a military resurgence in their country would provoke other Asian-Pacific countries to form an anti-Tokyo coalition that might eventually strangle Japan.[10] While balancing is sometimes inefficient,[11] prompt and efficient anti-hegemonic balancing against Japan is virtually assured by the lingering legacy of fascist Japan's Asia policy in the 1930s and early 1940s.

Present circumstances—a relatively weak China and Russia, an engaged but non-threatening United States, and the region's historical fear of Japanese military power—thus rule out an unprovoked Japanese military buildup, leaving Japan dependent on others for protection and unable to qualify as a hegemonic candidate. A change in these circumstances, however, could spark a *reactive* Japanese rearmament, discussed below.

If Japan is an overachiever that has to a large degree transcended its handicaps, China has long been a perennial underachiever. Despite its large territory and population, substantial natural resources, and the economic vigor demonstrated by Chinese everywhere except inside the People's Republic, China's various economic development strategies have posted disappointing results since the intrusion of the West during the Qing Dynasty heralded the end of the ancient order.

But with the economic reforms implemented by Deng Xiaoping and his protegés, China now shows signs that it is beginning to realize its economic potential. China's economy grew by 12.8 percent in 1992, helped greatly by $11 billion in foreign investment, and by another 13 percent in 1993 (in contrast, Japan's economy grew just 3.3 percent in 1993).[12] The International Monetary Fund recently reported that based on "purchasing power parity" statistics, China has the world's third largest economy.[13] Even at a more modest annual growth rate of 8 to 9 percent, the target declared by China's economic czar Zhu Rongji, China's economy will double in size within nine years. Indeed, the biggest worry among the leadership in the former "sick man of Asia" these days is how to keep the economy from growing too rapidly.

China's sudden economic surge raises the possibility that early in the next century, China will be a more powerful country than Japan. To the "Japan As Number One" argument[14] that Japan will soon replace the United States as the world's strongest economic power, others reply that "Japan will never become number one. . . . China is growing so much faster that it will overtake Japan before Japan has a chance to overtake the United States."[15]

Taken as a whole, China is still profoundly poor, and probably faces many setbacks en route to prosperity. Several problems threaten to prevent China's growth into an economic superpower. The most serious is the possibility of fractionalization—the breakup of the Chinese empire into several autonomous states—a tendency that has been accelerated by China's recent economic success.[16] Another hurdle is continued state ownership of much of China's economy. Employing about one-third of the urban Chinese workforce, these state-owned industries are largely unprofitable; some 40 percent of them operated in the red in 1991. Yet Beijing is reluctant to shut them down, fearing massive unemployment and consequent social unrest.[17] Other difficulties include a chronically high population growth rate, which exacerbates unemployment and siphons capital investment away from industry and into less productive sectors such as housing and environmental protection; inflation, the "running dog" of rapid economic growth; and widespread official corruption and profiteering.[18]

Nevertheless, China holds several important economic and political advantages that may make Beijing's long-term prospects for an Asia-Pacific hegemony better than Japan's.

In the economic sphere, China combines its high growth rate with a large territorial and population base (in contrast with Japan's small territory and medium-size population). This gives China a huge potential domestic market—over a billion customers within its own borders. Indeed, the special economic zones on China's eastern coast already send many of their "exports" to the Chinese interior.[19] In contrast, Japan lacks a large domestic markets and is thus vulnerable to protectionism. China's natural resource endowments are also far superior to those of Japan. The Chinese are self-sufficient in food production and supply most of their own energy needs, while the Japanese depend heavily on imports.

Another possible Chinese economic advantage is what Andrew Brick terms "Greater China": a network of ethnic Chinese with proven entrepreneurial prowess throughout the region. Chinese minorities in Southeast Asia, most of whom still speak the dialects of their ancestral home provinces in the PRC, own disproportionately large shares of their adopted states' capital. In Indonesia, for example, where Chinese account for only 5 percent of the population, they control 75 percent of the country's wealth.[20] Given the choice of doing business with Japan or the PRC, the overseas Chinese are likely to prefer customers, suppliers, and investors with whom they share language, culture, and ancestry. The overseas Chinese network gives China a significant long-term edge in the competition to establish an economic empire in East Asia.

China also has an important political advantage over Japan. To dominate the region, either Japan or China would need much larger military forces. China's edge is that the region would be more accommodating to a buildup of Chinese military power than to a Japanese buildup. The reason is historical.

Although the foreign policy of the PRC has hardly been pacific, China's record of aggression pales in comparison with that of Japan in this century. Where China has been militarily assertive, as with its punitive invasion of Vietnam in 1979 and its recent threats to use force against Taiwan and rival claimants of disputed islands in the South China Sea, its neighbors have been relatively tolerant.

While the Japanese government has irritated other Asian countries by its seeming reluctance to acknowledge the full magnitude of Japan's atrocities during the Pacific War, the Chinese government has sought to assure the region that "China does not seek hegemony now, nor will it do so in the future, even when it is economically developed."[21] Beijing and its apologists have steadily counter-attacked the "China threat" argument as an attempt by anti-China Westerners "to sow discord between China and its neighboring countries and to destroy China's plans of reunification and economic development."[22] There is substantial sympathy for China's position within the region. For example, Singapore Senior Minister Lee Kuan Yew, the dean of Southeast Asian statesmen, said after Beijing lost its bid to host the 2000 Olympic Games, "America and Britain succeeded in cutting China down to size. . . . The apparent reason was 'human rights.' The real reason was political, to show Western political clout."[23] Malaysian Prime Minister Mahathir Mohamad displays a similar attitude. "The U.S. is saying we are threatened by China," he says. "But I don't see the threat from China as being any worse than the threat from the U.S."[24] Anna Dominique Coseteng, a Philippine senator, recently said that although the Chinese "have been around the Philippines for 3,000 years, [they] have not shown any signs of wanting to control government policies or interfere in our affairs."[25] Korean scholar Sang Joon Kim assures us it is "highly unlikely that china will use its power and resources to support an aggressive or expansionist policy."[26]

This is not to deny that East Asians are concerned about China's recent military upgrading program. They clearly are. But the predominant sentiment throughout the region is appeasement.[27] There is no serious support for any response stronger than trying to get the Chinese "incorporated into a multilateral security framework."[28] Thus, there is a double standard in East Asia: a Chinese military buildup, while not welcomed, is acceptable; a Japanese defense buildup is not. Several Asian countries have complained loudly even about Japan's participation in United Nations peacekeeping operations.

While a Japanese military buildup would likely galvanize the region into forming an opposing coalition, the region appears prepared to tolerate a Chinese buildup, and would probably not form a balancing alliance unless China's external behavior became significantly more threatening than it is now. China thus faces far weaker political constraints against building a superpower-sized military capability—an important prerequisite of hegemony—than Japan.

If China can avoid disintegration, its inherent long-term economic and political advantages justify the expectation that during the first decade of the next century the "Middle Kingdom" is likely to become the most powerful country in East Asia.

THE IMPACT OF A STRONG CHINA ON REGIONAL SECURITY

The prospect of Chinese dominance has important ramifications for peace in the region. A stronger China would endanger East Asian security in two ways. First, China would be tempted to establish a regional hegemony, possibly by force. Second, the rise of Chinese power might trigger a response from Japan, bringing East Asia under the shadow of a new bipolar conflict.

Economic Development and Chinese Foreign Policy

While some scholars argue that ancient China established a track record of benevolent hegemony,[29] two patterns in the foreign policy of the PRC suggest that neighboring countries might find life with a powerful China unpleasant. First, China has from time to time behaved in ways offensive to the rest of the world, seemingly undaunted by the possible consequences of negative global opinion.[30] Second, China has shown its willingness to use force to settle disputes, even when its own territory is not under attack.[31]

If a relatively weak and developing China has established such patterns, would a stronger, developed China abandon them? The question of whether economic development will make Chinese foreign policy more pacific or more assertive divides commentators roughly into two theoretical camps. The liberal position holds that prosperity will make China behave more peacefully, while realists argue that greater economic strength would embolden a unified China to expand its political influence in the region, perhaps to the grief of its neighbors. An evaluation of the primary arguments for both these positions suggests that the realists have the stronger case.

Two arguments are commonly advanced in support of the liberals' prosperity-causes-peace proposition. The first is that economic development leads to political liberalization, and with it greater government accountability to the demands of the mass public. Historically, democratic peoples have rarely if ever chosen to fight each other. Thus, peaceful relations could be expected between a democratized China and the United States, Japan, and the other liberalizing states in the region.[32]

Unfortunately, this prediction, and the argument upon which it is based, may never be tested. The establishment of a liberal democracy in China is extremely unlikely in the foreseeable future.[33] The obstacles are daunting, and since crushing the student rebellion in Tiananmen Square, Beijing has shown little interest in further political liberalization, many observers, including the

Beijing regime itself and many Chinese intellectuals, see "soft author-itarianism," in which the state allows considerable economic freedom but retains tight control over politics, as a more likely model for the Chinese than Western-style democracy.[34] In any case, prosperity will not automatically result in meaningful mass public input into China's foreign policy decisions. Without democratization within, there is not basis for expecting more pacific behavior without.

A second argument for the pacifying effects of Chinese prosperity is the interdependence argument. According to this view, China is aware that its economic development depends on maintaining financial, trade, and diplo-matic ties with other countries. Dependence on the outside world will there-fore, it is argued, deter Beijing from contemplating any acts that might offend foreign governments or jeopardize China's access to international capital, technology, and markets.[35] The same international links that promote Chinese prosperity also ensure Chinese docility.

Problems with the interdependence argument, however, weaken its per-suasiveness. First, economic interdependence may heighten rather than defuse political tensions.[36] The threat or practice of economic coercion has sometimes driven states to war. If used against China, this strategy might backfire, pushing Beijing to try to establish direct control over the foreign resources and markets the Chinese consider vital to their well-being.

A second weakness of the interdependence argument is that in China's case, the deterrence value of interdependence is severely limited. In the past, the liberal capitalist countries have proven greatly reluctant to pressure Beijing, and this pressure, when applied, has produced poor results. Western govern-ments easily succumb to the ageless warning against "isolating" China; Japan, the first to break ranks and lift post-Tiananmen trade sanctions against China, opposes "applying an abstract yardstick of human rights to foreign aid."[37] For their part, the Chinese leaders have learned from past experience that the threat of collective international punitive action against them is largely a paper tiger.[38] In the most recent confirmation of their view, the perpetrators of the Tiananmen massacre were first runners-up in the competition for the right to host the 2000 Olympic Games.

Finally, interdependence may be doomed by its own success. Throughout its modern history, China has been an economically backward country trying to catch up with the earlier-industrializing West and Japan. This has been a common goal of the various developmental strategies pursued by the PRC since its inception.[39] An "open door" to the international economy, with heavy dependence on imports of capital and technology and exports of low-to-middle-end manufactures, is China's most successful strategy to date. But dependence means vulnerability. Like all national governments, the Chinese leaders are naturally inclined to "control what they depend on [from abroad] or to lessen the extent of their dependency."[40] Dependence is a necessary evil, part of the price that capital-poor, developing economies must pay to achieve rapid modernization. The security threat of vulnerability to economic coercion is compensated for by the security benefit of a growing economy, the basis of future military and political strength. Enmeshment in the world economic system also promises quicker development than the alternative strategy of autarky. The opportunity costs of interdependence thus remain low for developing countries, while the costs of securing their own sources of necessary resources are prohibitively high. But as a developing country becomes strong and wealthy relative to the other states in the system, both the benefits it realizes from interdependence and the costs of establishing its own sphere of influence decrease. Today's weak China has to suffer the vulnerabilities of interdependence, but tomorrow's strong China will not. The more powerful China grows, the less it needs the aid and approval of the other major powers to get what it needs. Over the long term, interdependence cannot offer other countries much hope of reining in a burgeoning China.

Realists would not in any case expect prosperity to make China more pacific. If the international behavior of states is strongly influenced by threats and opportunities governments perceive in the international system, as realists assume, then China's growth from a weak, developing state to a stronger, more prosperous state should result in a more assertive foreign policy. Specifically, says Christopher Layne, "rising powers," or states that have acquired the prerequisites of major power status, "seek to enhance their security by increasing their capabilities and their control over the external environment."[41] Strong countries are also more assertive than lesser powers in both defining and defending their interests.[42] As China fulfills its economic potential, it will conform to these patterns. A growing economic base will increase opportunities for China to establish greater control over its environment, while simultaneously decreasing the costs of doing so. An economically stronger China will begin to act like a major power: bolder, more demanding, and less inclined to cooperate with the other major powers in the region.

The realist argument has powerful historical support. A stronger China will be subject to the same pressures and temptations to which other economically and militarily powerful countries of recent history succumbed, including Britain, Nazi Germany, the Soviet Union, and the United States. Each sought to dominate the part of the globe within its reach (although the particular character of each hegemony varied, from relatively benign to malign).

China Is Prone to Using Force

The impact of a strong China or Asia-Pacific security becomes more clear if we compare the consequences of a dominant China with those of a dominant Japan. For several reasons, a strong China is more likely to use force in pursuit of its goals in the region than a strong Japan, even a powerfully rearmed one.

First, while the Japanese government is democratic and stable, the Chinese government is a typical Third World regime: authoritarian and unstable. Steven David argues that these latter characteristics create war-proneness.[43] David points out that since Third World governments are not democratic, their accountability to the mass public is limited, which increases the possibility that ruling elites will go to war for their own purposes against the wishes of the majority. An authoritarian regime may even embark on hostile overseas adventures against its country's interest if the regime expects this will help it maintain its own political power. Militarism and hyper-nationalism, partly facilitated by state control of the media, are more prevalent in the Third World, making their populations more supportive of adventurism. Finally, the leaders of Third World states are more likely to undertake aggressive action abroad to divert the public's attention from domestic political problems.

China is subject to all of these factors. Both its state and society are unstable. A single party monopolizes power, suppressing serious dissent, and authority is located in persons rather than institutions. Presiding over a sprawling, largely destitute, populous empire, the central government lives in constant fear of insurrection. To the familiar problems of poverty are now added the new problems of rapid, uneven economic growth, including massive corruption and a growing disparity between the rich and the poor. Consequently, as David Shambaugh observes, China may "become more confrontational externally, even as it becomes more fragmented internally."[44]

A second reason why China is more likely to use force than Japan is that China is a dissatisfied power, while Japan is a status-quo power.[45] Japan has benefited enormously from the current international order, it is relatively comfortable with interdependence,[46] and it has a constitution that forbids offensive military action. China, on the other hand, is still trying to recover territory and prestige lost to the West during the *bainiande ciru* ("century of shame"). China's irredentist claims have brought sharp disagreements with Britain, Taiwan, Vietnam, Japan, India, and Malaysia, among others. Its fear of exploitation and conquest by foreigners remains strong.[47] The Chinese leadership perceives the international environment as primarily hostile, and their own place within it insecure. The Soviet Union is gone, but the Chinese believe the United States "has never abandoned its ambition to rule the world, and its military interventionism is becoming more open."[48] Beijing is deeply resentful of attempts by the United States and others to foment "peaceful evolution," which Chinese leaders fear will result in social and political chaos and the destruction of their plans for China's economic development. Although they have submitted out of necessity, the Chinese remain highly averse to interdependence, and to subjection to international norms and regimes.[49]

Accordingly, unlike Tokyo, the Chinese government sees the use of force as a serious policy option. Indeed, Chinese leaders speak much more belligerently at home than abroad.[50] Even in official public statements, China continues to review its threat to attack Taiwan if the island declares itself independent of the mainland, and refuses to rule out the use of force to settle the South China Sea islands dispute.

Finally, China is better able to mobilize its population for war than Japan. As we saw above, Japan would have difficulty fielding large armies for self-defense, let alone foreign military adventures. Thomas Berger concludes that even if the Japanese government decided to undertake a major military buildup, "given the existing culture of anti-militarism they would encounter strong opposition from the general populace as well as from large sections of the elite."[51] This is a formidable barrier to Japan's use of force in defense of its interests overseas.

China, however, has no such problem. The multi-million-member People's Liberation Army has obediently carried out a variety of unsavory orders from Beijing, including the attacks by PLA "volunteers" on American and South Korean troops in Korea, the occupation of Tibet, the punitive incursion into Vietnam, and the slaughter of unarmed demonstrators in Tiananmen Square. It could be counted on to enforce China's hegemonic imperatives as well.

If China is prone to using force, Chinese economic development carries with it the problem of making more force available for Beijing to use.[52]

Japan's Response to Chinese Growth

China and Japan are natural rivals. Both the Japanese and the Chinese see themselves as rightful leaders of the region. Historical and geographic factors in the Sino-Japanese relationship make them highly susceptible to conflict.

One of the most important historical factors is the memory of the Pacific War, during which Japan invaded and pillaged much of China. Recent Sino-Japanese relations underscore the fact that a past history of conflict between two nations makes them more likely to perceive each other as security threats, increasing the possibility of future conflict between them.[53] Since the war, the Chinese have been extremely sensitive to, and highly critical of, hikes in Japan's defense spending, the deployment of Japanese peacekeeping troops overseas, and other indications of increased Japanese military activity. Many Chinese seem convinced that a rearmed Japan means a militaristic Japan.[54] For their part, the Japanese have expressed concern over China's recent assertiveness, including Beijing's pushy approach toward resolving ownership over the disputed Spratly Islands; recent Chinese reiteration of ownership of the Senkaku Islands, which Japan also claims to own; and expansion of China's capability to project military power, including the acquisition of in-flight aircraft refueling technology. In August 1992, Tokyo publicly warned China against purchasing an aircraft carrier, which the Chinese were rumored to be considering. The legacy of the Pacific War seems to have reinforced the security dilemma, causing China and Japan to interpret all military activities by the other side as offensive threats.

Another potential source of Sino-Japanese tension is competition for Southeast Asia. Ancient China and modern Japan have each claimed a sphere of economic influence in this resource-rich and rapidly industrializing region of nearly half a billion people. With powerful and growing export-oriented economies, both China and Japan have voracious appetites for raw materials and a pressing need to expand their share of overseas markets.

China and Japan also have similar but competing strategic interests in the region. One such interest centers on the South China Sea. The Spratly and Paracel Islands, claimed by China for their potential as oil fields, fisheries and military bases, straddle the key sealane between the Strait of Malacca and Japan, the route traveled by ships bearing some 90 percent of the oil the Japanese consume. The combination of technological improvements now underway in the Chinese military and the construction of air and naval bases on Chinese-occupied islands will soon give China the ability to restrict the flow of shipping through the South China Sea—in effect, to cut Japan's jugular vein.

Serious conflict in this potentially explosive relationship will be averted if both sides remain non-threatening. But the growth of China into an economic powerhouse might upset this fragile calm. If the important trends of the present continue into the near future, Japan and China will soon be concurrent great powers for the first time in history. Neighboring great powers without a more threatening common enemy are natural enemies of each other. With the warning of U.S. and Russian power in the region, Japan and China are each likely to identify the other as its most dangerous potential adversary, with negative consequences for their economic and diplomatic cooperation.

One of these consequences could be a major Japanese military buildup. The argument is often made that a stronger China is desirable as a potential balancer against Japan. But no "check" on Japanese military power is presently needed; the risk of encirclement provides sufficient deterrence. On the contrary, an increase in Chinese power will make large-scale Japanese rearmament *more* likely, not less. Japan's anti-militarist sentiment constrains the Japanese from making the first move. The Japanese would consider a large military buildup only if they felt seriously insecure. But a large increase in China's economic strength, coupled with a corresponding growth in Chinese military power, would give China the capability to threaten Japan's economic and political survival. In such circumstances, the Japanese would feel compelled to respond.[55]

China's rapid economic growth also raises the possibility of a regional power transition of the type some theorists have identified as extraordinarily dangerous.[56] In the power transition scenario, a major power with a relatively high growth rate is projected to overtake the slower-growing or declining dominant power. Political tensions between the two rise as the threatened dominant power fears it will lose its control over the international system, while the rising challenger begins to flex its newfound muscle by demanding self-serving changes in the system. Robert Gilpin says the natural consequence of these tensions is a "hegemonic war."[57] Although power transition theory deals with the international system, its logic also seems applicable to a regional rivalry for control of East Asia between a dominant but mature Japan and a rising China. The conclusion: serious political tensions between China and Japan are certain, and military conflict is likely, if China's economic power continues to grow rapidly relative to Japan's.

Although a delicate peace now prevails between China and Japan, it would probably not survive China's emergence as a top-rank economic and military power. The international systemic pressures that typically produce tensions in such cases will be intensified by Beijing and Tokyo's common but conflicting hegemonic aspirations and by their history of poor relations. It is important to note that a Sino-Japanese cold war would not require that Japan revert to the aggressive, imperialist foreign policy that it pursued during the Pacific War, only that it becomes a "normal" major power, counting military force among its strategic options.

In the U.S.-Soviet Cold War, each of the superpowers had its own distinct sphere of influence, and conflicts were generally limited to peripheral areas. This helped preclude a major war. In a Sino-Japanese cold war, however, Southeast Asia would be an area of primary interest to both contestants, increasing the chances of direct major power conflict. In this sense, the new East Asian cold war would be more dangerous than the previous Cold War.

CONCLUSIONS

China represents a greater long-term treat to East Asian security than Japan. If behavior reflects capabilities, China's potential to build a larger economy also makes it more likely to be assertive and uncooperative. China is more prone to using force than Japan, and will likely remain so after its economy has grown, because the Chinese government is authoritarian, unstable, wants to redress the status quo, and can mobilize large military forces with comparative ease. China is also harder to deter than Japan, because it is less vulnerable to economic coercion, and will be even less dependent on outside suppliers as its economy continues to develop. Furthermore, past experience gives Beijing good reason not to take the threat of economic sanctions seriously.

How should the United States and the other major Asia-Pacific powers prepare the for Chinese challenge? Three general strategies are possible. The first would be to suppress China's economic growth and thereby preempt its development into a superpower. This might be attempted through a cutoff of economic contact with China, similar to U.S. policies toward North Korea, Cuba and, until recently, Vietnam.

This option, however, stands little chance of success. An economic embargo is politically impossible in the case of China. Even if the governments in Asia, Western Europe, and North America could be persuaded that such a strategy was strategically sound, their fears of missed economic opportunities and cheating by coalition partners would remain major barriers. Furthermore, economic suppression of China, while perhaps precluding one form of security threat from China, would likely create others, including massive outflows of Chinese economic refugees, Chinese vulnerability to territorial challenges by bordering states, and the breakdown of centralized control over China's nuclear weapons arsenal. An economically retarded, chaotic China is scarcely more desirable than a highly prosperous, united China.

A second policy option would also aim at undercutting China's potential strength, but by another means: strategic economic engagement designed to increase regionalism within China's borders. The current trend in China is toward a decline in control by the central government in Beijing and greater leeway for regional authorities to run their own economic and political affairs.[58] The United States and other capitalist countries could attempt to foster this tendency by providing information and incentives to encourage their nationals who do business in China to target the regions most committed to free market reforms and least responsive to Beijing's control. China's capitalist business partners could also push for arrangements that would promote greater regional autonomy, undermining the central government's control over local prices, profits, and wages. The goal would be to strengthen the linkages between individual Chinese provinces and foreign states, and to weaken the links between the provinces and Beijing, making regional governors less likely to cooperate with attempts by the central government to marshal resources for campaigns of overseas conquest or coercion.

However, an open attempt by the United States and other foreign governments to foment fractionalization in China would also be counterproductive. This policy would convince the Chinese their worst fears of Western neo-imperialism were correct. Chinese nationalism would increase, and links between Beijing and the provinces would likely grow stronger rather than weaker as more Chinese saw the need to work together against the apparent attempt by foreigners to divide the conquer. Such a policy would also alienate America's Asia-Pacific allies, who would wonder why the more distant and powerful United States was taking such an aggressive approach when so many of them are prepared to accommodate a strong China. Without their cooperation, U.S. efforts to shape Chinese development could not succeed.

In short, openly attempting to thwart China's economic growth by imposing an embargo or encouraging national disintegration would probably not work, and would likely backfire by increasing Beijing's insecurity and hostility toward the West.

A third possible strategy for the major powers would be continue their participation in China's economic development, encouraging positive behavior when feasible (e.g., Most Favored Nation trade status as a reward for progress in human rights), and organizing an anti-China coalition only if and when threatening behavior occurs. While the free flow of capital and goods may be providing nourishment for a future hegemon, it also helps promote regional autonomy, political liberalization, and cross-cutting linkages between various parts of China and the outside world. From a political standpoint, it is far better to rely on the free market than initiatives by foreign governments to achieve these goals. Nevertheless, this strategy requires the other major powers and the ASEAN states to be prepared to react swiftly to undue assertiveness by the stronger China of the near future. A powerful China provides another reason for a continuing U.S. military presence in the region. It may also breathe new life into the shaky U.S.-Japan alliance. In the meantime, multilateral security regimes might focus on persuading China to limit its power-projection weapons systems and to agree to shared or divided ownership of the South China Sea Islands.

In the absence of an ideal solution, continuing to abet China's growth, while hoping defensive balancing will not be necessary, is the least problematic option for the outside world. Continued and unrestrained economic engagement conveys implicit acquiescence to the possibility of an economically and militarily powerful China, with all its attendant risks. But this approach has its positive points as well: it is the least threatening from China's perspective, and it allows for the possibility that unrestrained trade and investment will continue to weaken the central government's control over the provinces, reducing Beijing's potential for foreign aggression. This strategy also recognizes the limits on the ability of outside countries, even powerful ones, to manipulate China. Michel Oksenberg correctly points out that "America has periodically sought to produce a China more to its liking. The efforts have always ended in massive failure."[59] It may well be inescapable that China's destiny remains in its own hands.

From the point of view of the rest of the world, the ideal China, perhaps, would be a medium-sized China, with an economy and military forces about the size of present-day Japan's. While continuing to export goods of increasing quality, the more prosperous China could also provide surplus capital for investment abroad and a vast market for foreign imports, finally fulfilling the dream of nineteenth-century Western traders. The Chinese might also maintain qualitatively improved but numerically smaller military forces structured for rapid deployment to China's borders and coastal waters, but not far beyond. This mid-size China would be a prominent economic and political player in the region, engaging in diplomatic give-and-take with the other major powers, but not a hegemon.

Unfortunately, current developments foretell an economically gigantic China with a historic fear of foreigners, a distaste for cooperation, and an interest in developing a blue-water navy and long-range air combat capabilities.[60] These may be the first signs of what will develop into the greatest threat to the region's stability since the Pacific War.

NOTES

1. There are a few recent studies which mention, but do not analyze in detail, the possible threat posed by a stronger China. See Gerald Segal, "The Coming Confrontation Between China and Japan," *World Policy Journal,* Vol. 10, No. 2 (Summer 1993): Zakaria Haji Ahmad, "Japan and China in Pacific Asia's Evolving Security Environment," *Global Affairs,* Vol. 8, No. 1 (Winter 1993), pp. 27, 28; A. James Gregor, "China's Shadow Over Southeast Asian Waters," *Global Affairs,* Vol. 7, No. 3 (Summer 1992); and Nicholas D. Kristof, "The Rise of China," *Foreign Affairs,* Vol. 27, No. 5 (November/December 1993). Kristof hints at two theoretical assumptions that might provide a basis for understanding China's external behavior in the future: he writes that China has "a sense of wounded pride, the annoyance of a giant that has been battered and cheated by the rest of the world." China will "seek a more powerful role, because that is what great powers are supposed to do" (pp. 70, 72). His conclusions, however, are very general: he says China may try to "resolve old quarrels in its own favor," including attacking Taiwan, but also that Chinese foreign policy will not be aggressive or irresponsible (pp. 59, 70–72). William H. Overholt briefly, but directly, examines the impact of a wealthier China on regional security; Overholt, *China: The Next Economic Superpower* (London: Weidenfeld and Nicolson, 1993), chap. 6. Overholt, however, emphasizes the positive consequences of a developed China, not the potential dangers.

2. Works that support the view of Japanese dominance in Asia are Chalmers Johnson, "Where Does Mainland China Fit in a World Organized into Pacific, North American, and European Regions?" *Issues & Studies,* Vol. 27, No. 8 (August 1991), p. 12; Walden Bello, "Trouble in Paradise," *World Policy Journal,* Vol. 10, No. 2 (Summer 1993); and Steven Schlosstein, *The End of the American Century* (New York: Congdon and Weed, 1989).

3. Frank Gibney, *Japan: The Fragile Superpower* (Tokyo: Charles E. Tuttle, 1987).

4. Andrew Pollack, "A 'Made in Japan' Label Is Getting Harder to Find," *International Herald Tribune,* August 30, 1993, p. 1.

5. Bill Emmott, "The Limits to Japanese Power," *Pacific Review,* Vol. 2, No. 3 (1989), p. 179.

6. Associated Press, "Japan may face claims of up to $290b from WWII victims," *Straits Times* (Singapore), September 9, 1993, p. 4.

7. George Friedman and Meredith LeBard, *The Coming War with Japan* (New York: St. Martin's Press, 1991), p. 386.

8. A recent poll asked Japanese, "What will you do if Japan is attacked by a foreign country?" Less than half of the respondents said they would fight the invaders; most of the remainder responded, "I don't know." Paul D. Scott, "The New Power of Japan," *Pacific Review,* Vol. 2, No. 3 (1989), pp. 187, 188n. See also Peter J. Katzenstein and Nobuo Okawara, "Japan's National Security: Structures, Norms, and Policies," *International Security,* Vol. 17, No. 4 (Spring 1993), p. 101.

9. The main arguments in Japan against rearmament tend to be economic and political rather than ethical. Katzenstein and Okawara, "Japan's National Security," p. 116.

10. As the Japanese discovered earlier in the century, threatening states generally prompt other states to balance against them. See Stephen M. Walt, *The Origins of Alliances* (Ithaca, N.Y.: Cornell University Press, 1987), pp. 17–26.

11. John Mearsheimer, "Back to the Future: Instability in Europe After the Cold War," *International Security,* Vol. 15, No. 1 (Summer 1990), pp. 15–16.

12. Carl Goldstein, et al., "Get Off Our Backs," *Far Eastern Economic Review,* July 15, 1993, p. 69; "Prices and Trends," *Far Eastern Economic Review,* Jan. 27, 1994 p. 58.

13. Susumu Awanohara and Lincoln Kaye, "Number Games," *Far Eastern Economic Review,* July 15, 1993, p. 74.

14. Terminology borrowed from Ezra F. Vogel, *Japan As Number One* (New York: Harper & Row, 1979).

15. Segal, "The Coming Confrontation Between China and Japan," p. 27.

16. Ibid., p. 27.

17. David Shambaugh, "China in 1991: Living Cautiously," *Asian Survey,* Vol. 32, No. 1 (January 1992), p. 26.

18. K.C. Yeh, "Macroeconomic Issues in China in the 1990s," *China Quarterly,* No. 131 (September 1992), pp. 503–504, 516.

19. Bruce Cumings, "The Political Economy of China's turn Outward," in Samuel S. Kim, ed., *China and the World* (Boulder, Colo.: Westview, 1989), pp. 217, 218.

20. Andrew B. Brick, "Chinese Water Torture: Subversion Through Development," *Global Affairs,* Vol. 7, No. 2 (Spring 1992), p. 97.

21. The quotation is from Chinese Foreign Minister Qian Qichen, in Michael Richardson, "China Said to Court Asians as a Buffer Against U.S.," *International Herald Tribune,* July 24–25, 1993, p. 1.

22. Wei Zhengyan, "China's Diplomacy in 1993," *Beijing Review,* January 17–23, 1994, p. 15.

23. *Straits Times,* October 14, 1993, p. 1.

24. "Give Bosnia Back," *Asiaweek,* August 11, 1993, p. 21.

25. "A Colossus Stirs," *Asiaweek,* January 27, 1993, p. 25.

26. Sang Joon Kim, "Korea, China and a New Order for Peace in Northeast Asia," *Korean Journal of International Studies,* Vol. 24, No. 2 (Summer 1993), p. 137.

27. Yong Pow Ang's commentary is typical: "Rather than fret over China's defence build-up, the ASEAN countries would do well to accommodate the inevitable rise of China as a regional superpower." Yong, "ASEAN Should Accommodate China's Rise as Superpower," *Straits Times,* August 10, 1993, p. 27.

28. Yoichi Funabashi, "The Asianization of Asia," *Foreign Affairs,* Vol. 72, No. 5 (November/December 1993), p. 84.

29. Chen Jian writes, "Territorial expansionism or imperialism as known in the West was never an active part of Chinese civilization." Chen, "Will China's Development Threaten Asia-Pacific Security?" *Security Dialogue,* Vol. 24, No. 2 (June 1993), p. 194.

30. A. James Gregor makes this observation in "China's Shadow Over Southeast Asian Waters," *Global Affairs,* Vol. 7, No. 3 (Spring 1992), p. 5.

31. China's incursion into Vietnam in 1979 was evidently intended to punish Hanoi for invading Cambodia. China entered the Korean War to rescue its communist ally North Korea. The Chinese have also used force against Vietnam to defend their disputed claim to the South China Sea islands; territorial self-defense might be claimed in that case, but only dubiously.

32. See, for example, Winston Lord, "China and America: Beyond the Big Chill," *Foreign Affairs,* Vol. 68, No. 4 (Fall 1989); and Gaston J. Sigur, "China Policy today," *Department of State Bulletin,* Vol. 87, No. 2119 (February 1987). The literature on the war involvement of democracies is summarized in Nils Petter Gleditsch, "Democracy and Peace," *Journal of Peace Research,* Vol. 29, No. 4 (November 1992).

33. See, for example, Shambaugh, "China in 1991," p. 31.

34. See Denny Roy, "Singapore, China, and the 'Soft Authoritarian' Challenge," *Asian Survey,* Vol. 34, No. 3 (March 1994).

35. An example of this view is Kim, "Korea, China, and a New World Order," pp. 135–137.

36. Stephen Van Evera, "Primed for Peace: Europe After the Cold War," *International Security,* Vol. 15, No. 3 (Winter 1990/91), p. 33n. Michael W. Doyle adds that the pacifying effects of interdependence are minimized in relations between "liberal" (e.g., the United States, Japan, Western Europe) and "nonliberal" countries (e.g., China). "Kant, Liberal Legacies, and Foreign Affairs, Part 2," *Philosophy and Public Affairs,* Vol. 12, No. 4 (1983), p. 326.

37. Then–Prime Minister Kiichi Miyazawa, quoted in Lin Binyan, "The Beijing-Tokyo Axis Against Human Rights" *New Perspectives Quarterly,* Vol. 9, No. 1 (Winter 1992), p. 32.

38. Deng himself reportedly dismissed the possibility of serious international sanctions by saying the world finds China "too big a piece of meat." Roger W. Sullivan, "Discarding the China Card," *Foreign Policy,* No. 86 (Spring 1992), p. 21.

39. Cumings, "The Political Economy," pp. 204, 205.

40. Kenneth N. Waltz, *Theory of International Politics* (New York: McGraw-Hill, 1979), p. 106.

41. Christopher Layne, "The Unipolar Illusion: Why New Great Powers Will Rise," *International Security,* Vol. 17, No. 4 (Spring 1993), p. 11.

42. Jack Levy, *War and the Modern Great Power System, 1495–1975* (Lexington: University Press of Kentucky, 1983), pp. 11–19; Layne, "The Unipolar Illusion," p. 8n.

43. Steven R. David, "Why the Third World Still Matters," *International Security,* Vol. 17, No. 3 (Winter 1992/93), pp. 131–140. In specifying which states make up the "Third World," David explicitly excludes China (p. 127). Nevertheless, I categorize China as a Third World state and find David's observations applicable to China.

44. David Shambaugh, "China's Security Policy in the Post-Cold War Era," *Survival,* Vol. 34, No. 2 (Summer 1992), p. 89.

45. Segal, "The Coming Confrontation Between China and Japan," p. 29.

46. Japanese scholar Seizaburo Sato says most Japanese now accept the idea that "the international game has changed from a gamed based on military power, to a game based on economic capabilities." The Japanese therefore accept interdependence, not only because it is believed to uphold peace, but also because they "realize that other countries are also dependent on Japan." Indeed, "for Japanese, interdependence is an improvement on vulnerability." Seizaburo Sato, "Japan Ascendant," *Peace and Security,* Vol 7, No. 1 (Spring 1992), p. 4.

47. In official Chinese commentaries, for example, Western criticism over Chinese human rights abuses, China's treatment of Tibet, and similar issues is inevitably attributed to alleged Western plans to divide and weaken China.

48. The quotation is from a high-level Chinese report leaked to the press. Nicholas, Kristof, "The Rise of China," *Foreign Affairs,* Vol. 72, No. 5 (November/December 1993), p. 73.

49. Michael Oksenberg, "The China Problem," *Foreign Affairs,* Vol. 70, No. 3 (Summer 1991), p. 10; Shambaugh, "China's Security Policy," pp. 92–93.

50. An example: during a speech to the People's Liberation Army general staff in late 1992 that was later leaked to the Hong Kong *South China Morning Post,* Chinese President Yang Shangkun said the Chinese government had decided to acquire an aircraft carrier and to settle the Spratly Islands controversy by force if Vietnam did not accept Chinese terms by 1997. He also reportedly said, "Hostile forces in the international arena might get burned if they don't behave well," and specifically mentioned the United States

as a potential opponent. Report in the *South China Morning Post,* reprinted as "China Prepared to Use Force, Says Yang in Touch Speech," *Straits Times,* December 15, 1992, p. 1.

51. Thomas U. Berger, "From Sword to Chrysanthemum: Japan's Culture of Anti-militarism," *International Security,* Vol. 17, No. 4 (Spring 1993), p. 147.

52. This is because, as Stephen Walt notes, "modern military power is based largely on industrial capacity." Walt, "The Case for Finite Containment: Analyzing U.S. Grand Strategy," *International Security,* Vol. 14, No. 1 (Summer 1989), p. 11.

53. David J. Myers, "Threat Perception and Strategic Response of the Regional Hegemons: A Conceptual Overview," in Myers, ed., *Regional Hegemons: Threat Perception and Strategic Response* (Boulder, Colo.: Westview, 1991), p. 13.

54. See, for example, Sun Zhengao, "The Security Situation in Northeast Asia," *Korean Journal of International Studies,* Vol. 24, No. 2 (Summer 1993), pp. 164–165.

55. Thomas Berger concludes that for domestic reasons, "it is highly unlikely that the Japanese would set out to become a military superpower." Nevertheless, "if a serious threat to Japan's security arose" and if the United States were unwilling or unable to guarantee Japan's protection, "the Japanese government would be compelled to consider a dramatic expansion of Japan's military capabilities." Berger, "From Sword to Chrysanthemum," pp. 147–148.

56. A.F.K. Organski and Jacek Kugler, *The War Ledger* (Chicago: University of Chicago Press, 1980); Robert Gilpin, *War and Change in World Politics* (Cambridge: Cambridge University Press, 1987).

57. Gilpin, *War and Change in World Politics,* pp. 208–209.

58. Segal, "The Coming Confrontation Between China and Japan," p. 27; Harry Harding, *A Fragile Relationship* (Washington, D.C.: Brookings Institution, 1992), p. 305.

59. Oksenberg, "The China Problem," p. 14.

60. Michael T. Klare, "The Next Great Arms Race," *Foreign Affairs,* Vol. 72, No. 3 (Summer 1993), pp. 136–152; Gregor, "China's Shadow Over Southeast Asian Waters," pp. 7–8.

China's Illusory Threat to the South China Sea

Michael G. Gallagher

The rebirth of Chinese power after five hundred years of decline is one of the major events of this decade: "The rise of China, if it continues, may be the most important trend in the world for the next century."[1] And indeed, on the economic side of the ledger China has turned in a stunningly impressive performance over the last fifteen years. Economic growth has averaged 9 percent since 1978. China's 1993 growth rate was 13 percent.[2] In 1994, industrial output is expected to top 15 percent. Fast-paced economic growth has made mainland China a favorite of foreign investors. In the first nine months of 1993, $15 billion (U.S.) was spent by overseas investors in the China market.[3]

China's leadership has apparently decided to invest a portion of that new wealth in a major upgrading of the combat power of the People's Liberation Army (PLA). Special attention is being paid to the buildup of air and seapower. This combination of rapid economic growth and increasing military strength has many, in Asia and elsewhere, wondering exactly what the Chinese intend to do with their newly acquired power: "China has increasing weight to throw about. But its neighbors still question whether this weight will be thrown behind efforts to build a more secure and stable Asia."[4]

One focus of the concern over Chinese intentions is the Spratly Islands. At the far end of the South China Sea from the Chinese mainland, this collection of stony outcroppings and islets is perhaps the main source of international tension in Southeast Asia with the end of the Cold War. In a world of shrinking natural resources, the mainland Chinese have clearly stated what flag they think should fly over the potentially oil-rich island group: "these islands and reefs are within Chinese territory and other countries are definitely not allowed to invade and occupy them."[5] Ominous statements of that sort have

Michael G. Gallagher, Ph.D., International Studies, University of Miami. "China's Illusory Threat to the South China Sea," *International Security,* Vol. 19, No. 1 (Summer 1994): 169–194. © 1994 by the President and Fellows of Harvard College and the Massachusetts Institute of Technology.

driven people to worry that China's growing economic and military strength may tempt it to expand at the expense of its neighbors in Southeast Asia. "Beijing's buildup on Hainan and Woody Island [the largest island in the Paracels group], signal[s] an inclination to dominate the South China Sea by force rather than negotiate shared control with the other claimants to the Spratlys."[6]

The head of the Malaysia Institute of Maritime Affairs, Hamzah Ahmad, feels that China is seeking to replace the United States and Russia as the region's main military power. "China should not attempt to revive the Middle Kingdom mentality and expect tribute from Southeast Asia," he declared in October 1993.[7]

But fears of a looming conflict over the Spratly Islands may be premature. China's huge size and tremendous numbers may no longer be a decisive advantage in the competition for the control of the Spratly Islands. The growing wealth of its maritime rivals, and their willingness to invest in high-technology weaponry, combined with serious political constraints, both international and domestic, on overseas adventures, have diminished any military advantages China might at one time have enjoyed over its neighbors.

This paper is divided into four sections. The first discusses the basis for the dispute over the Spratly Islands, and includes an examination of the territorial claims of China and its rivals, the significance of the Spratly Islands dispute in international politics, and what tactics the Chinese have used in the past to exert their control over the contested islands. The next section analyzes the military balance between China and some of its smaller neighbors. Their military modernization efforts are described briefly, and the potential problems facing the Chinese in any military operations against the Spratly Islands are analyzed. The section that follows it describes some of the international political and economic constraints on aggressive action in the South China Sea. The concluding section discusses the domestic problems now facing China and how they might affect Chinese behavior with regards to the South China Sea.

BACKGROUND OF THE DISPUTE

To a casual observer, it might seem strange that the Spratly Islands could be the flashpoint for a major international confrontation. Of the 230 islands that make up the Spratly group, only seven are more than 0.1 square kilometers in area.[8] Thity is the largest island in the group; claimed by the Philippines, it is less than one mile long and just 625 yards wide.[9] Many of these so-called islands are merely rocky outcroppings that are underwater at high tide.

These minuscule islands, however, possess significance well beyond their actual size. The islands sit astride sea routes through which twenty-five percent of the world's shipping passes, including the supertankers carrying the petroleum that fuels the economies of Japan, Taiwan, and South Korea. Large quantities of oil may also lie beneath the islands as well; a December 1989

Chinese report claimed that the sea floor surrounding the Spratly Islands may contain from 1 billion to 105 billion barrels of oil.[10] In addition, the area is a rich fishery: 2.5 million tons of fish were harvested from the waters around the islands in 1980.

China's growing economic success and its huge and expanding population suggest why China would be excited by the opportunity to gain control of such large, virtually untapped natural resources. The Chinese assert that their claim to the Spratly Islands dates back 1700 years to the time of the Han Dynasty. But the only independent confirmation of Chinese claims to the Spratlys dates from 1867, when a British survey ship discovered a group of fishermen from Hainan working the area's rich fishing grounds.[11] Despite the sparseness of historical evidence to support their claims to the islands, the Chinese have been forthright about their intention to claim those resources. In February 1992, China's National People's Congress passed a declaration stating that the Spratlys Islands were an integral part of Chinese territory. China's claims to the Spratlys are easier to understand when one realizes that the Chinese regard control of the ocean's resources as vital to their nation's continued existence.[12]

Claims to the resources of the South China Sea have been backed by China's willingness to use force to compel recognition of its rights. In January 1974 Chinese forces drove South Vietnamese naval forces out of the Paracel Islands after a sharp clash in which one South Vietnamese corvette was sunk and two destroyers were damaged. Chinese and Vietnamese forces skirmished a second time in the South China Sea in March 1988. This time the two navies fought over the disputed Johnson Reef in the Spratly Islands, far to the south of the 1974 Paracels clash. Chinese forces sank three Vietnamese supply ships, killed seventy-two Vietnamese, and captured nine.[13] By the end of 1988 the Chinese had occupied six atolls in the Spratly Islands. China continued its expansionist activities in the Spratlys when it occupied Da Lac reef in July 1992. Vietnam swiftly protested the Chinese move, demanding that the Chinese remove their forces from the disputed reef. By spring 1992, the prospect of an armed clash over who controlled the Spratlys was drawing the attention of Japan and the United States. During a spring 1992 visit to Malaysia, then U.S. Undersecretary of Defense for Policy Paul Wolfowitz declared that the parties to the dispute "must not resort to military force to try to sort that mess out."[14]

Along with the use of force, China has throughout the 1970s and 1980s used fishing fleets, the dispatch of "oceanographic" vessels carrying high-ranking naval and civilian personnel on cruises through the disputed areas, and the construction of airfields, blockhouses, and other facilities in both the Paracels and Spratly Islands to make China, if not first claimant on the scene, at least the party on the spot with the most muscular presence. China may be practicing Cold War "salami tactics," absorbing the South China Sea in small bits so as to avoid a violent response from potential adversaries.

During the 1970s, Vietnam was China's only competitor in the Paracels. In contrast, presently China must share the Spratly Islands with other nations. China has garrisoned seven atolls, but Vietnam has occupied twenty-one atolls, the Philippines has placed troops on eight, and the Malaysian flag flies over two atolls.[15] Although outside confirmation for Chinese claims to the Spratly Islands date from the 1860s, other countries can marshal evidence to support their claims as well. Vietnamese claims to the islands date from 1862 and 1865, when cartographic surveys of the South China Sea showed the islands as part of Vietnam. The Philippines' claims date from 1938, when Manila tried to interest Japan in a joint occupation.[16] In 1971, Philippine President Ferdinand Marcos fairly summed up the non-Chinese view of the Spratly dispute when he declared the islands "derelict and disputed."[17]

Apart from the declared parties to the Spratly dispute, any reasonable examination of the situation in the South China Sea must consider the attitudes of both the wealthiest and the largest of the Association of Southeast Asian Nations (ASEAN) states, Singapore and Indonesia. Among the nations of Southeast Asia the tiny city state of Singapore is by far the most prosperous and technologically advanced, but its government is acutely aware of its dependence on the unimpeded flow of shipping through the Malacca Straits and the open waters of the South China Sea beyond. The Singaporean Air Force chief, Brigadier General Bey Soo Khiang, expressed his nation's anxieties concerning its vulnerability in post-Cold War Asia in an early 1993 speech. "The reduction of the American military presence in the Asia-Pacific region is likely to be destabilizing. . . . We will then have a region fraught with potential for a competition for influence. To avert becoming another Kuwait, or suffering the tragedy of being bullied by a bigger and stronger power, countries will attempt to strengthen their national resilience."[18]

Indonesia, freed from fears of foreign domination by its huge size and a population of 180 million, nonetheless has always been jealous of its prerogatives as the largest power in Southeast Asia. Remembering Indonesia's disastrous relations with China in the 1960s, which culminated in the overthrow of President Sukarno, the generals in Jakarta probably feel that they have every reason to be wary of China's intrusion into the South China Sea. Nervousness over Chinese expansionism certainly pushed along Indonesia's February 1993 stopgap purchase of thirty-nine vessels from the former East German navy and the follow-on plans to construct twenty-one modern frigates in local shipyards.[19] Indonesia's concern for its image as the great regional power also displays itself in its representatives' public attitudes towards attempts to enhance military and political cooperation in Southeast Asia. "We don't want to see the region amalgamated," one Indonesian diplomat bluntly stated during ASEAN's May 1993 foreign ministers' meeting held in Singapore.[20]

THE MILITARY EQUATION

Table 1 suggests that China would be capable of bringing vastly superior military strength to bear in any armed confrontation over the Spratly Islands. Overwhelming numbers would support China's leaders if they one day decided to expel rival claimants from the disputed islands.

The bulk of China's modern weaponry has been purchased at garage-sale prices from the increasingly decrepit military of the Russian Republic. Over the last two years the PLA has bought up to $2 billion worth of Russian arms. These include one hundred A300 SAM missiles and twenty-six Su-27 Flanker fighter aircraft.[21] Combined with an inflight refueling capability, which the Chinese have acquired from the Iranians, the highly maneuverable, Mach 2-plus Flankers could provide air cover the Chinese warships flying from airfields on Hainan Island. As of April 1993 the Chinese were said to be negotiating with the Russians for an additional twenty-six Flankers and two Kilo-class diesel-powered submarines, which would provide a much-needed upgrade for the PRC's submarine fleet, most of whose boats are based on 1950s Soviet designs. Other deals rumored to be under discussion include the acquisition of another seventy Flankers, fifty Mach-3 MiG-31 high-altitude interceptors, additional Kilo-class submarines, and an undisclosed number of Tu-26 Backfire long-range bombers.[22] Armed with anti-shipping cruise missiles, the Backfires would be a serious threat to shipping as far south as the Malacca Straits.

Since China is still a relatively poor nation, the best way for it to acquire a modern air force may be to build a foreign-designed aircraft locally. A recent story reported that the Russians had offered to develop for the Chinese air force

Table 1. Naval and Air Forces Available to China, Selected ASEAN Countries, and Vietnam

	Combat Aircraft	Large Warships	Patrol Craft	(SSM)	Submarines
China	5000	54	860	(207)	46 + 5 SSN
Malaysia	69 + 6 armed helos	4 frigates	37	(8)	0
Singapore	192 + 6 armed helos	6 corvettes	24	(6)	0
Indonesia	81	17 frigates	48	(4)	2
Vietnam	185 + 20 armed helos	7 frigates	55	(8)	0

Notes: Aircraft totals include naval air forces; patrol craft include gun and torpedo boats; SSM = Surface-to-Surface Missiles, SSN = attack submarines

Source: Compiled from International Institute of Strategic Studies, *The Military Balance 1993–94* (London: Brassey's, 1993), pp. 145–165.

a brand new fighter for as little as $500 million.[23] With performance falling between the MiG-29 and the MiG-31 high-altitude intercepter, the proposed aircraft would have Russian electronics and engines, but would be built in Chinese factories upgraded by Russian engineers. The Chinese were supposedly planning to produce the new aircraft at the rate of 100–150 a year, according to the Russians, but considering China's fiscal and technical constraints, a more realistic figure may be fifty aircraft a year.[24]

However, China's rivals for control of the Spratly Islands have not been standing idly by while the PRC stockpiles weaponry. In July 1993, Malaysia announced its decision to buy eighteen MiG-29s and eight McDonnell Douglas F-18s as part of its military modernization program. Although the exact dollar amount of the MiG-29 deal remained undisclosed, the Russians, eager to dispose of an estimated one hundred MiGs left undelivered by the collapse of the former Soviet Union, offered Malaysia generous terms in return for the sale, including the manufacture of spare parts either through a joint partnership or a local Malaysian company.[25] In June 1992, GEC-Marconi of the United Kingdom agreed to build for the Royal Malaysian Navy two modern frigates for approximately $425 million.[26] Equipped with *Seawolf* missiles capable of knocking down both aircraft and low-flying cruise missiles, and with *Exocet* anti-shipping missiles, these up-to-date vessels, operating in conjunction with the new MiGs and F-18s and the missile-armed patrol craft already in Malaysia's possession, would provide a credible defense of Malaysia's claims in the South China Sea. This would be particularly true if the frigates and the new fighter aircraft were based at Jesselton, in the Malaysian province of Sabah on Borneo. From Jesselton it is only 250 miles to the easternmost fringes of the Spratly group, a very short flight at Mach 2-plus speeds, and only half a day's steaming time for the new frigates when they enter Malaysian service in the second half of this decade. Malaysia intends to build a potent military force by the first few years of the twenty-first century, having announced plans to jump the percentage of its growing GDP that it spends on military affairs from 2 percent to 6 percent over the next 10–15 years.[27] By the early 2000s, Malaysia could be the owner of a military machine that, at least in qualitative terms, would be the equal of any country in region, including China.

Singapore is an often overlooked factor in Southeast Asia's military balance. With a population of only 2.5 million, the tiny city-state is in the process of building a military force to match the growing sophistication of its economy. With 192 aircraft (including F-16s and E2C early warning aircraft) and a high level of training, Singapore's air force is already the most potent in Southeast Asia. The Navy's six *Victory*-class corvettes and six *Sea Wolf* missile patrol craft are armed with U.S. *Harpoon* and Israeli *Gabriel* anti-shipping missiles.[28]

Singapore's industrial base is annually becoming more capable of supplying the armed forces' needs from domestic sources. The local defense industry is dominated by Singapore Technologies Incorporated. Singapore Technologies is a holding company with forty-six subsidiaries, 12,000 employees and $1.2 billion (U.S.) in annual sales.[29] Local shipyards are producing *Victory*-class corvettes for home use and for export. The local armaments industry is now capable of manufacturing 155mm heavy artillery, composite armor panels for the Singaporean Army's armored personnel carriers, and improved antitank missile warheads. Local industry, in cooperation with local and foreign firms, has developed extensive maintenance and refit capabilities for both ships and aircraft. In 1991, plans were made for the purchase of twelve additional F-16s to enhance the air force's striking power. More significantly for any future operations in the South China Sea, Singapore announced plans to buy two more maintenance E2C early warning aircraft, creating a total force of six.[30] Each twin-engine E2C is capable of tracking up to 250 potential airborne targets simultaneously and, if based at nearby airfields (e.g., Malaysian Sarawak), would be able to loiter in the vicinity of the Spratly Islands, giving adequate warning of the approach of any hostile forces.

Economically, Indonesia is still lagging behind star performers like Malaysia and Singapore, but its military does have its modern components. Alone among ASEAN states, Indonesia operates its own submarine force, and possesses an inflight refueling capability. The Indonesian air force also flies twelve F-16s, while the navy's frigates and patrol craft are armed with *Exocet* and *Harpoon* anti-shipping missiles.

By the year 2000, moreover, the island nation's poverty may be a receding memory for many of its citizens. With an average annual growth rate of 5.5 percent, and an export economy shifting from reliance on oil to increasing emphasis on manufactured goods, Indonesia is likely to have the money available for continued military modernization. An agreement earlier this year to purchase up to one-half of the old East German Navy and plans to construct 21 modern frigates are signs that Indonesia's rulers are committed to a strong modernization effort. While the East German warships are obsolescent, they do provide a welcome increase in the Indonesian navy's numbers. (Modernizing these aging vessels, particularly the 16 *Parchim*-class frigates may, however, turn out to be prohibitively expensive.[32]) Along with boosting the size of its navy, Indonesia is giving its air force greater striking power with the June 1993 agreement with Great Britain to purchase Hawker Hunter light attack aircraft, scheduled for delivery in 1996.[33]

GEOGRAPHY

Geography is another difficulty the Chinese must cope with in the event of an armed confrontation over the Spratly Islands. The main Chinese naval bases in the South China Sea, Yulin on Hainan Island, and Zhanijiang, the headquarters of China's South Seas Fleet on the mainland, are much farther from the disputed islands than are the bases of potential enemies. Chinese surface forces facing serious opposition in the waters surrounding the Spratly Islands would require effective air cover in order to survive. Currently, the People's Liberation Army Air Force (PLAAF) lacks modern aircraft with the range, speed, and maneuverability necessary to protect a large Chinese naval force operating in the Spratly group. The Flankers and the Backfire bombers discussed earlier would certainly help reduce Chinese problems in this area, but would by no means solve them.

The initial order of twenty-six Flankers, even with inflight refueling capability (which the Chinese do not have yet on a large scale), would not be able to provide more than a very small force, reduced further by the usual difficulties concerning maintenance, to cover Chinese ground and naval forces in the Spratly Islands. Even with the seventy additional Flankers and the introduction of the projected Russian-designed, Chinese-produced fighter aircraft mentioned above, the Chinese could still face serious difficulties in providing effective air cover over the Spratly Islands. Again the question of inflight refueling capacity dominates any discussion of Chinese air operations in the South China Sea. Even with a sizable tanker force available, which is a highly questionable proposition before the early 2000s, the Chinese would still not be able to mount more than limited aerial operations over the disputed islands. The tanker aircraft themselves would also be vulnerable to attack, while they were in transit over the open waters of the South China Sea, from long-legged aircraft such as the MiG-29 and the F-18.

Since it is likely that Chinese naval forces would have to operate in the vicinity of the Spratly Islands with only limited air support, they would often be forced to fend for themselves in the event of air attack. Here Chinese prospects are dismal. Chinese naval vessels are adequately equipped with short-range antiaircraft guns, but ships equipped with modern antiaircraft missile systems are virtually nonexistent. At the start of 1994, in the entire People's Liberation Army Navy (PLAN) there were only four ships—a *Jiang-dong*-class frigate, two *Jiangwei*-class frigates, and one brand new *Luhu*-class destroyer—equipped with surface-to-air missile (SAM) systems.[34] In 1993, China commissioned the first of the *Luhu*-class guided-missile destroyers. A substantial improvement over previous classes of Chinese surface warships, the *Luhus* are still only equipped with French-made *Crotale* SAM systems. The *Crotale's* seven-nautical-mile range would provide little defense against aircraft mounting 50–100-mile-range *Exocet* and *Harpoon* missiles.

With the demise of the Soviet Union, China now has the world's second largest submarine fleet, after the United States. But all of the PLAN's diesel-powered boats are based on 1950s Soviet designs. Only forty-six of the fleet's one hundred boats are on active duty.[35] As for the five Chinese-built *Han*-class nuclear attack boats in PLAN service, only two boats are believed to be fit for duty due to maintenance and technical problems.[36] Additionally, the twin afflictions of obsolescence and poor maintenance may make Chinese submarines excessively noisy when submerged, making China's submarine fleet vulnerable to modern anti-submarine warfare technology. Chinese acquisition of Russian *Kilo*-class boats would only mitigate, not entirely solve this problem. Limited funding makes it unlikely that China would be able to purchase more than a few of these modern vessels, and the establishment of a shipyard to construct the submarines on Chinese soil is unlikely before the late 1990s at the earliest. If tensions over the Spratly Islands erupt into a crisis over the next several years, China could find itself in the unenviable position of being able to field only a relatively small amount of mostly foreign-manufactured modern weaponry, operating far from any safe haven, against potential adversaries armed with increasingly up-to-date equipment, much of it manufactured locally.

MILITARY MODERNIZATION

China's lack of SAM-equipped warships and its creaky submarine fleet only serve to highlight a fact that is often left out of any discussion about China's ability to threaten its neighbors militarily: the PLA is very large, but is deficient when it comes to the sinews of warfare in the 1990s.

Chinese military technology is still as much as twenty years behind the West. One major obstacle is lack of money. The 1992 PLA budget stood at $7.4 billion (U.S.), or double its 1988 level.[37] The total cost for the initial buy of twenty-six Sukhois and two Kilo boats is expected to be in the $1.5–2 billion range.[38] Even though expenditures for arms purchases are likely to be spread out over a period of several years, such amounts would still represent a sizable chunk of the PLA's procurement budget.

China's military industry has a well-documented history of problems with reverse engineering. The most modern domestically designed aircraft is the J-8II, an F-4 equivalent based on a 25-year-old design. The PRC is supposedly developing a Tornado equivalent, the H-7, which may first have flown in 1989. The Chinese claim the H-7 will enter squadron service by the mid-1990s. The H-7 is rumored o be short of lightweight composite materials in its airframe, and not to have a fly-by-wire flight control system.[39] Sometimes Chinese copies of foreign-designed weapons never see the light of day: Chinese duplicates of the Soviet T-62 tank and the MiG-23 fighter-bomber are examples of weapons that never reached the production line. One reason for these failures may be that the PLA has the tendency to rush a new weapon into service without a thorough debugging.[40] Lack of extensive automation or computerized quality control also hamper the PLA's efforts to close the technology gap with the outside world.

Modern Chinese-produced weaponry has often proved itself ineffective. Towards the end of the 1991 Gulf War, Iraqi shore batteries fired two of

China's much-publicized Silkworm missiles at the battleship USS *Wisconsin* and its escorting destroyer, HMS *Gloucester*. One missile disintegrated and fell into the sea. The second missile was shot down by a *Sea Dart* missile fired by the *Gloucester*.[41]

Ironically, Chinese efforts to cannibalize the military technology of the old Soviet Union may not help the PLA very much in its drive to upgrade its combat power. First, it was not just Chinese, but also Soviet equipment that failed to affect the outcome of the Gulf War: Iraqi tank crews watched impotently as the shells from the guns on their supposedly first-line Soviet-made T-72 tanks bounced off the armor of the oncoming American M1 tanks.[42] Secondly, the tremendous economic problems bedeviling the Russian Republic, along with the independence of the former Soviet republics, has reduced the Russian military to a state bordering on collapse. Whatever political order rises from the ruins of the former Soviet Union, the sprawling Soviet-era military research and development apparatus will require many years to rebuild. Russian military procurement has, according to one source, been cut "savagely," falling 32 percent in 1991, and by another 68 percent in 1992.[43] Unless the PRC can overcome its inability to successfully develop and, especially, to mass-produce modern military equipment, the PLA faces the high probability of merely being locked into a higher level of technological obsolescence than is now the case.

INTERNATIONAL CONSTRAINTS ON CHINESE BEHAVIOR

Great powers are often viewed by their smaller neighbors with deep suspicion, and the fear that one nation will become overwhelmingly powerful tends to drive that country's rivals into each other's arms.

Starting in the early 1970s, the Five Power Defense Arrangement (FPDA) has provided an embryonic network for military cooperation among ASEAN and outside powers. Including Singapore, Malaysia, Britain, Australia, and New Zealand, the FPDA has over the last twenty years sponsored joint air exercises at the Payar Lebar airport in Singapore, including 1992 exercises that involved aircraft from Malaysia, Singapore, and Australia.[44] In July 1992 Vice Admiral Soedibyo Rahardjo, the chief of staff of Indonesia's armed forces, and Brigadier General Lee Hsien Yang of Singapore, the armed forces chief of staff and son of Singapore's former prime minister Lee Kuan Yew, signed an agreement to establish joint anti-piracy patrols between their two nations. The two countries' navies agreed to set up a direct communication link to coordinate action against the growing threat that piracy poses to the region's shipping. The signing of the anti-piracy accord coincided with the seventh bilateral air exercises between Indonesia and Singapore. Interestingly, the exercises included simulated attacks on shipping.[45]

Singapore-Indonesian defense cooperation goes beyond agreements over piracy and bilateral air exercises, however, extending to the development of a joint bombing range on Sumatra.[46] While the 1992 anti-piracy agreement and the joint air exercises hardly represent military cooperation on the scale of the NATO Cold War alliance, they have laid down a foundation on which future cooperation could be built.

But the ASEAN nations are still reluctant to transform what has been an economic and political relationship into a military one. At a 1992 conference on regional security held in Singapore, Lt. Colonel Philip Su, then Singapore's assistant chief of the general staff, expressed the hope that bilateral military exercises would be transformed into multilateral ones. Colonel Su even raised the possibility of the joint development of weapons systems, but stopped short of suggesting that ASEAN become a full-fledged military alliance, saying that given the lack of a clearly defined enemy, a treaty of military alliance, rather than bringing ASEAN states together, might only drive them apart.[47]

Such public disavowals may be only to provide cover for ASEAN members, particularly Indonesia, that are fearful of the loss of sovereignty that the establishment of a formal alliance, with its joint command arrangements and frequent consultation among members, might entail. For despite Colonel Su's protestations that a formal military arrangement among ASEAN states would lack a discernible adversary, China is the only plausible target for any ASEAN military cooperation. Japan, despite its impressive economic power, is likely to remain a military dwarf as long as the U.S.-Japan security treaty remains intact. Trade differences aside the United States supports Japan's campaign for a seat on the UN Security Council, and continues to seek Japan's cooperation on a broad array of political issues ranging from North Korea's nuclear program to dealing with prickly regional leaders like Malaysia's Prime Minister Mohammed Mahathir.[48] Suggesting that not everyone in the region is frightened of Japan, one proposal floated at a January 1992 regional conference in Kuala Lumpur called for a regional ASEAN defense force equipped by Japan on a concessionary basis.[49]

From the standpoint of international public opinion, the ASEAN states are in a much better position *vis-à-vis* China than Vietnam was in the 1970s and 1980s. Chinese moves against Vietnam during that period were based on a unique set of circumstances: China's 1974 gains in the Paracels were acquired at the expense of the soon-to-be-extinct government of South Vietnam, which had been nudged a pariah in the court of international public opinion. Even in the United States, South Vietnam's only ally, there was an overwhelming desire to purge as quickly as possible the painful and divisive memories of the war. In their plans to destroy South Vietnamese ambitions in the Paracels, the Chinese could also count on their new strategic relationship with Washington. Having already given up its South Vietnamese allies for lost, the United States would hardly be in the mood to jeopardize its new quasi-alliance with China against the Soviet Union.

In 1988, a communist-ruled Vietnam was again an international outcast due to its 1978 invasion of Cambodia. Two hundred thousand Vietnamese troops were mired in a protracted guerrilla war against the Khmer Rouge. China used Thailand as a conduit for funneling weapons to its Khmer Rouge allies. Mikhail Gorbachev's Soviet Union, Hanoi's main armorer and banker, was in full retreat from superpower status and was attempting to shrink its international commitments as rapidly as possible. The security of their erstwhile ally was not uppermost in the minds of Soviet policy makers as they sought to rebuild their relationship with their old rivals, the Chinese. The Chinese had astutely judged the international situation to be favorable to them before they drove the Vietnamese Navy away from Jones Reef in the Spratly Islands. They had displayed similar good judgment during their 1979 invasion of Vietnam, when they refrained from aggressive action in the South China Sea, for fear of bringing the then–vastly superior Soviet fleet down on their backs in defense of Moscow's Vietnamese clients.

Since the 1979 Chinese invasion, Vietnam has pulled out of Cambodia and opened its economy to foreign investment. With the lifting of the U.S. trade embargo in early 1994, this new cloak of international acceptance may give Vietnam greater protection against Chinese aggression, despite a 50 percent reduction in its armed forces, than at any time since the immediate aftermath of the 1979 Sino-Vietnamese War, when Hanoi enjoyed both military superiority over the PLA and the benefit of a security treaty with the now defunct Soviet Union.

Vietnam's ASEAN neighbors may also be able to draw upon international respectability. With the exception of the Philippines, all the ASEAN states are enjoying rising levels of prosperity. Forms of government range from Malaysia's machine-style politics, to Indonesia's mild authoritarianism, to Singapore's nanny-style paternalism. While none of these governments is fully democratic, they present a more pleasant face to the world than China's present regime. Any major Chinese military action to clear its rivals out of the Spratly Islands is likely to cause a level of international protest second only to that which followed the Iraqi seizure of Kuwait. More importantly, given the island groups' strategic position astride main shipping routes, large-scale violence over the Spratly Islands has a good chance of bringing larger powers onto the scene.

Worried about potential for violence in post-Cold War Asia, the governments of Singapore, Thailand, and Malaysia have offered port facilities to the United States. Even Indonesia, usually among the most reluctant of ASEAN members when it comes to inviting outsiders to assist in the region's troubles, signed an agreement in the fall of 1992 allowing the United States Navy the use of the state-owned Ptpal dockyard in Surabaya.[50] With Thailand, the United States carries out forty mostly small-scale joint exercises every year.

Depending on the magnitude of the problem, the United States might simply decide to increase its arms sales to the countries that felt most anxious about Chinese intentions. This policy has been followed for many years with regards to Taiwan. Along with the October 1992 agreement to sell Taiwan 150 F-16 fighters, the United States has quietly shared Patriot missile technology with the Republic of China and has licensed the construction of *Perry*-class frigates in Taiwanese shipyards. Additional U.S. moves to bolster Taiwan as a counterweight to mainland Chinese ambitions include discreet talks with Taiwan's military leadership and the agreement to sell Taiwan sixty-eight Supercobra attack helicopters.[51] All the ASEAN states already use at least some American equipment, so a policy of containing China by building up the militaries of its rivals would be relatively easy to implement.

Apart from military and diplomatic maneuvers to block any threat from China, the ASEAN states are trying to deter any aggressive moves in their direction by fostering economic ties with the Chinese. Singapore has sought to broaden economic ties with the PRC: Lee Kuan Yew recently set off for China with 150 senior government and business officials in tow. In May 1993 a Singaporean delegation signed an agreement in China to develop a 27-square mile zone near Suzhou. The Suzhou development zone has already attracted $1.1 billion in investments, mostly from overseas Chinese investors, and may garner up to $20 billion. In June 1993, Prime Minister Mahathir of Malaysia signed $600 million worth of agreements in China. He declared it his most successful trip as prime minister. Malaysian exporters are finding that China's rising living standards are taking up some of the slack as Japan's economy was stalled.[52]

The ASEAN states' growing economic ties with China raise the following question. Given the economic carrot the Chinese can dangle in front of the business people of Southeast Asia, wouldn't it be easier for the ASEAN countries to go along with China's claims in the South China Sea rather than put an increasingly profitable relationship at risk?

However, the Spratly Islands sit astride vital sea lanes and possess important natural resources. A nation, if it has the mans, will usually seek to prevent a hostile power from gaining control of important lines of communication and natural resources. For example, for centuries it was standard British policy to prevent enemy nations from gaining control of the Low Countries, which would have threatened London's control of the North Sea and the English Channel. And as noted above, the ASEAN states possess ever more capable military forces. Given the obvious technological defects of Chinese naval and air forces, there is no real reason for China's neighbors in Southeast Asia to submit to Chinese bullying. In fact, if a confrontation does take place in the South China Sea over the next several years, China's opponents, aware of the low technological level of China's sea and air forces, may simply decide that China is bluffing.

Also, while China can provide ever more lucrative opportunities for trade and investment, the China market is not the only game in town. Singapore, for example, is the world's largest manufacturer of computer hard disk drives, and has large markets in North America, Europe, and Japan. In 1993, Singapore's exports to China surged by 77.2 percent, but they also jumped by 38 percent with Japan, and a healthy 58 percent with Malaysia.[53] Malaysia's electronics industry accounts for 36 percent of its manufacturing, an grew at a 25 percent annual rate in 1993; it still depends more on exports to Japan, America, and Europe than on the China market.[54] The Lippo group, a growing Indonesian multinational corporation, does a great deal of business in China, but apparently tries to limit its exposure in China by having some projects financed mostly by foreign partners: "We see ourselves as a bridge for overseas capital looking to get into China," said James Riady, Lippo's deputy chairman.[55]

But if Southeast Asian governments should keep in mind their nations' economic interests in dealing with China over the South China Sea, why shouldn't Beijing consider its own trade and investment interests when deciding what action to take over the Spratly Islands? By the fall of 1993, $83 billion (U.S.) in direct investment had been pledged to the China market by foreign investors.[56] In November 1993, German companies signed $2.8 billion worth of contracts with Chinese customers.[57] The big Thailand-based conglomerate Charoen Pokphand (CP) has plans in the works for a $3 billion petrochemical plant near Shanghai.[58] China desperately needs foreign capital to finance its infrastructure development, including its power needs. The Nomura Research Institute calculates that China needs 20,000 megawatts of new generating capacity per year, but domestic producers can only supply 12,000 megawatts.[59] Thus China must seek out overseas investors. Two Chinese firms, the Harbin Group and Shanghai United, have signed technology transfer agreements with Westinghouse. Another Chinese firm, the Dongfang group, is hoping for joint venture agreements with Siemens, Hitachi, and General Electric.[60]

A stable international environment is usually viewed as beneficial to trade and foreign investment. Given both economic and military risks, Chinese leaders would have to ask themselves if islands that are barely noticeable on the map are really worth the risk of even a temporary disruption of the impressive flow of foreign investment into their country.

DOMESTIC CONSTRAINTS ON CHINESE BEHAVIOR

In addition to economic enticements, rivals with growing arsenals, and diplomatic difficulties, problems within China itself may place additional limits on Chinese actions beyond the borders of the PRC. Indonesian and Malaysian strategists have pointed out that China's defense spending has grown by 20 percent over the last two years, but what they have failed to discover (or to mention) is where the new money is going within the PLA's sprawling infrastructure. Public statements concerning the PLA's post-Cold War strategy constantly say that China needs to form a well-equipped rapid reaction force designed to be deployed quickly to trouble spots on China's frontiers. But of the 3 million PLA soldiers now on active duty, less than one-fourth are in units scheduled to be modernized. With the government paying only a portion of their operating expenses, these units are being forced to go in to sideline business activities. The newly modernized units are reportedly to be stationed across China, but there is to be an especially heavy concentration of modernized units in Northeast China to defend Beijing.[61] These units are also receiving much of the modern equipment that is reaching the PLA. Chinese strategists say that the three armies are deployed to defend China's capital from any possible threat from the increasingly run-down Russian Far Eastern Command. But with such a large part of the PLA left out of the modernization effort, the primary mission of the three armies may be to protect the Chinese leadership from any future internal unrest.

Chinese society has developed a web of hairline cracks from the frenetic pace of the transition from a command to a free-market economy. China's fast-growing economy has sparked an urban inflation rate of 20–26 percent annually.[62] A similar burst of inflation in 1988 helped set the stage for the uprising in Tiananmen Square in 1989. With private enterprise comprising an ever-growing share of China's GDP, power is flowing out of Beijing into the provinces and the hands of individuals. Thriving Guangdong Province, for example, gets only 3 percent of its investment capital from the central government.[63] In 1992, Guangdong provincial officials decided that the central government charged too high a price for oil, and purchased a tanker-load of Kuwaiti oil instead. In a 1992 incident, officials in Hunan province were so upset by neighboring Guangdong's attempts to bypass them by buying rice directly from Hunanese farmers that they ordered regional PLA troops to the Guangdong-Hunan border to block rice shipments. Guangdong officialdom responded with its own mobilization.[64] This renewed provincial rivalry coincides with a growing income gap between prosperous coastal provinces like Guangdong and Fujian, and poverty-stricken interior provinces like Gansu, which in 1991 had a per capita income of $75, compared to $350 in Shanghai.[65]

People in China are no longer dependent for their livelihoods on the *Danwei,* the state-controlled work units that formerly dominated every aspect of a worker's life. Many state employees nowadays just stop by their workplaces to pick up their paychecks, which merely supplement the income from the jobs they hold in the bustling private sector. In a society where housing and medical care were once virtually free, enterprises are prodding their employees to buy their own housing, and doctors and nurses are now demanding bribes for treatment.[66]

Entire villages of illegal migrants from the countryside have grown up on the fringes of most large Chinese cities. Since these places do not have Communist Party-run street committees, it has become very difficult for Chinese Public Security to control the transients' comings and goings. China may have up to 100 million people drifting across the country in search of work.[67]

Moreover, ten percent of the urban population may be underemployed. China's long history is dotted with great rebellions whose basic material was the jobless and the homeless. The Chinese government's disquiet over the situation was reflected in the Shanghai newspaper *Wenhuibao:* "The floating population, which exists without the normal controls, is fertile soil for the growth of secret societies. If they get together and form organizations, then the large group of people without a steady income will be a great threat to stability. If they join with the millions of unemployed in the cities, then the results will be even more unimaginable."[68]

The people left behind in the villages of China's vast countryside are also feeling the effects of their nation's rapid economic development. Widening economic opportunities have led to rampant official corruption, much of it in the countryside. Local officials extort money from the peasants under the guise of special "taxes," including fees levied on old radios and televisions, and forced "loans" from peasants to local bureaucrats in return for dubious IOUs.[69] In some parts of the countryside, refusal to give in to this extortion can lead to jail, with one's family forced to pay in return for one's release. Hong Kong newspapers reported 200 incidents of peasant unrest in 1992 alone.[70] The most dramatic incident took place in 1993 in Sichuan Province's Renshou County. Thousands of peasants showed their outrage over an excessive road-building fee by storming local government offices and taking local officials hostage. People's Armed Police units dispatched to quell the rioting were themselves cornered by large mobs of any peasants, which they dispersed with tear gas.[71] The destruction of the old social contract, the epidemic of petty corruption, and the creation of a huge class of undocumented and possibly uncontrollable transients are trends, that, if they continue over the next few years, are likely to divert the attention of China's leadership far away from the reefs and islets of the Spratly Islands.

It could be argued that a short, sharp war in the South China Sea might be just what China's leaders need to divert the Chinese people's attention away from problems at home. History is filled with such instances: for example in 1982, Argentina's military junta thought an easy victory over the tiny British garrison in the Falklands would shore up its shaky position at home. But the wars that China has fought since 1949 indicate a different pattern. Chinese leaders seem to like having their domestic house in order before they tackle foreign enemies. When China entered the Korean War in November 1950, communist control of the mainland was unchallenged. Chiang Kai-shek and the remnants of the Nationalist armies had fled to Taiwan in disarray; although ragtag groups of Nationalist soldiers were still loose in the remote jungles of Southwest China, they posed no threat to the Communists' domination of mainland China. China intervened in Korea strictly for reasons of international prestige and national security. Mao Zedong felt that China could not tolerate the destruction of a fellow communist government in North Korea by the U.S.-led United Nations forces. More importantly, with the Americans driving towards the Yalu River, the Chinese government was anxious about the potential threat to Manchuria, China's main industrial region.

China's last war, the 1979 invasion of Vietnam, was also fought against a background of foreign threats and domestic peace. In December 1978, Vietnam had invaded Cambodia and toppled from power Beijing's Khmer Rouge allies. Vietnam's principal ally and China's main adversary, the Soviet Union, had taken over the former U.S. Navy base at Cam Ranh Bay. China's leaders fearing Russian encirclement and disturbed by what they believed to be a steep decline in U.S. ability to fend off Soviet expansionism after the fall of South Vietnam, felt they had to go to war to demonstrate to their enemies that China could deal with challenges to its security without outside assistance.

Within China itself, however, the political situation was calm. Deng Xiaoping and his fellow economic reformers had swept most of the remaining Maoists from power and had tightened their control over the government. In 1978, Deng Xiaoping had started the program of economic reforms that was to make China one of the great economic success stories of the 1990s.

China's quiet intervention in the Vietnam War during the 1960s was the only occasion when Beijing has intervened militarily beyond its frontiers during a time of domestic crisis. The Cultural Revolution, Mao's last great effort to ideologically purify China and eliminate his political enemies, riddled China with factional feuds from one end of the country to the other. Fighting took place in China's far-western province of Xinjiang. In 1967, regional PLA units stationed in the big industrial city of Wuhan revolted against Beijing in support of local government leaders. Despite the turmoil, the Chinese dispatched 50,000 engineering and air defense troops to North Vietnam. The reasons for that deployment were the same ones that led to the Korean War intervention: defense of an ally and worries over the security of Chinese territory from foreign attack. China's relations with the United States had been in a deep-freeze since Korea. With the U.S. Air Force bombing Hanoi and the Americans sending 500,000 troops to South Vietnam, China's leaders decided not to take any risks with their nation's security.

But the 1965–68 deployment was limited in nature and for purposes of deterrence only. At the beginning of 1965, for example, the Chinese and North Vietnamese air forces conducted joint exercises which were restricted to within twelve miles of the Chinese border.[72] Chinese air defense and engineering troops arrived in North Vietnam with no fanfare, and fired on American aircraft only in self-defense or in the defense of their North Vietnamese allies. Beijing was very careful to signal to Washington the exact conditions under which it would enter the war in force: "The Chinese People's Liberation Army now stands ready, in battle array. We shall not attack; if we are attacked, we will certainly counterattack."[73]

Chinese officials who pushed for a more aggressive policy towards the United States could find themselves in serious trouble. Luo Ruiqing, the PLA Chief of Staff in the mid-1960s, clashed with Defense Minister Lin Biao over the seriousness of the threat to China posed by the American buildup in Vietnam. Both men agreed that some danger existed, but Luo argued for increased defense spending to counter what he felt to be the heightened danger of American attack. Mao Zedong, not wishing to be distracted from the crisis of the Cultural Revolution, sided with his protege Lin,[74] and Luo Ruoqing was relieved of his command in 1966. After the Tet offensive in early 1968, the Chinese, seeing that the United States was looking for way out, withdrew their forces from North Vietnam.

What the examples of Korea and the two wars involving Vietnam show is that Chinese leaders carefully balance China's domestic situation against the nature of any external threats. In both the Korean War and the 1979 invasion of Vietnam, domestic stability in China allowed Beijing a free hand overseas. Only in the case of the 1965–68 intervention in Vietnam did Chinese leaders decide to involve themselves on foreign soil while their country suffered from domestic conflict. Even then, the Chinese dispatch of troops to North Vietnam had limited defensive goals, was carried out quietly, and was quickly terminated once the danger of a U.S. attack on China had died away. This suggests that Beijing will behave cautiously if faced with the combination of internal unrest and the threat of foreign war.

CONCLUSION

Today, the PLA's largest source of relatively modern military technology is the military-industrial complex left behind by the former Soviet Union. The generals of the PLA should not forget the uselessness of Soviet armor during the Gulf War. Geography also argues against easy Chinese success in any military operations against the Spratly Islands. Even if all the reported sales of Russian military equipment are consummated, China, due to the distance of the Spratly Islands from major Chinese bases, would find it difficult to maintain a continuous air umbrella with a large force of aircraft over the ships of its South Sea Fleet. Considering the PLAN's lack of SAM-equipped warships, the absence of effective air cover might place the PLAN in the same fatal situation as the *Prince of Wales* and *Repulse* were fifty years ago when Japanese warplanes sent them to the bottom of the South China Sea. Even if the PLAN had many SAM-equipped vessels on hand, they might not help Chinese forces operating in the vicinity of the Spratly Islands. Much of China's weaponry, as we have already seen, is simply not very good. Results for the Chinese could be disastrous if they came up against a force armed with even a small number of "smart" weapons. Such a situation is almost certainly unavoidable since China's regional rivals are growing in both wealth and technological prowess. During the 1982 Falklands War, fewer than half a dozen Argentine aircraft armed with *Exocet* missiles sank the modern British destroyer *Sheffield* and several other vessels. A few more hits, particularly on one of the all-important aircraft carriers, could have cost Britain the war. China is so poorly equipped for the type of short, destructive high-tech fighting that was the hallmark of the naval warfare around the Falklands that one analyst recently declared: "An expansionist maritime policy is not an option given the current state of the [Chinese] fleet's equipment and training."[75]

The ASEAN states are slowly moving in the direction of increased military cooperation, with China being the only possible target of such efforts. The fast-paced economic growth of most ASEAN states has made them very popular with foreign investors, particularly those from Japan and Taiwan. Their economic star status, in tandem with the Spratly Islands' location along important sea lanes, almost certainly guarantees a major international outcry and open-handed assistance for these states in the event of aggressive action by China. China could face the same type of diplomatic isolation and dropoff in foreign investment that it suffered in the wake of the massacre in Tiananmen Square. Even Vietnam, with its new openness to foreign investment, would no longer be the isolated target of opportunity it once was. Violent Chinese action in the Spratly Islands would make other nations believe that China was an East Asian version of Saddam Hussein's Iraq, shattering China's carefully crafted public relations image as a poor nation lifting itself up by its own efforts to join the ranks of the advanced nations.

The force of domestic pressures may set another obstacle in the path of China's maritime ambitions. Much of the PLA's re-equipment program and troop deployment patterns may be at least partially dictated by the need to guard against new outbreaks of internal disorder. Eleven Chinese provinces suffered from peasant unrest in 1992.[76] Brought on by the most spectacular economic transformation since Japan finished its modernization at the beginning of this century, the shredding of China's social fabric is likely to continue. In the last few years of the twentieth century, the PLA and its political masters may have little time for foreign adventures.

If the mainland Chinese want to acquire a larger slice of the resources of the South China Sea, they are probably going to have to negotiate for it. Perhaps in recognition of this situation, the Chinese in August 1993 opened talks with Vietnam aimed at sorting out the two sides' territorial claims in the South China Sea.[77] China's ASEAN neighbors, along with efforts to widen economic ties with China, are engaged in diplomatic efforts of their own to head off any potential crisis. Over the last eighteen months, Singapore, Malaysia, and Indonesia have pushed for exchange visits of defense officials and officers with China in the hope of reducing chances for any misunderstandings.[78]

Broadening opportunities for trade, continued negotiations, and the deterrents to Chinese action already discussed make it unlikely that a major military confrontation over the Spratly Islands will erupt in the near future. The situation should be monitored carefully, however. Since its creation in

1949, the People's Republic of China has often displayed great astuteness in the conduct of its foreign policy. The opening of relations with the United States in the 1970s and China's use of the 1990–91 Gulf Crisis to pull itself out of the public relations quicksand of Tiananmen are proof. But the Chinese retain the very human capacity for self-delusion. China's last war, the 1979 invasion to "punish" Vietnam, cost the PLA heavily. A month of heavy fighting bought the Chinese 20,000 casualties and little else. The Chinese were forced to withdraw behind their borders without the satisfaction of having inflicted serious damage on the bottle-hardened Vietnamese army. But considering the rewards of continued peace, outsiders can hope that Chinese decision makers will avoid past mistakes and what could be a major tragedy not only for China, but for the prosperity and stability of East Asia as well. A war over the dribs and drabs of land that make up the Spratly Islands would be a sorry way indeed to start off the Pacific Century.

NOTES

1. Nicholas D. Kristof, "China's Rise," *Foreign Affairs,* Vol. 72, No. 5 (November/ December 1993), p. 59
2. Ibid., p. 61.
3. "China Speeds on to the Market," *The Economist,* November 20, 1993, p. 35.
4. "A Job for China," *The Economist,* May 1, 1993, p. 18.
5. John Garver, "China's Push Through the South China Sea: The Interaction of Bureaucratic and National Interests," *The China Quarterly,* December 1992, p. 1015.
6. Michael T. Klare, "The Next Great Arms Race," *Foreign Affairs,* Vol. 72, No. 3 (Summer 1993), p. 142.
7. "Trick or Treat," *The Economist,* July 10, 1993, p. 29.
8. Stephen Parksmith, "Spratly Claims Conflict," *Asian Pacific Defence Reporter: Annual Reference Edition* (1993), p. 48.
9. Parksmith, "Spratly Claims Conflict." Thity's small size certainly makes it useless as a site for an airstrip, unless one is using light fixed-wing aircraft, helicopters, or VTOL aircraft, of which China has none. Along with the runway itself one has to have an airfield infrastructure as well.
10. Garver, "China's Push Through the South China Sea."
11. Parksmith, "Spratly Claims Conflict," p. 48.
12. "In order to make sure that the descendants of the Chinese nation can survive, develop, prosper and flourish in the world of the future, we should vigorously develop and use the oceans." Garver, "China's Push Through the South China Sea." p. 1019.
13. Michael Richardson, "Spratlys Increasing Cause for Concern," *Asian Pacific Defense Reporter,* October–November 1992, p. 37.
14. Ibid.
15. Parksmith, "Spratly Claims Conflict," p. 49.
16. Ibid.
17. Ibid.
18. Denis Warner, "Interdependence a Regional Cornerstone," *Asian Pacific Defense Reporter,* February–March 1993, p. 16.

19. Tai Ming Cheung, "Instant Navy," *The Far Eastern Economic Review*, February 18, 1993, p. 11.
20. Michael Vatikiotis, "The First Step: ASEAN Takes the First Step on Security Concerns," *Far Eastern Economic Review*, June 3, 1993, p. 18.
21. Tai Ming Cheung, "Sukhois, Sams, Subs: China Steps Up Arms Purchases From Russia," *Far Eastern Economic Review*, April 16, 1993, p. 23.
22. Michael Richardson, "China's Buildup Rings Alarm Bells," *Asian Pacific Defense Reporter*, February–March 1993, p. 11.
23. Tai Ming Cheung, "China's Buying Spree," *Far Eastern Economic Review*, July 8, 1993, p. 24.
24. Ibid.
25. Michael Mecham, "Malaysia Buys MIG-29s, F/A18Ds," *Aviation Week and Space Technology*, July 5, 1993, p. 25.
26. "Frigates for the Royal Malaysian Navy," *Asian Pacific Defense Reporter*, June–July 1992, p. 31.
27. "Russia Muscles In," *The Economist*, July 17, 1993, p. 34.
28. International Institute for Strategic Studies (IISS), *The Military Balance 1993–94* (London: IISS, 1993), p. 160.
29. David Boey, "A Firm Product Base," *Jane's Defense Weekly*, April 4, 1993, p. 37.
30. Tai Ming Cheung, "Staying Smart," *Far Eastern Economic Review*, May 12, 1992, p. 18.
31. IISS, *The Military Balance, 1993–94*, p. 149.
32. Tai Ming Cheung, "Instant Navy," p. 11.
33. "Minister Views Purchase of UK Jet Fighters," Jakarta Radio, June 15, 1993, Foreign Broadcast Information Service: East Asian Edition, No. 114 (June 16, 1993), p. 40.
34. R. N. Moore, *Jane's Fighting Ships, 1993–94* (Coulsdon, Surrey, U.K.: Jane's Information Group, 1993), pp. 117, 127.
35. Tai Ming Cheung, "Lacking Depth," *Far Eastern Economic Review*, February 4, 1993, p. 11.
36. Ibid.
37. Tai Ming Cheung, "Sukhois, Sams, Subs."
38. Ibid.
39. Richard A. Bitzinger, "Arms to Go: Chinese Arms Sale to the Third World," *International Security*, Vol. 17, No. 2 (Fall 1992), p. 98.
40. Ibid., p. 99.
41. Norman Friedman, *Desert Victory: The War for Kuwait* (Annapolis: Naval Institute Press, 1991), p. 210.
42. Ibid., p. 234.
43. "Russia's Armed Forces: The Threat That Was," *The Economist*, August 28, 1993, p. 18.
44. Denis Warner, "First Big Steps Towards Regional Security," *Asian Pacific Defense Reporter*, June–July 1992, p. 11.
45. Michael Richardson, "Crackdown on Piracy," *Asian Pacific Defense Reporter*, October–November 1992, p. 34.
46. Tai Ming Cheung, "Staying Smart."
47. Warner, "First Big Steps," p. 10.
48. "That's What Friends Are For," *The Economist*, February 26, 1994, p. 34.
49. Michael Vatikiotis, "Brave New World," *The Far Eastern Economic Review*, January 30, 1992, p. 19.

50. Michael Richardson, "Indonesia Opens Commercial Door to U.S.," *Asian Pacific Defense Reporter,* October–November 1992, p. 33.

51. Gary Klintworth, "Rich, And Now Powerful," *Asia Pacific Defense Reporter,* October–November 1992, p. 36.

52. "Trick or Treat," *The Economist,* July 10, 1993, pp. 28–29.

53. N. Balakrishnan, "High Octane Growth," *The Far Eastern Economic Review,* January 20, 1994, p. 44.

54. Ibid.

55. "Southeast Asia's Octopuses," *The Economist,* July 17, 1993, p. 62.

56. "China Speeds on to Market," p. 35.

57. Ibid.

58. "Southeast Asia's Octopuses," p. 61.

59. "Power Surge: Electricity in China," *The Economist,* March 19, 1994, p. 82.

60. Ibid.

61. These units are the 38th Army at Baoding in Hebei Province, the 39th Army at Dalian in Liaoning Province, and the 54th Army at Xinxiang in Henan Province. Tai Ming Cheung, "Quick Response," *Far Eastern Economic Review,* January 14, 1993, p. 19.

62. "China Prepares for a Summer of Discomfort," *The Economist,* April 9, 1994, p. 35.

63. "Cut Along the Dotted Lines," *The Economist,* June 26, 1993, p. 35.

64. Ibid.

65. Ibid.

66. "Why China's People are Getting Out of Control," *The Economist,* June 12, 1993, p. 42.

67. Ibid.

68. Ibid.

69. Anthony Blass, Carl Goldstein, and Lincoln Kaye, "Get Off Our Backs," *Far Eastern Economic Review,* July 15, 1993, p. 68.

70. Ibid.

71. "The Revolt of the Peasants," *The Economist,* June 19, 1993, p. 33.

72. Allen S. Whiting, *The Chinese Calculus of Deterrence: India and Indochina* (Ann Arbor: University of Michigan Press, 1975), p. 175.

73. According to Whiting, this statement meant that China would not enter the war unless it was physically invaded: "This wording excluded any ground combat with American troops unless and until American troops crossed the border" into China. Ibid., p. 185.

74. Gerald Segal, *Defending China* (Oxford: Oxford University Press, 1985), p. 169.

75. Moore, *Jane's Fighting Ships: 1993–94,* p. 55.

76. Blass, Goldstein, and Kaye, "Get Off Our Backs," p. 68.

77. Politics and Current Affairs Section, *The Economist,* August 28, 1993, p. 4.

78. Michael Richardson, "China's Military Secrecy Raises Questions," *Asian Pacific Defense Reporter,* June–July 1993, p. 24.

Broken Promises: Hong Kong Faces 1997

Martin C.M. Lee and Tom Boasberg

During a century and a half of British colonial rule, the people of Hong Kong have been denied the experience of democratic government. At the same time, however, this bustling port city has established itself as the freest place in Asia—not only for trade and commerce, but also with respect to such personal and civil liberties as the right to a fair trial and freedom of the press. The people of Hong Kong are determined to expand their rights to include that of democratic self-government, for they fear that without democratic elections they may lose the rule of law and human rights guarantees that they have long enjoyed and so highly cherish. In three short years, sovereignty over the six million inhabitants of Hong Kong will be transferred from Britain to the People's Republic of China (PRC), and neither China nor Britain is honoring their joint promise that Hong Kong could look forward to exercising full autonomy over its own internal affairs. If this promise remains unfulfilled, then the light of freedom and hope that Hong Kong represents for China's 1.1 billion people may well be extinguished.

In 1984, the government of the People's Republic of China and Great Britain signed the Joint Declaration on the Future of Hong Kong, in which Britain pledged to transfer sovereignty over the Crown Colony of Hong Kong to the PRC on 1 July 1997. In the Joint Declaration, China promised that Hong Kong would retain its capitalist economy for at least 50 years after 1997, and that the people of Hong Kong would be allowed to govern themselves in all matters except defense and foreign affairs, which would be the responsibility of the central government in Beijing. Deng Xiaoping encapsulated the PRC's declared intentions in a trio of four-Chinese-character phrases: Beijing's policy toward Hong Kong would be grounded on the principle of "one country, two systems," meaning that "Hong Kong people will rule Hong Kong" with a "high

Martin C.M. Lee, Chair of the United Democrats of Hong Kong, and Tom Boasberg, J.D., Stanford Law School. "Broken Promises: Hong Kong Faces 1997," *Journal of Democracy,* Vol. 5, No. 2, April 1994: 42–56.

degree of autonomy." For its part, Britain promised that it would use the 13-year transition period between the 1984 Joint Declaration and the 1997 transfer of sovereignty to transform its unelected colonial administration into a government democratically elected by the people of Hong Kong.

Ten years after the Joint Declaration, however, and only three years before the handover, it has become clear that neither Britain nor China is going to honor the promises that each made in the Joint Declaration. Almost before the ink was dry on the treaty, the PRC Government began to backpedal from its promises of self-rule for Hong Kong. The Beijing-drafted Hong Kong Basic Law, which is to serve as the territory's post-1997 constitution, reneges on the Joint Declaration's promise of democratic elections and ensures that Beijing will be able to exercise authoritarian control over Hong Kong. As 1997 draws closer, the communist regime's threats and meddling grow stronger by the day.

In order both to appease the PRC and to maintain control over Hong Kong during the twilight of its colonial rule, Britain has disavowed its own transition responsibility of developing democratic institutions in the colony. It has promised Beijing that it will allow for no more than a third of the colony's 60-seat legislature (known formally as the Legislative Council, or Legco) to be democratically elected before 1997, and executive power remains firmly in the hands of the British governor appointed from London. While Hong Kong's latest governor, former Conservative party chairman Chris Patten, has angered Beijing by proposing some modest last-minute democratic reforms, the fury probably has more to do with Patten's rhetoric and style than with the actual content of his limited proposals.

It is imperative that Britain use the final years of its rule to respond at last to Hong Kong's need for genuinely democratic institutions. China, likewise, must be persuaded to amend its authoritarian Basic Law and allow Hong Kong the autonomy promised in the 1984 treaty. If the PRC attempts, as it is now threatening, to impose its dictatorial rule on Hong Kong, there will likely be serious conflict between the communist government and the well-educated, cosmopolitan, and heretofore free people of Hong Kong.

THE JOINT DECLARATION

Hong Kong's three parts—Hong Kong Island itself, the Kowloon Peninsula, and the New Territories (the area between Kowloon and Mainland China that constitutes approximately 90 percent of the colony's total land mass of just over a thousand square kilometers)—were acquired by Britain through three separate nineteenth-century treaties forced on China's Qing emperors. While Hong Kong Island and Kowloon were ceded in perpetuity to Britain in 1842 and 1860 respectively, the decaying Qing Dynasty in 1898 granted Britain only a 99-year lease over the New Territories. It is this lease that expires in 1997. Although the communist leaders who founded the PRC in 1949 never recognized the legitimacy of these three "unequal treaties," neither did they seek to force Britain out of Hong Kong. From 1949 to his death in 1976, Chinese Communist Party (CCP) chairman Mao Zedong's position on Hong Kong was simply that the PRC would take back Hong Kong "when the time is ripe." The usefulness of Hong Kong as a source of foreign currency and a window on the world apparently outweighed the insult that the British colony's existence presented to the CCP's nationalist and socialist principles.

In September 1982, Britain's then-Prime Minister Margaret Thatcher made her first visit to Beijing to raise the question of Hong Kong's future with Chinese leader Deng Xiaoping. Fresh from Britain's victory over Argentina in the Falklands War, Thatcher adopted an aggressively nationalistic pose, stressing Britain's sovereign treaty rights to rule Hong Kong rather than the rights of the people of the territory. In two years of difficult Sino-British negotiations that followed the Thatcher visit, Britain offered to recognize the PRC's formal sovereignty over Hong Kong in exchange for continued British administration of the colony after 1997. China refused, insisting that Hong Kong was part of Chinese national territory that Britain must return. In two years of talks, no representatives of Hong Kong's six million people were ever consulted or allowed to play any part; all discussions took place in secret between British and PRC diplomats.

In September 1984, Britain and China initialed the Joint Declaration in which Britain agreed to transfer sovereignty over Hong Kong in 1997 and China made detailed promises as to how it would implement its stated policy of "one country, two systems." Despite its obligations under the UN Charter and the International Covenant on Civil and Political Rights, Britain refused Hong Kong the right to determine its own fate. The people of Hong Kong never had a chance to vote on or amend the provisions of the Joint Declaration. it was presented as a "done deal" made by the outgoing and incoming sovereign powers.

Nevertheless, the detail and substance of the Joint Declaration exceeded Hong Kong's expectations. The Joint Declaration proclaims that after 1997 Hong Kong will become a Special Administrative Region of the PRC, and that it "will enjoy a high degree of autonomy, except in foreign and defense affairs, which are the responsibilities of the Central People's Government." The Declaration promises Hong Kong wide-ranging economic autonomy, avowing that the territory can keep its capitalist economy, remain a free port, retain its own currency, participate in multilateral organizations such as the General Agreement on Tariffs and Trade (GATT), have independent finances, and remain free from any taxes from Beijing. On the whole, therefore, the treaty makes clear the importance that China places upon Hong Kong's remaining the capitalist engine that has done so much to help drive China's remarkable post-1979 economic growth.

While the political and legal autonomy granted to the territory under the Joint Declaration is not quite so extensive, the treaty's provisions do establish the system under which "Hong Kong people will rule Hong Kong." According to the Joint Declaration, the Legislative Council, which in 1984 was entirely appointed by the colonial government is to be fully elected by 1997. The chief executive (the post-1997 governor) is to be selected "on the basis of the results of elections or consultations held locally." Although this clause leaves Beijing able to refuse to allow elections for the chief executive in favor of a controlled "consultation" process, the treaty at least requires that the legislature be fully elected and that executive authorities "abide by the law" and "be accountable to the legislature."

Equally important, the territory is to continue to be governed under its existing common-law system, and the "laws currently in force in Hong Kong will remain basically unchanged." As the treaty stipulates: "Rights and freedoms, including those of the person, of speech, of press, of assembly, of association, of travel, of movement, of correspondence, of strike, of choice of occupation, of academic research, and of religious belief will be ensured by law." In order to guarantee that these freedoms do not share the fate of the similar list of promised freedoms enumerated in the PRC's Constitution, the Joint Declaration provides that Hong Kong's courts shall continue to be independent of the government. Although the Chinese government was not prepared to allow appeals from Hong Kong courts to the Privy Council in London to continue after July 1997, it did agree to Hong Kong's establishment of its own Court of Final Appeal. This new court is to have the power of final judgment over Hong Kong law; to bolster its independence from the government, it is allowed to invite distinguished foreign judges from other common-law countries to sit on its benches.

Perhaps the greatest flaw of the Joint Declaration is that it gives to China's National People's Congress (NPC), and not to the people of Hong Kong, the task of embodying the treaty's provisions in a "Basic Law" that will serve as the territory's post-1997 constitution. Although it may have been somewhat naive to expect the communist regime to fulfill its promises, the great detail of the Joint Declaration and its status as a binding international treaty nonetheless created high hopes among the people of Hong Kong. The last decade, however, has demonstrated just how unfounded such hopes really were.

DEMOCRATIZATION VERSUS "CONVERGENCE"

After the signing of the Joint Declaration in September 1984, Britain was faced with the responsibility of reforming its colonial government along democratic lines. In particular, the British had to transform the wholly appointed Legco into a wholly elected one by 1997. As Richard Luce, Minister of State with Special Responsibility for Hong Kong, pledged to the House of Commons on 4 December 1984, during the ratification debate on the Joint Declaration: "We all fully accept that we should build up a firmly based democratic administration in Hong Kong in the years between now and 1997."

While Britain's original intentions may have been good, it soon retreated in the face of China's vociferous objections and the colonial government's own reluctance to share political power with local Hong Kong representatives. Further pressure against democratization emanated from members of the colony's business elite, who traditionally had been appointed to the colonial Legco and feared the prospect of open democratic competition. In 1985, therefore, Britain contented itself with introducing indirect elections to Legco through extremely limited constituencies such as business and finance groups and professional associations. Britain labeled these rotten boroughs—most of which had less than a thousand voters—as "functional constituencies." Their introduction was only a slight improvement over the colonial appointment system.

Within months after the introduction of these indirect elections, Britain's new special minister for Hong Kong, Timothy Renton, was summoned to Beijing. He returned to Hong Kong in January 1986 announcing that thenceforth Britain's primary transition responsibility would be not building democratic institutions but rather achieving "convergence" with Beijing's plans for Hong Kong after 1997. Convergence was necessary, Renton argued, to achieve a "smooth transition" in 1997. This passive and shortsighted notion has remained the touchstone of British policy ever since. Its inevitable result has been to allow Beijing to dictate pre-1997 policy for Hong Kong, for any failure by the colonial government to confine its reforms within the limits set down by Beijing would damage the paramount goal of convergence in 1997. In 1988, therefore, after the colonial government conducted a sham public review to determine whether to introduce democratic elections to Legco, colonial officials chose to defer to China's objections to democratic reform. Though numerous independent surveys showed a strong majority of Hong Kong citizens favoring democratic elections, the colonial rulers declared that opinion in Hong Kong was too "divided" to permit such democratic elections before 1991—more than halfway through the 13-year transition period!

Meanwhile, in Beijing, the NPC was drafting the Hong Kong Basic Law. In order to give the appearance of Hong Kong participation, the NPC gave 23 places on its 59-member drafting committee to representatives from Hong Kong—after making sure that most of these were longtime pro-Beijing loyalists. As the drafting process proceeded, it soon became apparent that Beijing had no intention of living up to the Joint Declaration's promises of political and judicial autonomy. Most striking was Beijing's contention that the promise of "elections" to Legco did not in any way imply open and direct balloting. Rather, communist leaders argued that "indirect" elections were more desirable and pointed approvingly to the easily controllable "functional constituencies" that the British had introduced in 1985.

As the drafting process neared its close, the PRC and Hong Kong alike were profoundly shaken by the Chinese democracy movement that captured the world's attention in the spring of 1989. Inspired by the courageous example of the students in Beijing's Tiananmen Square, over a million of Hong Kong's people poured into the colony's narrow streets on two successive Sundays in late May to support the students' call for democracy in China. After this call was stifled by the brutal Tiananmen Square Massacre of June 4, a great wave of anger and fear toward the government that would rule them in eight years' time swept over the colony's residents.

The massacre in Beijing and the ensuing repression throughout the Mainland greatly strengthened Hong Kong's desire for a democratic political system capable of safeguarding human rights. Even Legco, which still lacked any democratically elected members, began arguing for democratic reforms that Beijing and London had already rejected. The Council unanimously agreed that Britain should allow for at least half of Legco to be democratically elected before 1997, and called on China to provide that the entire Legco membership and the chief executive be democratically elected by 2003.

Both Britain and China, however, turned a deaf ear to such pleas. Hong Kong's reaction to Tiananmen raised for Britain the disturbing possibility that a democratically elected legislature in the colony would object heatedly to the terms of the 1997 handover. For Britain to be seen remanding an unwilling Hong Kong into the hands of a communist dictatorship with a known lack of regard for its treaty commitments under the Joint Declaration would be a foreign relations disaster. It became imperative, therefore, for Britain to ensure itself the cover afforded by a majority of yes-men in the colony's legislature. In Beijing, the resurgence of hard-liners following Tiananmen only stiffened the regime's opposition to democratic reforms in a territory where a million people had so recently come out to demand that the CCP give up its grip on China.

Unbeknown to people in Hong Kong, Britain and China began secretly to collude for the purpose of formulating a response to the colony's call for democratic reforms. In February 1990, the two governments reached a secret deal not fully disclosed until almost three years later: Britain agreed to allow no more than a third of the Legco to be democratically elected before 1997, and also promised to raise no objections to the inclusion in the soon-to-be-completed Basic Law of severe restrictions on the democratization of the territory after 1997. In April, the NPC finally promulgated the Basic Law. As widely expected in Hong Kong, the NPC had designed an authoritarian system with power concentrated in the hands of a Beijing-appointed chief executive subject to few checks or balances from the legislative or judicial branches. In a strong display of dissatisfaction with this projected constitution, Hong Kong's Legco moved on 4 April 1990—the date of the Basic Law's promulgation— to call on Beijing to amend many of its central provisions.

THE BASIC LAW

As Hong Kong's future constitution, the Basic Law will go into effect at the moment of turnover on 1 July 1997. It is the hope of Hong Kong that the Chinese government will agree to amend this severely flawed document before then, yet the PRC's leaders have repeatedly stated that amendments are impossible—indeed even illegal—before 1997. Most troubling is the degree to which the Basic Law departs from the Joint Declaration. In order to understand what China plans for Hong Kong after 1997—and to see how greatly this differs from what was promised in 1984—one need only briefly examine some core provisions of the Basic Law.

A) *Election of the Legislature:* Despite the Joint Declaration's promise that the Hong Kong legislature "shall be constituted by elections," only a third of the legislators chosen in 1997 are to be democratically elected. The rest are to be selected via "functional constituencies" and an undefined "Election Committee" which presumably will be under Beijing's control. While the Basic law provides for marginal increases in the number of democratically elected legislators in future years, there is no promise that more than half the legislature will ever be democratically elected. The PRC government seems intent on controlling a legislative majority through its supporters in the territory.

B) *Appointment of the Chief Executive:* The chief executive, who will possess many of the same wide-ranging powers as the current colonial governor, will not be democratically elected, but rather will be selected by a Beijing-controlled "Election Committee" similar to the one that will select members for the legislature. Appointed by the central government in Beijing, the chief executive, also will be removable only by Beijing.

C) *Accountability of the Chief Executive:* While the Joint Declaration provides that executive authorities up to and including the chief executive "shall be accountable to the legislature," the Basic Law gives Legco no power to pass a vote of no confidence in the chief executive, even as it arms the chief executive with the power unilaterally to dissolve the legislature should it fail to pass an "important" bill. Just as significantly, the chief executive has the power to block the introduction of any bill by a legislator if the chief executive deems the bill in question to be "relating to government policies"—a potentially all-encompassing prohibition.

D) *Restrictions on the Judiciary:* Although the Joint Declaration promises that Hong Kong courts will have the "power of final adjudication," the power of interpretation over the Basic Law—the territory's own constitution—ultimately rests not with Hong Kong courts but with the Standing Committee of the National People's Congress. This severely limits the ability of the courts to ensure governmental compliance with the Basic Law, thus calling into question the viability of the rule of law in Hong Kong. It also means that the final arbiter of the constitutional rights of the people of Hong Kong will be the communist legislature in Beijing. Beijing furthermore has reserved to itself the power to declare null and void any Hong Kong law (whether passed before or after 1997) that it deems to be in conflict with the Basic Law, a power that it has already stated it will use to repeal Hong Kong's Bill of Rights. Finally, Beijing, with London's blessing, has reinterpreted the power given under the Joint Declaration to Hong Kong's post-1997 Final Court of Appeal to "invite judges from other common-law jurisdictions to sit on the Court." Under the new interpretation, the Court will be able to invite one foreign judge at most.

THE 1991 ELECTIONS

Slightly more than a year after the promulgation of the Basic Law, in September 1991, the people of Hong Kong were finally given the opportunity to elect 18 of the 60 members of the Legislative Council democratically. The election turned into a contest between advocates of democracy (viewed with hostility by Beijing and London) and those who favored good relations with Beijing above democratic reform. The democrats' campaign theme was very clear: Hong Kong must proceed with democratic reforms before 1997 even though such reforms might alienate Beijing and be dismantled in 1997. The democrats' chief opponents, most of whom had the backing of pro-Beijing groups and business associations, opposed further reforms and placed their emphasis on good relations with China and a smooth transition in 1997.

Despite the funding edge enjoyed by the pro-Beijing and business-backed candidates, the democrats swept the election. Of the 18 seats, democrats captured 17, with the United Democrats of Hong Kong winning 12. Not only was the margin of seats won overwhelming, but within individual constituencies leading democrats outpolled their rivals by margins of over 2 to 1. Governor David Wilson, one of the main architects of Britain's policy of appeasement toward China, was surprised by these results, but waited only days to appoint 17 antireform representatives to Legco as a counterweight to the elected democrats. These appointees almost immediately formed a coalition with the business representatives chosen through the functional constituencies to build an antireform majority within Legco.

Equally important, the British government decided to break with longstanding practice in cases of decolonization and refused to name any local democrats to the colony's Executive Council (Exco), which serves officially as the governor's cabinet and in practice makes decisions by majority vote that he is bound to follow. As the British prepared to pull out of other former colonies (such as Ghana, malaysia, and Kenya), they had always appointed leading winners of the first democratic legislative elections to the Executive Council—both to lend legitimacy to the sunset regime and to prepare locally elected leaders for the task of governing. In Hong Kong's case, however, China's strong objections to the appointment of democrats, along with Governor Wilson's lack of enthusiasm for sharing power with elected leaders vigorously opposed to his appeasement policy, led to a British refusal to name any democrats to Exco and allow for the start of self-government.

THE ARRIVAL OF GOVERNOR PATTEN

Soon after the Tory victory in Britain's April 1992 general election, Prime Minister John Major named his close personal friend and former Conservative party chairman Chris Patten as Wilson's replacement. Patten, who had failed to hold onto his own parliamentary seat in the elections, represented a departure from the pattern set by his predecessors. He was not a Mandarin Chinese-speaking diplomat whose career had been built by promoting smooth Sino-British relations, but rather a consummate politician who at the time of his appointment had practically no experience in Hong Kong or Chinese affairs.

When Patten arrived in Hong Kong in July 1992, he found a colony that had changed vastly in the ten years since Britain had initiated negotiations with China over its future. The PRC's own successful experiments with economic reform had spurred a tremendous business boom in Hong Kong during the 1980s, and by 1993 the colony's per capita GDP exceeded that of Britain itself. Though business had suffered a brief downturn following the Tiananmen Square Massacre of 1989, China had rebounded to emerge as the world's fastest-growing economy by 1992. As the principal source of China's foreign investment capital and the port through which it ships most of its exports, Hong Kong has reaped great dividends from China's growth. As Hong Kong investors poured their money into the Mainland, and as Hong Kong manufacturing companies moved their operations into neighboring Guangdong Province to take advantage of low land and labor costs, the economic border between Hong Kong and the Mainland began to fade; economists now speak of the flourishing Pearl River Delta as a single economic unit.

While business confidence in the colony was at an all-time high at the time of Patten's arrival, the same could not be said for political confidence. Dissatisfaction with Britain's policy of appeasement and fear of Communist China's plans for 1997 and beyond led many in Hong Kong to demand that the new governor reverse his predecessors' policy of seeking to squelch democratic reforms. Shortly after Patten took office, all 18 democratically elected members of Legco, in a rare unanimous action, signed a letter calling on him to resist Beijing's pressure and allow at least half of Legco to be democratically elected before 1997. Simultaneously, polls showed Hong Kong residents saying yes by a 7-to-1 margin when asked if the new governor should introduce democratic reforms even at the expense of antagonizing the PRC.

The feeling in Hong Kong could be summarized simply: if we whose own futures are at stake are willing to stand up to Beijing, why should Britain be so unwilling?

Faced with these pressures in Hong Kong and increasingly aware of the international criticism of Britain's appeasement of Beijing, Governor Patten decided on a course of limited democratic reform. By agreeing to Beijing's demands on the most important subjects but still making substantive reforms, Patten hoped that he might square the circle and satisfy both the gerontocrats in Beijing and Hong Kong's young middle class. He began by bowing to Beijing on the two most important issues of democratic reform. In October 1992, in his first Policy Address to Legco, Patten announced that despite the unanimous wish of Legco's democratically elected members, Britain would not allow more than a third of Legco to be democratically elected before 1997. Nor, he added, would he appoint any democratically elected representatives to the Executive Council. With these two strokes, he denied Hong Kong the opportunity for any meaningful degree of democratic self-government before 1997, just as China wished.

To compensate, Patten hoped to enlarge the numbers of electors represented in the indirect-election constituencies of Legco. According to the Basic Law, in 1997, only 20 of Legco's 60 members are to be democratically elected; 30 are to be chosen through the functional constituencies, and the remaining 10 are to be picked by the nebulous "Election Committee." In their secret deal of 1990, Britain and China had agreed that if the 1995 Legco elections (the last under British sovereignty) followed these proportions, then China would allow this Legco to continue in office for its full four-year term ending in 1999. This was known as the "through-train" arrangement, from the term for the Hong Kong-Guangzhou express rail service.

Patten's approach centered on broadening the extraordinarily narrow franchise in the rotten boroughs of the functional constituencies and defining the rules for the yet-to-be-established Election Committee. Patten planned nine new functional constituencies (making a total of 30) to be elected through the suffrage of Hong Kong's 2.7 million working adults. His decision to preserve the 21 existing functional constituencies represented a major concession to Beijing and Hong Kong business interests. Second, he proposed that Hong Kong's Election Committee, which would choose ten Legco members in 1995, be composed of local district representatives who themselves would be democratically elected. Under Patten's plan, then, 39 of Legco's 60 seats (the 20 directly elected, the 9 new functional constituencies, and the 10 filled by the Election Committee) would be open to widespread suffrage. Given the democrats' overwhelming success in the 1991 Legco elections, it was a real possibility that they could capture more than 30 of these seats in 1995, giving them a thin legislative majority and creating a nightmare scenario for Beijing.

Beijing reacted furiously to Patten's proposals, and the PRC media made him the object of an almost comically vitriolic propaganda barrage. Patten's extremely limited reforms became the focus of a major international dispute between Britain and China. China's rage stemmed from several sources. First, Beijing's leaders bitterly resented Patten's direct and unsparing verbal style. Second, Beijing was not prepared to countenance the possibility that Hong Kong democrats might gain a majority in Legco. Third, and most important, after a decade in which Britain's colonial leaders had bowed to Beijing's every wish and solved all problems secretly through Sino-British diplomatic channels, Patten was attempting to chart a new course and proposing to allow Hong Kong's Legislative Council to make its own decision on the issue of democratic reform.

SECRET NEGOTIATIONS

After six months of shrill invective, Beijing switched tactics and agreed to enter into negotiations with Britain over the Patten proposals. The communist leaders hoped either to make Patten back down or to stall him long enough to kill the reforms. To respond to this ploy, Patten in April 1993 announced that the decision on the reforms was no longer going to be for Hong Kong's Legislative Council to make. Rather, he committed Britain to private talks with Beijing aimed at forging a compromise between the sovereign powers.

These negotiations would be handled by Britain's ambassador to the PRC. The need for secrecy, Patten stated, meant that Britain would not inform the Hong Kong public or even the Legislative Council about the course of the negotiations that would determine their future. In falling back upon the discredited practice of secret Sino-British dealings, Patten failed to understand the strategy of China's leaders.

For almost eight months, PRC negotiators stonewalled in round after round of secret Sino-British talks in Beijing. The Chinese rejected out of hand Patten's proposals to broaden the franchise in the functional constituencies or the Election Committee. In addition, the PRC leaders insisted on retaining the right to prevent Legco members deemed by the Chinese to be "unpatriotic" (i.e., not under Beijing's direct control) from keeping their seats after the 1997 handover. The communist regime, in other words, was determined to throw the Hong Kong democrats off the trans-1997 "through train" in midpassage.

Britain, not surprisingly, found China's position unacceptable: if the British were expected to shape the 1995 Legco elections to guarantee a pro-Beijing majority, then China could at least allow the minority of democrats elected to retain their seats. What the "through-train" approach gives Britain, after all, is an excuse to retreat from its promises of pre-1997 democracy for Hong Kong. Despite the Hong Kong democrats' insistence that Britain's priority should be the establishment of democracy before 1997, Britain has long made the self-serving argument that it is "better for Hong Kong" to sacrifice the "lesser" goal of pre-1997 democracy in order to achieve the "greater" goal of convergence and a smooth transition in 1997. Yet with China declaring its refusal to accept the "through-train" approach, Britain can no longer justify its failure to hold democratic elections now.

As of this writing Patten has finally agreed to introduce his proposals to Legco—nearly 18 months after his initial promise that this would be a matter entirely for Legco to decide. Patten's latest plan, however, appears to be to introduce his proposals and then to allow or even tacitly encourage the current pro-Beijing majority of Legco to gut them by making amendments palatable to Beijing. Such a reliance on Britain's own colonial appointees would be extraordinarily cynical. It is clear that at least 17 of the 18 democratically elected members of Legco support the reform proposals. Indeed, the democratically elected representatives believe that Mr. Patten's plans are far too limited, and intend to offer amendments to make at least 30 Legco seats democratically elected by 1995. Patten still retains enough influence over several appointed Legco members to obtain their support for his original proposals (indeed, Legco passed resolutions supporting the reforms on three separate occasions in late 1992). Now, however, he appears content to let the colonial appointees amend the heart out of the reforms. He would then be able to tell the world that Britain had done its part by introducing the reforms, and to lay the blame for their failure squarely on the timidity of Hong Kong's own Legislative Council.

LISTENING TO THE PEOPLE OF HONG KONG

The great irony of Patten's policies is that, while he deserves credit for attempting to broaden the franchise even slightly, the means that he has used tend to undermine Britain's most important duty of decolonization—namely, establishing the institutions that will allow Hong Kong to realize its promised autonomy. Patten's most damaging mistake has been his decision to shut Hong Kong's democrats completely out of the Executive Council. Rather than increasing the authority and democratic composition of Exco in preparation for 1997, Patten has taken ever more personal and direct control over Hong Kong's executive branch. The result is that, as 1997 approaches and the people of the territory are supposed to be learning how to manage their own affairs, their decisions are being made for them by an Englishman who will definitely leave in three years' time. Those who will stay behind have no part in policy making. Consequently, the policy decisions of the Hong Kong government are increasingly viewed by the territory's citizens as Patten's personal decisions made with Britain's interests rather than Hong Kong's interests in mind.

Under the Joint Declaration, reforms to Hong Kong's electoral laws are entirely internal matters for Hong Kong to decide; they have nothing to do with the defense and foreign affairs that are to be managed by the sovereign governments. Yet after initially promising to allow the Hong Kong Legislative Council to decide on the reforms for itself, Patten erred grievously be reneging and opening up more secret Sino-British negotiations closed to the people of

Hong Kong. By allowing the political-reform debate to be transformed into a diplomatic conflict between Britain and China, Patten has taken the whole fight out of Hong Kong's hands. Faced with the impossible choice of supporting either their old colonial or new communist sovereign, the people of the territory view the dispute with increasing skepticism and have little confidence that either Britain or China will act in their interest.

At a time when it is crucial that Hong Kong learn how to govern itself and to negotiate for itself with Beijing, the British have stymied any such development. Within Hong Kong, all major decisions are made by the British colonial governor with little or no input from Hong Kong's elected representatives. In all matters relating to their post-1997 future, the people of Hong Kong are allowed to play no part; everything is handled in secret between British and Chinese diplomats. Sadly, the Joint Declaration's promise that Hong Kong citizens would be allowed to manage their own affairs has never seemed more empty.

With only three years to go before the 1997 handover, Britain must immediately abandon its failed policy. It has already wasted ten years in unavailing attempts to appease China's opposition to political reform. In the 1991 elections, the people of Hong Kong clearly revealed their belief that genuine democratic reforms must be undertaken before 1997, even at the expense of upsetting PRC leaders. The importance of Hong Kong's economy to China's economic reforms (along with the huge sums invested in the territory by Mainland enterprises and individuals) has given Hong Kong confidence that it can stand up for itself; one indication of the territory's growing self-assurance is that in the year and a half since Patten made his proposals, the Hong Kong stock market has more than doubled in value.

Britain must respond to the aspirations of the people of Hong Kong and fulfill the promises it made when it decided in 1984 to hand the territory's six million people over to China. Patten must appoint democratically elected local leaders to the Executive Council, and he must led such a locally constituted government stand up for itself and deal with Beijing. Hong Kong's affairs must be decided by the people of the territory, not by British and Chinese diplomats meeting behind closed doors 1,400 miles away. Equally important, Patten must also accept Hong Kong's demand for genuine democratic elections to Legco, for only then can Legco represent the people of the territory and hold accountable the Beijing-appointed post-1997 chief executive. Given the common view of Hong Kong's democratically elected representatives, Patten must not back away from reforms under the tired old rubric of "Hong Kong's desire for a smooth transition." Hence, he must not let the spring of 1994 go by without ensuring that at least his modest reforms become reality.

Patten himself has said that he knows he will be judged on the degree to which he implements the Joint Declaration. If he fails to establish constitutional institutions whereby Hong Kong people will truly rule Hong Kong with a high degree of autonomy, he will be adjudged to have failed in his duty to Hong Kong. The best scenario would be if Beijing were to agree to accept those institutions and allow them to continue after 1997 on the "through-train" arrangement. It is quite unlikely, however, that PRC leaders will reach such an agreement with Chris Patten in the near future.

The worst scenario would be for Patten, in blind pursuit of "convergence," to reach an agreement with Beijing that would preclude the establishment of democratic political arrangements. Such a "compromise," advocated by many British businessmen and by many of the Sinologists in Britain's Foreign Office, would only ensure that Hong Kong would have no democracy either before or after 1997. It would be far better for Britain, if it cannot obtain China's assent even to modest democratic reforms, to follow Hong Kong opinion anyway and implement such reforms before 1997. Then at least the hope would remain that circumstances could change by 1997, and that Beijing might become reluctant to make its first act of sovereignty the summary ejection of all members of Hong Kong's elected institutions.

At present, Beijing's policy toward Hong Kong remains in the hands of aging communists who, in the power vacuum created by Deng Xiaoping's failing health, are reluctant to do anything more than rely on hard-line dogma. Beijing's leaders must be persuaded that authoritarian tactics and lack of respect for Hong Kong's pluralism will only backfire and lead to conflict and instability in the territory. Deng Xiaoping's original pledge of "one country, two systems" still holds promise for Hong Kong, where the great majority of the people take pride in their Chinese nationality, but are equally devoted to protecting their personal and economic freedoms. Yet this policy needs to be implemented: Hong Kong must be allowed to practice its own separate economic and political systems.

China must agree to amend the territory's post-1997 constitution. The Basic Law is undemocratic, unacceptable to the people of Hong Kong, and unable to preserve the rule of law in the territory. The demise of the rule of law will gravely threaten Hong Kong's status as an international financial center where all investors and financial institutions heretofore have been confident of fair and equal treatment in local courts. China must listen to the people of Hong Kong: we understand our own society best and are in the best position to draft a constitutional framework that will allow for our continued success. If China continues to refuse to honor the Joint Declaration's provisions for political and legal autonomy, then the people of Hong Kong will not enjoy "one country, two systems" and the right to manage their own affairs with a "high degree of autonomy." Rather, Hong Kong will run the risk that it could soon become little different from China's Special Economic zones—with capitalist economics and communist politics. Such a result would be a tragedy not only for the people of Hong Kong but for the cause of democracy throughout the entire Pacific Rim.

Development and Democracy: Are They Compatible in China?

Yongnian Zheng

Democracy's failure to develop in contemporary China gave rise to an intense debate between the advocates of neoauthoritarianism and of democracy in mainland China.[1] Because of the government's crackdown against the 1989 democracy movement, this debate inside China was interrupted for a while. Yet both within China and among Chinese abroad, the debate is being revived. The state's measures for economic and political stabilization and their relative success have led scholars and many politicians, both old and young, to conclude that China needs an authoritarian regime for fast and stable economic growth.

Neoconservatism is becoming popular among Chinese scholars.[2] In contrast, liberal intellectuals who are travelling in the West argue that a centralized state is unnecessary for fast economic growth; economic growth can be reached only after the collapse of this centralized state.[3] Other scholars contend that China cannot go forward in a pluralistic democracy and support stable economic progress without implementing a federal political system, requiring a fundamental loosening of central control.[4]

The purpose of this article is to provide a structural perspective to Chinese democracy. It argues that the development of democracy in China cannot be understood by assessing liberalism as a result of economic development alone. Instead, democratic development must be considered in the context of the connections between the state and development, a form of state-society relations. Those relations present external circumstances for democracy as a political system. Changes in state-society relations in China have originated from economic growth in the reform years.

Yongnian Zheng, former Assistant Professor at Beijing University, "Development and Democracy: Are They Compatible in China?," *Political Science Quarterly,* Vol. 109, No. 2, 1994: 235–259.

The article is divided into two sections. The first will examine changes in state-society relations and their meaning for democracy. The second section will explore why changes in state-society relations have not led to democracy.

REFORMS, DEVELOPMENT, AND CHANGES IN STATE-SOCIETY RELATIONS

In post-Mao China, the Four Modernizations of industry, agriculture, the military, and science and technology have highest priority in state agendas. Although the state legitimatizes the "fifth modernization"—that is, political democratization—economic growth is doubtless the state's most important goal. The achievement of this specific and narrow goal must be judged quite successful. A World Bank 1990 country study reports:

> Over the last decade, China's GDP growth rate has averaged 9.5 percent per annum. Investment was high throughout and was matched by a strong savings performance, which contained the need for external borrowing. Industrialization and modernization increased the competitiveness of China's manufactures in the international market and merchandise exports grew from $18.3 billion in 1980 to $52.5 billion in 1989. China's share of international trade rose from 0.97 percent to 1.7 percent during the same period. The average income of the 800 million rural population more than doubled and absolute poverty receded nationwide. In 1988, some 13 percent of rural households fell below the poverty line, compared with 17 percent in 1981. Infant and child mortality declined, the rate of population growth was slowed and universal education of five years was achieved.[5]

In post-Mao China, politics slowly receded in importance as the Chinese leadership implemented a new political line stressing a pragmatic approach to rebuilding the country's economy, rather than the class struggle which prevailed in Mao's time. From the 1978 Third Plenum onward, various strategies of economic growth have been established in Beijing. Farmers and nonagricultural (industrial, commercial, transport) enterprises now have greater freedom to determine the composition and pricing of outputs, to retain profits, and to decide on the disposition of retained earnings. Administrative decentralization has transferred more of the authority to plan and manage economic activity from the central government to provincial and local bodies. Central control over the economy has been scaled back by reducing the number of commodities, the volume of production subject to mandatory plan targets, and the share of key products distributed through state controlled channels. Resources previously monopolized by the state have been transferred to enterprises and rural producers.

The Deng Xiaoping regime proposed an anti-egalitarianism line at the beginning of the 1980s.[6] The most obvious consequences of this new economic line is the formation of a multifaceted economy. Although China remains an economy where public ownership is dominant, the government has permitted other forms of ownership, including private, cooperative, foreign joint venture, and so forth. According to an official's incomplete statistic, up to 1987 there were 225,000 private enterprises and 3.6 million employees.[7] China has also accelerated its international economy because of the post-Mao regime's open door policy. Western influences have been penetrating China's old protective isolationism. China's external trade, now equivalent to over a quarter of the GDP, has opened up the economy significantly. The creation of several Special Economic Zones with adequate infrastructure, legislation governing foreign investment, and the steady elaboration of laws defining the rights of overseas businesses operating in China have helped attract a large volume of foreign capital. Meanwhile, there has been progress in Chinese technology. From 1981 to 1986, China introduced more than 2,100 foreign technological items, not including items at the local level. These items cost more than 9 billion U.S. dollars.[8]

With economic development, political changes have also been introduced into Chinese political life. Although it is hard to believe that China's political system is becoming a liberal one, China's political system is departing from the old totalitarianism and is tending to be more authoritarian. Harry Harding calls it a "consultative authoritarian regime" characterized by "a significant departure from the totalitarianism of the past but not yet a fully democratic, or even a quasi-pluralistic, political system. . . . It is increasingly consultative in its recognition of the need to obtain information, advice, and support from key sectors of the population, but still authoritarian in its desire to suppress dissent and maintain ultimate political power in the hands of the party."[9]

According to Harding, China's political reform in the post-Mao period can be categorized in terms of five aspects: encouragement of a reconciliation between the party and society by reducing the scope and arbitrariness of political interference in daily life; expansion of opportunities for popular expression in political affairs, albeit with limits on the reform and content of political expression; efforts to revitalize all institutions of governance by restaffing them with younger and better educated officials and by granting them greater autonomy from party control; measures to restore normalcy and unity to elite politics so as to bring to an end the chronic instability of the late Maoist period and create a more orderly process of leadership succession; steps to redefine the content and role of China's official ideology so as to create a new basis for authority in contemporary Chinese politics.[10] Although the state adopted these reform measures to cope with a serious political crisis and maintain party governance, the establishment of these measures created the possibility for further political changes. For example, changes of the cadre system introduced a strong potential element for changing the old political system, even though the party reformed the cadre system in order to revive itself and promote economic progress.

The Chinese political system is not a liberal one, but individual leaders are becoming liberal. They were recruited into the system because of their performance and their better education. They represent a liberal force in the system. Compared to the old generation of leaders, newly recruited cadres can tolerate differences and have less ideological loyalty. They are thus liberal toward individual citizens' diversified behavior, although they have vague attitudes toward democracy.

China's political system is changing institutionally bit by bit if not systematically. For example, China has carried out a local direct election system: delegates to middle-level people's congresses are selected by direct election. Meanwhile, the National People's Congress (NPC) has extended its functions in China's politics. Today it has established a number of functional standing committees to consider and discuss state matters regularly.[11] In addition, other consultative mechanisms such as "democratic parties," the Chinese People's Consultative Conference, and some professional academic associations and research institutions are also encouraged to participate in politics through discussing political agendas, initiating or considering state policy, and providing information for the state's decision making.[12]

The role of China's media is undergoing changes. Although the media are still not an independent mechanism in shaping political agenda, they have played some part in promoting change before the June Fourth 1989 crackdown. First, they encourage transparency in state policy making. The media are becoming involved in almost every major conference, reporting ideas expressed. Second, the media connect voices from above and below. They have been an important channel for individuals, especially intellectuals, to participate in politics. Third, they occasionally reveal corruption among state officials. As a well-known journalist writes, "[In the past], the media have become more and more directly involved in the country's highest level party affairs, governmental affairs, even legislative and judicial activities. They actively build a bridge between people and government, between masters and servants. They have been an important channel to guarantee the people's right to know, to participate in and discuss politics and to supervise state politics."[13]

Economic growth and political progress have had a great impact on individual behavior and thus have significance for China's fifth modernization—democracy. China is now transforming from a planned economy to a mixed one. The market is playing an increasingly important role. In contrast to the planned economy, the base of a market economy is that every human being, as an owner of property, is economically independent and chooses how to cooperate with others in production (division of labor). The market economy is characterized by free choice. Individual initiatives are important. With economic development, economic rationality is changing human relationships and other human behavior and making human beings equalize. Although a market economy also leads to income difference and creates new kinds of difference, it does not create an unequal society, but rather changes the base of inequality. Under a market economy, inequality based on official rank and other political factors is replaced by inequality based on income and other economic factors, less by political factors. What is important for individuals is that they can change their social status by creating economic opportunity using their ability. They can try to get what only those who controlled political resources and thus controlled economic resources could get in the Maoist old days.

Survey data show that individual economic and political values are changing in contemporary China. Since 1978, Chinese living standards have been rising fast because of economic reform. Economic reform on the one hand increases uncertainty and risk in individual life; but on the other, it brings an individual hope and a possibility to develop oneself and realize one's expectations. In terms of individual values, most younger people are open minded in their choice of employment and their consumption preference. A survey demonstrates this trend (see Table 1). Most individuals prefer to take some risk to increase their income and raise their social status. In terms of age groups, 62 percent of young people chose the risky job. This rate is much higher than that of middle-aged and older people. This demonstrates a generation gap in individual values. Also, traditionally, China emphasized frugality. Individuals were asked to control their desire and reduce their consumption. The increased open-mindedness toward consumption among younger persons reflected by the data is the result of the past years of economic progress.

Values are becoming more individualistic. The data reveal that the generation gap is growing. When asked, "What do you think is improper behavior in daily life?" 46 percent of those 45 years old and younger chose "interfering in other people's privacy." Only 22 percent of those 40 years old and older selected this answer. When asked, "What do you think is most important in your life?" 40 percent of those 45 years old and younger chose "friends' confidence and respect of other people" and 20 percent of those 45–60 years old selected the same answer.[14] Table 2 reveals that most young people tend to pay more attention to their own interests. Concerning a possible promotion, we can see that 66 percent of those 30–45 years old chose "try to get myself selected" while 53 percent of those 46–60 years old selected the same answer. Compared to older people, fewer young people chose "to give up the opportunity." This reveals that individual interest is more important to the younger generation.

The data presented in Table 3 demonstrates that political values are also changing, particularly attitudes toward the socialist state. Although most people still identified with the socialist state in 1987, nearly half the interviewees were already indifferent to it. After the death of Mao, Deng's regime faced a serious political crisis—a crisis of political identity. Deng and his reformist successors carried out a series of measures to revive people's confidence in the socialist state.

With progress in economic reforms, individuals gradually increased their income and raised their living standards. Politically, they had relative freedom

Table 1. *Individual Values in China*

Q. 1. "There are two kinds of jobs. From the first, you can get high income and more opportunities to raise your social status. But you have to work hard and also risk losing your job. From the second, you can only get lower income but you do not need to work hard and you will not lose your job. If you have to choose between them for yourself or your children, which will you choose?" *The Result:* *

		The First %	The Second %
Age:	18–30	62	31
	31–45	47	46
	46–60	48	45
	60 and over	42	51
Whole survey		54	39

Q. 2. "Mr. Zhang bought a watch several years ago. It works well now but is old-fashioned. He wants to buy a new one. What would you do? *The Result:* *

		Get a New One %	Use the Old One %
Age:	18–30	53	47
	31–45	41	59
	46–60	38	62
	60 and over	22	78
Whole survey		47	55

* $N = 4,124$

Source: Adopted from Shang Xiaoyuan, *Zhongguoren de ziwo yizhixing renge* [*The Chinese Self-Controlling Personality*], (Kunming, Yunnan People's Publishing House, 1989), 222, 223.

to pursue their own businesses and express their own ideas without state interference. Most of them then held positive expectations for a socialist state and believed that China could resolve her problems within the existing framework. Yet compared to Mao's time, individual loyalty to the socialist state is weakening, especially among young people.

Another nationwide survey among urban citizens also confirms this tendency. When interviewees were asked, "Do you think that 'Love the socialist motherland' is the most important basic morality?" the distribution of those who answered "yes" was: only 28 percent among people 18–30 years old; 38 percent among those 31 to 45 years old; 46 percent for persons 46

Table 2. *Individual Values in China*

Q. "There is an opportunity for a promotion in a unit. Both Mr. Zhang and his close friend Mr. Wang are qualified for the promotion, but only one can be selected. If you are one of them, what will you do?"
The Result: *

Age	*Try to Get Myself Selected* %	*Give Up* %
30 and below	67	22
31–45	66	26
46–60	53	40
60 and over	51	44

* *N* = 4,124.

Source: Adopted from Shang, *Zhongguoren de ziwo yizhixing renge,* 228.

to 60 years old; and 52 percent for those 60 and over.[15] For most individuals, what is important is not what form of state they should have and what ideological principles they should obey, but rather what form of state and what sort of principles will actually promote economic growth and bring about social change.

A change in individual attitudes toward the existing political institutions also has occurred. Data reveal that most people have recognized that to reform the party is the most crucial of all political reforms. Only 15 percent believe that the NPC has played an important role, 46 percent believe that it has played an unimportant role, and 23 percent believe that it has not played any essential role in Chinese politics. Only 39 percent have high expectations for the NPC and believe that only by improving the NPC can Chinese democracy be achieved. Another 39 percent do not have high expectations for the NPC, because to improve the NPC is only one aspect of democracy. Fully 14 percent feel that under the existing regime there is no possibility for people's delegates to represent people's real interests. Thus, to rebuild the NPC is not the starting point of political democratization in China. Instead, China needs to make more efforts to construct the instruments of democracy.

A most dramatic change occurred in individuals' faith in the Communist party (the CCP). The party has faced serious criticisms from individuals since the reform began. Only 30 percent think the party's performance has been satisfactory, and 62 percent think not. This striking change in individuals' faith in the party has made the party much less appealing not only to nonparty individuals, but even to some party members. Fully 57 percent do not expect to be a party member. Another 43 percent of party members are no longer

Table 3. *Individual Attitudes toward the Chinese Socialist State*

Q. "Are you proud of the Chinese socialist state?"
R. Yes: 54%; no: 45% (*N* = 1,721)

Q. "Do you agree with the following statement: 'In China, what is important is not to follow strictly some basic principles but to develop the economy and raise people's living level'?"
R. Yes: 56%; no: 44% (*N* = 1,510)

Q. "Does the CCP's performance satisfy your expectations?"
R. Yes: 30%; no: 62% (*N* = 1,419)

Q. "Do you want to be a CCP member?"
R. Yes: 43%; no: 57% (*N* = 1,230)

Q. "Are you proud of yourself as a party member?"
R. Yes: 56%; no: 43% (*N* = 472)

Q. "Do you think the CCP members have played a vanguard role?"
R. Yes: 18%; no: 78% (*N* = 1,404)

Q. "Are you satisfied with the CCP's ultimate goal?"
R. Yes: 65%; no. 29% (*N* = 1,405)

Q. "Are you satisfied with the CCP's current line and policy?"
R. Yes: 57%; no. 38% (*N* = 1,405)

Q. "Are you satisfied with the CCP's social development goal?"
R. Yes: 52%; no: 47% (*N* = 1,405)

Q. "How do you evaluate the role of the People's Congress?"
R. Functions well: 16%; functions poorly: 23% (*N* = 1,709)

Q. "Do you have expectations that the People's Congress can play an important role in the building of Chinese democracy?"
R. High expectation: 39%; no expectation: 14% (*N* = 1,600)

Q. "Do you agree with the statement that one main reason that China has developed so slowly is its political institutions?"
R. Yes: 72%; no: 28% (*N* = 1,369)

Q. "Do you think now it is necessary to reform the Chinese political system?"
R. Yes: 67%; no: 19% (*N* = 1,337)

Q. "Do you agree with the statement that China needs democracy?"
R. Yes: 75%; no: 19% (*N* = 1,391)

Source: The data are based on 1987 political culture and political attitude survey.
Adopted from Min Qi, *Zhongguo zhengzhi wenhua* [*Chinese Political Culture*], (Kunming Yunnan: Yunnan People's Publishing House, 1989), 33, 35, 98, 99, 101, 64, 66, 83, 179.

proud to be party members. Only 18 percent believe that party members have a vanguard role; 78 percent think they have not. In addition, many individuals begin to cast doubt on the party's ultimate goal, that is, leading the country toward a communist society. Nearly 29 percent are not satisfied with the party's ultimate goal; 47 percent are not content with the party's social de-velopment goal, and 38 percent are not comfortable with the party's line and policy.

Discontented with the state's behavior, individuals assign high priority to institutional reforms. Almost three-quarters argue that the political system itself has led to China's slow pace of progress. Two-thirds contend that it is necessary to reform the political system. Democracy is a desirable alternative. Three-quarters believe that China needs democratic politics, despite their varying views of democracy.

OBSTACLES TO DEMOCRACY

This article so far has demonstrated the impact of economic progress on state-society relations in China. I contend that the introduction of the market economy has given rise to new social forces and attitudes. In this section, I will examine why changes in state-society relations did not lead to the establishment of democracy.

Three theories have been relevant for understanding the conditions for democracy. First is a theory that perceives democracy as a form of government likely only in market or capitalist economies. The second views democracy as more likely to be sustained in wealthy or economically developed societies. The third posits that well established political traditions of compromise politics and of checks and balances on central power help countries evolve into democracies. Taken together, all these theories suggest a logical connection between democracy and market economy.[16] Atul Kohli summarizes:

> Capitalism, as an economic system based on private property, provides a fundamental check on state power. It generates a "private sphere" of social and economic activity separate from the "public sphere." And it is this separation between the public and the private realms that is an initial and necessary condition for the evolution of democracy as a form of limited government. Moreover, the division into the public and the private realms makes the sphere of legal and political equality somewhat separate from that of substantial social and economic inequalities. Separating political equality from economic in-equalities not only lays the basis for legitimate elected governments in inegali-tarian societies. It also opens up the hope and opportunity . . . of modifying inherited inequalities through the use of democratic state power.[17]

An understanding of the development of associations between capitalism and democracy can shed some light on why economic growth did not lead to democracy in China.

Why did economic growth liberalize politics a bit but not democratize China's political system? This article argues that the development of democ-racy in China cannot be understood by reviewing democracy as a result of economic development alone. Instead, democratic development must be con-sidered in the context of the connectedness between the state and development. The state in a developing country like China is not only an agent of political order; it is also responsible for facilitating socioeconomic development. In other words, differing from states in the West, state authorities in China have to generate capitalism and economic development. The state thus faces a dilemma between economic development and democracy. The state must attempt to establish legitimacy and order, on the one hand, and has to promote socioeconomic changes from above on the other. But the state authorities often find that these two sets of goals are in conflict. Whereas democracy tends to require that the state accommodate many competing demands, effective performance of developmental functions pushes the state to stand above society in order to act as a rational agent of change. This tension seems to be irreconcilable in China's case. The state often enforces its rational order on society, which tries to free itself from the state.

Democracy requires a nonpolitical, a societal sphere. Development, however, demands that the state penetrate into society. In other words, both economic growth and creation of civil society are political tasks. The state is thus in command of socioeconomic change. State domination of society makes it difficult for democracy to develop. Democracy is thus more likely to be a gift of the political elite to the society and less likely to be a political system that significant social forces create of their own volition as the West demonstrated.[18]

Having these theoretical considerations in mind, I turn to analyze the state-development association and its meaning for democracy. To do this, I consider politics as an independent variable. This is because I believe that economic reform heavily signifies interest redistribution; it thus creates political opposition. While the nature of the problem is essentially economic, the key to the nature, scope, and pace of reform lies in the political realm.

One school of thought has contended that China's reforms did not spring from "a massive spontaneous surge of the Chinese peasantry back to family farming."[19] Instead, the idea of family farming came from high authorities, who used the usual machinery of command to make a reluctant peasantry accept the new system. Harry Harding focuses on the role of Chinese elites in reforms. It seems to Harding:

> [The] objective problems at the time of Mao's death still do not explain the extent of the reforms that have occurred under Deng Xiaoping. . . . The immediate cause of reform was the existence of a reform faction within the Chinese Communist Party, its successful struggle to gain supremacy over more conservative rivals, and its skillful strategy to launching and sustaining a bold program of political and economic renewal.[20]

Leadership does matter in Chinese reforms. The sources of the reform ideas of leadership are thus a crucial variable in interpreting the nature of their reform and strategy. Past experience of the post-Mao reform leadership determines that they give high priority to economic construction rather than political rebuilding.[21] The Deng Xiaoping regime has been committed to market economy and economic growth. Political reform should thus be subordinate to economic growth. The state in its relations with economic development has not only to promote the development of the market, but also to make strategic plans for economic progress. The state must use its administrative mechanism to protect the development of market mechanisms. Administrative power should be strengthened in order to provide favorable conditions, especially stable politics, for market development. Without such a political instrument, both "reform" and "open door" are impossible.[22] The reforming coalition does believe that political reform or political development itself is desirable, because "without political institutional reform, the achievements of economic institutional reform cannot be secured. Also, economic reform will not be able to continue further."[23] On the other hand, "without democracy, there will be no socialism and socialist modernization."[24] A precondition of political development, however, is the provision of very favorable conditions for economic progress. Political stability must be given highest priority. "[China's] modernization needs two prerequisites. One is international peace, and the other is domestic political stability. . . . A crucial condition for China's progress is political stability."[25] Without stable politics domestic construction is impossible, let alone an "open door" policy.[26] So, if political reform or democracy undermines political stability, it is not worthwhile. In other words, an authoritarian regime is desirable if it can produce stable politics. In this context, "bourgeois liberalization" is harmful because it often leads to political discontent, even political demonstrations. Deng explains, "Why have we [the state] treated student demonstrations so seriously and so quickly? Because China is not able to bear more disturbance and more disorder."[27]

Furthermore, in this view, state constraints must be considered as an important variable in explaining state-society relations. Mao's legacy had greatly constrained the post-Mao regime's strategic alternatives for economic development. The regime was able to make policy independent of social forces, but it could not escape from its past inheritance. Deng's coalition chose decentralization as a development strategy mostly because of past experience. The Chinese economy, as many authors point out, had undergone several reforms before Deng's regime began economic reforms. During the Great Leap Forward and the Cultural Revolution, Mao found fault with highly centralized planning, so he sought to rely on the initiative of the localities. Provinces, counties, and communes were encouraged to be self-sufficient. By the 1970s at least, China's economy had a "cellular" quality.[28] Under such a cellular economy:

> Localities acted like entrepreneurs: developing local industries, providing coordination, finding customers, etc. The impact on the nature and operation of the economy was profound: central ministries and planning organs already weakened by the turmoil of the Cultural Revolution lost major sinews of financial and material allocative powers; important centrally managed industries found themselves in competition with localities for needed materials; local

investment soared; protectionism hampered the movement of goods between localities; and finally, where goods were exchanged, the medium was not always the plan. There was informal bartering and bargaining between economic or government units.[29]

This trend was not arrested in the post-Mao period. Instead, it accelerated. Deng's early reform decentralized power to the level of local government. But the reformers' goal is to decentralize power to individual enterprises and allow industrial enterprises to act according to economic criteria and to stop submitting to outside administrative interference. Enterprises were therefore permitted to retain more of their profits instead of remitting them to the central government. This measure was supposed to give enterprises the financial resources to make independent decisions and reward them for economic success. But this attempt to decentralize economic decisions to enterprises ran afoul of the growing power of local government, which did not want individual enterprises to retain profit. Instead, local governments began bargaining with the central government over profit retention and seized decision-making power in the enterprises. This intervention inhibited the more efficient behavior that reforms sought to elicit from industry.

On the other hand, decentralization has caused the decline of state fiscal resources. The consolidated government budget as a share of national income went down from an average of 38–49 percent in the late 1970s to 24–25 percent in 1988–1989. Decentralization enabled local governments to pursue pet projects, squandering funds needed for energy and transport infrastructures. Consequently, decentralization rather than promoting reform has limited its progress. In order to introduce a true market economy, Beijing has to free individual enterprises from local administrative meddling and regain control over funds for central investments in the infrastructure. The state must first recentralize in order to deepen decentralization, as many authors suggest.[30]

A decentralization strategy will necessarily lead to the rise of civil society. China's short-term economic growth doubtless has had a close relationship with this development strategy. But because this reform measure in concerned with interest redistribution, local governments, as interest maximizers, took over power that the state wanted to dispense to individuals. As a consequence, decentralization has given rise to localism. This localism is as follows:

> First, the state reforming policies lack administrative authority and are often distorted due to the disturbance of "countermeasure" [of local governments]. Every locality has its own policy and behaves on its own will. Central-local relations are thus difficult to coordinate. Second, localism is a self-interested phenomenon. Third, [localism] promotes mutual comparison among localities. Every locality develops its economy blindly, overlaps in its construction, extends extra-budget construction on an unlimited scale, and focuses on short term investment. . . . Fourth, local protectionism is becoming popular. This protectionism cuts off a primitive unified market, which is underdeveloped, into various small pieces. . . . Localism has made it difficult to distribute resources and adjust industrial structure rationally. It is also a trauma for a developing market.[31]

The attempts at decentralization have resulted in macroeconomic as well as institutional imbalances, which in turn led to economic instability. The lag between administrative decentralization and the creation of an institutionalized capacity for macromanagement gave rise to excessive monetary expansion that stoked inflation. Because of slow progress toward nationally integrated and competitive markets that would supplement the now diminished planning mechanism as a source of discipline, decentralized industrial management has permitted provincial bureaucracies to push ahead with unsustainable rates of expansion. These and other economic problems ultimately turn into political problems. The state must take various measures, both political and economic, to stabilize its economy. These measures often have a major impact on the progress of civil society. For instance, the state's recentralization efforts after the crackdown on the 1989 democracy movement constrained the development of both local economy and new political forces.

Equality is another important variable in understanding the relation between state control and economic progress. For the reform coalition, the market is necessary for Chinese economic growth, but the market economy develops unevenly. This has significant political consequences. Smooth and fast development of a market economy requires relatively equal interest distribution among various social groups and areas. State interference is needed to achieve such a distribution. Deng's coalition has used uneven development strategy, breaking from Mao's egalitarian legacy. This strategy has been followed by the household responsibility system, industrial contract system, Special Economic Zone policy, the coastal development policy, and others. The state, however, must avoid extremely uneven income distribution and economic development, because development without basic equity will lead to political instability for China, which has such a long egalitarian tradition.[32] Given an extremely uneven economy, the state's effort to achieve basic equity will necessarily hinder fast progress of a middle class, which has been a basic pillar of democracies in the West, because the state needs to transfer wealth from the rich to the poor, from rich regions to poor areas.

In the last analysis, every developing state needs to achieve at least three goals in the course of modernization: growth, equality, and control. Politics is embedded in all three goals. In other words, the achievement of these goals is a political task. While these three goals are in theory complementary, in practice they often conflict. The state needs to adjust its policy priority repeatedly. Democracy, which means competitive politics, often becomes a victim of conflicting goals.

CULTURAL CONTEXT

I have considered democracy in the context of economic development. In this section, I will examine another important variable—political culture—and its meaning for democracy. The political culture of a society has been defined by Sidney Verba as "the system of empirical beliefs, expressive symbols, and values which defines the situation in which political action takes place."[33] I have argued that democracy in China is more likely to be a gift of the elite to the society. Society's attitudes toward and demands for democracy are thus important, because elites often are reluctant to give such a gift to society if there is no pressure from society.

Data demonstrates that most Chinese are still authoritarian and conservative, as Table 4 shows. We can see most individuals selected "diligence," "frugality," "pragmatism," and "conservatism" as individual values. Only 3 percent chose "risk taking." A 1986 survey shows 69 percent of urban citizens prefer "a stable life and rich material interests"; 14 percent prefer "independence and freedom from other's control."[34] A 1985 survey shows 80 percent of people prefer "a stable life but less opportunity to increase income." Only 19 percent prefer "an unstable life but more risk and opportunity to increase income."[35]

Individuals' basic values necessarily have economic and political meaning. For instance, although a little inflation does not affect their living standards very much, most individuals cannot understand price reform. Surveys were made in 1985 after the state implemented a non-staple food price reform. When asked to answer the question, "Some argue that the price reform will be ultimately favorable for the country's economic prosperity: do you think it is true?" 77 percent answered yes. When asked, "Do you think this price reform

---

Table 4. *Authoritarian Orientation in China*

Q. "Among the values listed, which do you think can exemplify individual values best?"
The Result: *

Value Items	%
Diligence	56
Frugality	49
Pragmatism	40
Conservatism	37
Obedience	35
Personal connections	28
"Face" saving	28
Sociability	7
Risk taking	3

* $N = 4,124$

Source: Adapted from Shang, *Zhongguo ren de ziwo yizhixing renge,* 30.

will facilitate the country's economic institutional reform?" 85 percent believed that it would bring a great or positive impact on economic reform, and only 13 percent argued that it would fail to promote, even slow, economic progress. However, only 31 percent believed that further price reform was necessary; 27 percent argued that further price reform should not be implemented within one or two years; 40 percent argued that the state should not carry out further price reform for a long time. A 1986 survey among Tianjin citizens demonstrates that 63 percent preferred not to increase their wages rather than to raise prices.[36]

In terms of their political values, most individuals show their strong need for the state. Most individuals have high identification with the state. While many people are no longer proud of or are indifferent to the socialist state (as already demonstrated), most people still have high loyalty to the Chinese state. Fully 75 percent of individuals contend that one should love the state even if he or she is disappointed with it. Also 86 percent believe that there is no reason for one to betray the state, even though it cannot satisfy one's needs and expectations. Most individuals think that they should hold high accountability to the state. The government's authority is unquestioned and viewed as beneficial. Also 74 percent believe that they should trust in and obey the government, because the ultimate goal of the government is to serve them. Half believe what they have is given by the government, and 69 percent still indicate they had confidence in the central government.

Data also demonstrates that most individuals have high identification with leaders. Answers to the following questions demonstrate this trend. When peasants were asked (n. 466), "Do you agree with the statement that a given cadre can be a lifelong cadre if he or she performs well?" 60 percent of them said yes and 40 percent no. When questioned, "When disagreements exist, what do you think should be followed? A. majority rule; B. everyone can follow his or her own will; or C. listening to the leaders' opinions;" the result is: 44 percent of individuals (n. 1,689) believe majority rule should be followed; 15 percent selected the second alternative, and 25 percent selected the third. When questioned, "Do you think the CCP's leadership is necessary; 30 percent believe that it is necessary now but will be unnecessary in the future; only 10 percent believe that it was necessary in the past but unnecessary now.[37]

State-centered individual values are also revealed in individual attitudes towards democracy. Although the 1987 survey shows that 75 percent believe that China now needs democracy, they identify with the state's explanation of democracy. Their conceptions of democracy more or less reflect the official definition of democracy, such as democratic-centralism, the mass line, "be master in one's own house" (*dangjia zuozhu*), and "make decisions for people" (*weimin zuozhu*). Also 25 percent of individuals believe in the concept of democracy under the leadership of centralism; 19 percent think democracy is to listen to and extensively solicit mass opinions; 12 percent consider democracy is a system in which people are the masters of the nation; 11 percent conceive of democracy as being a master for the sake of the people; 11 percent accept that democracy means that people have the right to participate in the management of social life; 7 percent believe democracy means the limitation and separation of political power.[38]

It is important to look at college students' conceptions of democracy, because they are an integral part of the Chinese intellectual class that has been a major force in the struggle for democracy. Their conceptions of democracy can not only influence present politics, but also determine the future model of Chinese democracy to a large extent. A 1986 Beijing University survey reveals some basic attitudes towards democracy. We can see that college students are optimistic about Chinese democracy. Most of them believe that democracy can be achieved through long-term endeavors even though China has a long nondemocratic tradition; that there are positive correlations between democracy and law; that democratization within the Communist party in power and its structure necessarily influences and conditions the whole process of democracy; and that a market economy is the basis for socialist democracy, because prerequisites of a market economy are freedom, equality, and competition, which are also essential for democracy.

However, most college students still identify with the official ideology of democracy. Fully 68 percent of Beijing University students believe that democracy is of a class character. They emphasize "the government of law not the government of man," "incorruptible and intelligent government," "democratic centralism," and "equal opportunity." But they overlook "periodic elections," "power checks and balances," and other important values.[39]

There is a great gap between liberal intellectuals and the masses. Intellectuals are more idealistic about democracy, while the masses focus more on material interests. Consequently, intellectual movements in the past years of reform did not attract a great part of the masses throughout the country. Surveys show, although most people understand student movements, they will not participate in such actions.[40]

CONCLUSION: PROSPECTS OF CHINESE DEMOCRACY

I have examined Chinese democracy in the context of state-society relations. Now we can see that democracy in China faces a number of structural obstacles. The first is the commanding position that the state occupies in relation to the society. The state's superior positioning is essentially antidemocratic; but is not easily done away with, because it is historically inherited. Because of Mao's legacy, China has often lacked economic dynamism. A cellular economy has made it hard to develop a unified market. Thus political action has been a primary source of dynamism. The state authority needs not only to provide public order but also to be responsible for facilitating economic progress.

The state simultaneously seeks different goals such as economic growth, equitable distribution, political stability, and national unification. These goals often conflict with each other. Democracy or human rights frequently become the victims of other goals. As one scholar argued in the mid-1980s, "except in the very long run, rapid development and human rights are competing concerns."[41] Although the Chinese leadership realizes the importance of political reform, it gives high priority to economic growth. Many leaders believe that if China is going to achieve high rates of economic growth, it will have to be a development-oriented authoritarian government. Democratic governments will be too soft and hence unable to mobilize resources, curtail consumption, and promote investment to achieve a high growth rate. An authoritarian system is more likely than a democratic one to be compatible with greater economic equality among different regions and individuals.[42]

As the economy develops, social forces are likely to develop and strengthen in relation to the state. But these developing social forces do not have enough capacity to build national coherence, mobilize resources, organize for task achievements, and provide economic dynamism. Consequently, the state must perform these functions. These social forces might produce pressure from below, but they are still controlled by the state. Democracy is likely a business of the state. The masses often enter politics only when elites mobilize them for their own political purpose. There have been spontaneous movements initiated by social forces, but they are not able to contest the state.

There is also a cultural dimension. Although I do not believe that culture is a determinant variable, it does influence Chinese democracy. The masses' strong identification with the state will necessarily strengthen the state's commanding position and weaken social forces.

It is economic progress that has more significance for Chinese democracy, however. First, the state must change its basis of legitimacy. As data demonstrate, the old basis of state legitimacy is being weakened by economic development and political change. The state has tried to introduce a new basis of its legitimacy, that is, to accelerate the country's economic growth and to carry out limited political reform and let people's delegates have a say in politics to some extent. But the state-society relation has not been institutionalized. The 1989 democracy movement revealed the tension between the two. Since 1989, the state has had to implement further economic reform in order to improve its relation with the mass. Second, there is great potential for the rise of a counterelite. The Communist party is declining fast, although it still rules the country, and any other independent parties are still prohibited. But more and more individuals no longer believe that the ruling party is able to meet their expectations. Further, the leadership is no longer unified. There is also the possibility that the existing elite will be challenged by those who are alienated from the existing system or who rose from the masses as a result of liberalizing the existing system. Third, the state must change the basis of political agendas. In the past, almost all political agendas were set forth by the state. That time is gone now. The state is still playing an important role in establishing national agendas, but it has to pay attention to society, because without support from society, the state policy may not be successful.

Finally, with economic progress and political change, more individuals, especially intellectuals, are tending to be liberal. Although this does not mean that they will actually participate in politics, their being liberal is a potential pressure on the state to prepare channels for their possible participation. Therefore, democracy's failure to develop does not mean that China is not able to develop it. Its failure is due to some structural obstacles, which are difficult to eliminate in a short period of time. However, further economic progress will necessarily deepen changes in state-society relations, which will push China toward democracy.

NOTES

1. On the debate between Chinese neoauthoritarianism and democracy, see Mark P. Petracca and Mong Xiong (Yongnian Zheng), "Chinese Neo-Authoritarianism: An Exploration and Democratic Critique," *Asian Survey* 30 (November 1990); 1099–1117; Barry Sautman, "Sirens of the Strongman: Neo-Authoritarianism in Recent Chinese Political Theory," *China Quarterly* 129 (March 1992): 72–102; Liu Jun and Li Lin, ed., *Xin quanwei zhuyi: dui gaige lilun gangling de lunzheng* [Neo-authoritarianism: A Debate on Theories of Reforms] (Beijing: Economic Institute Press, 1989); *Guoqing yanjiu* [China Study], March 1989 (This issue includes many essays on the debate between neo-authoritarianism and democracy); Wu Guoguang, "Ziyou: tuijin zhongguo xiandaihua zhuanxing de jiben daoxiang" ["Freedom: Basic Orientation of Promoting the Transformation of China's Modernization"] in Chen Yizi, et al., ed., *Zhongguo dalu de gaige yu fazhan* [Reform and Development in Mainland China], (Taibei: Guiguan Book Company, 1991), 123–152; Wen Guanzhong, "Zhongguo de ziyou jingji yu zhengzhi zhuanzhi" ["The Chinese Market Economy and Authoritarianism"] in *Zhishi fenzi* [The Chinese Intellectual] 26 (Winter 1992): 45–48; also, many essays on neoauthoritarianism written by Chinese abroad appear in Qi Mo, ed., *Xin quanwei zhuyi: dui Zhongguo dalu weilai mingyun de lunzheng* [Neo-Authoritarianism: Debates on the Future China] (Taipei: Tonson Books, 1991).

2. About the rise of neoconservatism in recent China, see, "Dalu xin baoshou zhuyi de jueqi" ["The Rise of Neo-Conservatism in Mainland China"] *Zhongguo shibao zhoukan* [Chinese Times Weekly], part 1 and 2, 26 January 1992 and 1 February 1992.

3. See Li Xianglu, "Weishenma shuo fenquan gaige de fangzhen shi zhengque de" ["Why Do We Say that the Decentralization Line for Reform is Correct?"], *Chinese Intellectual* (Fall 1940). Li argues that only after the state's control over the country is seriously weakened, is it hopeful for Chinese market economy and democracy. Zhang Xin, "Quyu jingji zizhi de kexingxing" ["On Implementing Regional Economic Autonomy in Mainland China"] in Chen Yizi, et al., eds., *Zhongguo,* 51–66. Zhang contends that a centralized state is the main obstacle to Chinese economic take-off. After the collapse of this state, "the invisible hand, the market, will lead individual self-interested behavior to an effective resource allocation for the whole society." Within every economic region, citizens have rights to choose their own economic, political, and any other

institutions. Every autonomous region can issue its own currency, make its own development strategy, have independent international trade, and determine whether or not to be independent from other regions. In a word, it is an independent economic "state." Yang Xiaokai, "Zhongguo jingji tizhi gaige de jiaoxun" ["Lessons from Chinese Economic Institute Reforms"] in Chen et al., eds., *Zhongguo*, 99–122. Yang suggests that China will speed up its economic development if the country is divided into various small states.

4. See Yan Jiaqi, former adviser of Zhao Ziyang and director of the Institute of Political Science of Chinese Academy of Social Sciences, *Lianbang Zhongguo guoxiang* [On Federal China] (Taipei: Lianjing Book Company, 1992); "Minzhen mubiao: jianli zhongguo lianbang" ["The Goal of the Front for Chinese Democracy: Establishment of a Chinese Federation"], *Shijie Ribao [World Journal]* (New York), 4 August 1989, 1; "Ruhe kandai ershishiji de zhongguo lishi?" ["How Should Twentieth-Century Chinese History Be Looked At?"] *Shijie Ribao (World Journal)*, 14 September 1989, 16; Jiang Meiqiu, "Zhongguo minzu goucheng yu weilai de lianbangzhi geju" ["The Structure of Nationalities and the Future Federal System in China"], papers of the Center for Modern China, no. 8, June 1991.

5. *China: Between Plan and Market* (Washington, DC: The World Bank, 1990), xxi.

6. See *Selected Works of Deng Xiaoping (1975–1982)* (Beijing: Foreign Language Press, 1983), 163–64. Deng says, "In economic policy, I think we should allow some regions and enterprises and some workers and peasants to earn more and enjoy more benefits than others in accordance with their hard work and greater contribution to society. If the standard of living of some people is raised first, this will inevitably be an impressive example to their 'neighbors,' and people in other regions and units will want to learn from them. This will help the whole national economy to advance wave upon wave and help the people of all our nationalities to become prosperous in a comparatively short period."

7. Liang Zhuanyun, "Woguo siying qiye de fazhan qingkuang he guanli zhong de wenti" ["The Development of China's Private Economy and Its Problems in Management"] in The Research Group for China's Private Economy During the Seventh Fie-year Plan, ed., *Zhongguo de siying jingji* [China's Private Economy], (Beijing: The Chinese Academy of Social Sciences Press, 1989), 8.

8. Shen Qiuchang, *Jishu yinjin yu xiandaihua* [*The Introduction of Technology and Modernization*] (Chongqing, Sichuan: Chongqing Press, 1989), 10.

9. Harry Harding, "Political Development in Post-Mao China" in A. Doak Barnett and Ralph N. Clough, ed., *Modernizing China: Post-Mao Reform and Development* (Boulder, CO: Westview Press, 1986), 33.

10. Ibid., 17.

11. On the NPC reforms, see Kevin J. O'Brien, *Reform Without Liberalization: China's National People's Congress and the Politics of Institutional Change* (New York: Cambridge University Press, 1990).

12. On the role of Chinese intellectuals in policy making, see Carol Lee Hamrin, *China and the Challenge of the Future: Changing Political Patterns* (Boulder, CO: Westview Press, 1990).

13. Hou Jun, *Piruan de yulun jiandu* [*Weak Supervision From Public Opinion*], (Beijing: Chinese Women Press, 1989), 86.

14. Shang Xiaoyuang, *Zhongguoren de ziwo yizhixing renge* [*The Chinese Self-Restraining Personality*] (Kunming, Yunnan: Yunnan People's Publishing House, 1989), 225, 38.

15. Ibid., 231.

16. See Charles Lindblom, *Politics and Markets: The World's Political-Economic System* (New York: Basic Books, 1977), esp. part v; Samuel Huntington, "Will More Countries

Become Democratic?" *Political Science Quarterly* 99 (Summer 1984): 193–218; B. Moore, *Social Origins of Dictatorship and Democracy* (Boston: Beacon Press, 1966), esp. chap. 6.

17. Atul Kohli, "Democracy and Development" in John P. Lewis and Valeriana Kallab, eds., *Development Strategies Reconsidered* (New Brunswick, NJ: Transaction Books, 1986), 165.

18. Ibid., 168.

19. Kathleen Hartford, "Socialist Agriculture is Dead; Long Live Socialist Agriculture! Organizational Transformations in Rural China" in Elizabeth J. Perry and Christine Wong, eds., *The Political Economy of Reform in Post-Mao China* (Cambridge, MA: Harvard University Press, 1985). An alternative line of thought contends that the rural reform was initiated by the peasantry, but it does not deny the role of the state in promoting reforms. See John P. Burns, "Chinese Peasant Interest Articulation" in David S. G. Goodman, ed., *Groups and Politics in the People's Republic of China* (Cardiff, Wales: University College Cardiff Press, 1984), 126–51; Daniel Kelliher, "The Political Consequences of China's Reforms," *Comparative Politics*, 18 (July 1986): 479–493.

20. Harry Harding, *China's Second Revolution: Reform After Mao* (Washington, DC: Brookings Institution, 1978), 39. Also see his "Political Development in Post-Mao China" in Barnett and Clough, eds., *Modernizing China*, 13–37.

21. See E. Perry and C. Wong, "The Political Economy of Reforms in Post-Mao China: Causes, Content, and Consequences" in Perry and Wong, *The Political Economy of Reform in Post-Mao China*, 1–27; Steven M. Goldstein, "Reforming Socialist Systems: Some Lessons of the Chinese Experience," *Studies in Comparative Communism* 21 (Summer 1988): 221–237.

22. Deng Xiaoping, *Deng Xiaoping wenxuan* [Selected Works of Deng Xiaoping] (Beijing: Renmin Chubanshe, 1983), 364. Also see, Zhang Bingjiu, "Jingji tizhi gaige yu zhengzhi tizhi gaige de jincheng yu xietiao" ["Processes and Coordination of Economic and Political Institutional Reforms"] in Liu and Li, eds., *Xin quanwei zhuyi*, 1–26. Wu Jiaxiang, "Xin quanwei zhuyi shuping" ["A Critique of Neo-Authoritarianism"] in ibid., 34–38; and Wu, "Xin quanwei zhuyi yanjiu tigang" ["An Outline of Neo-Authoritarianism Study"] in Liu and Lin, eds. *Xin quanwei zhuyi*.

23. Deng Xiaoping, *Jianshe you Zhongguo tese de shehui zhuyi* [Building Socialism with Chinese Characteristics] (Beijing: Renmin Chubanshe, 1984) 138.

24. Deng, *Wenxuan*, 154.

25. Deng, *Deng Xiaoping tongzhi zhongyao jianghua* [Important Talks of Comrade Deng Xiaoping] (Beijing: Renmin Chubanshe, 1988), 8, 13.

26. Deng, *Wenxuan,* 156.

27. Deng, *Deng Xiaoping,* 13.

28. See Harding, *China's Second Revolution;* Audrey Donnithorne, "China's Cellular Economy: Some Economic Trends Since the Cultural Revolution," *The China Quarterly* 52 (October–December 1972): 605–619; Nicholas Lardy, "Centralization and Decentralization in China's First Management," *The China Quarterly,* 61 (March 1975): 26–60, and *Economic Growth and Distribution in China* (New York: Cambridge University Press, 1978); Michel Oksenberg and james Tong, "The Evolution of Central-Provincial Fiscal Relations in China, 1971–1984: The Formal System," *The China Quarterly* 125 (March 1991): 1–31.

29. Goldstein, "Reforming Socialist Systems," 226–227.

30. On decentralization and its result, see ibid., 221–237; Daniel Kelliher, "Political Consequences," 479–493; Barry Naughton, "False Starts and Second Wind: Financial Reforms in China's Industrial System" and Christine Wong, "Material Allocation and

Decentralization: Impact of the Local Sector on Industrial Reform" in Perry and Wong, *Political Economy of Reforms,* 223–252, 253–278; Barry Naughton, "The Decline of Central Control over Investment in Post-Mao China," Dorothy Solinger, The 1980 Inflation and the Politics of Price Control in the PRC," and David Bachman, "Implementing Chinese Tax Policy" in David M. Lampton, ed., *Policy Implementation in Post-Mao China* (Berkeley: University of California Press, 1987), 51–80, 81–118, 119–153; and Christine P. Wong, "Central-Local Relations in An Era of Fiscal Decline: The Paradox of Fiscal Decentralization in Post-Mao China," *The China Quarterly* 128 (December 1991): 691–715.

31. Huang Shiqing and Zhang Dehua, "Xianshi xuyao quanwei, quanwei xuyao zhiyue" ["Reality Needs Authority, and Authority Needs to Be Checked"] in Liu and Li, *Xin quanwei zhuyi,* 295–296. Also see Wang Huning, "Zhongguo bianhua zhong de zhongyang he difang zhengfu de guanxi: zhengzhi de hangyi" ["The Changing Relationship Between China's Central and Local Governments: Connotations of Politics"], *Fudan daxue xuebao* (Journal of Fudan University, Shanghai), no. 5 (1988): 1–8; "Jifang pingheng: zhongyang yu difang de xietong guanxi" ["Balance between Centralization and Decentralization: Coordinative Relationship Between Center and Locality"], *Journal of Fudan University,* no. 2 (1991): 27–36.

32. Huang Shihua and Zhang Deqing, "Xianshi xuyao quanwei," 298. Also, World Bank, *China: Between Plan and Market,* 55–58.

33. Sidney Verba, "Comparative Political Culture" in Lucian W. Pye and Sidney Verba, eds., *Political Culture and Political Development* (Princeton, NJ: Princeton University Press, 1965), 513.

34. The Institute of Chinese Economic Institutional Reform Studies, "Renmin dui jiage gaige de shehui xinli fanying: ba chengshi diaocha" ["People's Social Psychological Reaction to Price Change: A Survey in Eight Urban Cities"] in *Shehuixue yanjiu* [Studies of Sociology] no. 6 (1987).

35. The Institute of Chinese Economic Institutional Reform Studies, *Gaige: women mianlin de tiaozhang yu xuanze* [Reform: Challenges and Choice Facing Us] (Beijing: Chinese Economic Press, 1986), 87.

36. Ibid., 75–88.

37. Min Qi, "Zhongguo zhengzhi wenhua" [*Chinese Political Culture*] (Kunming: Yunnan People's Publishing House, 1989), 40, 190, 104.

38. Ibid., 181.

39. Zhang Tao, "Daxuesheng dui minzhu de renshi, qinggan yu pingjia," ["University Student's Perceptions and Valuation"] in *Political Science Studies* (Beijing: The Chinese Academy of Social Sciences, 1989), 18–22.

40. Min Qi, *Zhongguo zhengzhi wenhua,* 125–127, 185.

41. Jack Donnelly, "Human Rights and Development: Complementary or Competing Concerns?" *World Politics* 36 (January 1984): 255.

42. Those concerns are especially emphasized by the neoauthoritarian or the neoconservatism school and recognized by many leaders. About the content of this line of thinking, chiefly see Chen Yuan, "Woguo jingji de shenceng wenti he xuanze—guanyu woguo jingji fazhan geju he yunxing jizhi de ruogan wenti" ["Deep problems in our economy and choice—on some problems about the situation of our economic development and operating mechanism"], unpublished papers for internal use of government officials, March 1991; and The Department of Thought and Theory of China's Youth, "Sulian jubian zhihou zhongguo de xianshi yingdui yu zhanlue xuanzhe" ["China feasible countermeasures and strategic choice after dramatic changes in the Soviet Union"], unpublished papers for internal use of government officials, 9 September 1991.

How and Why China Succeeded in Her Economic Reform

Gregory C. Chow

INTRODUCTION

In the late 1970's the world discovered an economic miracle in the rapid economic development of four economies of East Asia: Hong Kong, Singapore, Taiwan, and South Korea, known as the four little dragons in the annals of economic development. In the early 1990's the world witnessed another economic miracle in the rapid development of mainland China and its successful transformation from a planned economy to a market economy. This miracle was the more noticeable in view of the problems facing many formerly socialist countries in Eastern Europe and Northern Asia. Ever since economic reforms began in 1978 in China, rapid economic growth has followed, at the average rate of growth of 9.5 percent per year in real national output in the first decade. During the first two years of economic reform the former Soviet Union and several Eastern European economies experience substantial decline in real output. This paper is an attempt to characterize the reform process in China since 1978 and draw some lessons from its success. The first section describes the major institutions in the Chinese economy which needed to be transformed. The second section follows by listing the major steps taken in the Chinese reform process. The third section summarizes several major characteristics of the reform process and draws some lessons from the Chinese experience.

WHAT ECONOMIC INSTITUTIONS TO REFORM

To describe briefly the economic institutions that needed to be reformed, let us start with the supply side of the market. By Chinese official statistics, which

Gregory C. Chow, Department of Economics, Princeton University, "How and Why China Succeeded in Her Economic Reform," *China Economic Review,* No. 2, 1993: 117–128. Copyright © 1993 by JAI Press, Inc.

follows the statistical system of the former Soviet Union, national output is divided into the five sectors of agriculture, industry, construction, transportation and commerce. In 1978 when reform began, these five sectors accounted respectively for 32.8 49.4, 4.2, 3.9 and 9.8 percent of national income (see State Statistics Bureau, 1991, *Statistical Yearbook of China (SYB 1991,* p. 35). Collective farming prevailed in agriculture under the Commune system which had been introduced in 1958 during Chairman Mao's Great Leap Forward movement. Of the total labor force of 401.5 million in 1978, 306.4 million or 76.3 percent were laborers in rural areas while 95.0 million were classified as staff and workers. Of the latter 74.5 million or 78.4 percent worked in state enterprises and the remaining 20.5 million worked in collective enterprises in cities and towns (*SYB 1991,* p. 95). In 1978, 77.6 percent of gross output value of industry was from state enterprises (*SYB 1991,* p. 396). Thus most of industry and other nonagricultural sectors consisted of state enterprises which were not operated for profit and were under the control of central planning, although the degree of control was not necessarily complete. In sum in 1978 most of China's productive units in agriculture, industry and the other sectors were not operating for profit as in a market economy.

Turning to the demand side, consumer demand in urban areas was controlled by the government in three essential aspects.

1. Housing of staff and workers was assigned by the unit in which they worked with negligible rent (averaging about three to four yuan RMB per month, the official exchange rate being 1.9 yuan per one U.S. dollar). There was no market for urban housing.

2. Important food items including grain, meat and oil were rationed at below market prices.

3. The purchasing power of the urban consumer was controlled by controlling the wage rate. Demand for materials by production units was controlled by the State Bureau of Supplies in the State Council which allocated inputs in production as a part of central planning.

With controlled allocation of many consumer and produced goods, prices of these goods were also controlled by the government. Agricultural products were purchased by government procurement units at regulated procurement prices. These products were distributed to urban consumers at below market prices under a rationing system. Prices of inputs including electric energy, raw materials, mineral products and transportation services were in many instances set below market prices as a form of subsidies to producers. That these prices were below market was evidenced by their rapid increases during the 1980's after the beginning of price reform (see State Statistics Bureau, 1989, p. 29). Thus the price system in 1978 failed to perform its function to regulate supply and demand as in a market economy. Note, however, that in spite of the government's attempt to control prices through the Administration Bureau for

Commodity Prices in the State Council, market forces did work to a significant extent to influence the relative prices of industrial and agricultural products. As the output of industrial products increased relative to agricultural products between 1952 and 1978, the relative price of industrial products declined. Output indices in 1978 (with 1952 = 100) were 1679.1 for industry and 161.2 for agriculture. Price indices in 1978 (with 1952 = 100) obtained by taking the ratios of outputs in current prices to outputs in constant prices (*SYB 1991*, p. pp. 32–33) are 77.0 for industry and 179.9 for agriculture, reflecting the changes in relative supply and demand. For relative change in demand, see Chow (1993, Section V.C).

Besides the supply and demand of current output, capital formation in 1978 was heavily controlled by the government. Net capital formation is measured by accumulation in official statistics, which amounted to 108.7 billion RMB, as compared with 188.8 billion for consumption in 1978 (*SYB 1991*, p. 40). Of the 108.7 billion, 84.7 billion was accounted for by state enterprises, 3.6 billion by urban collectives, 16.9 billion by rural collectives (mainly agricultural communes at the time) and 3.5 billion by individuals (see Chow, 1993, Table IV). These statistics show the importance of capital formation in nonagricultural state enterprises where investment projects required the approval of the State Planning Commission and the provincial and local units under its control. The banking system did not perform the functions prevailing under a market economy. The People's Bank controlled the supply of currency. However, the total supply of credits to state enterprises was regulated by the State Planning Commission through the approval of their budgets. The banking system played a passive role in providing whatever funds to the enterprises as they were approved. Commercial banking did not exist and played no active role in providing funds for investment. The People's Bank accordingly did not function to regulate the supply of such funds. State enterprises did not seek outside funding through the financial market for stocks and bonds. Foreign investment was practically nil in 1978 (see *SYB 1991*, p. 629).

Foreign trade was directed by central planning in 1978. When construction projects were included in a five-year plan, some required the imports of foreign capital goods and materials. Certain consumption goods in the plan had to be imported, including food grain when domestic supply was insufficient. All these projected imports required the use of foreign exchanges, which has to be earned by the planned exports of domestic goods. Exports, imports and the demand for and supply of foreign exchanges were incorporated in a foreign trade plan which was part of China's economic plan. In the State Council, the Ministry of Foreign Trade directed the affairs of foreign trade, supervising the Bureau of Import-Export Control and the General Administration of Customs and assisted by the State Administration of Exchange Control. The official exchange rate was set below market; at the official rate of 1.9 RMB per U.S. dollar, the Chinese people could not obtain U.S. dollars without the approval of the government. Imports were restricted and exports were managed by the government. In 1978 foreign trade totalled 27.25 billion RMB, with 13.97 billion exports and 13.28 billion imports, and accounted for 10.3 percent of national income of 164.4 billion (*SYB 1991*, p. 615).

If the non-market economic institutions described above had to be changed, the government economic planning apparatus had to be changed also. It included not only the Economic Planning Commission, but also the various industrial ministries in the State Council, each directing the state enterprises of the corresponding industry, the banking system and the ministries and bureaus related to price control and foreign trade. The nature of government planning had to be changed from directing the economic activities of Communes and state enterprises to regulating their activities through a system of economic incentives.

HOW ECONOMIC REFORM WAS ACHIEVED

Before describing the steps taken since 1978 to change the economic institutions, it is useful to characterize the political environment surrounding the reform. Two characteristics of the political environment deserve to be noted: the stability of the political institutions and the large amount of popular support for economic reform. The political institutions in China since the death of Mao Zedong in September 1976 have been quite stable. In spite of some political struggles at the top after Mao's death, which led to the downfall of four top leaders known as the Gang of Four and the rise of Deng Xiao-ping at the expense of Hua Guofeng, the heir designate of Mao, the political system did not change. After Deng gained power in 1978, the country had learned the bitter lessons from the political upheavals of the Cultural Revolution of 1965–1975. Party leaders, government officials at all levels and the Chinese population were eager to have political order and economic reform as they had learned the shortcomings of the planning system. In 1978, the "Four Modernizations" in science, agriculture, industry and defense originally suggested by Chou En-lai in 1964 were put forth as a program for the modernization of China.

Historians would attribute much of the credit for the successful economic reform in China to the able leadership of Deng Xiao-ping and Zhao Ziyang, with the former providing overall leadership and the latter implementing concrete reforms. Although Deng, Zhao and other leaders were confident of the general direction of reform toward a more market-oriented economy, in the sense of reducing central control and providing economic reward to individuals and economic units willing to produce more, they were not sure of exactly what economic institutions to establish. The procedure followed was one of experimentation. A favorite saying wa "touching the rocks as you cross the river," deciding on the next step only after you have completed the previous step.

Economic reform officially began with the decision of the Third Plenary Session of the Central Committee of the 11th Congress of the Chinese Communist Party in December 1978. (In January 1979, official diplomatic relations with the United States were established.) For excellent surveys of China's economic reform, see Perkins (1988) and Vogel (1989, Chapter 3). There were three major steps in this reform.

1. The adoption of the responsibility system in agriculture. Collective farming under the commune system was generally recognized to be inefficient in 1978. Reform of the commune system occurred initially in 1978 when commune leaders in some regions recognized that they could fulfill their assigned output quotas for delivery to the government procurement departments by reorganizing the commune internally following and improving upon the practices of private farming in the 1950's. In essence, under the responsibility system, each farm household was assigned a piece of land and was held responsible for delivering a given quantity of output to the commune to satisfy the latter's output quota. After fulfilling its output quota, the farm household could keep the remaining output for its own consumption or for sale at the market at market prices. The institution amounted to private farming with the farm household paying a fixed amount of rent for use of the land in the form of an output quota. Observing the success of the locally initiated experiments, the Fourth Plenary Session of the Central Committee of the Eleventh Communist Party Congress officially adopted the responsibility system as a national policy in September 1979.

2. Was to allow private markets and small private enterprises to flourish. Rural markets used to exist in China in the 1950's. Once the farmers were allowed to dispose of their above-quota output, rural markets grew rapidly after 1978. Farmers also extended their productive activities to more profitable products such as ducks and cash crops, using privately owned trucks for transportation. In the meantime private restaurants, repair shops, peddlers, stores, and street markets developed in urban areas. In two to three years one witnessed the growth of light industries in both rural and urban areas in the form of small collectives owned by several persons. Traditional handicraft manufacturing in rural areas and small clothing factories in urban areas were examples. The rural collectives later turned out to be an important part of Chinese industry.

3. Reform of state enterprises which progressed in several stages. For small enterprises, the principle of the responsibility system in agriculture was quickly put into practice. The idea was to allow the manager, like the farm household, to reap all the profits after paying a fixed rent to the

government. State-owned stores, restaurants, small factories and later hotels were in fact privatized by the responsibility system, where the managers were often selected by auction. The right to operate a business for profit was leased to a manager who was willing to pay the highest. A nominally state-owned enterprise was being operated for profit like a private enterprise. Gradually in the 1980's, some managers became entrepreneurs who used their own and borrowed funds to purchase assets to establish their own private enterprises. (*New York Times,* Sunday, February 14, 1993, p. 1, carried a story of an entrepreneur who founded and managed a domestic airline.)

While it was easy to adopt the responsibility system to small state enterprises, it was not easy, and in the early stage of reform not intended, for large enterprises. Only after years of experience of reform did the government attempt to apply the responsibility system to large state enterprises. Reform of state enterprises began in late 1978 when six pilot enterprises in Sichuan Province were given certain autonomy and allowed to retain a part of the profits. By the end of June 1980, 6600 industrial enterprises which produced 45 percent of the output value of all state-owned enterprises were allowed to make certain output, marketing, and investment decisions and to retain a part of their profits. By the end of 1981, some 80 percent of state industrial enterprises were affected by the reform. The main elements of early industrial reform included:

  i) a certain autonomy regarding the use of retained profits, production planning, sales of output, experimentation with new products, and capital expansion;

 ii) adoption of features of an "economic responsibility system" by assignment of identifiable tasks to lower level units and payment to them according to productivity;

iii) increase in the role of markets;

 iv) the streamlining of the administrative system at local levels for enterprises under local control; and

  v) the encouragement of the establishment of collectively owned enterprises (Chow, 1985, pp. 148–151).

Reform in the industrial sector turned out to be more difficult than in the agricultural sector. It was much easier to make small farm households behave like private enterprises in a market economy than to make large state enterprises so behave for four types of reasons.

  1. Ideologically, members of the Communist Party of China believed in the ownership and the control of the means of production by the state. They were unwilling to surrender control of large state enterprises to

nongovernment individuals and allow them to keep substantial profits for themselves, as in the case of small farms.

2. Politically, government bureaucrats were unwilling to give up their power and vested interests by allowing the state enterprises to operate independently. Economic ministries tended to hold on to their control over the operations of the state enterprises. The bureau of material supplies tended to retain its control over the distribution of major material inputs.

3. Economically, large industrial enterprises were more dependent on factors outside their control then were small household farms. Given a piece of land, a farm household could produce as it pleased, subject to climatic conditions. A large industrial enterprise needed the supplies of equipment and of material inputs produced by other enterprises. The entire system of pricing and distribution of industrial products and material inputs had to be changed to provide more autonomy to the state enterprises.

4. Administratively, the efficient operation of a large industrial enterprise was much more difficult than operation of a small farm. Chinese managers often did not have sufficient knowledge and experience to run a modern enterprise as an independent entity. Even with additional training, managers and administrators of state enterprises were reluctant to give up their old habits of dependence on the economic ministries. The mode of operation of a large economic organization was difficult to change. This is true for a large american corporation and for a large Chinese state enterprise.

To carry out further economic reform, a Commission for Restructuring the Economic System was established at the State Council in 1982, headed by Premier Zhao Ziyang, and listed in the organization of the State Council as the first Commission, above the Planning Commission, to signify its importance. This Commission had the responsibility to draft reform proposals and carry out the approved proposals through the Planning Commission and the relevant ministries. By 1983, however, reform of state enterprises did not appear to have increased the efficiency of state enterprises significantly. I estimated a Cobb-Douglas production function for Chinese state industrial enterprises using data up to 1981 (Chow, 1985, pp. 123–126) and later found the same production function to fit the post-sample data for 1982, 1983 and 1984 very well (Chow, 1988). I also estimated production functions for the entire Chinese industry using data from 1952 to 1980, and found total productivities for the post-sample years of 1981 to 1985 to change by –0.006, 0.001, 0.042, 0.104, and 0.202 (Chow, 1993, Table XIII). Total productivities for agriculture increased by 0.077, 0.181, 0.269, 0.422 and 0.436 in 1981 to 1985 as estimated by Chow (1993, Table XI) and by 0.105, 0.203, 0.270 and 0.406 in 1981 to 1984 as estimated by McMillan, Whalley, and Zhu (1989, p. 794).

Perhaps observing the limited progress in the reform of state enterprises and stimulated by further success in the agricultural sector, the 12th Central Committee of the Chinese Communist Party as its Third Plenary Session on 20 October 1984 adopted a major proposal to achieve overall reform of the economic structure. Economic reform in China in the late 1980's were based on this major decision. Implementation was to be formulated and carried out to a significant extent during the seventh Five-Year Plan of 1986 to 1990. Seven key elements of the decision of 20 October 1984 concerning reform of the economic system were to:

i) give individual state enterprises autonomy in decisions regarding production, supply, marketing, pricing, investment, and personnel as independent profit-seeking economic units;

ii) reduce the scope of central planning and, except for certain major products, change the method from mandatory planning to guidance planning;

iii) allow prices of more products to be determined by the forces of demand and supply rather than by central control;

iv) develop macroeconomic control mechanisms through the use of taxes, interest rates, and monetary policy under an improved financial and banking system;

v) establish various forms of economic responsibility systems within individual enterprises to promote efficiency and encourage differential wage rates to compensate for different kinds of work and levels of productivity;

vi) foster the development of individual and collective enterprises as supplements to the state enterprises; and

vii) expand foreign trade and investment as well as technological exchanges.

An often-quoted slogan to capture the essential characteristics of the reform was, "Invigorate the microeconomic units. Control by macroeconomic means."

Under the Decision of October 1984, the responsibility system in agriculture was to be introduced in the management of state enterprises by allowing subunits of each enterprise to act independently through contracts with the enterprise. This provision should be distinguished from the policy of allowing the enterprise itself to have financial independence after paying a fixed rental to the state as in the case of individual farms. The distinction was made partly because the state enterprises are much larger than the individual farms and the management of these enterprises could not be permitted to use the possibly very large profits as freely as the individual farm households could. It was not until 1986 that a major attempt was made to introduce the responsibility system to the level of the state enterprises themselves rather than their subunits. By 1986, some small state-owned commercial and industrial enterprises were leased to the managers who were given almost complete control of the profits after paying rent to the government. A number of successful cases, with tremendous increases in outputs and profits, were well publicized in the news media. The "contract responsibility system" was then introduced in 1987. The main feature of this system was to let the management and workers sign a contract with the state or provincial government to lease the enterprise, paying fixed amounts of taxes in the forthcoming years (often five) of the contract and keeping the remaining profits for distribution among the management and workers in a way agreed upon by their mutual consent. Customs and workers' consent limited the amount a manager could draw as salary. However, profits could be used for distribution to management and workers often in the form of durable consumer goods. Even though this system might look attractive on paper, in practice the results were not entirely satisfactory. The management and workers often complained that the fixed taxes imposed by the state or local government were too large, leaving too little profit for them; they would prefer to pay a fixed percentage from their profits, thus avoiding the risk of paying taxes if the enterprise operated at a loss. Also, limited compensation to management who attempted to increase profits might affect their incentives. See Byrd (1991) for a study of market reform for state industrial enterprises in the 1980's.

A fourth step in economic reform was to allow more prices to be determined by the market forces of supply and demand. This was also accomplished in stages, sometimes by the government setting prices closer to market prices and sometimes by letting prices be determined freely in the market. An example of the former was the increase in procurement prices for agricultural products from an index of 217.4 in 1978 to 265.5 in 1979 and to 301.2 in 1981 (*SYB 1991*, p. 230). An example of the latter was the policy to allow farm products in rural markets to be determined freely. Controlling the prices of certain government distributed products while allowing them to be set in free markets led to a two-tier price system. The welfare effect of such a system was debated by economists. While granting the virtue of free market prices, some criticized the simultaneously existing controlled prices. When the government was the purchaser of certain products at below market prices, the seller essentially paid a tax to the government. If the quantity of government purchase was fixed, it amounted to a lump sum tax which does not have adverse incentive effects. When the government was the seller of certain products at below market prices, as in the case of material inputs to state enterprises, the purchaser received a subsidy. If the quantity for sale was fixed, it might not have an adverse incentive effect. If the quantity can be increased by negotiation, the purchaser would have an incentive to resell the extra quantities in the free market to make a profit. State enterprises receiving supplies from the government at below market prices did resell some of them in markets; they also had a competitive edge over other enterprises not receiving the subsidy. Overall, it appeared that the ill effects from subsidies might be outweighed by the positive effects of making the products available in free markets to benefit the consumers or producers. The October 1984 Decision of the Central Committee of the Communist Party singled out price reform as one of its important components. The decontrol and resetting of prices have continued until today.

A fifth step of reform was the decontrol of supply of consumer goods. As the supply of agricultural products increased rapidly since 1978 and became available in free markets, rationing of food items for urban consumers and rationing of cloth became unnecessary in the middle 1980's. Supplies of durable consumer goods such as watches, bicycles, electric fans, sewing machines, refrigerators, and television sets also increased rapidly in the early 1980's, making government control of their distribution unnecessary. Government supply of housing to the urban population has taken much longer to decontrol because the total supply of housing could not be increased as rapidly as other consumer durables and because the government was unwilling to abandon the virtually free housing provided for the urban population. The commercialization of housing still goes on as of 1993, with more and more urban families buying their apartments by installments from their working units at below market prices and some rich families buying their apartments at market prices.

As the sixth step in the reform process, China expanded foreign trade and encouraged foreign investment in an open-door policy. An excellent analysis of foreign trade reform can be found in Lardy (1992). Exports were decentralized as provincial and local government units as well as collective and private enterprises were given authority to promote exports. Restrictions on imports were also reduced. The official exchange rate for the Chinese currency was lowered several times from 1.9 U.S. dollars in 1980 to 5.6 U.S. dollars in 1993 to approximate more closely the market rate. As a result the ratio of foreign trade to national income increased from 10.3 percent in 1977 to 38.5 percent in 1990 (*SYB 1991,* pp. 32 and 615). Foreign investment also increased rapidly, from a negligible amount in 1978 to 10.3 billion U.S. dollars of foreign funds utilized in 1990 (*SYB 1991,* p. 629). Special economic zones were established to encourage foreign investment as foreign investors were given favorable tax concessions and a suitable infrastructure to establish their enterprises. Foreign trade and investments have performed three significant functions in China's economic development.

1. Foreign investment augments domestic investment in the process of capital accumulation while foreign trade expands China's production possibility frontier inclusive of trade.

2. Foreign investment and trade are channels through which updated technology and management practices are introduced into China in the process of learning by doing.

3. Joint venture, foreign enterprises, and foreign trade provide competition to Chinese state and collective enterprises, forcing them to be more efficient, and at the same time put pressure on the Chinese price system to reflect the forces of demand and supply.

The seventh step of the reform process was to change the government planning process to suit the more market-oriented economy. Central planning through providing output targets and approving investment budget of state enterprises was being shifted to the regulation of more autonomous and financially independent enterprises through taxation and the control of credits. The People's Bank was to play a more important role as a central bank in regulating the supply of money and credit, after being officially declared to be a central bank in 1982. Commercial banking was to be developed. Banking reform was progressing only slowly as the existing specialized banks under the control of the People's Bank did not change to modern commercial banks rapidly. The staff of these banks had neither knowledge and experience nor incentives to function as commercial banks in a modern market economy. Once given autonomy, local banks tended to extend loans and credits to local collective enterprises as personal favors or to promote economic growth of their own region. When inflation became more serious in 1985 and especially in 1988 as a result of overexpansion of money and credit, the People's Bank's only resource was to rely on administrative directives to assign credit quotas to the branch banks in different regions. In both instances, the administrative directives of the People's Bank succeeded in controlling inflation within one year. Modern commercial banking regulated by a central bank is still in the process of being developed in 1993, as are stock markets in Shenzhen (the economic zone bordering Hong Kong) and Shanghai.

In October 1992, some 14 years after the official beginning of economic reform introduced by the Third Plenary Session of the Eleventh Central Committee of the Communist Party in 1978, the Congress of the Communist Party was able to adopt a resolution urged by Deng Xiaoping to declare that China's economy is a socialist market economy. By that time, over 65 percent of China's national output was produced by profit-seeking economic units. In 1992, real national income increased by 12 percent by official statistics, with most observers projecting a 10-year growth rate averaging seven to nine percent. Private enterprises were flourishing. China already became an essentially market economy.

Having summarized the seven steps taken to achieve reform toward a market economy, I would like to discuss the main characteristics of the reform process.

1. To be noted is a strong support of the country for the reform. The strong support by political leaders, government officials at different levels and by the population at the initial stage of the reform was already mentioned.

After the success of the responsibility system in agriculture, the vast majority of the farmers who made up nearly 80 percent of China's population became strong supporters of the reform thus assuring no return to collective farming under the commune system. Urban industrial reforms, though less successful, made the urban population much better off than before in terms of the increase in income through increases in wages and bonuses distributed from increased profits, the availability of consumer goods, the freedom to travel and the opportunity to engage in private enterprises. The major discontent of part of the urban population occurred in the Fall of 1988 when inflation was at an annual rate of about 18 percent by official statistics and when government corruption became a major issue, contributing to demonstrations led by university students in Beijing and other cities in the Spring of 1989. Soon after the demonstrations were suppressed by force on June 4th, causing much criticism of the political leaders from around the world, the Chinese people continued to support economic reform. They cheered when Deng made a speech in Shenzhen in January 1992 urging the speeding up of the reform process. They cheered when the Party Congress adopted the resolution to declare China a market economy in October 1992.

2. The reformers only knew the general direction of reform but did not have a detailed blueprint. They admitted that they did not know the answers to what the final system ought to be. They learned as they experimented and observed, touching the rocks as they walked across the river. As a result, China has developed a market economy with its own characteristics, as alleged by a slogan of the Community Party. A notable feature is the flexible form of state and collective enterprises whose managers seek profits as in private enterprises. Another is the limited formalization of legal institutions under which economic transactions take place, although the legal system is being transformed.

3. Closely related to the second, is the extensive use of experimentation and practical experience. The official adoption of the responsibility system in agriculture by the Party Central Committee in 1979 was based on successful experiences in the communes of several provinces. Further success led to the adoption of the responsibility system for small enterprises. Reform in granting autonomy to state industrial enterprises started by experiment with six pilot enterprises in Sichuan in 1978 and some 6600 enterprises by June 1980. Expansion of rural and urban markets, of private and collective enterprises, of private housing, of foreign trade and investment and of special economic zones all proceeded in stages after successful experimentation. Successful experimentation helped the reformers not only in deciding what to adopt, but also in unifying skeptics in the Party and the government to support the reform.

4. Related to the third, is the pragmatic attitude of the reformers who are free from ideological restraints. This attitude was probably influenced by the attitude of Deng and Zhao. By pragmatism is meant the willingness to adopt whatever works with little ideological constraint. While conducting a workshop for officials of the Commission for Restructuring the Economic System in 1987, I was much impressed by a remark made by a member of the workshop: "Nothing prevents us from adopting in our socialist system anything that works well under a capitalist system." He probably would not have used the word "capitalist" in 1982. As Deng was quoted often since the late 1970's, "We don't care whether a cat is black or white as long as it catches mice." Of course the ideology of Communist Party members has changed greatly in the 15 years of reform since 1978 as Chinese practice changed, but it was practice that led the ideology and not the other way around, following the principle of "seeking truth from facts" advocated by Deng.

5. The absence of any drastic changes in the political system. The Communist Party continued to rule China, although political authorities have become more decentralized, with provincial and local governments now exercising more power and a richer population outside the Communist Party exercising more economic power and enjoying more economic and political freedom. For evidence of increase in economic and political freedom, compare the amount of domestic and foreign travel and the contents of the writing by Chinese intellectuals between 1978 and 1993.

The above five characteristics are on the side of gradualism in economic reform as opposed to shock treatments. Gradualism was needed to secure the support of Party and government officials and of the population for the reforms, to help the reformers decide what reforms to adopt, to change the existing institutions such as state enterprises and banks to modern institutions, to allow consumers and producers receiving subsidies or entitlements to adjust to the competitive force of the markets, and to enable new enterprises and new entrepreneurs to develop as they were developed in other market economies all through history. Economic institutions require time to acquire the necessary human capital. By the government simply announcing a new set of rules, small private enterprises and state banks cannot change rapidly to an entirely new pattern of behavior as a result of institutional inertia and the lack of the required human capital. Rapid price changes often amount to the government taking away economic entitlement from its people which is difficult to accomplish it Western market economies including the United States.

The Chinese economic reformers have taken a course of gradualism because of these difficult problems associated with rapid changes. Some of these problems may also exist in other countries attempting to reform their economies.

REFERENCES

Byrd, W.A. (1991). *The market mechanism and economic reforms in China.* Armonk, N.Y.: M.E. Sharpe, Inc.

Chow, G.C. (1985). *The Chinese economy.* New York: Harper & Row.

——. (1987, January 16). Development of a more market-oriented economy in China. *Science 235,* pp. 295–299.

——. (1988). Economic analysis of the People's Republic of China. *Journal of Economic Education 1*(1), 53–64.

——. (1993). Capital formation and economic growth in China. *Quarterly Journal of Economics. 108*(3), 809–842.

Lardy, N.R. (1992). *Foreign trade and economic reform in China, 1978–1990.* New York: Cambridge University Press.

McMillan, J., Whalley, J., & Zhui, L. (1989). The impact of China's economic reform on agricultural productivity growth. *Journal of Political Economy, 97*(4), 781–807.

Kristof, N.D. (1993, February 14). Entrepreneurial energy sets off a Chinese boom. *The New York Times,* p. 1.

Perkins, D. (1988). Reforming China's economic system. *Journal of Economic Literature, 31*(2), 601–645.

State Statistics Bureau. (1989). *Price statistics yearbook of China 1989* [in Chinese]. Beijing.

State Statistics Bureau. (1991). *Statistical yearbook of China 1991.* Beijing.

Vogel, E. (1989). *One step ahead in China.* Cambridge, Mass.: Harvard University Press.

Incremental Changes and Dual-Track Transition: Understanding the Case of China

Fan Gang

In 1993, China registered the highest GNP growth rate (13.4%0 in the world and a recognizable acceleration of market-oriented reform. In the previous year, a kind of market economy ('socialist market economy') was officially adopted by the ruling Communist Party s the goal of system reform. As some formerly socialist countries are still suffering from economic recession and political turmoil, China has suddenly become a 'model' for successful economic restructuring, e.g. Chen *et al.* (1992), and Gelb *et al.* (1993).

The goals of this paper are twofold. First, it explains the fundamental causes and characteristics of China's gradual market-oriented reform strategy. Second, the paper identifies the problems that the gradual reform strategy has left for further reforms.

The problem of policy choice is studied by focusing on two related questions. The first question is why 'shock therapy' could not be accepted by the Chinese in the late 1970s or even now, and why 'gradualism' was not acceptable or is no longer acceptable in some other nations in the late 1980s. The second question is why China has been successful so far in conducting its 'gradual reform' in the 1980s, while others failed during the same period. The first question is about the 'acceptability' of different reform approaches, and it is the subject of Section 1. The second question is about the 'feasibility' of different reform approaches, and is discussed in Section 2.

The gradual reform strategy has delayed the resolution of several fundamental issues. The postponement of reforms in these areas has created forces that are destabilizing the economy. Section 3 discusses the problems of the

Fan Gang, Chinese Academy of Social Sciences, "Incremental Changes and Dual-Track Transition: Understanding the Case of China," *Economic Policy*, December 1994: 100–122.

'dual-track' system, and Section 4 traces the post-1978 output cycles to the decentralization policies of the reform programme.

1. ACCEPTABILITY: THE POLITICAL ECONOMY OF REFORM

1.1. The Pre-Reform Economic Situation

China's overall economic reform has never been 'radical' as compared with Eastern European countries and the Former Soviet Union (EEFSU). Political reform has yet to take place after fifteen of years economic reform; mass privatization is not ont he agenda; price reform has been gradual; exchange rates were not unified until very recently; and so on. The general objective model is the ambiguous 'Socialist Market Economy.'

Gradualism was adopted at the end of 1978 not because there were no proposals for more radical reform programmes but because a majority of society and the leadership were not in favor of them. The fact was that the Chinese economic situation in the late 1970s was 'too good' for a radical reform package to be adopted. Following the end of the decade-long Cultural Revolution in 1976, China registered 7.8% national income growth in 1977 and 12.3% in 1978 before the reform started in 1979. At that time, most ordinary people had not yet totally lost their trust in the old system because, first, they had not suffered zero or negative income growth like the Eastern Europeans and Russians did, and, second, they felt that the Chinese technocrats had had no chance to carry out their 'optimal' economic plans due to the frequent political upheavals since the late 1950s. It was hence popularly believed that the most important problem for the economy was the failure of the 'political-struggle-first' doctrine; and not defects in the basic institutional structure of the system. Such 'methodological mistakes' could easily be overcome by concentrating on economic construction.

The noticeable recovery of economic performance immediately after the end of the Cultural Revolution seemed to many people evidence of the virtues of the old system. It was hence natural for a majority of people not to choose an abrupt change of their life when their real income was not only growing but was also expected to continue to grow under the current regime. Compared with the seventy-year old Soviet system which finally ran into keep crises in the late 1980s, forty years of socialist history was too short to exhaust the energy of China's economic machines.

In contrast, a radical reform programme was actually demanded by the EEFSU societies in late 1980s after their political change. In 1989 when the revolution took place, the gradual approach was unacceptable to the majority. The Russian referendum in April 1993, 3 years later, still supported the radical approach. Similarly, the economists who designed the 'shock therapy' package could not have sold it to the EEFSU societies if there were other alternatives under the prevailing circumstances (the lack of real authority of central government, for instance). Furthermore, gradual reform had been tried before the 1989 social crises. The previous gradual reforms were undertaken not because people were myopic or 'conservative' but because the old system at that time had not yet entered its terminal crisis. China's old system (the state sector) has not yet reached its end even after fifteen years of reform. What has happened in China so far is mostly the growth of a new system paralleling the old one.

The hypothesis advanced here is that the radicalness or gradualness of the reform process is a function of, among other things, the extent to which the economy has stagnated and declined on the even of the reform. Specifically, the lower is the growth potential of the old system, the stronger are the incentives and the willingness to pursue radical reform.

1.2. The Ceaselessly Changing Objective Models

China's gradual reform also has been characterized by gradual changing of its reform objectives. Unlike the majority of Pole and Russians who wee clear about their desire to 'return to Europe' and to adopt a private market economy, the Chinese had neither a clear idea nor consensus about where to go. What the Chinese knew was merely that the conventional centrally-planned system was not working well and that some changes were necessary in order to promote economic growth.

Consequently, China has proceeded through a lengthy path of readjusting reform objectives, from 'a planned economy with some market adjustment', to 'a combination of plan and market', and now to 'a socialist market economy.' The changes in objectives reflect, first, the increasing knowledge in China about the merits of different resource allocation mechanisms, and, second, and most fundamentally, the changes in the social balance between various interests groups and the changes of economic structure resulting from the process of reform and development itself. As the non-state sector grows rapidly and the state sector continues to decline, people become more convinced about the superior efficiency of the market system and hence offer less resistance to more profound changes.

1.3. The Rule of Government

The discussion above suggests that 'gradualism' is less an 'adopted approach', or 'chosen strategy', but more of an *ex post* description of an unintended evolutionary process. Very few people really knew in 1978 how to implement gradual reform. Participants might have known what the first 'piece' should be, but might not know what the next piece should be. Indeed the term 'piece-meal approach' is a more accurate description than 'gradualism'.

For example, the rural 'household contract responsibility system,' which later turned out to be the most important step in starting the whole reform process, was banned by the government in 1979 and only 'adopted' later after it had become widely practiced by the peasants. Again, when the rural economy was liberalized, few policy-makers would have predicted that there would be a dynamic rural industry sector. In fact, most policy-makers and some leading pro-reform economists were against the development of township and village enterprises (TVEs) for a long time. More recently, the retrenchment programme of 1989–91 included serious measures to crack down on TVEs and private businesses in order to increase the dominance of the state sector. These measures were abandoned later only because the state authority could not afford the sharp fall in tax revenue caused by the crack-down.

Another example is that even to date, the leadership and many reformists are still convinced that expanding state-owned enterprises' (SOEs') autonomy without changing ownership is the way to perfect the system of socialist ownership and to solve the current problems in the SOEs. They put their major effort into reforming the state sector and left the non-state sector to grow 'spontaneously' by itself. It is hence ironical that the development of the non-state sector has been counted by the Chinese policy-makers as one of their major achievements.

1.4. Decentralization and Bottom-up Innovation

Do Chinese policy-makers have something to offer for improving reform methodology? Perhaps.

One notable feature is the pragmatic and flexible attitude of the Chinese government. As it did not see the need to clarify everything in concepts before taking actions, it did not spend much time on argument ('No argument [on principles]' has even become an official approach in dealing with controversies) and simply allowed different norms to exist ('groping for stone to cross river'). When something new but controversial appeared, the 'no-encourage-ment-but-no-ban' policy was applied. This may not be the best way to deal with the transformation, but under certain circumstance, it may create the conditions for a better approach to emerge.

While the decentralization of decision-making powers to local govern-ments and enterprises under the unchanged public ownership framework have created a number of new problems (to be discussed in Section 4), it has turned out to be a dynamic mechanism for various new forms of economic arrange-ments to emerge. Experiments of different reform programs at various levels were encouraged; 'special economic zones' were set up; various 'special treatments' to different regions were extended; and local initiatives were respected.[1]

Now, more and more Chinese people understand that the market cannot be planned or created in planned ways. What needs to be planned may be only the first of several steps toward removing restrictions to institutional innovations by ordinary people and putting reform vehicles on track.

2. FEASIBILITY: THE DIFFERENT STRUCTURAL CONDITIONS

2.1. The Pre-existence of a Repressed Non-state Sector

The different fates of gradualism in different countries at various times were actually pre-determined by their initial economic structures (Fan, 1993; and Sachs and Woo, 1994). Gradualism is more possible in an under-developed (under-industrialized) economy with a huge surplus rural labour force like China than in an 'over-industrialized' and 'over-state-sector-dominated' country like Poland. Until the end of the 1970s, Chinese peasants' incomes were declining (absolutely and relatively) compared to those of the urban population. The pre-existence of a repressed sector—peasant agriculture as in China— in which people earned a stagnant subsistence income and had a strong demand for change and new opportunities, provided a labour force that was ready to pursue new economic activities. It was the development of a new non-state sector emerging from a previously repressed non-state sector that made the first stage of reform a Pareto improvement.

The different approaches to reform may also be defined in terms of ways of dealing with the old system. If it were feasible to develop a new non-state sector first, the original state sector could (and, maybe, should) be kept alive for a while in order to avoid immediate resistance from the people who still benefit from it. If, however, the new sector cannot be established without moving resources from the old sector, then political reform must come first before any real economic reform (cutting subsidies to the SOEs, for instance) can be undertaken.

One important question is: can the new sector develop fast enough to outpace the increasing need to keep the declining old sector alive? As long as the state sector is dominant but suffering losses, it will use every possible means (explicit or implicit) to extract subsidies from the other sectors. Furthermore, it will win in policy-making if 'majority rule' is followed.[2] Thus, if the new sector cannot grow fast enough and become strong quickly enough to retain some of its surplus (after paying for the subsidies) to add to its capital accumulation, it will always be repressed and not attractive enough to draw out more state employees.

From this perspective, China had two special conditions that permitted incrementalist reform. First, China stated reform when the state sector was not so worn down that it needed heavy subsidies like the former Soviet firms in the late 1980s. In 1978, subsidies to loss-making SOEs accounted to only 3.21% of GDP, an amount that was easily covered by moderate growth. Second, rural reform and liberalization of private economic activities in the presence of a huge rural labour surplus could generate growth rapid enough to outpace the speed at which the subsidies to SOEs were increasing.

2.2. The Government's Authority

Another condition favorable for gradualism is the political continuity of the government. The Chinese government never lost the administrative ability to control the reform path and to keep changes moving gradually. Furthermore, it did not totally denounce the old system and announce a commitment to something totally different. In contrast, a government, that was established through political revolution and owed its legitimacy to the promise of a radically new system, would not be able to make changes gradually and still maintain its authority. The lesson appears to be that under 'post-revolutionary' conditions, gradualism is not only unacceptable but also infeasible.

2.3. The Path of Least Resistance

The fact that Chinese reform started in agriculture has led many observers to conclude that the optimal reform strategy would have a 'leading sector approach,' e.g. Chen *et al.* (1992). I offer two comments about this recommendation.

(1) When the economy as a whole has not run into an overall systemic crisis that requires an overall radical reform programme, remedial measures will be demanded and carried out on a sector-by-sector basis. From the political perspective of implementing sequential reforms, the most important feature of the leading sector is that it is the sector with the least resistance to reform and therefore the easiest sector in which to carry out reforms. An early success is important in persuading the other sectors also to adopt the reforms. This is why gradual reforms in China have been taken in an 'easy-to-hard sequence,' see Zhang (1993). So if gradualism is the only acceptable and feasible strategy, one should find out which sector is of 'the least resistance' and start reform there.

This reasoning suggests that Goldman's (1991) conclusion that the agricultural sector should always be the first to be reformed makes as little sense in political terms as it does in economic terms. There is no basis to believe that the agricultural sector in an industrialised country like the Czech Republic would automatically be the sector most eager to undertake reform. Woo (1994) stresses the above political consideration to explain the sequencing of reforms, and he advances the hypothesis that the largest sector is generally the most 'reform-demanding' sector because its crisis by definition is the gravest one faced by the economy.

(2) For an economy which is not significantly differentiated in terms of ownership, development level, income disparity, labour mobility, or relationship with the state, the 'leading sector approach' would not work. The resistance to reform in this case may be evenly distributed and no sector can play a 'leading role'. In this case, to choose a particular sector to start the reform may create more rather than less conflict.

3. THE DUAL-TRACK TRANSITION

3.1. Honoring Previous 'Implicit Contracts'

The 'dual-track system' in China was first used in price reform and it has been extended to cover almost all economic transactions.[3] The most important dual-track system has been the reform of the ownership structure which has created a dual-track economy: the development of a new system that parallels the unreformed old system. China's rapid economic growth can be attributed mainly to the dynamic development of the 'new track non-state sector' which consists of private and semi-private enterprises, community-owned rural industrial enterprises, foreign joint-ventures and individual businesses.

The virtue of the dual-track system is that it honors the 'implicit contract' previously set according to socialist principles. The implicit contract guarantees the worker that, regardless of her work effort, she would receive at least the minimum wage and various benefits which include health insurance, free housing, retirement pension and jobs for her children. Even though this implicit contract system may reduce the efficiency of the market economy, it has to be recognized that it has already become part of people's vested interests. To keep the 'old track' is to respect the vested interests under the old system. The gain from the maintenance of the distorted incentives is that the resistance to reform is reduced. This explains why governments have tended to pursue a dual-track approach to reform if at all possible. It is only when this approach fails and the old government collapses, that the new government—free of the obligation to respect previous contracts—can pursue radical reforms and enter into new contractual obligations.

3.2. Convergence of the Two Tracks?

The real question is not whether the government should follow a dual-track system, but whether the two tracks should converge into one as rapidly as possible. The success of dual-track transition depends mainly on the success of the new track. If the growth rate of the new sector is higher than that of the old sector, then the old system will, in the long run, shrink to zero as a proportion of the economy. In other words, if the old system stops expanding and everything else grows, a dual-track transition will end in the space of one generation, without explicit reform actions having been taken against the old system.

Price reform has followed this idealised dual-track transition for a number of markets. In 1992, most Chinese provinces removed all controls on food prices. This was the 'final punch' of a process of step-by-step price reforms over the past ten years. When convergence of the two tracks finally took place, the food products sold at officially fixed prices accounted for less than 15% of total consumption and the free market prices were about twice the official prices. Naturally, under these conditions, the 'final punch' did not cause 'shocks'.

A similar thing happened in the foreign exchange market. The unification of the official exchange rate and the 'swap market exchange rate' occurred at the end of 1993 when the differential between the two rates was about 50%. But at that time, only 20% of foreign exchange transactions were still subject to the official exchange rate. In this case, it is noteworthy that the 'rationed' component of foreign exchange sales did not decrease in absolute size over time, it only shrank relative to the size of the 'new track'.

In practice, an expansion of the old system (in absolute size) has occurred quite frequently. This is because the state has used the revenue from the more productive new sectors both to compensate those who suffer losses because of the transformation and to expand the old inefficient sector. The latter type of subsidy is usually justified on the grounds of strengthening the competitiveness of the SOEs through technological upgrading. The result is that the old track has not shrunk proportionately as rapidly as it should have.

From a supply-side perspective, the non-state sector has become the major contributor to China's GDP—52% of industrial output in 1992, and an estimated 37% in 1993. In 1992, about 80% of the increment of GDP was from the non-state sector. On the expenditure side, however, the state sector has remained dominant. In 1993, 79% of total bank credits went to the state sector.[4] In 1993, over 70% of total social investment in fixed assets was for projects in the state sector. This was a higher share than in the previous year. The number of state employees as a proportion of the total labour force has not changed in the past 15 years, in some years, it even increased. The number of state enterprise has also increased.

Corruption is another reason for the survival and expansion of the 'old track'. For example, in the process of price reform, the old track was frequently expanded not only because of pressures from SOEs seeking more resources at low official prices, but also because of rent-seeking by government officials. The higher the share of production that is designated as 'planned sales', the higher will be the free market price, and, hence, the greater the amount of resources that can be diverted to the corrupt officials. The result was that for a long time, planned sales were not fixed as they were supposed to be, but increased instead. Sometimes what shrank was the 'market track' instead of the 'planned track'. This is one of the reasons why the dual-track price system has lasted for so long.

The lesson is clear: the most important challenge in a gradual transition may not be how to speed up the growth of the new track, but how to assure that the old track does not grow as well. The old track cannot be simply ignored as many advocates of gradual transitions have suggested, because it will not wither away voluntarily. It may, on the contrary, not only prosper as a parasite of the new track because of its considerable political clout but many also metastasize and crowd out the new track.

3.3. 'Transitional Corruption' and 'Spontaneous Privatization'

Corruption is no doubt a source of economic distortion, income disparities and social unrest. But it appears that wide-spread corruption may be unavoidable for a declining public ownership economy during the transformation. 'Capitalistization' (Zhang, 1993) of some government officials, openly or underground, may be the way to make everyone better off, because it shifts officials from previous positions under the old system to new ones with a minimum of resistance.

Wang and Li (1993) have estimated that, in 1992, official corruption, wage-drift ('wage eats profits and capital'), and stealing has siphoned off at least 100 billion yuan worth of state assets, or about 5% of total state assets. A survey in Shanxi province shows that up to 40% of state assets has been dissipated in the past 10 years. Meanwhile, household savings in the form of both bank deposits and financial assets have increased rapidly. For an economy in which mass privatization with a fairer redistribution of property rights could not be accepted, such gradual 'spontaneous privatization' seems to be an unavoidable part of the process of moving towards the market. The unpleasant possibility during the historical stage of 'initial capital accumulation' is that the big money may be the most 'dirty' money.

It is imperative that legal protection of private property rights be quickly established in order to reduce the 'decapitalization' and 'capital flight' that are occurring. It recent years, personal purchases of luxury consumer goods have been running disproportionately high for the level of overall economic development, and Hong Kong banking sources have estimated that about US$10 billion of capital fled abroad annually. Capital flight amounted to one-third of the gross capital inflow in 1993. This suggests that private property rights have not been sufficiently protected and private investment in the domestic market has not been properly encouraged.[5]

The present level and form of 'transitional corruption' have not given rise to many problems, because many corrupt officials used their power and privileges to obtain money from the state for their own businesses and then left their positions in the government. One cannot be sanguine, however, that the nature of corruption will not evolve into types that would stop economic growth. One such danger lies in the conversion of planning power into 'licensing power'. The disturbing signs are that the approval process has become longer in recent years for many kinds of business and projects, and that the number of profit-oriented companies run by government departments have increased greatly. There is a positive sign, however, in that the demand for further changes is also increasing.

3.4. Remaining Hardcore Problems and 'Sequential Features'

The gradual approach in its essence is an 'easy-to-hard' reform sequence. It starts with the easy problems and leaves the hard problems until later. In contrast, the radical approach tackles the hard problems at the beginning. As the question of which approach is better can be answered only after all problems have been solved in both approaches, one should therefore be very careful when making comparisons in the middle of the reform process.

In terms of economic optimality, a 'hit-the-core-problems-first' radical programme is more justifiable because it maximizes efficiency gains and minimizes implementation costs of the reform. On the other hand, an 'easy-to-hard' gradual programme is more justifiable on the grounds of minimizing the political costs of reform.[6] Clearly, the reform cost are different in different economic and political situations. So an 'optimum sequence' cannot be defined without specifying the circumstances under which the reforms are being implemented.

The three most hardcore problems remaining in the Chinese economy today are: (1) factor price reform, including interest rates and prices for oil, coal and some other basic raw materials; (2) Ownership reform of the state sector, including the state-owned banks (SOBs); and (3) Government reform, including reform of the fiscal system.

4. DECENTRALIZATION AND MACROECONOMIC STABILIZATION

4.1. Decentralization and Liberalization

For a centrally planned economy, market-oriented reform must involve the decentralization of decision-making powers. The broader definition of decentralization may include removing restrictions to private activities, or more generally, all kinds of non-state[7] economic activities, and decentralizing decision-making powers to individuals and private business people. The narrower definition of decentralization, however, may only refer to granting decision-making powers to the lower-level state agencies from the central authority, i.e., to local governments, to state-owned enterprises (SOEs) and to state-owned banks (SOBs, plus other state financial institutions if any). In short, it is decentralization within the state sector without change of ownership structure. Under this narrower definition of decentralization, actions of removing restrictions to private economic activities should be referred as 'economic liberalization'.

Decentralization within the state sector and economic liberalization of private activities may be correlated with each other. When the local governments have autonomy to pursue their own interests, they may find that it is in their interests to promote and protect local private or non-state business, as long as the latter would provide more 'local revenues'. This is one of major reasons why the non-state sectors have been developing so rapidly. On the other hand, decentralization within the state sector may encourage so-called 'spontaneous privatization' as it may result in the spread of corruption and 'flowing out' of state assets to private hands or the 'capital depletion' of state enterprises. But decentralization within the state sector itself is not as the same thing as liberalization of private activities.

4.2. Decentralization within the State Sector

The reform of the state sector so far has mainly remained a process of decentralization without change of ownership.[8] It has involved almost all decision-making on production, pricing, investment, trade, expenditure, income distribution, taxation, and credit allocation. The following institutional innovations have played important roles in the process:

(a) The 'Budgetary Contracting System' (BCS, since 1980, see Zhong, 1990).[9] This was the major device for re-shaping fiscal relations between central and local government. Under the BCS, the central government shares revenues (taxes and profit remittances) with local governments in the following way: (1) The central and local governments collect revenues on separate tax bases according to the administrative subordinate relationship (different levels of government tax different payers); (2) Each provincial government signs a contract with the central government fixing the amount of revenue remittances for a specified period of time. for provinces that run budget deficits, the contract will be on the subsidies to be transferred by the centre to local government.

(b) The 'Contract Responsibility System' (CRS, since 1983) for state enterprises. Under this system, SOEs pay a fixed amount of taxes and profits to the state and retain the rest for themselves. In principle, as long as SOEs can deliver the tax-cum-profit remittances specified in the contracts, the government will not interfere with their operations.

(c) Direct borrowing. Since 1985, state grants for operating funds and fixed asset investments have been replaced by bank loans. Local governments and SOEs are allowed to borrow directly from banks. The proportion of SOEs' funds that is raised externally has been increasing dramatically over the years (see Fan and Woo, 1993). Since 1991, local governments and SOEs are also allowed to borrow directly from workers, households, and other institutions. Similarly, the local branches of the central bank (People's Bank) and the state specialized banks are also allowed some discretion in formulating their lending policies.[10] The fact is that direct credit control (through 'credit quotas' or 'credit ceilings') imposed by the central authority has been in force most of the time.

The decentralization reforms have created a 'decentralized state sector'. 'Autonomous' local governments, SOEs and local SOBs have increasingly important roles in determining resource allocation, while the central authority has become less influential in resource allocation within the unchanged ownership framework. It should be noted, however, that the giving up of power by the centre has not always been voluntary. The impetus for decentralization at later stages has been pressure from local governments and SOEs. The step-by-step reform in the past 14 years has often reflected erosion of the resistance of the central authority to these pressures for decentralization.

Many people still believe that a market system could be created by changing managerial incentive systems and that a market economy could be compatible with state ownership. Many economists (Chinese and foreign) have praised the decentralization and measured the progress of reform by the amount of decision-making powers that have been given up by the central government. The decentralization reform may have improved the technical efficiency of the state sector.[11] But if we look at the allocative efficiency and intertemporal stability, it must be understood that the decentralized state sector is the major institutional cause of macroeconomic instability and of the divergent development of regional economies. In addition to the ordinary factors of structural changes in the 'take-off' stage of economic development, China's increasing inflation and fluctuations are to a great extent caused by the redistribution of fiscal power, increasing budget deficits, growing subsidy credits ('policy loans') to state enterprises, and the phenomenon of 'locally initiated monetary expansion'.

4.3. The Redistribution of Fiscal Power and Central Budget Deficits

The fiscal situation can be summarized by two facts: total government budgetary revenue declined from 31% of GNP in 1978 to 16.6% of GNP in 1992; and central budgetary expenditure fell from over 60% of total budgetary expenditure in the 1970s to 39.7% in 1992.[12] The relative fall in budget revenue is due to two major reasons: the fall in revenue remitted by SOEs and the rise of the 'revenue-hiding-in-local-economies' phenomenon.

Despite the (possible) improvement in productivity, the profitability of SOEs has been deteriorating since the decentralization reform. Wage payments, bonuses, fringe benefits, and 'publicly-financed consumption' (which are often disguised as costs) have increased dramatically and disproportionately. The overcompensation of workers has caused profits remitted to the government to decrease as a proportion of total value-added (see Fan and Woo, 1993). Budget subsidies to loss-making SOEs have also increased. Besides, under the enterprise 'Contract Responsibility System' (CRS), the amount of emitted taxes and profits are pre-set. So when production grows, remittance will fall as a proportion of total revenue. Meanwhile, under the CRS, SOEs are still not responsible for their losses in practice even though they are supposed to be in theory. For those enterprises that make unexpectedly large profits, their revenue remittances do not increase beyond the contracted amounts. Consequently, government revenue is destined to fall because of this institutionalized asymmetry.

The central government revenue is mainly dependent on taxes and profit remittances from the large and medium-sized SOEs. But since the financial performance of these enterprises has been below average, there has been a fall in central government revenue relative to total revenue.

Another cause for the relative decline in total budget revenue and central budget revenue is the change in central-local fiscal relations. Under the 'Contracting Budgetary System' (CBS), the amount of revenue transfer between local and central government is also pre-set by contracts that were determined by a one-to-one bargaining process between the central and provincial governments. (The provincial governments would then negotiate tax contracts with the lower down local governments). As the negotiated amounts are heavily influenced by the tax payments of the previous periods, central revenue growth has not kept up with the growth of the local economies. Moreover, to retain more revenues in the local economies, local governments have increasingly concealed their revenue bases. Local governments would allow local enterprises to under-report their taxable revenues and, in return, the enterprises would make contributions to local development projects when the local governments indicate their needs for funds. Such types of concealed-revenue arrangements have played increasingly important roles in the recent development of local economies. According to some surveys, such concealed funds amounted to 40–70% of the explicit revenue of local governments (Sen and Zhu, 1993).[13] If this kind of 'out-of-budget' local government revenues were added to the total government revenue, government revenue would not have fallen so much.

As a result of the decline in budget revenue, budget deficits and government borrowing from the banks have been rising. Furthermore, central government support for the development of poor regions has tapered off.

4.4. Subsidy Credits

An increasingly significant cause of inflation is the increase in policy loans to loss-making SOEs. The SOEs have gained more and more autonomy, but their budget constraint has remained soft. With the government's ability to subsidize the loss-making enterprises declining, bank loans have become a more important means of keeping these enterprises afloat. It is estimated that one-third of SOEs have explicit losses, and that another one-third of SOEs have 'hidden losses' which refer to the accumulation of unpaid inter-enterprise debt. It is well known that the reported explicit losses understate the true losses substantially. According to a 1992 survey of 300 large and medium-sized SOEs carried out by the State Economic and Trade Commission, the average ratio of total debt to total assets was 180%. Other surveys suggests that the ratio was almost up to 200%.

As the policy loans are something of a 'must', the central authority have encountered a dilemma in macroeconomic stabilization. It wants to curtail monetary expansion to cool down the over-heated economy, but it is not able to reduce credits to loss-making enterprises which are using these credits to maintain the wage levels of their employees. So, in practice, a tight credit policy hurts only profitable enterprises.

4.5. Locally Initiated Monetary Expansion

The most important cause of inflation and economic fluctuations in the past decade has been monetary expansion initiated by pressures exerted at the local level. Decentralization reform has produced strong 'local public-ownership economies.' Each region is led by a coalition of local governments, SOEs, and SOBs, and the regions compete with each other for bank credits to finance local growth. It is not market competition that they engage in, but competition under soft budget constraints.

Under the centrally planned system, regions would constantly demand for more investment projects. Now, under the decentralized system, they can make most decisions on investment by themselves.[14] Great pressures are put on the local banks for investment loans and in most cases local banks collude with the local governments and local enterprises. Diversion of credit and innovative financing have become common practices since the early 1980s. Innovative financing has taken forms that include requests for more credits from the central monetary authority, issuance of de facto 'IOUs' to depositors, and misappropriation of funds from central projects to local projects, leaving the central projects to be financed by additional credits (see Zhong and Hong, 1990, and Oi, 1992). Since 1991, local governments and SOEs have also had the right to issue bonds to the public.

It is extremely difficult to test the hypothesis that the increase in money supply since 1978 has, to an increasing extent, been initiated by the local governments and SOEs. What we do know is that the actual money supply has always been greater than the money supply target set at the beginning of the period, and that banks usually extended more credits than allowed by their credit quotas without obtaining clearance first. . . .

5. CONCLUDING REMARKS

My conclusion is that the economic transformation experiences to date do not show that either approach to reform, radicalism or gradualism, is unconditionally better than the other. Rather, by comparing the initial economic and social situations and special economic structures, the only conclusion is that each approach may be a 'constrained optimum" that reflects what is politically acceptable and economically feasible in each case. This does not mean that whatever happened was always right. It just shows that each approach has its own logic. Any comparison between Chinese reform and EEFSU reform is necessarily a difficult task. There have been only three years of radical reform in EEFSU. China, on the other hand, has been implementing reforms for over 15 years. Initial successes of Chinese reform should not be misjudged as superiority.

By saying that both approaches to reform are 'constrained optimum', I am not saying that there is no need for improvements in reform strategies and implementation policies in both cases. Given that China is likely to stay on gradualism, there could be better gradualism. The policy recommendations presented here, for example, would render the reform process more efficient.

As pointed out above, there are several hardcore challenges facing China: ownership reform, macroeconomic stabilization, regional and rural-urban income disparity and political reform. Fortunately, positive signs are emerging.

Corporatization is becoming a widely accepted idea and ownership reform of the state sector is not only on the policy agenda but is also no longer a subject of political criticism. More and more state enterprises are being sold to, or merged with, non-state companies. Property rights in rural industries are being redefined and redistributed among members of local communities. Most important of all, knowledge about the market economy is rapidly growing. In short, China's market-oriented reform has become irreversible.

One thing is certain: any improvements of the situation in EEFSU (such as what has happened in Poland) will accelerate Chinese reform by giving China lessons on how to deal with difficulties, and putting more pressure on the Chinese government to catch up faster with the West.

REFERENCES

Bowles, Paul (1989). 'Contradictions in China's Financial Reforms: The Relationship Between Banks and Enterprises,' *Cambridge Journal of Economics*.
Chen, Kang, Gary Jefferson and Inderjit Singh (1992). 'Lessons from China's Economic Reform', *Journal of Comparative Economics*.

Fan Gang (1995). 'Two Kinds of Reform Costs and Two Approaches to Reform' (in Chinese), *Economic Research Journal.*

Fan Gang and Wing Thye Woo (1993). 'Decentralized Socialism and Macroeconomic Stability: Lessons from China,' Working Paper No. 112, World Institute for Development Economics Research, The United Nations University, July.

Gelb, Alan, Gary Jefferson & Inderjit Singh (1995). 'The Chinese and East European Routes to Reform,' manuscript, NBER Eighth Annual Macro-economics Conference.

Goldman, Marshall (1991). *What Went Wrong With Perestroika?* Norton.

Jefferson, Gary, Thomas Rawski and Yuxin Zheng (1992). 'Growth, Efficiency and Convergence in China's State and Collective Industry,' *Economic Development and Cultural Change.*

Oi, Jean C. (1992). 'The Shifting Balance of Power in Central-local Relations: Local Government Response to Fiscal Austerity in Rural China,' mimeo, Harvard University.

Qian, Yingyi, and Xu Chenggang (1993). 'Why China's Economic Reforms Differ: The M-form Hierarchy and Entry/Expansion of the Non-state Sector,' *The Economics of Transition.*

Sachs, Jeffrey and Wing Thye Woo (1994). 'Structural Factors in the Economic Reforms of China, Eastern Europe, and the Former Soviet Union,' *Economic Policy.*

Sen, Tanzhen, and Zhu Gang (1993). 'A Study of Out-of-system Government Revenue of Township and Village,' *Jingji Yanjui (Economic Research Journal).*

Shi, Z. Jeffrey (1993). 'Reform for Decentralization and Decentralization for Reform: A Political Economy of China's R

Reform,' mimeo, University of Maryland.

Tang, Zongkun (1992). 'Decline of Profits and Reproduction Capability of State Enterprises' (in Chinese), *Jingji Yanju (Journal of Economic Research).*

Wang, Chenghua and Xintao Li (1993). 'The Losses of State Assets' (in Chinese), *Financial and Economics Studies.*

Woo, Wing Thye (1994). 'The Art of Reforming Centrally-Planned Economies: Comparing China, Poland and Russia,' *Journal of Comparative Economics.*

Woo, Wing Thye, Wen Hai, Yibiao Jin and Fan Gang (1994). 'How Successful Has Chinese Enterprise Reforms Been? Pitfalls in Opposite Biases and Focus,' *Journal of Comparative Economics.*

Xie, Ping (1993). 'Monetary Policy During the Transition towards the Market Economy,' Working Paper, The People's Bank of China.

Zhang, Weiying (1993). 'Decision Rights, Residual Claim and Performance: A Theory of How Chinese Economy Works,' Nuffield College, Oxford, mimeo.

Zhong, Pengrong (1990). *A Study of China's Inflation* (in Chinese), Jianxi People's Press.

Zhong, Pengrong and Tonghu Hong (1990). *Macroeconomics* (in Chinese), Beijing: Economic Sciences Press.

NOTES

1. This means that the 'M-form hierarchy' (Qian and Xu, 1993) is mainly the result of the decentralization reform rather than the pre-condition for a special approach to reform to be taken. As Zhang (1993) pointed out: 'It was (former) Premier Zhao Ziyang's strategy to use local governments to fight against more conservative central ministerial bureaucrats. To some degree this strategy was shared by Deng Xiaoping . . . As pointed out by Shi (1993), decentralization of reform government was a feature of the central leaders' style of governing the reform'.

2. Sachs and Woo (1994) argue that the pro-reform government should cut subsidies to push more state employees to leave the state sector for the more attractive non-state sector. The problem is whether the cuts would be accepted. The recent change in Russian government policies to the state sector shows how strong the state sector is. It seems that whether the state would cut the subsidies to state firms does not depend on its willingness to do so, but on the deterioration of the state's capacity to mobilize resources from the other sectors, i.e., tax the non-state enterprises.

3. The most noteable exception is credit markets where interest rates are still tightly controlled by the central government (although black market rates are widely in effect).

4. It should be noted that, as bank loans are given to state enterprises at low interest rates (about 10%), and the non-state sector is willing to pay higher rates (about 20%), the state enterprises re-lend some of these credits to non-state firms in the black market and earn interest differentials (that may be higher than their profits). No data is available on the volume of credits which have been 'transferred' in this way. But a reasonable estimate is no more than 30% of credits to the state sector.

5. Of course, if an individual's assets were proved after due process to be illegally obtained ('dirty'), they should be seized and the individual punished. If 'dirtiness' cannot be established, then the individual's assets should be protected as long as they stay reinvested in the national economy.

6. 'Political costs' of system reform refer to the economic resources wasted because of political conflicts. It may take the form of a reduction in output, and I have argued in Fan (1993) that this reduction is necessary to economic restructuring.

7. This term is quite often used by Chinese economists to refer to a broader range of economic organizations, from private businesses, cooperative firms, semi-private or shareholding companies, and collective or community-owned businesses such as Township and Village Enterprises (TVEs). These economic organizations are mostly new since the economic reform, and differ from state enterprises as they do not follow some regulations applicable to the state sector. Most forms of non-state enterprise are transitional—they are still evolving with the changes in the entire institutional environment.

8. Some fundamental steps towards reforming state ownership have taken place recently. The experimental 'share-holding' state corporations that was started in 988 allowed only 10% of shares to be sold to individuals. In 1993, comprehensive restructuring of state ownership was adopted by the Central Committee of the Chinese Communist Party (October, 1993) and the first Corporation Law was passed by the National People's Congress (December, 1993). Various experiments in corporatization will be made in 1994.

9. New changes are being attempted in taxation and revenue sharing. The new attempts include redistribution of tax revenues by categories (instead of by taxpayers) between central and local government in order to increase the share of central revenue, rebuilding the revenue transfer mechanism, and redefining the division of expenditure responsibilities between central and local government.

10. The local branches of state banks (the central bank and the state commercial banks) are to a great extent 'truly local.' The officials of local banks are part of a larger hierarchy, usually appointed by higher supervisors within the bank system. In reality, they are directly under the supervision of local authorities and benefit from local prosperity. They have generally always done their best to meet the loan requests of local officials and local SOEs, albeit somewhat constrained by central regulations—see Bowles (1989).

11. There are four major factors which determine the productivity of state enterprises: (1) management (operational incentive structure and decision-making process for 'agents');

(2) outside environment (planning or market); (3) technological inputs; and (4) the ownership form ('principal-agent' incentives and responsibility). Decentralization may improve the first three. That is why it is not surprising to observe improvement in SOEs' total factor productivity or technical efficiency (see Jefferson *et al.* 1992), but the extent of the improvement remains controversial (see Woo *et al.* 1994). These improvements, however, do not disprove the importance of the ownership factor, which may become the key 'bottle-neck' for further improvement.

12. Budgetary revenues includes domestic government borrowing, but excludes foreign debts (*Source: Chinese Statistical Yearbook* 1995).

13. That is, when the local government collects 100 yuan as 'budgetary revenue', it receives another 40 to 70 yuan as 'out-of-budget revenue'. They get 140 to 170 yuan in total.

14. Local autonomy on investment projects has expanded over time. For example, in 1984, the limit on investment projects that a provincial authority could approve was raised from RMB10 million to RMB30 million. In 1992, this limit was raised to RMB50 million. Furthermore, nearly all 'nonproductive investment projects' (apartment buildings, for instance) are under the jurisdiction of local governments. The result was that 82.7% of total investment in fixed assets in the state sector in 1992 was labelled 'local projects' (Tang, 1992), and there was a 45.4% increase in total investment spending by the state sector in 1992.

Editor's note: The original article was edited for publication here.

Public Law, Private Actors: The Impact of Human Rights on Business Investors in China

Diane F. Orentlicher and Timothy A. Gelatt

INTRODUCTION[1]

The astonishing brutality of Beijing's clampdown on pro-democracy advocates near Tiananmen Square four years ago placed human rights in the forefront of U.S. policy concerns in the People's Republic of China (PRC). Perhaps inevitably, the debate over U.S. human rights policy toward Beijing has had a profound impact on the expanding web of trade and investment between the United States and China—itself a central concern of U.S. policy. The Tiananmen incident thus wove together two strands of U.S. policy toward the PRC that had previously been thought to be unrelated, raising a raft of complex policy dilemmas to which satisfactory solutions still remain to be fashioned.

The focus of debate has been the annual renewal of China's most-favored-nation (MFN) trade status, but concerns about China's enduring human rights problems have pervaded virtually every aspect of U.S.-China trade and investment relations. However inconsistently enforced, sanctions ranging from a ban on military and high-technology sales to China[2] to a prohibition on involvement by the Overseas Private Investment Corporation in Chinese projects'[3] have been used to promote human rights improvements.

But if the most visible debates have centered on U.S. trade and aid policies, a potentially more far-reaching debate is taking place in the boardrooms of corporate America. From Levi Strauss & Co. to Phillips-Van Heusen,

Diane F. Orentlicher, Associate Professor of Law, Washington College of Law, The American University, and Timothy A. Gelatt, Adjunct Professor of Law, New York University, "Public Law, Private Actors: The Impact of Human Rights on Business Investors in China," *Northwestern Journal of International Law and Business,* 1993: 66–129.

from Sears,Roebuck and Co. to Reebok International Ltd., companies are asking how their role as investors can and should be shaped by human rights concerns in the PRC and other countries.

The answers that have emerged from these companies' deliberations reflect a pathbreaking reconception of corporate responsibility—one in which human rights occupy a central place. In March 1992, Sears, Roebuck and Co. announced that it would not import products produced by prison or other involuntary labor in China, and established a monitoring procedure to ensure compliance with its policy. In November 1990, Reebok International Ltd. condemned military repression in China and vowed that it "will not operate under martial law conditions" or "allow any military presence on its premises." Two years later, Reebok adopted a human rights code of conduct governing workplace conditions in all of its overseas operations, including those in China. Phillips-Van Heusen currently threatens to terminate orders from suppliers that violate human rights principles enshrined in its ethical code.[4] Adopting the most far-reaching policies, Levi Strauss & Co. and the Timberland Company apply human rights criteria in the selection of business partners, and avoid investing at all in countries where there are pervasive violations of basic human rights. In February 1993, the Timberland Company decided to end its sourcing from China. Two months later, Levi Strauss & Co. announced that it would end its relations with business partners in China, and would not initiate any direct investment there.

While these companies are in the vanguard of an emerging trend, their approach to human rights remains exceptional within the business community. Still, their initiatives have presented a bold challenge to the conventional view that business practice and human rights policy should remain largely separate, and have spurred a broader debate about the role of human rights in corporations' overseas investment decisions.

Should companies invest at all in countries, like China, where severe human rights abuses are pervasive? If they do invest, should they restrict their operations to areas of the country that have a comparatively good human rights record? Are there basic principles that transnational companies should observe to ensure, at a minimum, that they do not become complicit in a host government's abrogation of universally-recognized human rights? Should such principles be enforced by Executive or congressional fiat, or should companies take primary responsibility for policing themselves? How can companies that wish to factor human rights considerations into their business decisions be assured that they will not pay a price in lost investment opportunities or reduced market share?

This article addresses these questions in light of relevant principles of international law and U.S. foreign policy. A central thesis of this article is that businesses that may or do invest in China bear a responsibility to ensure that their actions do not, however, inadvertently, contribute to the systematic denial of human rights law provides an objective basis for identifying those responsibilities.

We also believe that, in some circumstances, companies that invest in China can and should play a more proactive role in advancing respect for human rights. This view is based, above all, on the unique influence of major foreign investors in China. Today, after a temporary downturn in business activity in the year following the Tiananmen incident, the U.S. business presence in China is at an all-time high. With total committed investment close to six billion dollars, in 1993 the United States is China's second largest foreign investor. In the 1980s, U.S. companies became one of China's top providers of foreign investment, technology and management expertise. Few sectors of U.S. industry are absent, with substantial U.S. investment projects across the length and breadth of the country. Major U.S. petroleum companies have been among the most active in both offshore and onshore explorations, as have the service companies that complement them. In locations from Beijing to Lhasa, from Guangzhou to Xian, U.S. companies manufacture everything from air conditioners to airplanes, from baby food to ball bearings, and from cars to computers. Major U.S. hotel chains are in business as investors, managers or both. U.S. companies involved in business projects in China include numerous household names—Boeing, H.J. Heinz, Coca-Cola, PepsiCo, 3M, Xerox, IBM and At&T, to name just a few—as well as a large number of smaller companies on and off the Fortune 500 list that have made important commitments to China. Thousands of U.S. managers and company representatives live in China and interact with Chinese business and legal officials on a daily basis.

The importance of this large and growing U.S. presence to China's drive for economic and technical modernization cannot be overestimated. With the renewed ascendancy of the pragmatic, economic reform-oriented elements in the leadership. China is now pressing its economic reform process full speed ahead. To advance that process, the PRC has an overwhelming need for the investment, technology and managerial skills that U.S. business has been providing. U.S. businesses are thus in a unique position to capitalize on their importance to China by upholding basic principles of respect for human rights in their daily business activities in China.

Greater involvement by the U.S. business community in promoting human rights in China is, to be sure, no substitute for the type of leverage that can and should result from well planned and appropriately defined governmental actions. We believe that more effective government action is likely to include measures that directly affect transnational corporations.

Indeed, a key premise of our analysis is that questions relating to the human rights responsibilities of transnational investors stand at the intersection of public and private spheres of law and policy. The powerful influence of transnational corporations on human rights conditions in the countries where they invest makes it both appropriate, and necessary, to assure that the behavior of these private actors comports with the human rights standards established by public international law and enforced by national law.

While the role of regulatory regimes—national and international—is an important part of any analysis of transnational corporations' human rights responsibilities, effective leadership in defining those responsibilities must come from the business community itself. In this, the challenges will be considerable. How to balance the imperatives of economic growth in a highly competitive international market against the most profound interests of human beings presents dilemmas to which no easy solutions suggest themselves. In the final decade of the Twentieth Century, the business community will be summoned to turn the same ingenuity and commitment that rebuilt Japan and Germany in the postwar years on the equally tortuous challenge presented by a country, like China, that is marred by systematic violations of fundamental rights, and at the same time is in massive need for support in reaching its development and modernization goals. By forging a new cooperation between business and the deepest interests of humanity, America's corporate leadership will continue in the future, as in the past, to promote basic standards of human decency across national borders.

I. HUMAN RIGHTS CONDITIONS IN CHINA AND THE U.S. RESPONSE

The current debate over corporate responsibility *vis-a-vis* human rights in China has been driven by three principal developments: 1) the persistence of systematic violations of basic rights in the PRC since the June 1989 crackdown near Tiananmen Square; 2) the inadequacy of U.S. as well as multilateral, sanctions in addressing those violations; and 3) the surge in U.S. business investment in China in recent years, and the correspondingly significant leverage that U.S. businesses have to promote improvements in China's human rights record. With violations persisting on a massive scale, U.S. companies that have substantial investments in China are being pressed to account for the human rights consequences of their China operations.

A. Human Rights Conditions in the PRC

Four years after the Tiananmen tragedy, the human rights situation in the PRC remains critical. Despite repeated pronouncements by Chinese officials that the cases of individuals involved in the Tiananmen affair have "basically been resolved,"[5] political trials of dissident figures involved in the 1989 events, Tibetan independence advocates, religious figures and other political offenders apprehended for reasons unrelated to Tiananmen have continued at a steady pace in the past year. Their trials have been characterized by repeated violations of China's own legal procedures as well as international standards of due process and fair trial procedures.[6]

Reports of maltreatment and torture of prisoners detained in China are widely documented. Severe restrictions on freedoms of expression and association guaranteed by the Chinese Constitution remain the order of the day. So, too, do lengthy periods of incommunicado administrative detention, not subject to any formal legal procedures, for those who challenge the political orthodoxy. Documentation of the extensive use of prison labor, operating under dismal conditions to produce profitable export goods, has focused attention on still another highly disturbing dimension of China's human rights situation.

Other human rights violations that have been particularly pronounced during the past several years have included the persecution of individuals for the exercise of religious freedom (guaranteed by the PRC's Constitution[7]) and the suppression of emerging expressions of minority rights in Tibet and other "autonomous regions" of China. On the religious front, the past few years have seen an intensification of the PRC authorities' crackdown on independent religious groups, Christians, Buddhist and Muslim, that refuse to practice their religion through official government-supervised bodies.[8] In Tibet there has been no let-up, and even some intensification, of the persecution of peaceful advocates of independence as well as those engaged in religious and cultural activities that threaten the dominance of PRC state control.[9] A major crackdown has also been underway in Inner Mongolia, where the authorities have disbanded associations formed to promote Mongolian language and culture and arrested peaceful advocates of greater ethnic rights for Mongolians in this "autonomous region" of China.[10]

The past few years have seen a newfound willingness of the Chinese government to engage in a measure of dialogue and exchange with foreign countries on human rights issues. The government has allowed a number of delegations from Australia, France, Britain and other countries to visit China on human rights missions in the past two years. These groups have, however, been hampered by limitations on contacts with individual dissidents and restricted access to judicial and prison facilities. They have had extensive discussions with relevant Chinese agencies about human rights issues, and in some cases have issued detailed and highly critical reports. The Chinese government, for its part, sent two academically oriented groups to the United States in the last quarter of 1991, and also sent groups to several European and Asian countries in 1992, to discuss human rights with academic bodies, human rights organizations, and members of the legislative and executive branches in those countries.

These initial efforts to address human rights questions through contacts and discussion are highly preferable to the previous approach of the Chinese government, which was to reject out of hand human rights as an issue for bilateral or international debate. But while the government has engaged in some measure of discussion of human rights, it continues both to deny that well-documented violations occur in China, and to reassert its position that China's domestic human rights record is an internal affair not subject to outside action. In November 1991, the PRC State Council issued a "Human Rights White Paper" that attempts, through a variety of techniques ranging from propagandistic rhetoric to outright distortion, to paint China as not only a leader in the guarantee of economic and social rights for its citizens but as a country where the criminal justice system, the policy toward religious believers and minority groups and other policies fully protect human rights.[11] This report was followed by two similar reports on the treatment of prisoners and the situation in Tibet.[12]

The approach taken by Premier Li Peng in his January 31, 1992 speech to the U.N. Security Council and by the Chinese delegation at the past several sessions of the U.N. Commission on Human Rights was to express a willingness for dialogue on human rights "on an equal footing" and up to a certain point, but to reject any criticism of human rights conditions in any country—including China's own practices in Tibet and elsewhere—as "interference in internal affairs" and a violation of sate sovereignty.[13] The PRC continued to press this position at the June 1993 World Conference on Human Rights in Vienna.[14]

B. The United States Response

Daily violations of human rights in China continue to evoke condemnation and concern in the United States and elsewhere. Despite concerted efforts by the PRC government to shed its pariah status, its human rights record remains a prominent concern of U.S. policy and a barrier to China's full partnership in the community of nations. When, for example, Beijing launched a massive campaign to be selected as host of the 2000 Olympics, U.S. Senator Bill Bradley (D-N.J.) mobilized Senate opposition,[15] and the House overwhelmingly adopted a resolution urging the U.S. member of the International Olympic Committee to deny China's bid.[16] But while human rights pressure has elicited some positive responses from Beijing, such as the periodic release of prominent political prisoners, the international community's response to ongoing violations in China has thus far been ineffective in ending broad patterns of abuse.

1. "Constructive Engagement": The Bush Administration

This was notably true of the Bush Administration's policy of renewing political and economic ties with the PRC that had been suspended following the

Tiananmen incident, relying on what it termed "a constructive policy of engagement with China" to address human rights concerns.[17] Then Secretary of State James Baker was acting in accordance with that policy when, in November 1991, he visited China. The circumstances surrounding Secretary Baker's visit seemed to underline the inadequacy of the Bush Administration's China policy. Flouting the U.S. government's asserted concern for human rights, the Chinese government detained two leading Chinese activists, Hou Xiaotian and journalist Dai Qing, to prevent them from meeting with the Secretary or his staff during their visit. Although Dai Qing was subsequently allowed to travel to the United States, she was temporarily prevented from reentering China when she sought to return home on May 30, 1992.[18]

While Secretary Baker raised human rights concerns during his visit, he left with little in the way of concrete improvements to show for his efforts. Although the Chinese government promised to stop exports to the United States of prisoner-produced goods, it was subsequently caught violating that pledge.[19] And while the government did produce a promised accounting for some 800 political prisoners, it "provided just the barest of information on each one, some of which has been proven incorrect," according to congressional officials cited by *The New York Times.*[20]

Bush Administration officials acknowledged that Chinese authorities made little progress in human rights in response to the Administration's efforts, and, according to *The New York Times,* "have taken actions that almost seemed designed to 'rub our noses in it,' as one official put it."[21] Nonetheless, the policy of "constructive engagement" was continued by President Bush through the end of his presidency.

2. Enforcement of Ban on Products Produced by Prisoners

The revelation in April 1991 that China was using prison labor on a significant scale to generate export earnings was a major factor in reviving attention, both in the United States and elsewhere, to China's continuing violations of human rights. In the United States, this issue raised a legal problem under the provisions of a 1930 statute, the Smoot-Hawley Tariff Act, which prohibits the import into the United States of products of convict labor,[22] and provided an important focus of debate on most-favored-nation status for China's exports to the U.S. in the past two years.[23] Prompted by these revelations, the U.S. Customs Administration initiated an investigation into the prison labor allegations. In the course of this investigation, specific Chinese products known to be produced with prison labor were barred from entering the United States.

In the wake of Secretary Baker's November 1991 visit to Beijing, it was announced that the United States and China had reached basic agreement on a memorandum of understanding that would allow the U.S. Customs Service to make inspections in China to assure that products being exported to the U.S.

were not produced with prison labor. It took another nine months before the agreement was actually signed, however, and in the period since then Chinese authorities have allowed U.S. Customs officials limited access to a handful of prison factories, vitiating the possibility of meaningfully monitoring compliance.[24]

3. The Congressional Challenge

During the Bush presidency Congress sought to invigorate U.S. human rights policy toward China by imposing sanctions more stringent than those adopted by the Administration.[25] But President Bush repeatedly thwarted these efforts by using his veto power to block key legislation and by making liberal use of the presidential waiver authority built into laws that Congress had enacted.[26] Still, the very threat of legislated sanctions elicited some human rights concessions from Beijing—notably including the release of prominent political prisoners during key periods of congressional debate—and concerned legislators helped maintain public attention to human rights conditions in China. In larger perspective, Congress' past efforts to fortify U.S. human rights policy toward China laid the groundwork for a more constructive Executive policy under the Clinton Administration, the basic contours of which are examined below. Further, by forcing President Bush to justify his opposition, those initiative triggered a rich public debate about U.S. human rights policy toward China.

One of the most significant results of that debate has been a reexamination of the relationship between human rights concerns and U.S. trade policy. Congress has sought to promote human rights in China by harnessing the potentially powerful leverage available by virtue of the United States' importance to China as its major trading partner. Inevitably, these efforts have drawn the U.S.-based business community into public debate about U.S. human rights policy toward China, and that community has emerged as a singularly important voice in the debate.

4. Most Favored Nation Trading Status

The most visible and important congressional initiatives have focused on the annual determination about renewal of the PRC's most-favored-nation (MFN) trading status, which gives China the lowest possible tariffs on its exports to the United States.[27] Several factors have elevated the importance of MFN status in the overall debate about U.S. policy toward the PRC. First, the granting of MFN status is far and away the most significant economic lever available to the U.S. government to promote human rights in the PRC. The United States is China's largest overseas market, giving China a surplus of some $18 billion in its trade with the United States in 1992.[28] The loss of MFN status would thus have a substantial impact on China's exports. Second, the U.S. business community regards continuation of China's MFN status as vital to its own economic interests. In its view, China's MFN status is the keystone of the U.S.-China economic relationship, and U.S. companies fear that nonrenewal of that status would imperil their access to China's vast and expanding market, as well as the continuation of investment and other business opportunities in China. In consequence, the U.S. business community has mobilized strong opposition to both congressional and Executive efforts that could threaten continuation of China's MFN status. Third, by law the President is required to notify Congress whether he plans to review China's MFN status on June 3 of each year—almost to the day the anniversary of the massacre near Tiananmen Square.[29] This coincidence has, together with the first two factors, lent special prominence to the annual debate over continuation of China's MFN status.

a. President Bush's Policy and Congressional Initiatives

In each year of his presidency following the Tiananmen incident, President Bush notified Congress of his intention unconditionally to renew China's MFN status. Each time, his stance triggered congressional efforts to link renewal to human rights improvements in the PRC. But while the resulting clash between Congress and the Executive focused public attention on deficiencies in the Administration's China policy, President Bush was able each year to secure unconditional renewal of China's MFN status despite congressional opposition. In 1990, the House passed two bills, one denying China MFN status and the other extending MFN until 1991, with renewal then conditioned on the satisfaction of strong human rights standards. The Senate did not consider either bill before adjourning. In 1991 and in the Spring of 1992, both the House and Senate enacted legislation attaching human rights conditions to renewal of China's MFN status. But the Senate version failed to marshal enough votes to override a presidential veto, issued in keeping with the Bush Administration's "constructive engagement" policy.

In the Summer of 1992, several congressional leaders sought to break the MFN impasse by introducing refined versions of earlier proposals to attach human rights conditions. Following President Bush's announcement on June 2, 1992 that he planned to extend MFN status to China for another year, a modified version of a proposal developed by the human rights organization Asia Watch was introduced by Rep. Nancy Pelosi (D.-California) and Rep. Don Pease (D.-Ohio) in the House of Representatives and my Majority Leader George J. Mitchell (D.-Maine) in the Senate. Each of these Congresspersons had been chief architects of the conditional approach to MFN in the past. The initiative abandoned the "all or nothing" approach built into existing MFN legislation, which had forced Congress to choose between unconditional renewal of MFN on the one hand and, on the other, non-renewal or renewal with conditions that would apply across the board—requiring penalization of China's reform-oriented privatizing economic sectors along with all others. The legislation sought to impose measurable and effective human rights conditions—the release of political prisoners, an end to religious persecution, and the like. China's failure to meet such conditions would result in the loss of MFN benefits only for exports of PRC state enterprises, from which the repressive regime derives the most significant benefit.[30]

Under these bills, exports that could be demonstrated to emanate from non-state enterprises—private businesses, collectives, and enterprises with foreign investment—would not lose the trade benefits. The legislation thus sought to penalize the government for failing to improve the human rights situation, while minimizing the risk of harming sectors of China's economy and society that contribute to liberalization. Significantly, too, this approach addressed one basis for opposition within the business community to earlier efforts to attach human rights conditions to MFN renewal—the potential loss of tariff benefits for products produced by joint ventures between U.S. and Chinese businesses. Like its predecessors, this legislative initiative passed both the House and Senate but failed in the Senate to override President Bush's September 28, 1992 veto by a margin of seven votes.[31]

On April 21, 1993, Congresswoman Pelosi and Senator Mitchell introduced in the House and Senate, respectively, bills patterned on the legislation they had introduced last year, with various technical refinements. Under this legislation, failure by the PRC to meet specific human rights conditions would result the following year in denial of MFN treatment to Chinese state enterprise products. The proposed human rights conditions included continued release of Chinese citizens detained as a result of nonviolent expression of political and/or religious beliefs, unrestricted immigration of PRC citizens desiring to leave China for political, religious or other valid reasons, and compliance by China with the August 7, 1992 Memorandum of Undertaking on Prohibiting Import and Export Trade in Prison Labor Products.[32]

b. President Clinton's Executive Order

By the time these bills were introduced, a new Administration had taken office. Although President Clinton had not yet made known what action he would take on renewal of China's MFN status, it seemed likely that he would reverse his predecessor's policy of unconditional renewal. As a presidential candidate, Bill Clinton had indicated that he was likely to support some form of human rights conditionality.[33] During the early months of the Clinton presidency, key members of his administration repeatedly indicated the President's intention to link continued MFN treatment to human rights improvements in China.[34]

On May 28, 1993, President Clinton issued an Executive Order that continued China's MFN status for another year, but set forth human rights conditions that China would have to satisfy to qualify for renewal in 1994.

The Executive Order identifies seven human rights criteria relevant to the renewal determination. Only two are cast as absolute requirements, and both of these criteria relate to preexisting requirements of U.S. law. The first, that renewal "will substantially promote the freedom of emigration objectives" of the Trade Act of 1974, in effect restates the criterion for renewal of China's MFN status already imposed by that law.[35] The second, that "China is complying with the 1992 bilateral agreement between the United States and China concerning prison labor," by its terms incorporates a preexisting commitment, which in turn implements the Smoot-Hawley law discussed in Part I.B.2. China is required to demonstrate only "overall, significant progress" in meeting the other five criteria, which relate to such goals as the release of political prisoners and access of international humanitarian agencies to PRC prisons.

Against a recent history of assurance to Chinese leaders that, whatever Congress may say or do, the U.S. President will stand by them, the MFN conditionality imposed by President Clinton signals a serious U.S. intention to demand meaningful human rights improvements in exchange for continued trade privileges, despite the generality with which the human rights conditions are expressed in the Order. At the same time, the leader-to-leader approach also is better suited to the type of flexibility that may be necessary in addressing the complex issues that are sure to arise during implementation of a conditional MFN approach. But if presidentially-mandated conditionality is preferable, it remains desirable for Congress to sustain pressure to move the Administration clearly in the direction to which the Executive Order points.[36] Whether the policy established in President Clinton's Order is effective will depend, above all, on actions taken by the Administration in the months ahead. In particular, the Administration should communicate to Chinese authorities clear standards by which the PRC's compliance with the Executive Order criteria will be evaluated, and should actively press for progress in satisfying those standards. Further, as elaborated below, the Executive Order opens a unique window of opportunity for the Administration to mobilize U.S. investors in China to act as a constructive force for human rights progress.

c. The Role of the Business Community

While views within the business community have not been monolithic, U.S. companies that invest in China have, on the whole, strongly opposed efforts to attach human rights conditions to renewal of China's MFN status. The loss of MFN status would directly affect some U.S. companies engaged in joint venture operations in China, resulting in some cases in a multi-fold increase in tariffs for joint-venture products destined for a U.S. market. But the chief concern of U.S. companies is that termination of China's MFN status would provoke retaliation against U.S. companies that invest in and send exports to China. U.S. companies have already experienced significant difficulties penetrating the China market when faced with competition from exporters in Japan and Europe, who enjoy a substantial advantage by virtue of their governments' export-assistance programs and often more flexible pricing policies. U.S. companies fear that political tension between China and the United States could only exacerbate these endemic commercial problems.

Demonstrating a sophisticated grasp of the U.S. political process, the PRC government exploited these apprehensions in the period preceding President Clinton's decision about renewal of China's MFN status. As the MFN debate approached, Chinese trade delegations went on a buying frenzy throughout the United States, spending more than $800 million for jetliners, $160 million for cars, and $200 million for oil exploration equipment. After years of favoring French and other non-American telecommunications companies for entry into this key part of the China market, the PRC concluded a major agreement with Hughes Space Communications Co. to build communications satellites worth $750 million. Though characteristically frugal, Chinese representatives offered to buy U.S. steel at slightly higher prices than those charged in Japan and Korea.[37] Throughout this process, China made it clear that it expected U.S. companies to lobby for continuation of its MFN status in return for its purchases. U.S. companies are "regularly threatened with cancellation of orders or loss of future deals if China loses its preferred status," according to business sources cited in *The Washington Post*.[38] The message was not lost on U.S. companies, who mounted a campaign of unprecedented scope and intensity to secure unconditional renewal of China's MFN status in the period leading up to President Clinton's determination on this issue.

By letter dated May 12, 1993, some 370 companies and business associations, representing virtually every U.S. company active in China, stated their case to President Clinton:

> . . . .We represent companies that exported products to China worth nearly $7.5 billion in 1992, and that employ an estimated 157,000 American workers producing those goods. We represent the aerospace industry which exported products to China worth over $2 billion in 1992, and which expects China to purchase approximately $40 billion in new aircraft over the next twenty years. We represent the farmers whose largest market for wheat is China. . . . America's economic stake in maintaining trade relations with China is high. Withdrawing or placing further conditions on MFN could terminate the large potential benefits of the trading relationship, lead the Chinese to engage in retaliatory actions that would harm U.S. exporters, farmers, laborers and consumers. . . . .[39]

But while emphasizing U.S. economic stakes, the signatories to this letter endorsed the human rights goals of the Clinton Administration's policy toward Beijing. Echoing arguments by spokesmen for business interests that had become increasingly common during previous debates about renewal of China's MFN status, they asserted:

> We in the business community . . . believe that our continued commercial interaction fuels positive elements for change in Chinese society. The expansion

of trade and free market reforms has strengthened the pro-democratic forces in China. . . .[40]

Significantly, the letter expressed agreement with the President "that the Chinese must continue to make progress in . . . human rights."[41]

However much the business community may have hoped to avoid MFN conditionality, it now has a substantial interest in assuring that China makes sufficient progress on human rights to avoid termination of its MFN status in 1994. In this setting, U.S. policy would be most effective if the political leadership in Washington actively encouraged U.S. investors in China to promote human rights there. The Administration should build on the asserted commitment to its human rights goals expressed in the above-quoted letter by urging the signatories actively to promote human rights progress in China. While some Administration officials have already done so in general terms,[42] these efforts would be most effective if those same officials developed concrete proposals for measures that U.S. companies can take to promote human rights in China, and urged the chief executive officers of major U.S. investors to undertake those measures or others more suited to the nature of their business relationships in the PRC.

5. Code of Conduct Legislation

While MFN conditionally has dominated the U.S. human rights policy debate about China, a little-noticed legislative initiative has introduced a new, and potentially vital, plank in the policy options. Senator Edward Kennedy (D-Massachusetts) and Representative Jolene Unsoeld (D-Washington) have agreed to sponsor bills, in the Senate and House respectively, to establish a voluntary code of conduct governing the Chinese operations of U.S. companies. By directly focusing on the role of U.S. corporations in addressing human rights concerns in China, this legislation sharpens the broader debate about corporate responsibility vis-a-vis human rights violations in the PRC.

a. Background and Overview

The Kennedy and Unsoeld initiatives build upon a similar effort by then-Congressman John Miller (R-Washington), who on June 21, 1991, introduced legislation[43] that would have established a set of human rights principles governing the conduct of U.S. companies with investments and other business operations in the PRC. On October 30, 1991, the bill passed the House as part of the Omnibus Export Amendment Act of 1991 and was subsequently taken up in a joint House-Senate conference. A conference bill passed the Senate on October 8, 1992, but failed to come to a vote in the House for reasons unrelated to the code of conduct itself. The discussion that follows is based upon the original Miller bill.[44]

The proposed code-of-conduct bill does not seek to impose sanctions on China for failing to meet human rights standards, nor does it discourage U.S. businesses from investing in China. Instead, the bill asks companies with a significant presence in China to adhere to a set of basic human rights principles, on a "best efforts" basis, in the course of their operations.

In this way, the proposed law seeks to assure that U.S. business activities in the PRC do not inadvertently encourage or themselves contribute to repressive practices, but instead make a constructive contribution to human rights. Under the proposed law, these goals would be promoted by encouraging U.S. nationals conducting industrial cooperation projects in China to adhere to nine principles that have the cumulative effect of (1) assuring that U.S. businesses operating in China extend to their foreign employees the same type of minimum human rights protections that they have long been required to provide to employees in the United States, such as protections against discrimination on the basis of religious beliefs, political views, gender and ethnic or national background; (2) assuring that the premises of U.S. business operations are not used in a fashion that violates fundamental rights (for example, the proposed code of conduct includes a pledge to discourage compulsory political indoctrination programs from taking place on the premises of U.S. nationals' industrial cooperation projects in the PRC); and (3) bringing the considerable—and indeed unique—influence of the U.S. business community to bear to promote an end to flagrant violations of human rights (for example, the proposed code of conduct urges U.S. nationals to use their access to Chinese officials informally to raise cases of individuals detained solely because of their nonviolent expression of political views).[45]

There are no penalties for failure to comply with the principles, and in this respect compliance with the code depends upon the voluntary efforts of U.S. companies. The bill itself is framed as a "sense of Congress that any United States economic cooperation project in the People's Republic of China or Tibet should adhere to." "Adherence" is defined as "agreeing to implement the principles set forth" in the bill, "implementing those principles by taking good faith measures with respect to each such principle," and "reporting accurately to the Department of State on the measures taken to implement those principles."

The bill imposes only two "requirements" on U.S. companies: 1) the U.S. parent company of a PRC investment project must register with the Secretary of State and indicate whether it will implement the principles; and 2) the parent company must report on an annual basis to the Department of State describing the China project's adherence to the code. The Secretary of State is directed to review these reports to determine whether the project is adhering to the principles, and may request additional information to supplement company reports. The Secretary is further required to submit an annual report to Congress and the Secretariat of the Organization for Economic Cooperation and

Development (OECD) describing the level of adherence to the principles by U.S. company projects in China.[46]

The code-of-conduct bill sets forth a constructive approach to what has often seemed an intractable problem of competing policy goals. In effect, the bill takes up the claim of the U.S. business community, repeatedly asserted in the context of annual debates over renewal of China's MFN status, that U.S. corporations can more effectively promote human rights improvements in China by remaining an active presence there than by severing or contracting ties. By encouraging U.S. corporations to adhere to basic human rights principles in China, the proposed law seeks to assure that U.S. investment does in fact have a constructive impact on human rights in China. At the same time, the bill would assure that U.S. investment in China does not undermine U.S. human rights goals by inadvertently lending support to the PRC government's ongoing violations of fundamental rights.

Nevertheless, while some members of the U.S. business community have expressed support for the principles established in the legislation, many others have spoken out against it. The critics have raised two principal objectives. The first, in essence, is that Congress should not dictate business practices to U.S. companies operating in China, and that the latter should not appear to be the "lackeys" of U.S. policy. According to one press account, a letter to U.S. Congressperson from the American Chamber of Commerce in Hong Kong charged that the bill "practically [makes U.S. business] appear to be agents of the U.S. government."[47]

In response to this concern, U.S. businessman John Kamm, a former Chairman of the American Chamber of Commerce in Hong Kong, approached the Chamber with a proposal for it to adopt the legislation's principles on a voluntary basis. Similarly, the office of Congressman Miller, who introduced the original version of the code-of-conduct legislation, held discussions with the U.S.-China Business Council in Washington, the leading U.S. organization representing U.S. investors in China, about the possibility of the Council's taking a similar step. In each case, business groups were urged to avoid congressionally-legislated principles by adopting similar principles themselves. None of these efforts has met with success, however. Instead, both the Chamber and the U.S.-China Business Council have raised numerous objections to the principles on substantive grounds.

The general tenor of substantive objections by members of the business community is that the code would require U.S. companies to take action that may be "impractical" or provocative, and that could jeopardize their position in China. This line of objection, which is more pronounced with respect to some provisions of the code than others, has often been backed by the claim that compliance with the bill's principles would require U.S. companies to violate Chinese law or policy.

A close examination of the proposed legislation suggests that these concerns are unwarranted. As detailed in the following section-by-section analysis of the code-of-conduct bill, nothing in the bill requires U.S. companies to violate Chinese law. Further, the bill grants companies wide leeway to avoid taking action that could imperil their business relationships in China, urging only that they endeavor, on a "best efforts" basis, to comply with and promote basic international standards in their Chinese operations. . . .

II. RESPONSIBILITIES OF THE BUSINESS COMMUNITY

As the discussion in Part I makes clear, the most important U.S. efforts to promote human rights in China have substantial implications for U.S. companies that export and invest there. In consequence, the business community simultaneously has emerged as a central voice in the domestic debate about U.S. human rights policy toward China, and has become the focus of debate about its own human rights responsibilities in the PRC. Though triggered by the unique confluence of U.S. policy interests in the PRC, the latter debate has implications reaching far beyond China, and indeed has inspired a broader reexamination of the human rights responsibilities of corporations that operate across borders.[82] Notably, some of the most developed thinking in this regard has taken place in the boardrooms of corporations. As elaborated below, a growing number of transnational companies have in recent years adopted human rights policies governing their overseas investment practices, and the trend has been toward adoption of increasingly stringent policies. Spurred in part by public criticism of corporations whose overseas investments appear to support repressive practices, these policies have, with some exceptions, emerged without substantial guidance from either the professional human rights community or the U.S. government about appropriate standards for corporate investment in highly repressive countries. And so, as one corporation after another seeks to meet its human rights responsibilities, there is a pressing need for clarity about what, precisely, those responsibilities are.

In addressing this issue, we begin by examining the sometimes conflicting values that have shaped recent debate about corporations' human rights responsibilities. Building on that analysis, we consider broader issues raised by efforts to promote human rights by regulating U.S. corporations' conduct overseas. Specifically, we address the question whether it is appropriate for a national government to promote values embedded in public international law by regulating private actors' conduct in another country.

A. Do Businesses Have Human Rights Responsibilities?

In considering the policy concerns that drive current debate bout corporations' human rights responsibilities, it is useful first to make clear what is *not* at issue. Business leaders now rarely press the claim, once commonplace, that social policy and corporate practice occupy distinct spheres—and that a rigid separation should be preserved.[83] Perhaps more to the point, at a time when consumers are increasingly assertive in demanding that the products they purchase be produced in a manner they deem "socially responsible," it is scarcely possible to draw a bright line between corporations' goal of maximizing profits and social expectations that they behave responsibly. Increasingly, public attention to such issues as the use of prison labor in products exported to the United States is making human rights a "bottom line" concern for multinational companies.[84]

Further, no company can afford to disregard the impact of massive human rights violations on the investment climate in a country where it may operate. The rule of law—the bedrock of human rights protection—is also essential to a stable and predictable environment for investment. One need only consider the devastating effect on the economies of the Latin American countries ruled by military dictatorships throughout the 1970s and, in many cases, into the 1980s to appreciate the correlation between massive human rights violations and investment risk.[85]

In part for these reasons, it is increasingly rare to hear business representatives claim that human rights issues are of no legitimate concern to corporations.[86] Still, the generalization that transnational investors may profit from a host country's respect for human rights—as well as their own adherence to human rights principles—is of scant value in addressing the question whether corporations have responsibilities in respect of human rights. In particular, the truism that corporate interests are in some respects well served by adherence to human rights standards provides no guidance in identifying corporations' responsibilities in situations where there is an apparent of genuine conflict between their business interests and human rights values.

Is there, for example, any principled reason to fault corporations for taking advantage of cheap labor in a developing country? Does the answer to this question depend on whether labor conditions fall below a minimum standard of acceptability? Do transnational investors in a nation like China bear some measure of responsibility for the country's human rights problems on the ground that their investments help sustain a highly repressive government? On the other hand, in today's economy, can U.S. companies afford *not* to invest in the world's largest and fastest-growing market? Does their investment indeed serve human rights goals—as many companies claim—as well as their economic interests?

These questions begin to frame the issues that are the pith of current debate about the appropriate role of businesses in responding to human rights violations in countries where they have substantial investments. No country has done more to sharpen that debate than China. It is the proverbial test case: how we define foreign investors' human rights responsibilities in China will serve as a critical precedent elsewhere. The current parameters of debate over corporations' human rights role in China are thus well worth examining.

As indicated in part I.B.4, that debate has revolved, above all, around the annual determination of China's MFN trade status. Though views within the business community have varied, the overwhelming majority of U.S. companies with substantial business activity in China have opposed efforts to attach human right conditions to renewal of China's MFN status. While their principal concern has been the impact of such conditions on their exports and investments,[87] corporate spokespersons have repeatedly invoked the rhetoric of human rights in support of their position. In particular, business representatives have opposed proposals to attach human rights conditions to renewal of China's MFN status on the ground that the very presence of U.S. companies in China has a liberalizing effect and that this presence should not be imperiled.

This assertion encompasses several distinct claims. In the context of China, business leaders have frequently asserted that the web of contacts between Chinese citizens and U.S. investors that develops in the course of business relationships promotes the transfer of liberal democratic values from this side of the Pacific to the East.[88] Further, advocates of "constructive engagement" also claim that transnational investment in repressive nations promotes greater integration of the host country in the international community, thereby enlarging its exposure to the shared values of civilized nations.[89] It is sometimes further asserted that liberal political values are an inevitable concomitant of a liberal market economy, and that transnational efforts to foster development of such an economy in China through expanded trade and investment practices will therefore promote political liberalization as well.[90]

A third and related claim is that U.S. investment in developing countries promotes economic growth, thereby fostering development of a middle class. Since, the argument continues, it is when this happens that citizens begin to assert demands for fundamental liberties, business investment spurs longer-term progress in respect of human rights. In the shorter term, foreign investment creates opportunities for employment that enhance the economic and social rights of the direct beneficiaries.[91]

There are compelling arguments, and cannot be readily dismissed. But are the claims justified?

It depends. Whether a substantial U.S. business presence contributes to improved human rights conditions or helps bolster a repressive regime depends on the particular circumstances of each country, the conditions under which businesses operate, and the behavior of the businesses themselves. When, for example, the manager of a joint venture operation discharges a Chinese employee because of government pressure based on the individual's support for democracy, that manager becomes an agent for the Chinese government's denial of internationally-recognized human rights. When, instead, a potential investor insists as a pre-condition of investing on assurances that its employees' right to freedom of association will be fully protected, that investor's presence may in fact help foster improved human rights conditions. But here, too, an investor's ability to promote human rights may vary widely depending on both the conditions in a host country and on the nature of its investment. A company with direct investments in a country may, for example, have greater scope to promote human rights than a corporation that merely utilizes contractors there.

The larger claim that investment in a country like China helps foster human rights improvements as a byproduct of its increased contact with individuals who subscribe to liberal values seems incapable of standing on its own as a justification for investment, if only because there can be no dispositive way of testing this claim. While some argue, for example, that areas of China with large levels of foreign investment, such as the southern provinces of Guangdong and Fujian, boast relatively good human rights records, there is significant evidence to the contrary. Recent reports indicate that in Guangdong, where both domestic economic reform and foreign business and investment activity outpace such reforms and activities in every other part of China, arbitrary arrests and violations of minimal due process rights have contributed to a prison population larger than that of any other province in China.[92]

The claim that enhanced employment opportunities made possible by foreign investment in and of themselves advance human rights is initially appealing, but proves problematic upon closer scrutiny. to the extent that the transnationalization of investment has engendered a global chase for the cheapest labor markets, international investment practices inevitably drive down wage levels as developing countries compete for foreign investment.[93] In this setting, it has become increasingly difficult to persuade governments of developing countries to respect internationally-recognized labor rights, particularly the right to receive a wage that meets the "basic human needs" of workers.[94]

In the longer term, this phenomenon has in many developing countries apparently retarded further expansion of the middle class, and instead has widened the economic gap between laborers and the management class.[95] Against this background, it is increasingly difficult to assume that investment in and of itself will promote expansion of a middle class, thereby enlarging the number of citizens who enjoy economic and social rights and simultaneously making it more likely that citizens will insist upon personal and political freedoms. In this respect too, then, whether foreign investment promotes human rights depends—in this instance, on whether the foreign investor assures adequate conditions of work, including fair wages.

While the impact of foreign investment on human rights thus cannot be captured by superficial generalizations, it is equally clear that transnational business practice can, and often does, have a direct and substantial impact on human rights conditions in a host country. The previously-noted example of an investor in China who is pressured to discharge an employee because of her political beliefs exemplifies the point, and other examples are seemingly infinite. It is precisely because (and when) investment practices have significant human rights consequences that it is appropriate to hold corporations responsible for those consequences. To the extent that their investment practices directly affect human rights conditions, transnational corporations have a corresponding responsibility to assure, at a minimum, that their operations do not contribute, however, inadvertently, to violations. As we elaborate elsewhere, the determination whether a company's investment practices contribute to human rights should, in highly repressive countries, include an analysis of whether the investment in and of itself makes a company complicit in pervasive violations. In Myanmar (Burma), for example, it is virtually impossible for foreign investors to enter a joint venture arrangement without having as a direct or indirect business partner the notoriously repressive military junta, the State Law and Order Restoration Council, and this should weigh heavily in prospective investors' decisions. More generally, substantial foreign investment may help stabilize a repressive regime that would otherwise be more responsive to human rights pressure.

As stated at the outset, we also believe that U.S. and other major investors in China should affirmatively promote human rights improvements there because they possess unique influence with the Chinese government. When U.S. corporations or individual business executives have undertaken affirmative measures along these lines, their impact has been substantial. Their accomplishments, examined below, make clear that private investors could have a singular impact on the state of human rights in China if they undertook to make human rights considerations a key component of their business strategies. The fact that the Chinese government publicly hails soaring levels of foreign investment for propaganda effect makes it all the more vital that foreign investors make clear where they stand on human rights.

B. Regulating Private Actors to Enforce Public International Law

Implicit in the foregoing analysis are several important assumptions: 1) There is now a set of "human rights" that can be readily identified and objectively defined; 2) It is appropriate to expect transnational corporations to curb otherwise permissible investment practices when they imperil basic rights; and 3) In the absence of adequate self-regulation by corporations, national governments may appropriately regulate corporate behavior to further human rights goals, even with respect to overseas conduct. All three of these assumptions are implicitly challenged by the charge, which has at times been put forth by representatives of the business community (as well as others), that efforts to link investment practices to human rights conditions is a form of cultural imperialism—a misguided effort to impose American values on other nations.

The answer to this claim is simple. Human rights are not exclusively American values; they are universal. International law imposes obligations on all states to respect certain universal rights.[96] As elaborated in Part III, those rights include a core set of rights relating to labor conditions, as well as more generally-applicable assurances of personal autonomy. These rights are defined in positive international law, and have long been the subject of international enforcement efforts.[97]

Although relevant international instruments typically establish duties on the part of *states* to respect individuals' rights, they also have significant implications for the behavior of non-governmental actors, including corporations. The key international human rights conventions typically require States Parties not only to respect the rights enumerated in the treaties, but also to "ensure" or "secure" those rights.[98]

That duty has authoritatively been interpreted to require States Parties to assert effective control over non-state actors to ensure that their conduct does not infringe individual rights recognized in the conventions.[99]

Still, complex issues are raised by the question of *which* government should regulate transnational companies to assure that they do not infringe human rights. It seems fairly straightforward that a national government, such as the PRC government, can and should act to ensure that non-state as well as state actors operating within its sovereign borders to not infringe internationally-protected human rights. By placing primary responsibility for assuring protection of human rights on the government that has control of the relevant territory, international law seeks to assure adequate protection while respecting national sovereignty. The problem, of course, is that governments like that of the PRC are often themselves chief violators of human rights. Far from assuring that non-state actors within their borders respect human rights, the Chinese government brings pressure to bear on business and other enterprises to carry out government policies that infringe protected rights.[100] In this setting, leaving regulation of corporate activities that affect human rights to the host government would effectively preclude adequate protection of those rights.

Further, even a government that is more inclined than that of the PRC to protect the human rights of its citizens may be hard-pressed to enact adequate legal protections against potentially harmful conduct of foreign investors. Intense competition among developing countries for foreign investment, combined with multinational corporations' search for countries that offer them the lowest costs—typically correlated with a comparatively low level of regulation—operate as powerful disincentives for underdeveloped countries to impose stringent requirements on foreign investors.[101] A compelling case can thus be made for holding national governments accountable for ensuring that the overseas conduct of their companies conforms with international human rights standards[102] or for developing an appropriate international regulatory regime.[103]

Policy considerations aside, it is clear that the United States has the power to regulate the overseas conduct of U.S. companies to assure their compliance with international human rights legal standards. Under the "nationality principle" of jurisdiction, the United States may regulate the overseas conduct of its nationals, including corporations.[104] Congress has in fact enacted numerous laws regulating the overseas conduct of U.S. corporations, governing such matters as their compliance with the Arab boycott of Israel and corrupt practices abroad.[105] There are, to be sure, limits on the extent to which the United States may regulate the overseas conduct of U.S. companies, particularly when a regulation would conflict with the law of the host state. In that situation, the host state's law generally should prevail.[106] (As noted elsewhere, none of the China-specific proposals advanced in this article would require U.S. companies to undertake action that conflicts with Chinese law.[107]) Further, while both U.S. and international law generally forbid otherwise permissible assertions of extraterritorial jurisdiction if they would be "unreasonable,"[108] the reasonableness of such regulations is determined by, *inter alia*, "the importance of the regulation to the international political, legal, or economic system," according to the *Restatement (Third) of the Foreign Relations Law of the United States.*[109] U.S. regulation of American companies' overseas conduct that aims to assure compliance with international human rights law would fall squarely within this measure of reasonableness. Indeed, the preemptory status of a core set of internationally-recognized human rights[110] would justify the United States in forbidding American companies from engaging in conduct abroad that breaches those rights, even if its prohibition conflicted with a host country's law.[111]

This form of extraterritorial regulation would be much in keeping with broader developments in transnational law. Municipal law that regulates transnational activities between non-state actors, as well as between such actors and state governments, occupies a growing area of transnational law.[112] While "formally regulat[ing] individual merchants outside national legal systems," that law "is ultimately dependent on them."[113] An important subset of this law regulates private actors to promote public policy values, and in this sense stands at the intersection of private and public international law. The emergence of this form of regulation is an inevitable concomitant of, and appropriate response to, the growing influence of non-state actors in countries other than their national state.[114] Such regulations may appropriately seek to shape state action in the host country by fostering "transnational patterns of interest"[115] that are likely to have this effect.

To say that it is appropriate for a government, such as the U.S. government, to regulate the overseas conduct of companies that bear its nationality does not necessarily mean that such regulation is the most desirable means of assuring conformity with international human rights standards by transnational companies. As with other aspects of corporate practice that have a significant impact on social policy, government regulation is necessary only when companies fail adequately to police their own behavior. Further, as we suggest in Part I.B.4.b-c, the government can effectively play a proactive role in encouraging the private sector to police itself.

In the section that follows, we examine the accomplishments of several corporations and individual business executives who have provided leadership in defining and implementing transnational corporations' human rights responsibilities. Building on their efforts, we then set forth general recommendations for businesses investing or considering investing in China and other countries scourged by pervasive human rights violations.

C. Business Initiatives to Promote Human Rights in China and Elsewhere

In the aftermath of the Tiananmen incident, a number of business executives and transnational corporations have sought to promote human rights in China. Perhaps the best-known individual initiative is the effort by U.S. businessman John Kamm to secure the release of persons detained for the non-violent expression of political opinion. Kamm, a long-time resident of Hong Kong, was general manager of Occidental Chemical Corporation Far East and was responsible for that company's considerable China operations when he began to address human rights violations in the PRC. At the time of the Tiananmen incident, Kamm was the chairman of the American Chamber of Commerce in Hong Kong, and in that capacity became an outspoken opponent of congressional efforts to attach human rights conditions to renewal of China's most favored nation (MFN) trade status. In testimony before Congress and in other fora, Kamm argued that the U.S. government should not adopt measures that could effectively sever China's trade relationship with the United States because, Kamm asserted, that relationship itself is an effective vehicle for liberalization. Believing that he had to gain human rights concessions from the PRC to avert congressional efforts to attach human rights conditions to renewal of China's MFN status, Kamm began to negotiate with Chinese authorities for the release of political prisoners in the course of his business visits to the PRC.

Kamm appears in fact to have been instrumental in securing the release of some political prisoners.[116] Kamm, who left Occidental and now combines business consulting with human rights work in China, has stated that neither the business activities of Occidental nor his private consulting business have been adversely affected by his human rights interventions.[117] In Kamm's view, he has been effective in his human rights efforts precisely because of his longstanding business relationship with the PRC.

At the level of corporate initiative, a growing roster of U.S.-based companies have adopted policies designed to address human rights concerns relating to investment in China and, in some instances, more globally. For example, on March 31, 1992 Sears, Roebuck and Co. announced that it had adopted a formal policy to assure that its imports from the PRC do not include products made by prison labor. The policy requires that all contracts that Sears signs for the import of products emanating from China include a clause stating that none of the goods subject to the contract have been manufactured by "convict or forced labor."[118]

The policy also asserts that "Sears employees may from time to time conduct unannounced inspections of manufacturing sites in mainland China to determine compliance with U.S. law as regards the use of forced or convict labor." Further, the policy requires Sears to maintain lists of its Chinese suppliers' production sites and to attempt to compile a list of the addresses of sites of forced labor in the PRC, so that the two lists can be compared.

The Sears policy was adopted in the wake of an announcement by Levi Strauss & Co. that it would apply human rights and related criteria in its selection of business partners. Formally adopted in January 1992, that policy has had a significant impact on Levi Strauss & Co.'s investment decisions *vis-a-vis* China.

The policy, which addresses "Business Partner Terms of Engagement and Guidelines for Country Selection," includes several human rights guidelines as well as guidelines on such matters as the environment. The five-point "Guidelines for Country Selection" include a provision asserting that Levi Strauss & Co. "should not initiate or renew contractual relationships in countries where there are pervasive violations of basic human rights."[119] Applying this provision, in late April 1993 Levi Strauss & Co. decided to begin a phased withdrawal from its operations in China, which involve sewing or finishing goods, a process that will continue to completion unless there is a substantial improvement in human rights conditions in the PRC. At the same time, the company decided that it would not initiate direct investment in China.[120]

Reebok International Ltd. adopted a human rights policy that responded to specific concerns raised by the human rights situation in China, and subsequently adopted a more comprehensive set of human rights principles governing workplace conditions in all of its overseas operations, including those in China.[121] The first policy, adopted in November 1990, provided:

1. Reebok will not operate under martial law conditions or allow any military presence on its premises.
2. Reebok encourages free association and assembly among its employees.
3. Reebok will seek to ensure that opportunities for advancement are based on initiative, leadership and contributions to the business, not political beliefs. Further, no one is to be dismissed from working at its factories for political views or non-violent involvement.
4. Reebok will seek to prevent compulsory political indoctrination programs from taking place on its premises.
5. Reebok reaffirms that it deplores the use of force against human rights.

Like Reebok International Ltd. and Levi Strauss & Co., both Phillips-Van Heusen and the Timberland Company have developed ethical guidelines governing their relations with suppliers, contractors and business partners.[122] Timberland's policy further bans the company from pursuing altogether business relations in a country "where basic human rights are pervasively violated." Although Timberland's human rights policy governs all of its overseas business relationships, the policy's development was driven by the company's desire to address issues raised by China in particular. In February 1993, Timberland decided to begin a gradual termination of its sourcing from China, a process it plans to complete by the end of 1993.

Variations among these three policies reflect each company's unique corporate values. All, however, do incorporate internationally-recognized human rights standards, and seek to assure that the companies' investment practices conform to those standards. . . .

If the principles proposed have a solid foundation in international law, they still have scant support in international practice—at least in the sense of universal compliance by multinational corporations with these standards. Indeed, as noted earlier the globalization of labor markets has, at least in some areas, served to drive down wage levels and to that extent has undermined international assurances of adequate pay. Thus, any meaningful effort to promote adherence to global principles along the lines suggested above would require coordination among companies from major investing nations.

The most appropriate forum for such coordination may be the Group of Seven Major Industrialized Democracies (G-7), whose members include Japan, Canada and the major industrialized democracies of Western Europe as well as the United States. The authors believe that the United States government should take the lead in urging other G-7 countries to agree to promote corporate adherence to international human rights standards along the lines outlined in Section B—and, indeed, to utilize all appropriate multilateral fora to promote such coordinated efforts.[158]

In particular, it is critically important to bring Japan along in any coordinated effort to apply human rights standards to investment in China, Japan, with the United States, is among the PRC's top few trading and investment partners, and U.S. companies are often in tight competition with their Japanese counterparts for the same contracts in the PRC. Japan's adherence to a set of human rights principles is thus clearly crucial. The United States should add this issue to the list of trade issues it is currently discussing with Tokyo. In this regard, it is relevant to note that in 1992 the Japanese government adopted new principles, which include a reference to human rights considerations, in its overseas development aid program.[159]

The proposals advanced in the preceding two sections seek to give substance to the general principle that corporations must assure that their own investment practices overseas do not contravene internationally-recognized human rights. To the extent that the principles proposed in Section B assume that corporations have already undertaken overseas investments, they beg the hard question whether there are situations in which corporations should, on human rights grounds, avoid altogether investing in a country.

Adherence to the principles proposed in section B would diminish the significance of this issue by seeking to assure that foreign companies' presence in a repressive country does not contribute to human rights violations and potentially contributes to improvement. Still, there may be times when foreign investment in itself contributes to violations, if only by bolstering a highly repressive regime that might otherwise be more responsive to internal or external pressures to ameliorate violations. Moreover potential investors may in some cases be able to exert considerable positive influence on a government if they make it known that their investment determination will turn, in part, on human rights conditions. Accordingly, if, as we have suggested, transnational companies' business decisions and practices should be guided by the principle that their conduct should not contribute to human rights violations and their influence should be harnessed on behalf of human rights, it surely is appropriate for companies to consider whether contemplated business decisions will have an impact on human rights conditions.

The approach taken by Levi Strauss & Co. serves as a useful model in this regard. As noted in part II.B., Levi Strauss & Co. has adopted a policy pursuant to which it will not "initiate or renew contractual relationships in countries where there are pervasive violations of basic human rights," and has determined that this standard is a bar to investment in both China and Myanmar (Burma).[160] At the same time, Levi Strauss & Co.'s "Business Partner Terms of Engagement" help assure that its operations in countries that have human rights problems—albeit not rising to the level of "pervasive violations of basic human rights"—do not contribute to violations, and instead help raise the level of enjoyment of basic rights in host countries. At noted in part II.B., Levi Strauss & Co. has effectively applied the latter criteria to elicit meaningful reforms in the employment practices of a number of business partners.[161]

Levi Strauss & Co.'s approach is based on the sound premise that a company's leverage to promote human rights is maximized when it combines a credible threat that it will terminate business relations either in a country or with individual business partners with identifiable criteria for non-termination, new investment, or contractual arrangements. Critical to the success of such a policy is Levi Strauss & Co.'s determination to identify specific conditions that must be satisfied—whether by a potential business partner or a country—to qualify for investment or business contracts.

Levi Strauss & Co.'s adoption of standards governing both engagement with individual business partners and investment in countries is a sophisticated approach to the vexing issue whether a company should invest at all in a repressive country. The Levi Strauss & Co. policy moves in a constructive fashion away from the "all or nothing" approach that has long characterized public debate about transnational investors' responsibilities *vis-a-vis* repressive governments. Total withdrawal from business and investment is reserved under this approach for countries where, in the company's estimation, "pervasive violations of basic human rights" make it impossible for Levi Strauss & Co. to play a constructive human rights role by investing there. The two-track approach embodied in Levi Strauss & Co.'s policy clearly has the potential to maximize its leverage to promote constructive change, while allowing the company appropriate flexibility to respond appropriately and effectively to myriad variations in relevant conditions.

While the proposals advanced in previous sections are universally relevant, meaningful efforts to implement them will require that transnational investors adopt policies that are responsive to the peculiar problems of individual countries.[162] With this in mind, we offer the following recommendations for companies that invest in China.

1. Endorse and Adhere to China Code of Conduct

We believe that the human rights principles set forth in the code-of-conduct legislation described in part I.B.5 represent minimum standards for U.S. and other foreign companies operating in China. Accordingly, we urge companies voluntarily to adhere to those principles, regardless of whether the legislation is enacted into law. The effectiveness of corporate adherence to these principles would be maximized if companies publicly acknowledged their adherence.

We also believe that these principles would be most effective if they were adopted by the American Chambers of Commerce in Hong Kong, Beijing, and Shanghai and the Washington-based U.S.-China Business Council to govern the activities of their member companies in China. The endorsement of human rights principles by these organizations would carry crucial significance both within the business community itself and with the Chinese government. Further, their adoption by the above-named organizations would expand the impact of the principles, since membership in these organizations is not entirely coextensive with corporations covered by the code-of-conduct legislation (principally because of *de minimis* limitations on investments covered by the legislation and similar jurisdictional provisions).

2. Assure Compliance with Code-of-Conduct Through Monitoring by Professional Organizations

Each of the professional organizations noted under our first recommendation should establish a human rights committee to oversee implementation by member companies of the code of conduct, as well as other human rights activities by companies. In the latter regard, these committees should act in a ombudsman's role to provide advice and counsel to companies that encounter human rights problems in their operations or need help in reaching relevant Chinese officials to discuss human rights, and generally should act as a clearing house for information and sharing of relevant experiences among member companies.

Member companies should be required to file with the associations' human rights committees annual reports describing their compliance with the principles endorsed by each organization. These reports would in many cases be the same as those to be submitted to the State Department under the code-of-conduct bill described in part I.B.5. In addition, member companies should be encouraged to submit, on an ongoing basis, reports describing particular problems or successes encountered in the course of their efforts to promote human rights, whether or not relevant to specific principles set forth in a code of conduct. Such reports would enable the human rights committees to consolidate experience and establish a data base of precedents that could be drawn upon in assisting member companies to deal effectively with human rights issues in their China business activities.

3. Work for Release of Political Prisoners

As indicated in part I.B.5.(8), we believe that companies could play a particularly constructive role in securing the release of persons detained solely because of peaceful political activities. We recommend that foreign companies operating in China "adopt" the cases of political prisoners held in the regions in which the companies' China operations are most substantial. When, for example, senior executives of major U.S. investors visit China, they should raise these cases in the course of their meetings with high-level officials in Beijing.

A few examples of situations in which U.S. companies active in China could exert their influence suggests both the magnitude of human rights violation in the PRC and the considerable impact that the business community could have in addressing them. The U.S. automobile industry has been among the most active investors in the PRC, providing China with badly needed capital, technology and management expertise to upgrade the country's moribund vehicle production industry for both commercial and industrial use. The Chrysler Corporation, for example, has an important cooperative project in Changchun, Jilin Province, often referred to as the "Detroit of China." In that city, Tang Yuanjuan, an assistant engineer at an automobile plant, was sentenced to 20 years' imprisonment in November 1990 for "counterrevolution" as a result of his activities in support of the 1989 democracy movement.[163]

General Motors has concluded a major investment project in Liaoning Province in northeast China, a province whose Lingyuan labor camp has been particularly notorious for the number of political prisoners held there and for its abysmal living and working conditions. One resident of the camp, Liu Gang, one of the 1989 student leaders, was reported to have had his arm broken by jail wardens and to have been force-fed when he attempted to go on a hunger strike last November to protest conditions in the camp.

The area comprising Shanghai and neighboring Jiangsu province, in the heart of China's richest agricultural region, is home to numerous important U.S. investment ventures: Hoechst Celanese manufactures ingredients for cigarette filters in Nantong; McDonnell-Douglas engages in coproduction of aircraft in Shanghai; also in Shanghai, Squibb, S.C. Johnson, and Johnson & Johnson have operations producing pharmaceuticals, medical products and various other items, and Xerox has a major joint venture project; Sheraton, Holiday Inn and other major hotel companies play a key role as investors and/or managers of major tourist hotels in this heart of China's tourist industry. This list could be continued at length.

In this same area, prisoners are detained for the non-violent expression of political opinion and the exercise of other internationally-recognized human rights. To cite just a few examples, Ma Zhiqiang, a worker from Shanghai in his late 20s, was arrested in June 1989, reportedly for attempting to form an independent trade union during the Spring 1989 democracy movement. Ma was apparently tried and sentenced to a five-year term on charges of "counterrevolution."[164] More recently, Fu Shengi, who had previously served two terms in detention for political dissidence, was sent to "reeducation through labor" for three years on June 26, 1993, for his peaceful activities in support of other political dissidents in Shanghai.[165] One of the individuals Fu was accused of "agitating" is a worker currently being held in a police-run mental institution in Shanghai, having attempted to form an independent trade union.

In Nanjing, Jiangsu province, Wu Jianmin, a 31-year-old worker in the Nanjing Passenger Train Factory, was sentenced to 10 years' imprisonment in April 1991 for starting a "counterrevolutionary organization"—the Democrats United Front. Yang Tongyan, an employee of the Jiangsu Academy of Social Sciences, was sentenced to 10 years' imprisonment in 1991 for founding the China Democracy Party.

In fact, one need look no further than China's capital city to find numerous examples of cases where U.S. companies with large-scale operations could play an effective role. As the nerve center of the 1989 democracy movement, Beijing has an especially large population of citizens held in prisons or administrative detention centers on charges stemming from their exercising the rights of free expression and freedom of association. Many have been detained in the past year—long after the Tiananmen incident—for ongoing attempts to promote human rights and political change. In addition to names relatively well known abroad, such as dissident leaders Wang Juntao, Chen Ziming and Ren Wanding, Beijing's political prisoner population includes less known individual such as Zhang Yafei and Chen Yanbin, student organizers currently serving 11- and 13-year sentences, respectively, for "counterrevolution." More recent additions to Beijing's population of detained political activists include

Chen Wei, a former student at the Beijing University of Science and Engineering who was arrested (for the fourth time since June 1989) in May 1992 for his continuing involvement in underground pro-democracy activities, and Liao Jia'an, a graduate student at People's University in Beijing, who was active in study groups and publications that address democracy and political reform issues, and was recently tried for "counterrevolution."[166]

Examples of companies with major investment projects in Beijing that could take up these and other cases in the course of their interactions with Beijing and central authorities include Hewlett Packard, with a large-scale cooperative computer operation in the capital, Babcock & Wilcox, with a major joint venture producing boilers, and the PepsiCo Corporation, whose participation in the several Kentucky Fried Chicken and Pizza Hut outlets in Beijing (and numerous other projects in different parts of China) give it a particularly high profile.

4. Include Human Rights Considerations in Feasibility Studies

We further recommend that U.S. and other foreign companies contemplating activities in China include human rights considerations in the feasibility studies generally required for investment projects. Just as there is now generally included in such studies by U.S. corporations an environmental impact report, so too there should be a human rights impact report. Thus, for example, in considering an investment project in the new special economic zone reportedly being created in Tibet to attract foreign investment,[167] a potential investor should consider such matters as the impact of the project on improving working conditions and economic opportunities for ethnic Tibetans and the possibility of prison labor being exploited for the venture. If a competing investment opportunity is offered to the same company in, for example, the Shenzhen Special Economic Zone, the company should consider not only the comparative economic advantages of each option, but also pertinent human rights considerations.

In general, potential investors should favor investment opportunities in regions that have a relatively positive human rights environment. Competition among different locations in China for foreign investment dollars is the order of the day, as reflected in a steady stream of local regulations seeking to offer competitive deals on land fees, labor policies, tax incentives, and the like. Foreign companies should advance this competition by adding a new consideration to the list—human rights.

Decisions to invest in highly repressive regions should be made only with a strong and unambiguous, commitment to play a proactive role in promoting human rights improvements, and a willingness to pull out if such improvements do not materialize. For example, in an area like Tibet, a U.S. company should undertake an investment venture only if it is prepared to insist upon applying fair hiring practices that give an appropriate role to Tibetans in both management and skilled labor positions, providing training to Tibetans that is equal to that afforded Han Chinese staff, and making strong representations against any interference in peaceful activities of Tibetan staff, such as participating in study groups on Tibetan history and culture, and using the Tibetan language. Similarly, current and future investors in Tibet should use appropriate opportunities to request information about and release of those imprisoned for the peaceful advocacy of political views as well as for religious activities.

The point is that companies should consider, in advance of their decision on an investment project, the human rights conditions in the area where a project is contemplated and their potential ability to have a positive influence on such problems as may exist or arise. A decision *not* to make a particular investment would be appropriate if local human rights conditions were poor and the company's position in the contemplated venture or the economic importance of the project would not enable it to have a significant impact on human rights conditions. Similarly, a company should not undertake an investment in a highly repressive area if the benefit of the investment to the regime would likely outweigh any positive impact the project could have.

5. *Assemble Data on Human Rights Conditions by Region*

To facilitate investors' consideration of human rights factors, professional organizations, such as the American Chamber of Commerce in Hong Kong and the U.S.-China Business Council, that publish for their members periodic assessments of investment conditions in various parts of China should add human rights conditions to the factors they currently address—regulatory incentives, fiscal conditions, environmental issues, and the like. These human rights data should include such information as the nature of working conditions, discrimination against minority groups, and numbers of political prisoners in regions covered. Such reporting could draw on the extensive reporting of non-governmental human rights organizations and the State Department's annual human rights reports.

In addition, member companies should be asked to submit information concerning their observations about human rights conditions in areas where they operate. This information could significantly enhance the base of currently available information, as businesspersons employed full-time in China are in a position to develop greater familiarity with certain practices than representatives of organizations based outside China and of the U.S. government.

None of the proposals advanced in this section would require U.S. businesses or business associations to engage in activity that would violate Chinese law or policy. They would, however, go a long way toward assuring that U.S. business activities in China promote basic human rights values and do not in any way condone or participate in their violation.

CONCLUSION

A nascent corps of transnational businesses are establishing new mileposts for corporate responsibility in respect of human rights. Their initiatives have been shaped, above all, by the daunting challenges presented to foreign investors in China in the wake of the June 1989 clampdown by the PRC. But if their efforts have been largely propelled by Tiananmen, their impact will reach far beyond China. Indeed, the human rights policies adopted by these companies have already been extended beyond the PRC to the global market. And while only a small number of businesses have adopted comprehensive human rights policies, they already have succeeded in reframing the terms of debate within corporate boardrooms about the appropriate role of businesses in addressing human rights abroad. It is no small measure of their impact that the center of public debate has now shifted from the issue whether businesses should be expected to address human rights conditions in their overseas operations, to the question of what, precisely, their responsibilities are.

NOTES

1. A few portions of this article build upon an earlier study by the co-authors which was published by the International League for Human Rights, entitled GETTING DOWN TO BUSINESS: THE HUMAN RIGHTS RESPONSIBILITIES OF CHINA'S INVESTORS AND TRADE PARTNERS, July 1992 [hereinafter GETTING DOWN TO BUSINESS].
2. Appropriations Act of 1990, Pub. L. No. 101-162, § 610, 103 Stat. 988, 1038 (1989).
3. Foreign Relations Authorization Act, Pub. L. No. 1-1-246, § 902(a)(1)-(2), 104 Stat. 15, 83 (1990).
4. John McCormick & Mark Levinson, *The Supply Police: The Demand for Social Responsibility Forces Business to Look Far Beyond its own Front Door,* NEWSWEEK, Feb. 15, 1993, at 48.
5. Nicholas D. Kristof, *China is Reported to Plan Release of Some Political Prisoners Soon,* N.Y. TIMES, May 6, 1992, at A12. On February 17, 1993, Tiananmen student leaders Wang Dan and Guo Haifang were released from prison, both having served their full terms. The PRC government claimed that these releases left no "students" in prison from the Tiananmen incident, a claim that appeared to be patently untrue in light of information gathered by the human rights organization Asia Watch, and in any event is misleading in view of the large number of prisoners of conscience other than students—workers, intellectuals and others—who remain detained in the PRC for activities during and long after the 1989 events. *See* ASIA WATCH, HUMAN RIGHTS WATCH, ECONOMIC REFORM, POLITICAL REPRESSION: ARRESTS OF DISSIDENTS IN CHINA SINCE MID-1992 (1993) [hereinafter MAR. 1993 ASIA WATCH REPORT]; *Chinese Confirm Two Pro-Democracy Student Leaders Still in Jail,* ASSOCIATED PRESS, Feb. 26, 1993, *available in* LEXIS, Nexis Library, AP File.
6. See generally LAWYERS COMMITTEE FOR HUMAN RIGHTS, CRIMINAL JUSTICE WITH CHINESE CHARACTERISTICS: CHINA'S CRIMINAL PROCESS AND VIOLATIONS OF HUMAN RIGHTS (1993) [hereinafter LAWYERS COMMITTEE REPORT].
7. XIANFA [Constitution] arts, 4, 36, 48 (P.R.C.).
8. ASIA WATCH, HUMAN RIGHTS WATCH, FREEDOM OF RELIGION IN CHINA (1992); ASIA WATCH, HUMAN RIGHTS WATCH, CONTINUING RELIGIOUS REPRESSION IN CHINA (1993).

9. AMNESTY INTERNATIONAL, *People's Republic of China: Repression in Tibet,* A1 Index: ASA 17/19/92, May 1992. *See also* INTERNATIONAL LEAGUE FOR HUMAN RIGHTS, HUMAN RIGHTS VIOLATIONS IN TIBET, submitted to the Secretary General of the United Nations, Jan. 1992, reprinted in Situation in Tibet: Note by the Secretary-General, U.N. DOC. E/CN.4/1992/37, at 50; Nicholas D. Kristof, *Communist Party Chief Calls for a Purge in Tibet,* N.Y. TIMES, Feb. 14, 1993, at 11.

10. ASIA WATCH, HUMAN RIGHTS WATCH, CRACKDOWN IN INNER MONGOLIA (1991); ASIA WATCH, HUMAN RIGHTS WATCH, CONTINUING CRACKDOWN IN INNER MONGOLIA (1992).

11. Information Office of the People's Republic of China State Council, *Human Rights White Paper,* English translation in FBIS-CHI-91-225-S, Nov. 21, 1991, Chapters III, VI–VIII. For a critique of the White Paper's discussion of the Chinese criminal justice system, see LAWYER'S COMMITTEE FOR HUMAN RIGHTS, CHINA'S WHITE PAPER ON HUMAN RIGHTS: A CRITIQUE OF CHAPTER 4 ON GUARANTEES OF HUMAN RIGHTS IN CHINA'S JUDICIAL WORK (1992).

12. *See generally* Information Office of the PRC State Council, *Criminal Reform in China,* Aug. 1992; Information Office of the PRC State Council, *Tibet—Its Ownership and Human Rights Situation,* Sept. 1992, English translation in FBIS-CHI-92-197-S, Oct. 9, 1992.

13. U.N. ESCOR, 4th Sess., 3046th mtg. at 92–93, U.N. DOC. S/PV.3046 (prov. ed. 1992). *See* Zhang Zhengdong, *Unjust Cause Finds Little Support,* BEIJING REV., Mar. 22–23, 1993, at 10.

14. *See* Zhou Qingchang, *Western Views on Human Rights Opposed,* BEIJING REV. July 5–11, 1993, at 8; *Proposals for Human Rights Protection and Promotion,* BEIJING REV., June 28–July 4, 1993, at 8.

15. *See* Lena H. Sun, *China Pulls Out Stops in Olympic Bid: Political Factors Dominate in Beijing Try for 2000 Games, With Chances Uncertain,* WASH. POST, July 15, 1993, at D7.

16. Nicholas D. Kristof, *Whither that Torch? China's Burning to Have It,* N.Y. TIMES, July 28, 1993, at A4.

17. Thomas L. Friedman, *Bush Seeks Trade Benefits for China,* N.Y. TIMES, June 3, 1992, at A13.

18. Ms. Dai was allowed to return to China on June 7, 1992, to return to the United States in August 1992 and then to return permanently to China in early 1993. But the PRC apparently intends to continue to deny reentry to other dissidents who travel abroad. A December 1992 document issued internally by the PRC State Council reportedly establishes a blacklist of political dissidents who will not be allowed to reenter China after traveling abroad. Kang Tieshang, *Banishment and Exile: New Tactics for Dealing with Dissidents,* CHINA F., Mar. 30, 1993, at 5.

19. *See Bush is Setting the Bloodhounds on Beijing,* BUS. WEEK, Dec. 23, 1991, at 36.

20. Friedman, *supra* note 17, at A13. *See also* ASIA WATCH, HUMAN RIGHTS WATCH, EVIDENCE OF CRACKDOWN ON LABOR MOVEMENT MOUNTS (1992).

21. Friedman, *supra* note 17.

22. (Smoot-Hawley) Tariff Act of 1930, 19 U.S.C. § 1307 (1988).

23. *See* discussion *infra* part I.B.4.

24. Mike Jendrzejczyk, *No Waffling on China,* WASH. POST, Feb.16, 1993, at A13 (opinion piece).

25. For analysis of those sanctions, see GETTING DOWN TO BUSINESS, *supra* note 1.

26. For discussion of the latter, *see* GETTING DOWN TO BUSINESS, *supra* note 1.

27. Pursuant to a 1975 law, § 402 of the Trade Act of 1974, the President may not extend MFN status to countries with non-market economies that deny their citizens "the right

or opportunity to emigrate." 19 U.S.C. § 2432 (commonly referred to as the Jackson-Vanik amendment to the Trade Act of 1974). The President may waive this restriction if a waiver would "lead substantially to the achievement of the objectives" of the law. The first provision of the law asserts that its object is "[t]o assure the continued dedication of the United States to fundamental human rights." and MFN determinations have sometimes taken into consideration human rights considerations unrelated to emigration. Although China does not allow free emigration, the U.S. government has waived the Jackson-Vanik restriction since 1980.

28. Daniel Southerland, *Clinton Sending First Trade Delegation to China,* WASH. POST, Feb. 27, 1993, at C1.

29. The violent assault on pro-democracy activists in Beijing began on the night of June 3, 1989, and continued through June 4. Most of the killings occurred on June 4, 1989, and the incident is now widely referred to in China simply as "June 4."

30. Although economic authority in the PRC has become significantly diffused and products whose export is monopolized by one particular state agency have diminished in number and in percentage of China's trade, state enterprises at one level or another of the Chinese trade structure—whether central or local—still account for a significant proportion of China's exports to the United States and other countries. *See generally* NICHOLAS R. LARDY, FOREIGN TRADE AND ECONOMIC REFORM IN CHINA, 1978–1990 (1992).

31. The Senate voted to sustain President Bush's veto by a count of 59–40 on Oct. 1, 1992. 138 CONG. REC. S15957 (daily ed. Oct. 1, 1992).

32. 139 CONG. REC. S4662, H2023 (daily ed. Apr. 22, 1993).

33. *See* Jendrzejczyk, *supra* note 24.

34. In his first congressional testimony after being confirmed as U.S. Trade Representative, Mickey Kantor noted the repeated failure of the Bush Administration to impose conditions on renewal of MFN for China, and stated that "the Clinton Administration will address all of these concerns—human rights, [arms] proliferation, and trade—and we will address them aggressively." Michael Chugani, *U.S. Takes Tough Stand on Trade,* S. CHINA MORNING POST, Mar. 11, 1993, at 2. Secretary of State Warren Christopher told a congressional committee in March that "it is my hope that we can go forward with MFN this year but conditioned on [China] making very substantial progress." Michael Chugani, *U.S. Spells Out MFN Renewal Conditions,* S. CHINA MORNING POST, Mar. 12, 1993, at 2. In his Senate confirmation hearing, Assistant Secretary of State for East Asia and Pacific Affairs Winston Lord said that "conditional MFN is the position of the President and we wish to go forward on that basis, depending on events." Susumu Awanohara, *China Consensus,* FAR E. ECON. REV., Apr. 22, 1993, at 13.

35. *See supra* note 27.

36. Congress has made clear its support for President Clinton's initiative by overwhelmingly voting against a bill that would have superseded the Executive Order and immediately terminated China's MFN status. H.R.J. Res. 208, 103d Cong., 1st Sess. (1993).

37. Michael Weisskopf, *Backbone of the New China Lobby: U.S. Firms,* WASH. POST. June 14, 1993, at A12.

38. *Id.*

39. Letter from Business Coalition for U.S.-China Trade to President Bill Clinton (May 12, 1993), at 1–2.

40. *Id.* at 1.

41. *Id.*

42. During a briefing on the Executive Order, the Assistant Secretary of State for East Asian and Pacific Affairs, Winston Lord, said "[i]t would be very helpful indeed if the business community lobbied the Chinese government to make progress in these areas as effectively as they are lobbying Congress and the President. I think it would help American policy . . .[if U.S. Business leaders] would take actions and express their views to the Chinese on human rights concerns. . . ." Winston Lord, *Most Favored Nation Trading Status to China,* May 28, 1993, *available in* LEXIS, Nexis Library, Reuter Transcript File (State Department on-the-Record Briefing).

43. H.R. 3489, 102d Cong., 1st Sess. (1991).

44. It is the authors' understanding that the offices of both Senator Kennedy and Representative Unsoeld are likely to introduce legislation patterned on the original Miller bill.

45. Somewhat analogous codes have been developed to promote human rights in other countries. The best known of these are the Sullivan Principles for businesses operating in South Africa. First developed in 1977 and subsequently amplified, the Sullivan Principles were for many years adopted by corporations on a voluntary basis. In 1985, President Reagan issued an executive order that included a provision forbidding U.S. export assistance to any U.S. firm with 25 or more employees that had not adopted the principles enumerated in the Sullivan code. The Anti-Apartheid Act of 1986, which superseded President Reagan's executive order, incorporated the Sullivan Principles by, *inter alia,* requiring "[a]ny national of the United States that employs more than 25 persons in South Africa [to] take the necessary steps to insure that the Code of Conduct [based on the Sullivan Principles] is implemented with respect to the employment of those persons." Comprehensive Anti-Apartheid Act of 1986 § 207(a), 22 U.S.C. § 5034(a) (1988). Another precedent is the MacBride Principles, which set forth employment standards for companies operating in Northern Ireland. A number of city and state governments have enacted laws supporting the MacBride Principles (by, for example, threatening to bar firms that do not adhere to the Principles from city contracts).

46. The Secretary is also directed to encourage OECD nations to promote similar principles. An international approach to business efforts on human rights is essential if such efforts are to achieve meaningful success. *See* discussion *infra* part III.C.

82. *See* Frank Gibney Jr., *Questions About China: U.S. Companies Are Caught in a Debate Over Beijing's Human-Rights Record,* Newsweek (int'l ed.), May 17, 1993, at 40.

83. For a classic statement of the view that businesses should not be concerned with "social responsibility," see Milton Friedman, *The Social Responsibility of Business is to Increase its Profits,* New York Times, Sept. 11, 1970 (Magazine), at 32. This claim has long been discredited, at least in its most sweeping form, in part because it is hopelessly circular. Our beliefs about what are proper concerns of the business community are themselves social constructs, and have evolved significantly over time in tandem with broader changes in the social and political environment. Further, to the extent that this argument asserts that it is the role of government to fashion and implement policy—in this case human rights policy—it also necessarily concedes to government the right to further specific policies by, *inter alia,* regulating the practices of U.S. corporations. Examples of such regulation, from legislation restricting companies' ability to discriminate or pollute at home, to laws prohibiting corrupt practices by corporations abroad, are too numerous to leave any room for doubting the legitimacy of government efforts to advance social policies in part by regulating corporate behavior.

84. *See* McCormick & Levinson, *supra* note 4, at 48.

85. There are, to be sure, some apparent counter-examples of countries with strong economies despite serious violations of human rights—in Latin America, Chile under Pinochet stands out as a notable example. But those who might suggest that these economies are strong *because* the government denied citizens' fundamental rights pose a false dichotomy. One can hardly imagine that Augusto Pinochet's economic policies, to the extent they were successful, would have been less so had his government not "disappeared" and killed over 2,000 people. (Indeed, if it were necessary to prove that one needn't choose between economic growth and respect for human rights, Chile's economy has thrived under the democratic government of Patricio Aylwin, which succeeded the 17-year dictatorship of General Pinochet.)

86. *But see* Matthew Lippman, *Transnational Corporations and Repressive Regimes: The Ethical Dilemma,* 15 CAL. W. INT'L. L.J. 542, 549–50 (1985) (noting that executives of multinational companies "typically respond to criticism of their relationship with repressive regimes by pointing out that corporations are economic rather than political entities and that as such they should not be held responsible for the policies pursued by their host countries. . . .").

87. *See supra* part I.B.4.c.

88. *See, e.g.,* UNITED STATES-CHINA BUSINESS COUNCIL, CHINA POLICY: FOSTERING US COM-PETITIVENESS AND THE BILATERAL RELATIONSHIP; Testimony on U.S.-China Trade Relations, Statement of the Emergency Committee for American Trade on United States-China Trade Relations to Subcommittee on Trade of the Ways and Means Committee of the House of Representatives, June 8, 1993; Richard W. Younts, Senior Vice President and Corporate Executive Director International-Asia and Americas, Motorola, Before the Subcommittee on Trade, Ways and Means Committee of the House of Representatives, June 8, 1993 [hereinafter Motorola Testimony]; *see also, generally,* Barber B. Conable, Jr. & David M. Lampton, *China, The Coming Power,* FOREIGN AFF., Winter 1992/93, at 145, 146.

89. *See* Lippman, *supra* note 86, at 550.

90. Motorola. Testimony, *supra* note 88; THE ATLANTIC COUNCIL OF THE UNITED STATES & NATIONAL COMMITTEE ON UNITED STATES-CHINA RELATIONS, UNITED STATES AND CHINA RELATIONS AT A CROSSROADS, 20–28 (1993); *see also, generally,* Conable & Lampton, *supra* note 88, at 146.

91. *See* Lippman, *supra* note 86, at 550.

92. Carl Goldstein, *Two Faces of Reform: Guangdong's Economy Booms, But the Crime Rate Soars,* FAR E. ECON. REV., Apr. 8, 1993, at 15.

93. This point was developed by John J. Keller, a business executive, at a workshop on business investment and human rights in Asia convened by the Washington College of Law of The American University and Asia Watch in Washington, D.C. on February 26, 1993. *Cf.* Note, *Forum Non Conveniens and Multinational Corporations: A Government Interest Approach,* 11 N.D.J. INT'L. L & COM. REG. 699, 712–13 (1986) (discussing "industrial flight" phenomenon associated with heavily regulated industries).

94. *See* discussions *infra* part III.A.

95. Again, the authors owe this point to John J. Keller. *See* note 93, *supra.* Our analysis assumes that the local employment opportunities created by foreign investment in underdeveloped countries tend to consist overwhelmingly of non-value-added jobs.

96. *See generally* LOUIS HENKIN ET AL., INTERNATIONAL LAW: CASES AND MATERIALS 980–1001 (2d ed. 1987) [hereinafter INTERNATIONAL LAW]. The university of human rights was recently reaffirmed at the U.N.-sponsored World Conference on Human Rights, held in Vienna, Austria in June 1993. *See* Final Document of the World Conference on Human Rights, para. 3 (1993).

97. Internationally-recognized human rights standards have been incorporated into a broad array of federal laws governing U.S. foreign policy. *See* Diane F. Orentlicher, *The Power of an Idea: The Impact of United States Human Rights Policy,* 1 TRANSNAT'L. L. & CONTEMP. PROBS. 43, 48–49 (1991). Some state and city governments in the United States also have adopted policies designed to promote human rights in particular foreign countries. *See* Michael H. Shuman, *Two Wrongs Don't Make Human Rights,* BULL. MUNICIPAL FOREIGN POL'Y (Winter 1989–90), at 4.

98. *See, e.g., ICCPR,* art. 2(1), *supra* note 48, at 53, *European Convention for the Protection of Human Rights and Fundamental Freedoms,* art. 1, 213 U.N.T.S. 221 (*signed* on Nov. 4, 1950; *entered into force* Sept. 3, 1953); *American Convention on Human Rights,* art. 1(1), *adopted* Jan. 7, 1970, O.A.S. Official Records, OEA/ser.K./ XVI/1.1, doc. 65 rev. 1, corr. 1 (1970), *reprinted in* 9 I.L.M. 673 (1970).

99. See generally Diane F. Orentlicher, *Settling Accounts: The Duty to Prosecute Human Rights Violations of a Prior Regime,* 100 YALE L.J. 2537, 2568–80 (1991). Further, the ICCPR, *supra* note 48, makes clear that non-state actors may not interfere with rights recognized under the Covenant, Article 5(1) provides:

> Nothing in the present Covenant may be interpreted as implying for any State, group or person any right to engage in any activity or perform any act aimed at the destruction of any of the rights and freedoms recognized herein or at their limitation to a greater extent than is provided for in the present Covenant.

100. *See supra* text accompanying notes 54–55.

101. *See* Lippman, *supra* note 86, at 545; Jacqueline Duval-Major, Note, *One-Way Ticket Home: The Federal Doctrine of Forum Non Conveniens and the International Plaintiff* [hereinafter *One-Way Ticket*], 77 CORNELL L. REV. 650, 674–75 (1992).

102. For discussion of a national government's self-interest in regulating its companies' overseas operations, see *One-Way Ticket, supra* note 101, at 675.

103. One effort to establish international standards governing transnational corporations is the Draft U.N. Code of Conduct On Transnational Corporations, U.N. ESCOR Suppl (No. 7), U.N. Doc E/1983/Rev. 1 (Annex 11) at 12–27, *reprinted in* 23 I.L.M 626 (1984).

104. *See* Steele et al. v. Bulova Watch Co., 344 U.S. 280, 285–86 (1952); Skiriotes v. Florida, 313 U.S. 69, 73 (1941); RESTATEMENT (THIRD) OF THE FOREIGN RELATIONS LAW OF THE UNTIED STATES, § 402(2) (1987) [hereinafter RESTATEMENT]. The U.S. government has somewhat greater scope to regulate the conduct of foreign branches of companies incorporated in the United States than that of subsidiaries of U.S. companies that are organized under the laws of a foreign state. *See id.* § 414.

105. *See* INTERNATIONAL LAW, *supra* note 96, at 839.

106. *See* RESTATEMENT, *supra* note 104, §§ 441, 414 cmt. d.

107. *See supra* part I.B.5; *see also* discussion *infra* part III.E.

108. *See* RESTATEMENT, *supra* note 104, § 403 cmt. a.

109. *See* RESTATEMENT, *supra* note 104, § 403(2)(e).

110. *See* RESTATEMENT, *supra* note 702 cmt. n.

111. *See* RESTATEMENT, *supra* note 104, § 493 cmt. e,

112. *See* Anne-Marie S. Burley, *International Law and International Relations Theory: A Dual Agenda,* 87 AM. J. INT'L. L. 205, 230 (1993).

113. *Id.* at 232.

114. *Cf.* Susan Strange, *The Name of the Game,* in SEA-CHANGES: AMERICAN FOREIGN POLICY IN A WORLD TRANSFORMED 238 (Nicholas X. Rizopoulos ed., 1990) (discussing the erosion of national authority caused by the expansion of an "international business civilization").

115. Burley, *supra* note 112, at 232.
116. For example, *The New York Times* reported that the Chinese government announced on May 22, 1992 that it had released three elderly Roman Catholic clerics from detention, and noted that John Kamm had been lobbying for their release. Sheryl WuDunn, *China Releases 3 Catholic Priests Who Spent Decades in Detention,* N.Y. TIMES, May 23, 1992, at A3. *See also* Gibney, *supra* note 82, at 41 (estimating that Kamm's efforts "have contributed to the release of more than 100 students, priests and businessmen from Chinese jails.").
117. James McGregor, *Many U.S. Firms in China Keep Quiet About Success,* ASIAN WALL ST. J. WEEKLY, Nov. 11, 1991, at 16; Lena Sun, *The Business of Human rights,* WASH. POST, Feb. 25, 1992, at D1.
118. The reference to "convict *or* forced labor" is particularly important in light of revelations about the extent of forced labor practices in the PRC. According to Asia Watch, not only are prisoners serving court sentences required to work without compensation to produce goods from which the state profits, but so too are criminal suspects, including those in political cases, during lengthy periods of pre-trial detention. *See* ANTHEMS OF DEFEAT, *supra* note 55, at 104–11.
119. The human rights provisions of Levi Strauss & Co.'s "Business Partner Terms of Engagement" are set forth in Appendix A.
120. Levi Strauss & Co. has terminated its relationship with at least 30 suppliers and extracted reforms from more than 120 others. *See* McCormick & Levinson, *supra* note 4, at 49. The company has also pulled out of Myanmar (Burma) closed down operations in Bangladesh and temporarily suspended operations in Peru pursuant to its policy. *See* Gibney, *supra* note 82, at 40.
121. Those standards, adopted in December 1992, are set forth in Appendix B.
122. The human rights provisions of Phillips-Van Heusen's policy are set forth in Appendix C. Although Timberland has already begun to apply its policy, it has not, as of this writing, adopted its policy in final form. The company is expected to have done so by the time this article is published; copies of the policy will be available from the Office of Legal Counsel of the Timberland Company.
158. As previously noted, the code-of-conduct legislation sponsored by Senator Kennedy and Representative Unsoeld, respectively, directs the U.S. Secretary of State to encourage (OECD nations to promote similar principles for companies that invest in China.
159. Jendrzejczyk, *supra* note 24. For discussion of Japanese companies' role in undermining international sanctions imposed in the wake of the Tiananmen incident, see INT'L. LEAGUE FOR HUMAN RIGHTS, BUSINESS AS USUAL . . .?: THE INTERNATIONAL RESPONSE TO HUMAN RIGHTS VIOLATIONS IN CHINA (1991).
160. *See supra* note 120 and accompanying text.
161. *See supra* note 120.
162. The approach taken by Levi Strauss & Co. in implementing its ethical code exemplifies this recommendation. When the company decides to withdraw from a country that engages in "pervasive violations of basic human rights," it identifies concrete human rights reforms that must be made before it will reverse its decision. Those criteria are based upon a detailed analysis by corporate staff of the chief human rights concerns in the relevant country. Similarly, Levi Strauss & Co. identifies concrete human rights goals that it will attempt to promote in countries where it maintains an investment despite human rights problems.
163. *See* AMNESTY INTERNATIONAL, PEOPLE'S REPUBLIC OF CHINA: CONTINUED PATTERNS OF HUMAN RIGHTS VIOLATIONS IN CHINA, AI Index ASA 17/32/92, at 11 (1992).

164. *See* AMNESTY INTERNATIONAL, TORTURE IN CHINA, AI Index: ASA 17/5/92, at 32–33 (1992).
165. S. CHINA MORNING POST, July 12, 1993, at 1.
166. *See* MAR. 1993 ASIA WATCH REPORT, *supra* note 5, at 13–15.
167. *Tibetan Economic Zone Planned,* WALL ST. J., May 13, 1992, at A11.

Editor's Note: The original article was edited for publication here.

'Developmental Communities' on China's Coast

The Impact of Trade, Investment, and Transnational Alliances

David Zweig

Most observers of China would have predicted that China's externally oriented development strategy, especially the growth of foreign trade, private foreign investment, reliance on international financial institutions, and overall opening of communications to the outside world, would weaken the redistributive and allocative power of the institutions of state socialism and undermine the strength and legitimacy of the Chinese Community Party (CCP). This paper addresses that assumption by looking at the impact of foreign investment and foreign trade on rural communities in coastal China. Overall, it seeks answers to the following key questions. What institutions have emerged to link domestic China and the international system, who controls them, and how do the incentives they create influence domestic behavior? Second, have these linkages affected growth and inequality? Third, has the emergence of new transnational ties strengthened state power at the national or local level? Finally, has growth in China's foreign trade affected the relative strength of different industrial sectors, as well as national policy on industrial development?

Three general approaches offer different predictions about the expected impact of China's open policy. The dependency school believes that socialist states can better protect their national interests as they undergo incorporation into the international capitalist system.[1] This model would predict increased social unrest as the Chinese state, under pressure from international financial

David Zweig, Associate Professor of International Politics, Fletcher School of Law and Diplomacy, Tufts University, " 'Developmental Communities' on China's Coast: The Impact of Trade, Investment and Transnational Alliances," *Comparative Politics,* April 1995: 253–274.

institutions, scales back its welfare functions.[2] Since authoritarianism results from concerted export promotion, an export-oriented China should continue to suppress its working class.[3] Except for growth in a small urban core, a shift from planning to comparative advantage could expand poverty and inequality, especially in the rural hinterland.[4] And directing these changes might be a new alliance among international capital, the dependent state, and a new domestic class, taking China on a more "dependent development" trajectory.[5]

The literature on East Asian development would counter that openness is good for a state's economic development, while autarky retards it. But success needs good leaders, efficient bureaucrats, and a state capable of creating comparative advantage in exportable products. Combining some import controls with foreign investment, China could grow by employing an "export-led growth" strategy.[6] However, without a capitalist class and a freer domestic market, this growth might be more limited than in other, more capitalist economies.[7] Also, without an autonomous bureaucracy, which helped East Asia avoid the nepotism and protectionism that undermined Latin America's export strategy,[8] China would be hard pressed to end the subsidies which harm competitiveness. Borrowing from positive political economy, continued tariffs, quotas, and government intervention in the foreign trade regime should generate many negative consequences of a "rent-seeking society," creating incentives for domestic actors to pursue those "rents."[9] Nevertheless, successful growth, as in Taiwan and Korea, might lead to greater democratization without expanding rural-urban inequalities.[10]

Finally, the literature on international political economy would predict that the expansion of foreign trade would alter China's industrial structure, as low-end products find a market niche vacated by the increasingly advanced Asian economies.[11] Greater openness might alter the power distribution in the domestic regime and its policies,[12] leading to a more pluralistic society, with domestic coalitions that support foreign trade[13] and oppose protectionism[14] pushing their programs on to the national agenda.

The view from the grass roots both supports and challenges all three models. Unlike any other Communist system, China has proven remarkably adept at following an export-led development strategy.[15] Foreign trade has grown 16 percent a year since the late 1970s and is a key force behind China's remarkable economic boom. Second, rural industries in coastal areas are a key contributor to this growth, raising living standards for tens of millions of peasants. Third, the areas of deepest foreign penetration are also the areas of highest growth and have the most stable Communist Party systems. Finally, the incorporation of the countryside into the international market has strengthened its industrial base, improving its ability to compete with urban state-owned factories.

Driving this development is an alliance between local Communist Party officials and foreign investors. Sharing common interests—the expansion of foreign trade and use of rural joint ventures to reap large profits in China's domestic market—local party officials have used their relationship with foreign investors to increase their authoritarian power over the local community. Together, they have captured and shared "domestic rents" that emerge due to the mixed market/plan foreign trade system. And by undermining the center's institutional framework for monitoring foreign investment and trade, they have weakened the central state's ability to control its own foreign trade regime. The emergence of Communist Party-dominated, export-oriented "developmental communities," which use foreign trade and links with private investors to enrich their peasantry, strengthen their party authority, improve their industrial structure, and challenge the central state's control over China's external boundaries, is the subject of this paper, making it relevant to comparativists and international political economists.[16] In addition, the increased authority of the local party/state and its bureaucratic appendages, even as it internationalizes, suggests that the future path of China's development may differ significantly from other authoritarian states, such as Taiwan and Korea, whose export-oriented path to prosperity ended in political liberalization and democratization.

THE CONSEQUENCES OF EXPORT-LED GROWTH AND THE TRANSNATIONAL ALLIANCE FOR CHINA

The transnational alliance between local ruling authorities and foreign investors, as well as the emergence of export-oriented developmental communities in rural coastal China, has affected China's growth, industrial structure, regional inequality, central-local relations, and local political power.

First, rural communities that have aggressively and successfully entered the international market have grown remarkably. In rural areas along China's coast, exports have brought new markets, more jobs, and new wealth. The foreign exchange earned from these exports is now used to import new technologies and has thus altered the comparative advantage of township and village enterprises (or TVEs),[17] allowing them to compete more effectively with the heavily subsidized, state-owned enterprises (SOEs).[18] And because access to technology alters China's industrial structure, strong support for global interactions has emerged among local elites, factory managers, and even some TVE workers, consolidating China's open policy.

Second, the demands of foreign partners have increased the leverage of local party officials over the industrial work force. The result is a new, stricter management regime within rural enterprises and increased power for the local party/state over the local population. The foreign trade bureaucracy, part of the local state structure, has also expanded quickly in response to increased local demand for linkages to the outside world, increasing the number of agents in the local state government.

Third, joint ventures undermine central efforts to control the boundaries between the domestic and international economies. Under the former foreign trade regime, the central state managed China's foreign exchange reserves, reaped tax benefits, and kept foreign producers out of China's domestic market, thereby protecting SOEs. By offering local producers channels to export directly to foreign vendors, joint ventures allow domestic producers to evade state middlemen, their controls, and their fees. At the same time, elites in developmental communities serve as "linkage agents"[19] for foreign investors who want access to China's domestic market and the enormous "rents" available within China to those with better technology, efficiency, and products.[20]

Fourth, while expanded TVE exports have made the rural/urban gap in coastal China less meaningful, TVE exports and the growth of rural joint ventures have made the coastal/inland gap within rural China more salient. Preliminary data from the late 1980s show that TVE exports are predominantly coastal and that the gap is growing. Similarly, most rural joint ventures are in coastal regions. Even a power differential has emerged between the two regions: while exports, joint ventures, and rural industrialization are strengthening the local state in coastal China, slower growth and the pull of the coast are leaving a power vacuum in the rural parts of internal China.

CENTRAL STATE POLICY TOWARDS TVE EXPORTS: THEN AND NOW

After taking power, China's leaders adopted the Soviet strategy of centrally planned foreign trade, under which imports' primary purpose was to supplement insufficient domestic production. China exported only to earn the foreign exchange needed to buy those imports. Specialized foreign trade corporations under the ministry of foreign trade controlled all international commerce, including purchases of technology. To insure that domestic allocations followed the central plan and were not diverted by market scarcity, prices for exports were set by plan and ignored world prices. Overall, China's mix of exports did not reflect China's comparative advantage.[21]

However, initially China's Communist leaders did not eschew foreign transactions. Development in the first decade depended largely on one of the largest cases of technology transfer in world history, delivered by the Soviet Union and the eastern bloc and financed through Chinese exports.[22] But as Maoist predilections towards "self-reliance" emerged during the Sino-Soviet split, foreign trade in the 1960s and most of the 1970s played a minimal role in China's overall economic development.

In 1978 China started to dismantle the wall Mao had built around China's economy and society. Its outward-oriented development strategy emerged in 1978, and in early 1979 China invited direct foreign investment.[23] Enclaves, called "special economic zones," were opened on China's southern coast as a locus for this investment, and a new joint ventures law codified the opening. In 1984, fourteen coastal cities were opened for direct foreign investment, and in 1985 three river deltas, comprising over 100 million people, were opened as well. By 1991 foreign trade surpassed $134 billion, with an annual growth rate in 1985–1991 of 17.5 percent. Committed foreign investment was $47.9 billion.[24]

China's "open policy" involved a shift to an export-led growth strategy, combined with vestiges of an import substitution industrialization regime. Trade was decentralized to a growing number of local trade companies, and regular currency devaluations helped export prices mirror international prices. But China also introduced export and import licenses to control the volume and composition of trade.[25] The result was a partially reformed, mixed system, which like other "late industrializers" in East Asia combines import substitution and exports to generate rapid economic growth.[26] Thus, throughout the 1980s many new goods and resources entered and left China, not through free and open markets, but through bureaucratically controlled channels. Many export factories interacted with foreign traders only through specialized foreign trade companies. But in order to promote exports China allowed exporting enterprises preferred access to foreign exchange, foreign technology, and domestic energy and resources and instituted bonuses for managers of enterprises earning foreign exchange. These incentives helped trigger China's current export boom.

EXPORT-LED GROWTH IN RURAL CHINA: THE ROLE OF NATIONAL POLICY

Both national policy, which targeted the countryside for export promotion, and the rural areas' industrial structure made the countryside in coastal China one of the key actors and beneficiaries of the open policy.

From 1979 to 1985 central leaders ignored much of rural China as they opened coastal cities and zones to foreign trade.[27] TVE exports were controlled by county and provincial foreign trade departments and companies, as was their ability to import technology with foreign exchange they themselves had earned.[28] But after the mid 1980s rural industry became a key sector of China's economy, supplanting the state sector in such areas as consumer goods, textiles, and building materials.[29] By 1991 rural industry, excluding the rural service sector, accounted for over 26.6 percent of China's industrial production. By 1991, TVEs, including the service sector, employed 96 million workers and outstripped SOEs, which employed 60 million workers.[30]

While rural areas have been marginalized in many developing countries, China's rural coastal communities have been incorporated into the state directed, export-led growth strategy. Why? First, as trade theory suggests, the abundance of skilled, cheap rural labor offered China a comparative advantage.

But central planners, not rural or provincial elites, lobbied for expansion of the countryside's role in export promotion in order to solve rural China's surplus labor problem.[31] Also, SOEs were not responding to the demands of the foreign market, while TVEs were far more market-oriented.[32] Thus, in late 1987, when former party secretary Zhao Ziyang enunciated his coastal development strategy, whose purpose was to help China make up for missing the high growth stage in East Asia in the 1960s and 1970s,[33] the rural areas became a key focus of China's export-led growth strategy.[34] In 1988 the central government opened more of China's coastal rural areas to foreign investment and promised local governments and their exporting TVEs access to new technology on the same tax-free terms as SOEs. State regulations stressed the right of TVEs to use their retained foreign exchange for imports of technology, equipment, and raw materials, without bureaucratic interference.[35]

Initially, most leaders in industrialized rural localities resisted pressures to export. Many had strong ties with SOEs, and foreign trade was risky.[36] In response, the center employed policy instruments borrowed from Maoist political campaigns to push local governments to export.[37] These national pressures and local interests led to dramatic increases in the role of TVEs in China's exports. While TVE exports were only 4.5 percent of total exports in 1984–85, they comprised almost 26 percent of total exports by 1991. In 1990 TVEs produced nearly 75 percent of all of China's exported garments. Their role in direct foreign investment is also significant, especially in coastal China. By the end of 1991 TVEs had attracted $5.85 billion in overseas funds, or about 12 percent of total committed direct foreign investment.[38] By 1991 there were over 7,000 rural joint ventures, about one-fourth of the joint ventures in China.

THE EMERGENCE OF "DEVELOPMENTAL COMMUNITIES"

While national policy affects incentives and opportunities for communities to adopt developmental strategies, local factors, such as industrial structure, leadership, and location, affect local perceptions of emerging opportunities and determine how localities link themselves with the international market.

China's export drive has unleased natural energies extant in the TVE sector. TVEs have worked primarily under market conditions, outside the formal, hierarchically planned economy imposed by the central and provincial administration. Compared to SOEs, which are tightly administered by industrial bureaus at different levels of the administrative hierarchy. TVEs confronted fewer "supralocal" bureaucratic constraints as export opportunities emerged.[39] SOEs must meet a production plan before they can redirect their commercial interactions and restructure their production in line with foreign needs. Bureaus that monitor their behavior can constrain them through control over resources, capital, and marketing channels. Thus, the level of concentration of TVEs versus SOEs within a community can affect whether or not it can respond to emerging foreign trade opportunities.

Second, strategic positions, such as location on a river or the coast (which decreases the transaction costs of exporting) or control over harbors (which serve as channels for the flow of goods inland and overseas), can increase the impact of export-led growth on a community. Harbors need service industries and links to other cities through roads and railways, which under a planned economy increases state investment.[40] One may hypothesize that particularly in China, where the transport sector grew so slowly until the late 1980s, the open policy's stress on global linkages has redirected a significant proportion of state infrastructure investment into areas directly related t the export economy.

The fact that even within coastal rural China some localities opted for greater levels of global interdependence suggests that local leadership plays a critical role in determining which areas respond more rapidly to the opening. In these localities, which I label "developmental communities," entrepreneurial state officials at the village, township, and county levels recognized the potential for community growth and accumulation of personal wealth in global economic linkages, so they mobilized the community to seek these benefits.[41]

Drawing both on their control over TVEs and on taxes derived from them to establish what Oi calls "local state corporatism," as well as on the organizational and coercive power inherent in their roles as Communist Party officials, leaders of developmental communities mobilize factory workers, local officials, and other members of the local bureaucratic elite for a massive shift into the foreign trade realm.[42] In some cases, almost half of their GDP may go into exports. They centralize the foreign trade plan based on local, not national, interests, and they dramatically promote joint ventures throughout the rural community. They mobilize townships to prepare their best TVEs for joint venture partnership. Work regimens in factories are strengthened to reward productive workers and sanction laggards, in part to entice the foreign investor. Aware that technological innovation and movement up the product cycle are critical if they are to compete with heavily subsidized state-owned enterprises, as well as with other rural communities, officials push firms to increase exports and joint venture partnerships in order to import new technologies. To increase exports, these local governments subsidize their key exporting TVEs, offering lower taxes, easier access to cheap loans, raw materials at lower planned prices, foreign exchange, and technology. Those who do not respond risk their jobs.

Township officials and TVE managers also support this export fever. Why? Technologies that can be imported only by export-oriented TVEs enhance a firm's domestic competitiveness, and because foreigners buy them, export products' prestige increases in the domestic market, especially if they receive awards. Also, frequent domestic recessions cause TVE managers to seek alternative (export) markets. Joint ventures resolve many of these problems by creating new markets and by supplying both new technology, which can be imported at low tariffs if used for exports, and much needed capital. Joint ventures allow TVEs direct access to international markets.[43] Joint ventures receive important tax breaks, including the right to import cars duty free.[44] Having joint ventures in one's township is a status symbol for local cadres, a sign that they are "progressive" and that foreigners appreciate their management skills. In some localities cadres are given quotas for establishing joint ventures. There is also the increased opportunity for foreign travel and access to foreign exchange. Finally, some factories and local governments see joint ventures as a way to get access to rents that exist due to the partial nature of the foreign trade reforms.

Yet a sharp line divides insiders and outsiders in these communities. While nationwide controls on land sales and labor mobility are weakening, continued limitations on exchanges of land, labor, and capital in these communities, left over from the Maoist era, limit welfare benefits, high salaries, and public goods (such as access to schools) to members of the internal community. Whereas in a market economy, workers who relocate and pay local taxes have equal rights to welfare benefits in their new community, internal migrants in China remain "outsiders" under law, unless they are given (or purchase, often on the black market) local residence permits. Without such permits—and most county governments do not sell them officially—local governments can expel outside workers after they serve their economic purpose. Thus, while these communities import labor from China's hinterland to perform more menial work that the local community's peasant/factory workers no longer want to do, to date they do not have to fear that these outsiders will buy their way in. Building on what Shue calls the "honeycomb" nature of Chinese society which first emerged during the Maoist era,[45] these developmental communities remain relatively impenetrable and resist pressures from outside authorities in a way that suggests international boundaries more than domestic regions.[46]

ZHANGJIAGANG AND THE MAKING OF A DEVELOPMENTAL COMMUNITY

Zhangjiagang, which is situated on the south shore of the Yangzi river, a half-day upstream from Shanghai, was particularly qualified to respond to the state's call for export-led growth because of its leadership, its position in China's administrative hierarchy, its geographic location, and its industrial structure. It has a tightly knit local elite, which based on its unity, common purpose, and control over resources manifests the "corporate coherence" necessary for successful development.[47] Surrounded by other counties in southern Jiangsu, which began to industrialize in the mid 1970s, peasants and leaders in Zhangjiagang have taken many risks since the early 1980s to enrich their locality. Zhangjiagang officials are known throughout southern Jiangsu as very touch businessmen. Throughout the 1980s members of the community who had left in the 1960s during hard times returned home. In the early 1980s one thousand people returned yearly, but after 1986 Zhangjiagang limited returnees to managers, engineers, skilled workers, and other talented people, as well as the spouses of urban residents, thereby strengthening the meritocratic nature of its bureaucracy.

Zhangjiagang's administrative qualities make it an effective export community. Zhangjiagang was formerly Shazhou county, under Suzhou municipality. In 1986, due to the internationalization of its harbor, it was promoted within the urban hierarchical ranks to a "county-level" or third-level city. Because Zhangjiagang had been a county, there remains only one administrative level between the current city government and township leaders who directly administer the rural community and own its TVEs. Even before 1986, all township officials had been directly appointed by the county organizational bureau, which today in Zhangjiagang city's organizational bureau, so township officials owe their loyalty directly to today's city leaders. Moreover, city officials often rotate posts with township leaders, strengthening links between city and township leaders. Unlike "second-level cities," such as Suzhou, which have counties or district governments between themselves and the local townships, the close links between city and township cities in "third-level" cities make it easier for city leaders to mobilize the populace for export-led growth.

Third, Zhangjiagang's economy depends heavily on TVEs. In 1991, almost 60 percent of the total labor force (including officials and bureaucrats) worked in TVEs; they comprised 87 percent of industrial firms in the region. From 1974 to 1986, over two-thirds of rural labor left agriculture, of which 80 percent moved into the expanding TVE sector. But because of its reliance on TVEs, which were not part of the formal economic plan, there has been little provincial involvement in determining its products or the direction of its trade. For various political reasons, few factories owned by Suzhou municipality have branch plants in this area, furthering their autonomy from supraregional administrative interference. But because TVEs are so critical to the local government, when the economic retrenchment of 1988–89 dropped local GNP growth from 25 percent per annum to only 5.5 percent and industrial employment dropped 7.6 percent, the local government grabbed the new opportunities for growth emerging in export promotion and joint venture development. From 1990 to 1991 industrial employment increased by 19.8 percent due primarily to growth in exports.

Fourth, the regional policy environment is conducive to export-led growth. Suzhou municipality, where Zhangjiagang is located, responded more rapidly to the coastal development strategy than any other part of Jiangsu province, and far more than almost any part of China. Much of Suzhou's industrial production comes from TVEs in its surrounding counties, so what is good for TVEs is good for Suzhou's total industrial output.[48] Zhangjiagang also has excellent ties to the provincial leadership. The current provincial vice-governor responsible for external economic relations was the party secretary of Suzhou in 1988 and had been party boss of Zhangjiagang in the 1960s. When some provincial officials criticized Zhangjiagang for establishing too many joint ventures in 1988, he responded by making them a provincial model for others to follow. Suzhou outstripped the entire province in establishing joint ventures, although as of 1988 it trailed Nanjing (the provincial capital) in terms of total direct foreign investment.

Finally, Zhangjiagang's location on the south side of the lower reaches of the Yangzi river helped its infrastructure. The city has expanded its harbor since the mid 1980s; as of 1991 it possessed the seventh busiest container harbor port in China. As the harbor for the booming cities of southern Jiangsu—Wuxi, Suzhou, and Changzhou—it has received significant provincial and central financial support.

MOBILIZING THE EXPORT-LED GROWTH

Under the prereform trade regime, Zhangjiagang had limited contact with the outside world. All exports passed through Jiangsu province's foreign trade corporations or those in Shanghai and Suzhou, making officials in Zhangjiagang dependent on foreign trade officials for information about export markets. The role of exports in the locality's economic development was not significant through the mid 1980s.

Zhangjiagang officials feared global interdependence. As of 1987, when foreign trade first expanded, 90 percent of local leaders feared the international market.[49] Several TVEs had been cheated by Hong Kong businessmen, and in 1988 a sudden shift away from Chinese sources by American purchasers of latex gloves caught Zhangjiagang with containers full of unmarketable products.[50] Therefore, they diversified, and by 1991 only 10 percent of local officials disliked direct foreign investment.

The domestic climate for export promotion changed in summer 1988. Party meetings in Suzhou empowered localities to approve foreign investment projects under $15 million without higher level approval. Thereafter, Zhangjiagang's first economic meeting in January of each year no longer focused on agricultural development; instead, the January meeting's main goal was to promote export-led growth. Between 1989 and 1991 this meeting distributed 200,000 RMB to TVEs that earned the most foreign exchange. In 1990 Zhangjiagang's foreign trade bureau gave firms earning over US $10 million from exports two million RMB in subsidies for electricity and supplied cotton and silk at the low planned price. In 1989 township leaders who met their quotas for exports and joint ventures were awarded 1,500 to 2,000 RMB, ten months salary for an average TVE worker, while those who failed to meet these quotas were passed over for promotions.[51] The number of joint ventures in Zhangjiagang increased dramatically. With only two in 1987, Zhangjiagang established twenty-nine in 1988, nineteen in 1989, sixteen in 1990, and forty-eight through October 1991. By mid 1992 they had signed over 300 joint ventures contracts, more than any other county in China.

While TVEs hold a comparative advantage in labor intensive products, Zhangjiagang officials believe that higher value-added products will bring prosperity even faster. As TVEs move up the technology ladder and their need for labor decreases, officials look to the day when they send back "guest workers" who currently build the roads and perform menial labor. As they expel outsiders, only the local population will share the spoils of economic development. No doubt, if labor intensive exports shift inland, the hinterland will also benefit. But in the words of one official: "We want to be the Second World; internal China can be the Third World."

THE IMPACT OF EXPORT-LED GROWTH ON ZHANGJIAGANG

As Zhangjiagang's links to the outside world deepened, significant changes followed. Exports became the engine of local growth. Whereas in 1986 exports were only 8.7 percent of GNP, by 1990 they jumped to 33 percent. According to local data, by 1991 one out of every two RMB produced in Zhangjiagang was exported, for an annual growth rate from 1984 to 1991 of 62.7 percent.[52] Similarly, per capita exports rose in the same period by 68.2 percent. Given that from 1984 to 1991 GNP increased yearly by 20.1 percent, exports were promoting local economic growth.

Exports and joint ventures strengthened the power of the local state over society. Some local party bosses used joint ventures and the challenges of international competition to tighten discipline of the work force. By attributing the tougher rules to the foreign partner, one township party secretary stopped peasants from resisting his new, harsher work regimen. The emergence of the export economy allowed Communist Party secretaries the legal right both to intervene in management and to meet directly with foreigners in their role as "chairman of the board" of the township economic committee. Moreover, some managers in these joint ventures are members of the township management committee. Rather than emerge as an autonomous force undermining party control, they reinforce the ruling power hierarchy.[53]

Export growth has expanded the local state bureaucracy involved in trade. The city's foreign trade company, an agent of the provincial foreign economic relations and trade bureau, was set up in 1987 with seventy-four employees. It purchases goods in Zhangjiagang for the provincial foreign trade companies who must meet the provincial foreign trade plan. In 1989 the city's foreign trade company began to seek unfilled export contracts allocated to other regions in China. As a result, the number of sales agents in the city company doubled to 144.

In 1988 Zhangjiagang also established a "local" foreign trade company with twenty-two employees whose main purpose was to find export contracts outside Jiangsu province and Shanghai for Zhangjiagang factories. Sales representatives from the local foreign trade company travel all over China looking for export quotas, particularly in textiles, that are not being used. Only by buying quotas can they expand exports. While in 1988 they purchased 22 million RMB of exported commodities, in 1989 they bought 36 million, and in 1990 they bought 89 million. Their projection for 1991 was 150 million RMB.

Numerous functional bureaucracies, not initially established to promote trade and investment, caught the joint venture fever. Since the former director of the TVE bureau became head of the foreign affairs office, the office no longer keeps foreigners at bay; it now aggressively seeks their investments. The Taiwan office, formerly involved in political struggles with Taiwan, now promotes Taiwanese investment. Similarly, the local branch of the China travel service is now a trade promotion organization.

The internationalization of the harbor in 1982 led to a major inflow of state investment. As an international port under the administration of the ministry of transportation, its amenities for local citizens improved significantly. By 1991 the central government had spent over 100 million RMB in the harbor area. According to the director of the harbor commission, the state built a middle school especially for the harbor, whose materials, facilities, and teachers are all better than other schools in this area. They built a new hospital for the sailors, directed by the best doctor in the region, and people from all over Zhangjiagang have operations done there.[54]

The harbor brought 4,000 new jobs to the region, many of which went to peasants from nearby villages. High school graduates in the county seat also get jobs here. The plan is to turn the former small, rural community of 12,000 people into a thriving harbor city of 200,000 with a "bonded" duty free zone full of new factories funded by units from all over China seeking cheap land, low local taxes, and other exemptions available in a bonded zone. A four-lane highway was built from the harbor to the county seat to facilitate communications, and a new highway now links Zhangjiagang to Suzhou, replacing a narrow, winding rural road.

Foreign trade and foreign investment have increased the level of technology in Zhangjiagang's factories. One township, whose exports grew from 1.38 million RMB in 1987 to over 137 million RMB by 1990, imported 30–40 million RMB of equipment in both 1989 and 1990 and 64 million RMB in 1991. Zhangjiagang imported equipment for a small steel plant and received export quotas for steel in 1991 worth $US 8 million, a major accomplishment for a rural community. Joint ventures were bringing in more medium level technology, while in 1991 local meetings promoted high tech in the TVE sector.

The shift to export production was popular because it expanded and stabilized the TVE sector. But attitudes varied, based on people's position in the division of labor.[55] The sales director for a joint venture knew that strict management and better products strengthened his market position, and since he worked on commission, increased sales meant more money in his pocket. He also favored domestic sales by joint ventures—a policy which threatened the domestic monopoly of SOEs—because the foreign manager promised him a new motorcycle if his sales department reached its quota. A technician in another factory reported that under the old system his factory could not produce high quality goods, so salaries were unstable. Clear lines of authority under the new management system eased his work. For most managers, salary increases that come with directing a joint venture are strong incentives. However, one Chinese comanager complained that the Communist Party committee, which was his "boss," took most of his salary.

Although a worker in an export factory admitted that it had taken him two years to adjust to stricter management, he applauded these innovations because it ensured factory jobs for himself and his wife and increased his monthly salary from 70–80 RMB in 1988 to almost 300 RMB in 1991. However, in one village which planned to turn all four of its TVEs into joint ventures, party leaders did not want workers who feared the stricter regimen to withdraw from the new joint ventures, so workers in the first TVE that became a joint venture were not allowed to change jobs even though the new management system was much tougher. A dissatisfied worker admitted that despite his anger at having his salary cut he could do nothing; all jobs in the village were controlled by the party secretary, and he could not work elsewhere.

Export-led growth affected relations between Zhangjiagang and more distant communities. "Guest workers" from northern Jiangsu live on boats along the northern coast of the community and reclaim river beds for Zhangjiagang peasants to plant. In export factories, workers hired as cheap labor from Anhui, Sichuan, and Jiangxi provinces live in dormitories and work for the local community. Income gaps between these outsiders and community insiders living in two and three story homes remain points of social tension.

Income disparities within the province were growing as well. If one compares exports in Zhangjiagang with those in Nantong municipality and its key county, Nantong county, situated on the north side of the Yangzi river directly across from Zhangjiagang, the pace of growth, while also strong, has been dwarfed by the growth in Zhangjiagang. In 1984 Nantong municipality exported thirteen times the value of goods as Zhangjiagang; by 1991 Nantong exported only 72 percent more goods than its much smaller competitor across the river. Exports from Nantong had not slowed: from 1984 to 1991 annual growth in foreign trade for Nantong municipality was 21.5 percent. However, for Zhangjiagang it was an amazing 62.7 percent.[56] Nantong's GNP was also less closely integrated into the international market. Even after it was named an "open" coastal city in 1985, its exports as a percent of GNP remained approximately 15 percent and only in 1991 increased to 21 percent. Similarly, while Nantong county's exports jumped in 1984 and boomed again in 1988, the pace of growth, though impressive, was dwarfed by Zhangjiagang. While annual growth in exports in Nantong county from 1984 to 1991 was 24.6 percent and from 1988 to 1991 was 28.9 percent, in Zhangjiagang it was 62.8 percent from 1984 to 1991 and 37.1 percent from 1988 to 1991.

JOINT VENTURES, RENT SEEKING, AND THE ALLIANCE WITH FOREIGN CAPITAL

Because channels to the international system are critical for community development, Zhangjiagang has become a "linkage community" through which foreigners access China's domestic market on more favorable terms than the central state would prefer.[57] According to national policy, joint ventures get special tax privileges (three tax free years, two years with half taxes) only if the export 70 percent of production. Yet of eleven joint ventures visited in Zhangjiagang, five offered foreign partners the chance to sell 50 percent or more of their products domestically. And when challenged about the joint venture law, some local factory managers suggested they would find ways around it, insuring the joint venture both tax breaks and access to the domestic market.

Zhangjiagang officials are chasing two types of rents. The first is the rent that the provincial foreign trade company earns through its monopsony on foreign trade. The second involves sale of joint venture products which are in high demand in the domestic economy but whose importation is restricted by tariff barriers. Producers of these goods earn large profits in the domestic economy because the limited competition, due to import constraints, inflates the prices of these goods in the domestic market.

Rent Seeking in the Export Sector

Despite the decentralization of central controls over foreign trade, most TVEs must export through state-run foreign trade companies, which keep TVEs in the dark as to the international price of their product.[58] The rent the foreign trade company earns is the difference between the domestic price, which they may force down, and the international price, to which only they have access due to the limited market in export licenses.[59]

Local elites in Zhangjiagang try to bypass the foreign trade companies by establishing direct export channels through joint ventures. Some are simply nominal joint ventures. In one case of a joint venture with an overseas Chinese from the United States, the foreign partner played no role. He was a front for the joint venture, for which he receives a salary. But this joint venture allowed the Chinese director to export through his own contacts. In another case, a foreign businesswoman was invited to set up a joint venture with a tablecloth factory. The Chinese partner admitted that they wanted to circumvent the foreign trade corporation's controls, believing that their prices were more competitive than those offered for their products by the trading company. . . .

Rent Seeking in the Domestic Market

A second form of rent seeking derives from the mixed marketplace nature of the foreign trade system. In its efforts to limit imports, the Chinese state has imposed tariffs or import licenses to prevent the importation of producer goods, such as high conductivity copper wires, valves, or similar products which are in high demand as China tries to produce export quality machinery. The result is scarcity in the domestic market, making the domestic price, PD, higher than the international price, PW.[61] But the central government's desire for direct foreign investment creates channels for foreigners and TVEs to access these rents. With foreign technology and foreign management, workers in TVE joint ventures can produce high quality products. And while production costs may be too high for the international market, import restrictions make the quality and price of these goods so competitive in the domestic market that some Chinese believed that, even if they exported 70 percent of their production at a loss, they could still make a profit by selling 30 percent of their product domestically.

This "rent seeking" is part of Zhangjiagang's overall development strategy, for while trade restrictions prevent other regions of China from importing these products, joint ventures let /z make these high profits. According to one joint venture Chinese manager:

> Next year we will begin to sell about 20–30 percent of our product domestically. The foreign partner raised this, and we agreed. If we sell domestically, Chinese factories will know that their domestic costs are too high. When we began this business, we saw from our own firm's perspective there was a domestic market, so we decided to import to do the domestic market. . . . The state gets burned, ut it is good for our firm.

THE DOMESTIC IMPACT OF TRADE AND FOREIGN INVESTMENT: LESSONS FROM CHINA

Our three models addressed several core issues and generated competing hypotheses about them. Focusing on the forces favoring collective action, the literature on international political economy suggests that foreign trade, with its diverse impact on industrial sectors, will generate domestic alliances which lobby for preferred policy outcomes. Our study, however, shows that no collective action was generated at the macro level. The state had to mobilize the rural areas, even though their labor surplus gave them an important comparative advantage in foreign trade. Why? First, when markets are comprised o many small producers, firms are ill-equipped to promote their collective interests.[62] Individual costs are too high, and in the case of China peasants are poorly represented in Beijing by one weak functional ministry—the ministry of agriculture—that confronts dozens of well-placed functional and line ministries lobbying for urban and industrial interests. However, once the state changed the countryside's incentive structure, allowing it access to foreign exchange and technology, rural leaders responded.

Then community leaders displayed the capacity for collective action, including an alliance with foreign capital, as they sought to promote community interests. Perhaps the "rents" themselves, and the high costs of market entry, galvanized this collective behavior.[63] Thus, only the combined efforts of the county government, its trading companies (which must find foreign investors, export quotas, domestic markets, and foreign technology), and local enterprises controlled by township officials could generate the products, relationships, administrative protection, and information necessary to access the rents and to successfully implement local export-led growth. While the literature on international political economy asserts that private firms and the central state are the critical actors in successful "developmentalism," intermediate levels such a the community, below the central or provincial administration and above the firm, may be an equally, if not more, useful level of analysis in understanding how foreign trade generates collective action and how a large state successfully employs a strategy of "export-led growth." These communities may be China's "autonomous centers" of economic power that suppress social demand, increase savings, and promote growth.[64] Thus, late developers need not rely solely on the central state or greater centralization of resources to grow and compete in foreign trade; export-led growth combined with decentralization may propel local communities, which control their own enterprises, to promote their own interests and in turn increase national wealth. Despite Migdal's concerns, local "bosses" may not be counterproductive to economic development.[65] In fact, given the right incentives and organizational skills, local governments can be the driving force of export-led growth.

Totally different hypotheses about the impact of foreign trade and investment on growth and equality emerge from the dependency and East Asian models. The former predicted rural poverty and urban-rural inequality, while the latter predicted growth and perhaps greater equality. Our case shows that foreign trade can be enormously beneficial to rural areas, particularly those possessing a basic industrial structure or the capability to build one. Whereas nonindustrial hinterlands simply ship out their resources, in an industrialized countryside the added value is passed on to the community (and its leaders), and with it the possibility of technologically improving its industrial structure. The alliance with foreign capital thereby strengthens the countryside in its battle with urban workers and increases urban-rural equality.

Nevertheless, foreign trade and foreign investment can exacerbate regional inequalities. Spatial factors or endowments, such as good harbors or proximity to industrialized neighbors, which bring only limited financial benefits under a policy of economic autarky, become enormously valuable under export-led growth. Also, the pattern by which new foreign resources—technology, foreign investment, and information—enter the country affects development and quality, especially if the state allocates them first to certain sectors of localities.[66] The granting of legal "exemptions" from restrictive domestic laws—such a tax breaks or cheap, subsidized land prices for joint ventures—to special localities, such as "special economic zones" or "development zones," endows these localities with enormous "powers of attraction," making them not only the locus of foreign investment, but also the end point of investment by domestic enterprises seeking tax relief.[67] Imbued with all these benefits, as well as family networks to overseas investors, the coastal areas in China are far better situated for export-led growth than inland China.[68]

Whether local economies in China's rural hinterland are growing more slowly or are regressing is crucial. As Hirschman's tunnel metaphor suggests, people will tolerate being in a slower lane, but their situation becomes intolerable if their lane stops.[69] Most data suggest that inland areas are growing, but more slowly than coastal areas, and if estimates of the 60–100 million people in China's floating population are correct, their remittances may be an important source of investment for the rural hinterland. No doubt, this migrant labor creates a cash nexus between inland and coastal communities that allows coastal communities to reap the benefits of cheap labor. As controllers of export channels, they also benefit from the new imported technology that produces higher value-added goods. However, internal regions of a country can also be opened. The current phase of China's open policy—the expansion of roads and harbors up and down the Yangzi River, which runs through the heartland of China much like the Mississippi and the Ohio rivers—should decrease the transaction costs of foreign trade for several hundred million people. They, too, may benefit from export-led growth. But even if only the coastal areas grow dramatically, we are still talking about export-led growth's improving the lives of another 200–300 million people in East Asia, more than the population of Indonesia and perhaps double the population of Japan.

Finally, what is the relationship among foreign trade, foreign investment, and democracy? Both the literature on international political economy and the East Asia model suggest that foreign trade and growth can generate political liberalization, while the dependency model sees bureaucratic authoritarianism as a part of export-led growth. Yet in the Chinese case both processes may be at work, albeit at different levels. While foreign investment may strengthen village or community authoritarianism, these strengthened communities become more powerful vis-à-vis the central state's own institutions.

Thus, while peasant autonomy from the local party-state expanded under China's decollectivization, the export economy strengthens local party control over rural society. Moreover, few foreign investors are demanding increased rural democracy. Nor has industrialization triggered the growth of a private sector demanding greater pluralism. In 1989–90, local governments responded to central demands to constrain the growth of TVEs by closing private firms and protecting local state-owned ones.[70] Our findings, too, show that local controls over the inflow of new resources and the outflow of new products insure that most new opportunities created by the open policy are captured by the local state, not the private sector. Thus, it is no surprise to find that efforts by the ministry of civil affairs in China to introduce democratic procedures in the countryside confront stiffest opposition from wealthy, industrialized rural communities in coastal China.[71]

And even though developmental communities, with their economic power and international alliances, are undermining the central state's authority and its ability to mediate between the domestic and global economies, the weakening of the central state does not necessarily create democracy.[72] The strengthening of local community power creates a weaker center, struggling with increasingly ineffective tools to reign in powerful local party/state institutions that now draw more of their influence from global ties. No doubt, the lessons that an export-led strategy has taught China's rural elites about collective action may generate a more vocal and demanding populace, as the literature on international political economy would predict. Perhaps they will be a driving force in institutionalizing local representation of the center. But as long as formal access to central decision-making channels remains closed to subnational elites, developmental communities will pursue their interests in more parochial and economic ways, making the center increasingly superfluous.

NOTES

Thanks to Tom Bernstein, Margaret Pearson, and Dorothy Solinger for comments on the manuscript. Research was conducted in 1991–92 under a fellowship from the Committee on Scholarly Communication with China. Research arrangements were made by the Department of Foreign Students and Scholars, Nanjing University, the School of International Business, Nanjing University, and the foreign affairs offices of Jiangsu province, Zhangjiagang city, and Nantong municipality. The views expressed are the author's alone.

1. Fernando H. Cardoso and Enzo Faletto, *Dependency and Development in Latin America* (Berkeley: University of California Press, 1978).

2. See Norman Girvan, "Swallowing the IMF Medicine in the Seventies," in Charles K. Wilber, ed., *The Political Economy of Development and Underdevelopment,* 3rd ed. (New York: Random House, 1983), pp. 169–181.

3. Thomas E. Skidmore, "Politics and Economic Policy Making in Authoritarian Brazil, 1937–1971," in Alfred Stepan, ed., *Authoritarian Brazil: Origins, Policies, and Future* (New Haven: Yale University Press, 1973), pp. 24–25.

4. See Andre Gunder Frank, "The Development of Underdevelopment," *Monthly Review,* 18 (September 1966), 17–31.

5. Peter Evans, *Dependent Development: The Alliance of Multinational, State, and Local Capital in Brazil* (Princeton: Princeton University Press, 1979).

6. See Alice Amsden, *Asia's Next Giant: South Korea and Late Industrialization* (New York: Oxford University Pres, 1989); Robert Wade, *Governing the Market: Economic Theory and the Role of Government in East Asian Industrialization* (Princeton: Princeton University Press, 1990); and Chalmers Johnson, *MITI and the Japanese Miracle* (Stanford: Stanford University Press, 1982).

7. For the argument that growth depends on the private sector see Ziya Onis, "The Logic of the Developmental State," *Comparative Politics,* 24 (October 1991), 109–126.

8. Stephan Haggard, *Pathways from the Periphery* Ithaca: Cornell University Press, 1990).

9. Defined as "payments to owners of resources above what value would be in a market situation," "rents" are excess profits generated in a nonmarket situation because administrative controls prevent market entry by numerous firms whose competition would otherwise force down the price of the good. See Anne O. Krueger, "The Political Economy of the Rent-Seeking Society," *American Economic Review* (June 1974), 291–303.

10. Speare sees improvement in both rural and urban areas, although the countryside still lags behind the cities. Alden Speare, Jr., "Taiwan's Rural Populace: Brought In or Left Out of the Economic Miracle," in Denis Fred Simon and Michael Y. M. Kau, eds., *Taiwan: Beyond the Economic Miracle* (Armonk: M. E. Sharpe, 1992), pp. 211–233.

11. For the impact of external forces on economic structural change, see articles by Miles Kahler, Peter Evans, and John Waterbury in Stephen Haggard and Robert R. Kaufman, eds., *The Politics of Economic Adjustment* (Princeton: Princeton University Press, 1993). The seminal works on this subject are James R. Kurth, "The Political Consequences of the Product Cycle: Industrial History and Political Outcomes," *International Organization,* 33 (Winter 1979), 1–34; and Raymond Vernon, *Sovereignty at Bay* (New York: Basic Books, 1971).

12. Peter Gourevitch, "The Second Image Reversed: The International Sources of Domestic Politics," *International Organization,* 32 (Autumn 1978), 881–911.

13. Ronald Rogowski, *Commerce and Coalition: How Trade Affects Domestic Political Alignments* (Princeton: Princeton University Press, 1989).

14. Helen V. Milner, *Resisting Protectionism: Global Industries and the Politics of International Trade* (Princeton: Princeton University Press, 1988).

15. The most ardent advocate of this perspective is Yun-Wing Sung, "Exploring China's Export Drive: The Only Success among Command Economies," Hong Kong Institute of Asia-Pacific Studies, Occasional Paper No. 5, May 1991. While Sung attributed China's success to the role of Hong Kong, similar successes in central coastal China, such as the provinces of Zhejiang and Jiangsu, suggest that something internal to China and more generic than simply Hong Kong must form part of a complete explanation.

16. I borrow the concept of "development community" from Chalmers Johnson, who first characterized Japan as a "development state." See Johnson, p. 10.

17. Townships are the current name for the former "people's communes," established in 1958 during the Great Leap Forward, while in today's parlance villages refer primarily to multivillage units, the former Maoist "production brigades." For an analysis of these enterprises, see William A. Byrd and Lin Qinsong, eds., *China's Rural Industry: Structure, Development, and Reform* (Oxford: Oxford University Press, 1990).

18. Despite central state efforts since the early 1960s to suppress TVEs, they have flourished. See David Zweig, "Rural Industry: Constraining the Leading Growth Sector in China's Economy," in Joint Economic Committee of the U.S. Congress, *China's Economic Dilemmas in the 1990s: The Problems of Reforms, Modernization, and Interdependence* (Armonk: M. E. Sharpe, 1993), pp. 418–436.

19. The classic study of modes of "linkages" between the external and internal world in Karl Deutsch, "External Influences on the Internal Behavior of States," in Barry R. Farrell, ed., *Approaches to Comparative and International Politics* (Evanston: Northwestern University Press, 1966). For a more contemporary analysis, see Barbara Stallings, "International Influence on Economic Policy Debt, Stabilization, and Structural Reform," in Haggard and Kaufman, eds., pp. 41–88.

20. Using foreign technology, joint ventures create producer goods (or high quality consumer goods) necessary for China's modernization. But because China limits imports of many of these goods, keeping domestic prices artificially high, manufacturers of these products have short-term monopolies in the domestic market and receive the higher prices that monopolies create.

21. For a detailed discussion of the prereform foreign trade system, see Nicholas R. Lardy, *Foreign Trade and Economic Reform in China, 1978–1990* (New York: Cambridge University Press, 1992), ch. 2.

22. Barry Naughton, "The Pattern and Legacy of Economic Growth in the Mao Era," in Kenneth Lieberthal, Joyce Kallgren, Roderick MacFarquhar, and Fredrick Wakeman, eds., *Perspectives on Modern China: Four Anniversaries* (armonk, M. E. Sharpe, 1991), pp. 233–234.

23. An excellent discussion of China's process of opening is Jude Howell, *China Opens Its Doors: The Politics of Economic Transition* (Boulder: Lynne Rienner Publishers, 1993).

24. See *Foreign Broadcast Information Service, China Daily Report,* Mar. 9, 1992, p. 42.

25. This discussion of the foreign trade reforms draws heavily on Lardy, p. 44.

26. Partial reforms in Communist systems involve the coexistence of planning and market mechanisms, continued bureaucratic interference, mixed property rights, as well as "soft budget constraints" for firms. Decentralization often shifts controls to lower levels of the bureaucracy rather than to the production units. See Janos Kornai, "Hard and Soft Budget Constraints," in Janos Kornai, *Contradictions and Dilemmas: Studies on the Socialist Economy and Society* (Cambridge, Mass: MIT Press, 1986); David Zweig, "Dilemmas of Partial Reforms: State and Collective Firms versus the Rural Private Sector," in Bruce Reynolds, ed., *China's Economic Reforms* (New York: Paragon Publishers, 1988), pp. 13–39; and Christine P. W. Wong, "Between Plan and Market: The Role of the Local Sector in Post-Mao China," *Journal of Comparative Economics,* 11 (1987), 385–398. Vestiges of the planned system increase the value of personal relations as a grease in facilitating transactions and exchanges. See Dorothy J. solinger, *China's Transition from Socialism* (Armonk: M. E. Sharpe, 1993), pp. 107–126.

27. In 1985, then premier Zhao Ziyang called on rural China to turn its agricultural produce into exportable industrial products. But outside Guangdong province near Hong Kong, the effort was minimal at both the national and local levels.

28. In 1987, only 14.3 percent of all direct exports by TVEs throughout China did not pass through channels controlled by the ministry of foreign economic relations and trade (MOFERT). The data was calculated from *Xiangzhen qiye nian jian, 1978–1987* (township and Village Enterprises Yearbook, 1978–1987) (Beijing: Nongye chuban she, 1989), pp. 616–17.

29. Byrd and Lin, eds., *China's Rural Industry.*

30. *Xinhua Overseas News Service* (Beijing), Oct. 4, 1992.

31. Joseph Fewsmith, *Dilemmas of Reform in China: Political Conflict and Economic Debate* (Armonk: M. E. Sharpe, 1994), pp. 214–217. Shirk argues that provincial leaders or domestic interests have been the key to reform, while Solinger argues that central leaders are. See Susan Shirk, *The Political Logic of Economic Reform in China* (Berkeley: University of California Press, 1993), pp. 111–115; and Dorothy J. Solinger, *From Lathes to Looms: China's Industrial Policy in Comparative Perspective, 1979–1982* (Stanford: Stanford University Press, 1991).

32. According to Rawski, growth in China's exports since 1985 was due more to TVEs and foreign-funded enterprises than to state-owned industries. Thomas Rawski, "Export Performance of China's State Industries," unpublished manuscript.

33. Zhang Bolin and Tao Pengde, "Fazhan waixiangxing xiangzhen qiye de jige wenti," [Several Questions on Developing Outward-Oriented TVEs], *Zhongguo xiangzhen qiye lilun yu shijian* [Theory and Practice in China's TVEs], 1–2 (1990), 30.

34. Dali Yang, "China Adjusts to the World Economy: The Political Economy of China's Coastal Development Strategy," *Pacific Affairs,* 64 (Spring 1991), 42–64.

35. "Yinfa 'guanyu tuidong xiangzhen qiye chukou chuanhui rougan zhengce de guiding' de tongzhi" [Notification about the Rules on Some Policies to Promote Township and Village Enterprises to Export and Earn Foreign Exchange], in *Xiangzhen qiye nianjian, 1989* (Township and Village Enterprise Yearbook, 1989 (Beijing: Nongye chuban she, 1989), pp. 140–141.

36. Luo Xiaopeng, "Ownership and Status Stratification," in Byrd and Lin, eds., pp. 134–171.

37. David Zweig, "Internationalizing China's Countryside: The Political Economy of Exports from Rural Industry," *China Quarterly,* 128 (December 1991), 716–741. Even under Deng, "campaign-like" mobilization remains the tried and true method for obtaining economic policy compliance. See Tyrene White, "Postrevolutionary Mobilization in China: The One-Child Policy Reconsidered," *World Politics,* 43 (October 1990), 53–76.

38. *Foreign Broadcast Information Service, China Daily Report,* Mar. 9, 1992, p. 42.

39. See Anthony Leeds, "Locality Power in Relation to Supralocal Power Institution," in Aidan Southall, ed., *Urban Anthropology: Cross-Cultural Studies of Urbanization* (New York: Oxford University Press, 1973), pp. 15–41. For an application of this model to China, See Solinger, *China's Transition from Socialism,* p. 206.

40. See Zheng Hongyi, *Gangkou chengshi tansuo* [An Analysis of Harbor Cities] (Nanjing: Hehai daxue chubanshe, 1991).

41. Wade and White see the emergence of "developmental states" as "a process in which states have played a strategic role in taming domestic and international market forces and harnessing them to a national economic interest." In this case the local state harnesses domestic and international forces, both market and planned, to advance community economic interests. See Gordon White and Robert Wade, "Developmental States and Markets in East Asia: An Introduction," in Gordon White, ed., *Development States in East Asia* (London: Macmillan, 1988).

42. See Jean C. Oi, "Fiscal Reform and the Economic Foundations of Local State Corporatism in China," *World Politics,* 45 (October 1992), 99–126.

43. According to one TVE manager who had established two joint ventures, "the Chinese government doesn't allow us to do business directly with the outside world, so we must find foreign partners. . . . I must have the right to send people out of China for business." Interview BBXG/1992.

44. According to researchers in the ministry of agriculture, 50 percent of rural joint ventures were fronts whose sole purpose was to gain the right to import cars. Personal interview, December 1991. New policies ended car import benefits to joint ventures in July 1994.

45. Vivienne Shue, *The Reach of the State* (Stanford: Stanford University Press, 1988).

46. For a similar phenomenon in southern China, see Anita Chan, Jonathan Unger, and Richard Madsen, *Chen Village* (Berkeley: University of California Press, 1993); and Helen Siu, "The Politics of Migration in a Market Town," in Ezra Vogel and Deborah Davis, eds., *Chinese Society on the Eve of Tiananmen* (Cambridge, Mass. Harvard Contemporary China Series, 1990), p. 61–84.

47. See Peter Evans, "The State as Problem and Solution: Predation, Embedded Autonomy, and Structural Change," in Haggard and Kaufman, eds., p. 163.

48. In Deng's China, a locality's GNP is the key success indicator determining its leader's worth and promotions.

49. Interview with the local bureau of foreign economic relations and trade.

50. Zhangjiagang officials warned that, if foreign partners had too much control over imported equipment or materials, they could earn unfair profits. By investigating and consulting with foreign trade officials, these officials cut prices by 20 percent and saved $100,000. See Zhangjiagang City, Xizhang Town Economic Committee, "Banhao hezi qiye, gao hao waixiangxing jingji" (Run Joint Ventures Well, Develop the Foreign-Oriented Economy] *Jiangsu xiangzhen qiye* [Jiangsu TVEs], 3 (1991), 43–44.

51. The guidelines stipulated that in townships that exported 50 million RMB of goods, increased exports by 30 percent, and had one joint venture and per capita exports of 4,500 RMB, the township head and "the person making the contribution" would receive a bonus of 2,000 RMB. See *Jiangsu xiangzhen qiye* [Jiangsu TVEs], 5 (1989).

52. The ratio of exports to GNP is probably inflated as local exports in RMB are usually calculated in current prices while GNP is usually calculated in fixed prices, often based on 1980–81 prices. Personal communication from Nicholas P. Lardy, January 21, 1993. Whatever the exact ratio, exports became the engine of growth in Zhangjiagang.

53. For a comparison with managers in joint ventures in the urban sector, see Margaret Pearson, "Breaking the Bonds of 'Organized Dependence': Managers in China's Foreign Sector," *Studies in Comparative Communism,* 25 (March 1992), 57–77.

54. Interview with author, November 1991.

55. I was able to interview only two factory workers in private. One supported joint ventures, and one opposed them.

56. These data mirror Rawski's findings that after 1985 exports from SOEs grew at an average annual rate of 20 percent, a good record for developing countries. But this pace was dwarfed by the growth in TVE exports. See Rawski, "Export Performance."

57. Development Zones in the fourteen coastal cities also became "linkage communities." One zone director admitted that he encouraged foreign investors in his zone to sell domestically, even though they should have lost their tax free status. He needed their investments to pay for the zone's capital construction. Other counties, particularly in southern Jiangsu province, also tried to attract foreign investment by becoming "linkage communities."

58. In 1987 only 6.3 percent of direct TVE exports from Jiangsu province passed through channels not controlled by the ministry of foreign economic relations (MOFERT), compared with a national average of 14.3 percent. And while decentralization in foreign trade allowed 19.2 percent of TVE exports nationwide in 1989 to leave the country through non-MOFERT channels, only 8.7 percent of TVE exports from Jiangsu province passed through non-MOFERT channels, less than in any other major TVE exporting province.

59. According to David Dapice, "normal" trade companies charge competitive margins of 2–4 percent; anything more is rent. Personal conversation with the author. However, in China, FTCs are supposed to charge only 1–1.5 percent.

61. A similar problem emerged under Egypt's *infitah* or "open policy." The joint venture law allowed foreigners to establish import substitution firms, which earned high profits in a highly protected domestic market. See John Waterbury, "The 'Soft State' and the Open Door: Egypt's Experience with Economic Liberalization, 1974–1984," *Comparative Politics,* 18 (October 1985), 76.

62. Robert H. Bates, "Macropolitical Economy in the Field of Development," in James E. Alt and Kenneth Shepsle, eds., *Perspectives on Positive Political Economy* (New York: Cambridge University Press, 1990), pp. 41–43.

63. While I focused on the search for rents, Andrew Walder suggested that high entry costs into these new markets for the TVEs may have contributed to this collective action. Personal communication with the author.

64. Onis, "The Logic of the Development State."

65. See Joel Migdal, "Strong States, Weak States: Power and Accommodation," in Myron Weiner and Samuel Huntington, eds., *Understanding Political Development* (Boston: Little, Brown, 1987), pp. 391–434. While local governments may promote exports efficiently, weakened central control over imports and foreign loans complicates a state's balance of payments.

66. Universities that got World Bank loans developed much more quickly than those that did not. See Chen Changgui and David Zweig, "China's Higher Education and the Open Policy," paper presented at the Asian Studies Association National Meeting, Los Angeles, March 1993.

67. Under Egypt's *infitah,* special "open zones," with tax free status, changed incentives for domestic investors who demanded similar exemptions. Jeswald W. Salacuse, "Foreign Investment and Legislative Exceptions in Egypt: Needed Stimulus or New Capitulations," in Laurence O. Michalak and Jeswald W. Salacuse, eds., *Social Legislation in the Contemporary Middle East* (Berkeley: Institute of International Studies, University of California, 1986), pp. 241–261.

68. Overseas ties, a terrible liability in the Mao era, have become an important source of capital, status, and access to overseas travel. Yuen-fong Woon, "International Links and the Socioeconomic Development of Rural China: An Emigrant Community in Guangdong." *Modern China,* 16 (April 1990), 139–172.

69. Albert O. Hirschman, *The Strategy of Economic Development* (New Haven: Yale University Press, 1958).

70. See Susan H. Whiting, "The Comfort of the Collective: The Political Economy of Rural Enterprise in Shanghai," paper presented at the Annual Meeting of the Association for Asian Studies, Los Angeles, March 1983.

71. Lecture by Wang Zhenyao, Harvard University, March 3, 1994.

72. Thus, even without a capitalist class, foreign investors can find allies in a socialist system to help them undermine central efforts to control their activities. See Margaret Pearson, *Joint Ventures in the People's Republic of China* (Princeton: Princeton University Press, 1991).

Editor's Note: The original article was edited for publication here.

China's Urban Migrants—The Public Policy Challenge

Linda Wong

Since the mid-1980s, urban migrants have emerged as a new status group in Chinese society. Officially called *liudong renkou,* or floating population, the label is pinned on people who are not permanently registered in their current place of abode. Generally, such people have moved domicile over some distance, usually across a city or county, and are staying in a place on a temporary basis. Far from being a homogeneous group, the ranks include migrants, vagrants and even the *mangliu,* blind drifters who roam from place to place to seek their fortunes without any job offer or definite plans of survival.[1] The last few years have seen a growing number of migration studies published by Chinese and overseas authors. These have thrown valuable insight on, for instance, the pattern and character of population movements, their spatial distribution, migrant characteristics, causes, theories, problems and issues relating to migration. This study examines the complexity of urban migration from a fresh angle, that of public policy. As such, it does not set out to test any theoretical position. Rather the aim is to take an overview of the current situation, from the late 1980s to 1993, focusing on the challenge migrants pose to the state and civil society and the policy responses adopted so far. The paper first analyzes the problems and contributions brought by urban migrants. Second, using Guangdong as an example, it examines the measures adopted by state agencies and their effectiveness. The final section discusses the problems and prospects relating to urban migration. The paper concludes that public policy dealing with urban migrants is plainly inadequate. Urban migrants are still relegated to the margins of civil society. It is argued that unless their claims are recognized, urban migrants are likely to remain a thorn in governance and a threat to social stability.

Linda Wong, University Senior Lecturer, Department of Public and Social Administration, City Polytechnic of Hong Kong, "China's Urban Migrants—The Public Policy Challenge," *Pacific Affairs,* 1995: 335–355.

GENERAL BACKGROUND

Since 1958, the *hukou* (a household) system has functioned as the basis of public administration and determinant of living standards in socialist China. Under the Household Registration Regulations of 1958, every Chinese citizen is registered as a member of a *hukou,* a household. Urban dwellers are entitled to subsidised grain rations and other goods, work allocation by labour bureaux, subvented housing, social insurance, health care, and cultural and urban amenities provided at state expense. As such, urban household status has been closely linked to the state's rationing system of vital goods and services. Such practice is rapidly changing with the transition to market economy; for example, grain is no longer rationed. Besides, all births, deaths, marriages, even overnight visitors have to be reported to the local police, where the registers are kept. In this way, household registration abets public surveillance and law enforcement. In the countryside, the same rules apply. However, the rights that urbanites take for granted—guaranteed jobs, life tenure, access to services and the like—are denied to peasants. In the days of collective agriculture, commune members shared in whatever was produced locally but seldom enjoyed largesse from the state.[2] Apart from an egalitarian distribution of grain and collective income, and a system of basic education and health care, the range and quality of amenities available to peasants remained paltry.

Given the inferior conditions that exist in the countryside, a rush to the cities would be quite natural. This is what happens the world over. In China, however, this seemingly rational outlet was blocked until recently. Under the 1958 regulations, a change to nonagricultural household status (*nong zhuan fei*), though not impossible, in exceedingly difficult. Previously, even taking short trips required prior approval. In order to buy a train ticket or stay in a hotel, a traveller needed a letter from his work unit or rural authorities. Nor could one buy a meal in a restaurant if one forgot to bring one's ration tickets. Few could survive for long away from home. Consequently, the *hukou* system served as a means to control mobility and to prevent rural leakage into urban society. The net effect of such a policy was a more or less immobile population. In particular, rural to urban migration was virtually halted, except under the behest of the state.[3]

The economic reforms altered the social context and challenged this rigid rural and urban divide. The household responsibility system restored farm incentives and raised the efficiency of agriculture. Although agricultural diversification and the growth of rural industries and tertiary services yielded more jobs for peasants, the pressure of absorbing vast quantities of surplus rural workers was tremendous. At the same time, stopping peasants from responding to the gravitational pull of jobs and business outlets in towns and cities, especially places undergoing rapid growth, was no longer sensible. Thus in 1983, the state council allowed rural households, without changing their residence, to take up cooperative ventures in market towns. In 1984, peasants were officially permitted to work or do business in cities and towns provided they could raise their own funds, arrange their own food rations and find a place to live.[4] Even though peasants retain their rural status, setting up a new home in cities is no longer banned. Once such artificial barriers are removed, the floodgates of urban migration stand wide open.

In 1986, a survey of 74 cities and towns found that 3.6 percent of the population were temporary residents.[5] Shanghai city alone counted 1.83 million floaters and in Guangzhou, there were 880,000. In 1988, various estimates put the number of floaters at 50 to 70 million. Cities such as Beijing, Shanghai, Tianjin and Guangzhou all have over one million temporary residents.[6] Nightmare came in spring 1989. Within a period of two weeks, Guangdong province was flooded with 2.5 million floaters. Record numbers also poured into other big cities and towns. After 1989, the influx of roving transients became an annual event at the spring festival. In 1993, the opening up of Pudong district in Shanghai added another hot spot to the list of favoured destinations. Between 31 January and 1 February 1993, one million floaters invaded Shanghai, overtaking the record from Guangdong which had accepted the largest number of visitors in recent years.[7]

THE CHALLENGE OF PUBLIC POLICY

Urban administration in mainland China is a command structure presiding over a stable and immobile population. Municipal functions are organized on departmental lines but two mechanisms keep urban citizens subservient to state dictates. These are the ubiquitous presence of work units and neighborhood committees whose job it is to control employees and residents in such matters as work, welfare, family planning, public security, neighbourly relations, disciplining of miscreants and mobilizing citizen support for state policies. Nowadays urban work units (*danweis*) have lost much of their power over employees. Likewise residents' organizations have become less relevant in directing community life than in their heydays during the Cultural Revolution. With their major allies much weakened, state agencies have to rely on more direct methods of administering civil society. The arrival of uninvited guests, some on short stay and many becoming de facto dwellers, threw planning and administration into a quandary. Even though state agencies can dismiss them as having no claim on municipal resources, such being restricted to bona fide residents, migrants created demands that could not be brushed aside.

State transport agencies, primarily rail and coach services, are usually the first hit. Handling passengers many times their normal capacity, facilities are stretched to breaking points. For example, Beijing Rail Station was originally built to handle 50,000 passengers a day. In most days now, the average daily load is 170,000; at peak periods, 220,000 to 250,000. Faced with insatiable demands for services, severe overcrowding, delays and disorder are unavoidable. Another problem was revealed in Spring 1993. Between 27 January and 4 February, the railroads carried some 3.3 million passengers each day. To find extra capacity, freight transport was cut, holding up some 1,640 freight trains nationwide.[8] As a result, huge quantities of perishable goods rotted by the roadside.

Migrants aggravate the general shortage of transport facilities which routinely plague most Chinese cities. This fact was borne out by a 1987 survey on twenty-five cities which had over one million population. for their regular residents, these cities could attain only a per capita road space of 3.91 sq. metres and 6.77 public buses per 10,000 persons. With the addition of transients, the ratios dropped to 3.26 sq. metres and 5.64 buses respectively. This compounded the urban malaise of overpacked buses, reduced car speed and worsened traffic congestion.[9]

Besides transport, floaters, including tourists and people at meetings, consume massive amounts of goods and services. According to official estimates, an increase of every 100,000 visitors in a big city requires 50,000 kg of food grain, 50,000 kg of vegetables, 100,000 kilowatts of electricity, 24,000 kg of water and 730 public buses. At the same time, they also produce 100,000 kg of garbage and 2,300 kg of waste and sewage. It costs a big city an extra 60 million yuan per year to clean up the refuse left by visitors and migrants.

Other equally daunting problems include challenges to policies on employment, housing, law and order, family planning and relief.

The major reason for urban migration is the search for employment. In cities, work allocation by labour bureaux under the state plan used to be the only means of finding work. By the early to mid-1980s, self-employment and open recruitment by enterprises became commonplace. On the one hand, this meant more choice for job seekers and on the other, much-needed autonomy for work units. Nevertheless, employment creation relies heavily on state investment. Every year, some seven million urban school leavers join the job market, and labour departments have their hands full placing new entrants.[10] Although migrants do not qualify for work assignments, their presence causes labour bureaux additional work in planning and coordinating the use of import labour and regulating those who arrive unannounced. It also exposes them to charges of incompetence from urban residents who worry that newcomers will take their jobs and pull down wages. Such anxieties may be unfounded as migrants rarely compete for the same jobs with urbanites. Indeed they are ready to accept the dirtiest and lowest paid work that urban dwellers do not want and they are also likely to become self-employed, making life more convenient for city dwellers.

Shortage of housing is another predicament. Thirty years of underinvestment in urban construction has left Chinese cities notoriously short of decent dwellings for permanent residents. The deluge of poor homeless transients aggravates the crisis. As few can afford a bed in a hotel or guest house; many sleep rough. Some erect tents and shacks in twilight zones around cities while others rent private rooms from farmers in suburban areas. Very often, such accommodation is decrepit, overcrowded, lacking in basic amenities and is a menace to public health. One telling sign is that outbreaks of infectious diseases such as malaria and polio, which had hitherto been eradicated from city areas, have resurfaced recently.[11] Quite often, such problems are blamed on the habits of rural migrants rather than existing gaps in infrastructures.

Vagrants without jobs and other means of livelihood can be a threat to law and order. They are said to be responsible for between one-third to 70 percent of all criminal activities in Chinese cities, with offences ranging from theft, robbery, prostitution, to drug peddling, extortion and murder.[12] Again, most of the blame for the rising crime wave is pinned on the transients. Whether this is true or exaggerated is hard to tell. Nevertheless, the image of the floater as potential criminal breeds fear among city dwellers. This in turn rationalizes the prejudice of the receiving communities against them.

Another concern is that migrants have too many children. China's draconian population-planning policy tries to limit urban families to having only one child and rural couples two. Communes, urban work units and city neighbourhoods have been the main instruments of policy enforcement. When communes vanish, rural governments are less capable of enforcing this stricture, and migrants away from home escape this control.[13] Neither do they come under the power of work units and neighbourhoods. More significantly, 70 percent of city migrants are in the most fertile ge group (sixteen to thirty-five). According to official estimates, most of the unplanned births in cities are attributed to temporary residents.[14] Such hysterical labels as "above-plan birth guerrillas" or "corps that break the birth control policy" underscore state worry over unbridled fertility as well as the state's failure to manage the problem.

To rid cities of transients who become a public burden, the state has a policy of returning destitute vagrants to their native place. Before this is done, civil affairs departments have the job of running relief, reception and despatch facilities for them. They also provide re-education for mendicants, "professional beggars" and arrested prostitutes. Because of the sheer number of clients and small agency budgets, welfare centres are simply overwhelmed. Many repeatedly turn back the moment they are sent on their way. Some service recipients, unlike their predecessors who were genuine victims and were grateful for any help given, are unruly and hard to discipline. According to interviews with welfare officials in Guangdong, working with prostitutes is especially frustrating because most are willing operators and resistant to rehabilitation. Some regard their detention as a temporary respite or even look forward to being schooled by veteran sisters.[15] The difficulty of changing the behaviour of clients embracing a different value system should not surprise social workers. Counseling prostitutes to go straight, like taking up factory or service work, after earning easy money from the skin trade can be a futile business.[16]

Such problems, however, are only a part of social reality. Indeed, migrants make positive contributions to their home and host communities. At places of emigration, labour export is a good way of tackling rural unemployment, boosting local income from home remittances, and developing backward economies through the infusion of capital, skills, markets and management know-how. At the same time, areas that receive these migrants benefit a great deal. First, they fill job vacancies such as those involving cleaning, construction, weaving, textiles and nursemaids—the kinds of jobs that urbanites abhor. By taking such jobs, these rural migrants augment shortfalls in work places such as restaurants, guest houses and repair workshops. Second, they meet the manpower need in places undergoing rapid industrialization. Special economic zones and open cities could not grow as they did without their guest workers. In Shenzhen, for example, outside people greatly outnumber local inhabitants; in 1992, the special economic zone had two million temporary residents and eight hundred thousand permanent residents. Third, transients as consumers increase the demand for goods and services and thus the volume of economic activities. Their role in capitalization is all the more important because they pay for everything they need, rather than live off largesse from the state. Finally, their very presence helps to break down the schism that divides rural and urban society and the distance between different parts of the country. National integration is given a better chance when people actually mix and learn from each other.[17] Indeed, if newcomers are only liabilities to their hosts, their sufferance will be unimaginable. With this in mind, the dominance of negative stereotypes only makes sense against a perceived challenge to urban interests and the rigid pattern of governance.

MANAGEMENT STRATEGIES AND THEIR EFFICACY

The first step to cope with the migrant population was to introduce a system of registration for temporary residents. In July 1985, the Ministry of Public Security announced a set of temporary regulations. People visiting cities and town for three days or more are required to notify the local police. Outside visitors over age sixteen who intend to stay for more than three months have to obtain a temporary residence permit, *zanzhu zheng*. On 6 September 1985, the Twelfth Meeting of the Standing Committee of the Sixth National People's Congress promulgated the People's Republic of China Residents' Identity Card Regulations. These require all citizens over sixteen to apply for a personal identity card and empower the police to make identity checks. No doubt useful as a tool of law enforcement, the ID card is also a pass to mobility and business transaction. In place of a letter from one's work unit or village official, Chinese citizens can buy a rail ticket, check into a hotel, apply for a job or a business licence upon presenting this document.[18]

Since public administration has always been premised on a vigilant control of registered persons, the local authorities were completely unprepared to handle the arrival of masses of migrants. The best that could be hoped for was some sort of crisis management before more regular methods could be invented. In this regard, Guangdong presents a good case of early trials and subsequent routinization.

THE CASE OF GUANGDONG

When the reform started, Guangzhou played host to some 300,000 visitors per day (in 1980), mostly people on official business or visiting with relatives or friends. As early as 1982, the city's Public Security Bureau initiated regulations to register temporary residents. In 1985, daily visitors increased to 620,000; by 1988, to 1.17 million. The ratio of temporary residents to permanent residents increased from 1:10 to 1:2.77, the highest ratio in all China. At the end of 1992, the eight municipal districts of the city counted 1.6 million visitors, of which 1.34 million wee temporary residents and 0.26 million were tourists and people in transit.[19] For Guangdong as a whole, provincial officials estimated that there were 6 million migrants in 1993.

As said before, for Guangzhou and the rest of Guangdong province, anxiety turned into panic in the spring of 1989. The ferocity of the migrant invasion prompted immediate action from the provincial government.[20] On February 23, 1989, Governor Ye Xuanping chaired a telephone conference to work out plans to deal with the sudden surge of migrants. Emergency calls were made to the State Council and the provinces of Human, Sichuan, Guangxi and Henan to stop people from pouring into Guangdong. All work units within the province were forbidden to hire new outside labourers immediately. When current contracts expired, migrants could not be rehired. At the same time, work committees were set up in various cities and counties to send migrants back to their native place. Work teams were formed to expel new arrivals the moment they were found.

In the last few years, special squads made up of personnel from the municipal government, public security, transport, labour and civil affairs bureaux have mounted checkpoints along major routes during the peak arrival periods. All nonlocals who cannot produce the necessary papers—a temporary resident's permit, labour permit, work contract and ID card—are turned back on the spot. Dongguan city is particularly vigilant about such deterrence.[21]

After years of trial and error, Guangdong has greatly improved the methods of checking the seasonal migrant tides. Preparatory work usually begins well before Spring Festival. First of all, propaganda about the prohibition of unauthorized new labour is sent out via newspapers, radio and television within and outside Guangdong. Then, special committees responsible for handling the holiday inflows are set up to conduct on-site surveys to project the likely demand on transport services and deter potential newcomers. Such information permits the authorities, especially transport departments, to make realistic preparations. Additionally, Guangxi and Sichuan have also been persuaded to cooperate by not selling train tickets to any Guangdong-bound travellers who cannot produce a valid work permit or job contract.[22] At the same time, many big enterprises have started to book passages for their employees well in advance. The richer firms in the Pearl River Delta charter coaches for such trips. Nowadays, peak season congestion is still serious but not as nightmarish as before. Experience clearly helps. Another contributing factor is the changing pattern of arrivals. In Guangdong and elsewhere, migrant traffic occurs year round and is no longer restricted to the new year holidays.

Work related to migrants cut across many departments. To improve coordination, Guangzhou set up migrant management offices or committees (*wailai renkou guanli bangongshi/weiyuanhui*). In these, the local police play a leading role in registering the floaters and maintaining order. In suburban areas where the majority of newcomers stay in rented accommodation, private housing (mostly belonging to peasants) was placed under the supervision of the police and housing authorities. Landlords are asked to make sure that their tenants obey the law and keep public and private places clean.[23] In addition, they should make sure that married couples practice family planning, which will be discussed shortly.

Registering migrants is daunting work. As a first step, there must be accurate records on the number of newcomers and information about their plan of stay. Such statistics are usually hard to obtain. A survey conducted in December 1989 in Guangzhou found that 30 percent of migrant workers and 80 percent of short-stay visitors did not report their stay to the police as required under the law.[24]

Regarding the duration of stay, it was found that there were substantial changes before and after the reform. Before the reform, the typical visit was short; most left before three months had passed. In the early 1990s, 80 percent of floaters stayed for over three months. This is quite normal since employment contracts are usually for three years and farm leases, fifteen years.[25] It is a wild guess as to how many will eventually go home. In the Pearl River Delta, it is observed that many female guest workers go home to get married when they are in their early and mid-twenties. As far as the majority of guest workers are concerned, they are likely to stay as long as possible.[26] There are reports that many young women marry local men and settle down permanently. At the end of 1989, Dongguan City alone registered two thousand such marriages. In recent years, it is estimated that between eight and ten thousand female migrants in the delta region have married local men.[27] From my interviews with cadres and local residents, there is the view that outsiders are actually preferred over indigenous women for a number of reasons. First, many men find northern girls physically attractive. Second, some migrants are better educated than local women, and quite naturally, those with good education and skills are favoured. Finally, newcomers are not as demanding about such things as nuptial gifts, wedding banquets and furnishings for the new home. On the other hand, there are usually burdensome expectations coming after the marriage. Newly wedded wives often exert pressure on their husbands to remit money home, send for kith and kin later on and assist them in settling down.

Since most migrants enter the province to get work, control of employment practices is a priority. In 1982, seven government departments in Guangzhou issued a joint decree to the effect that this type of hiring could be allowed only with the approval of the county labour bureau and endorsement by the labour bureau and the municipal level. This did not appear to be too effective. Hence in 1986 the city government tightened the restrictions. From then on, state agencies, enterprises and army units were barred from taking on such employees directly without first submitting their manpower plans to the labour bureau for approval. A number of conditions govern the engagement of outsiders: they can take only those jobs that cannot be filled by local people; the work must be of a temporary nature; and employees must be over sixteen, healthy and in possession of a work permit from the county administration.[28] Still, such stipulations were not heeded by all enterprises. Some firms held on to their right over staff selection, dismissal and contract hiring as set out in the new labour regulations effective from October 1986. It was especially difficult to police the practice of nonstate units, in particular private firms and rural enterprises.

In order to strengthen the force of administrative orders, local authorities learnt that legally binding regulations were essential. In August 1988, Guangzhou promulgated its own Temporary Workers Management Regulations. The principle of hiring "within the city first and from the outside last" (*xian shinei, hou shiwai*) was to be strictly enforced. Now enterprises wishing to recruit out-of-town labourers must complete the necessary procedures in their local labour bureau, including the payment of management fees, and obtain work permits for such staff. Both parties must sign employment contracts that stipulate mutual rights and obligations. Within three days of signing on, the hiree has to apply for a temporary resident permit from the police on the strength of his temporary work permit. Penalties are also provided for enterprises which violate the requirements. Regular fines for offending units are set at twenty yuan per worker per day. In serious cases, more hefty fines will be imposed; in the worst scenario, private owners may have their business license revoked by the bureau of commerce. Two months later (October 1988), Zhuhai Special Economic Zone followed suit with its own set of regulations.

Prior approval from labour bureaux at city or county level had to be obtained before enterprises could do extraterritorial hiring.[29]

Erecting work barriers at the city level proved ineffective in deterring outside job-seekers, as the 1989 march on Guangdong showed. Semi-educated peasants from within the province and without would not heed obscure municipal rulings. What moved them was the affluence of the area, recounted by visitors' tales and press propaganda. After the battle at the Spring Festival, Guangdong found it imperative to lay down stiffer punishments in the 1990 Guangdong Temporary Regulations Governing Offences against Labour Recruitment Regulations.[30] Now enterprises will be fined 100 yuan a day for each peasant labourer hired from within the province if they failed to obtain permission from the county labour bureau. Illegal hiring of non-Guangdong natives (without prior approval from the provincial labour bureau) may result in fines of 300 yuan per worker per day. Fines are also slapped on firms that fail to sign employment contracts with temporary staff, do not pay management fees (to labour bureaux) or secretly put up job advertisements.

Apart from cash sanctions, other instruments are necessary. One helpful means is to organize labour imports in an orderly programme. In October 1991, Guangdong reached interregional labour exchange agreements with Sichuan, Hunan and Guangxi, from where the majority of Guangdong migrants hail. Another practice now is to prohibit "old" migrant workers who return from their annual home visits from bring in new job-seekers; offenders will have their contracts terminated.[31] In 1992, five more provinces (Guizhou, Jiangxi, Anhui, Henan and Hubei) exchanged labour coordination agreements with Guangdong. According to newspaper reports, these methods seemed to have worked. In 1992, migrant workers who entered Guangdong for the first time dropped 70 percent over the previous year; in spring 1993, the number further went down from 120,000 to 60,000.

In 1987, Guangzhou introduced birth control measures for married migrant workers. Temporary resident permits would only be issued to those who were certified by the birth planning agencies of their home counties as practicing contraception. Work units were forbidden to hire any married workers without a birth planning certificate and temporary resident permit. In 1989, a set of provincial regulations came into force. Nonresidents have to produce a birth planning certificate if they are married or a bachelor/spinster certificate issued by their home authorities if they want to apply for a job or obtain a temporary resident permit. Fenghe Cun, a village in the Haizhu District of Guangzhou, went even further. Nonresidents who do not have the required documents will not be allowed to live and work in the area. Above-plan pregnancies will result in dismissal if the woman refuses to have an abortion. Shenzhen's policies are equally tough. Without a birth planning certificate, an outsider cannot find work, operate a business, rent a room or get a driving licence. In addition, the

Special Economic Zone is very zealous in conducting identity checks, aliens unable to produce the plethora of papers—spinster certificate, birth planning certificate, border pass, temporary resident's permit, labourer's handbook— are to be taken into custody and eventually expelled.[32] According to frequent visitors to the city, such raids are common spectacles in the busy town centre.

Local measures were really not enough to address the problem of migration. On 9 September 1991, the State Council finally acted to approve the Floating Population birth Planning Management Regulations, which places such work on a firm legal footing. Coming into effect on 26 December 1991, the regulations give the State Population Planning Commission overall responsibility for birth control among floaters under active cooperation from local governments and all state agencies. Joint responsibility is now imposed on governments in the floater's place of permanent residence and current abode. The former has the job of issuing proof of birth planning while the latter performs the actual work of birth control, including education, inspection, supplying contraceptives and technical services, keeping up-to-date records and keeping the former informed of any changes of circumstances that have occurred. Before the newcomer can apply for work, temporary residence and a business licence, the newcomer must first hand in the home-issued birth control document to the birth planning office in the host area for verification and registration to obtain an inspection certificate. Without the new certificate, state agencies are forbidden to approve the relevant applications.[33]

The latest regulations address the problem of geographical and sectoral administration, which is extremely important in dealing with migrant matters. Clarification of roles and procedures is useful in removing ambiguities, plugging gaps and deterring evasion of duty. By including all fertile persons and not just married couples under it purview, the law reflects a more realistic approach to people's sexual behaviour and life styles. Nevertheless, the policy is obviously very difficult to implement. First, to be effective, state agencies must possess accurate data about the numbers and whereabouts of transients. At present, registration of migrants is far from universal. Many floaters, especially the *mangliu,* are far too mobile to come within the attention, not to say control,of the authorities. Second, interterritorial collaboration is particularly troublesome. For example, the exchange of information across long distances requires an inordinate amount of effort and cost, more so the task of sharing out expenses. Third, organisational barriers with the same locality cannot be easily overcome. Most places have not set up coordinating machineries with enough clout to effect interdepartmental cooperation. Indeed, the problem of fragmentation and autonomy of different functional and geographical systems (*tiaotiao kuaikuai*) is a major issue in Chinese politics and administration. In the area of population policy, these hurdles are even more formidable because the basis of management, milieu control, is destroyed when the link between resident right and physical abode is severed. Some places actually prefer not to know about birth transgressions by turning a blind eye to nonregistration or not permitting above-plan births to be registered. In many areas, success in enforcing family planning is one measure of cadre performance. Hiding such information from higher authorities is one way of escaping punishment.

In Guangzhou, the control of migrants who are found begging, working as underground prostitutes or who become mentally disturbed was authorized by municipal regulations decreed in 1985. They empower the police to round up such persons and turn them over to the civil affairs, health and judicial agencies for education, treatment, reform and repatriation. In 1987, tougher sanctions were imposed on vagrants who repeatedly defy repatriation orders, cheat money from people, withhold their true identity and become a public nuisance. Such persons were to be reeducated through labour (*laodong jiaoyu*) for a maximum period of five months. The implementation of the reception and despatch policy was divided between the public security and civil affairs bureaux. The police have the job of catching vagrants and deviants, investigating their backgrounds and providing escort. Civil affairs departments are responsible for direct supervision, providing education through labour and sending them home.[34]

It is widely acknowledged that the 1987 regulations are no longer adequate in supplying the policy framework for the relief and despatch programme. First of all, these do not provide clear definition of reception targets. As a result, the policemen on the ground rely on their own discretion to take people into reception or to let them loose. Second, with no power over intake, civil affairs bureaux at the receiving end of the process find it impossible to cope with the motley crowd sent by the police. As said before, many are tough customers and welfare officials find it exceedingly difficult to impose authority. In some reception and relief centres in Guangdong, civil affairs staff running the camp wear police uniforms. This does not fool their charges and the problem of authority is unresolved.

More intractable is the problem of resources. Both the police and civil affairs departments are understaffed and underfunded. Within the public security apparatus, there are no personnel specializing in vagrant policing. When the job of catching criminals is already too onerous, reception work naturally does not command priority. Because of the manpower stretch and worsening crime wave, some cities in the Pearl River Delta are bringing in armed police from outside Guangdong to do routine policing. In civil affairs departments, the shortage of money is even more acute. for most years, the entire civil affairs budget of the government averages some 1.6 percent of state spending.[35] The vagrant processing programme plays only a very small part in the administration of civil affairs, which covers duties such as dispensing relief and welfare services, registering marriages and societies, resettling and helping demobilized soldiers, fixing place names, mediating in territorial boundary disputes and running cemeteries and crematories. Manpower is likewise very short. Struggling under such restraints, both departments are not too zealous in tending to vagrants. Their experience teaches that the more people they process, the more money is required. More frustrating is the futility of the effort, which is very much like playing a cat-and-mouse game with determined clients straggling back the moment they are put on a train for home. Thus, in Guangzhou the number of vagrants taken into reception was a mere 6,449 against an estimated daily floating population of 914,220 in 1989.[36]

PROBLEMS AND PROSPECTS

Since 1949, China has been divided into two major classes—workers and peasants. As far as life styles and governance is concerned, the separation of the rural and urban masses makes China a country of two nations. The intrusion of peasants into urban society, alongside the emergence of new social strata such as the new rich, entrepreneurs and managers, adds diversity and complexity to the pre-existing class configuration. Despite the size of this influx, urban migrants take up a marginal position in Chinese society. Like new immigrants anywhere, integration with the host community is very difficult. Although not all migrants are country bumpkins and poorly educated, they are often much maligned and despised by urbanites who perceive them as competitors and a menace to the civil city life. Indeed their presence is not so much accepted as tolerated. Their welcome will last as long as their usefulness outweighs the troubles they bring.

From 1989 onwards, official and mass hysteria reached a crescendo around the spring festival. When the influxes became overwhelming, local authorities tried every means to stop their entry. In a way, new-year invaders are treated like unwanted cargo, to be dumped or shipped back to their place of origin as required. Some of the measure taken—like not selling train tickets to those without a work certificate, blocking carloads of new-arrivals and immediate repatriation—are o doubt desperate responses to desperate situations. Some of the local practices relating to birth control among temporary residents—like denying tenancies to people not carrying birth planning documents, terminating work contracts of female workers who become pregnant without authorization and requiring abortions of above-plan births—appear shaky on legal grounds and involve possible infringements of human rights. Similarly, banning recruitment of guest workers looks more rational on paper than during enforcement. It is virtually impossible to police the hiring behaviour of private firms as well as joint and rural enterprises. The most commonly used sanction, cash fines, may not be effective if bosses are bent on using cheap labour until they are found out or if violations are not reported in the first place. To state agencies and cadres straining under tight budgets, distancing themselves from the business of "non-belongers," such as turning a blind eye, allowing underreporting, or defining them as targets of some other departments, makes life a lot easier. Likewise, government planners will have a smaller headache when they serve only permanent residents. My interviews with officials in Guangdong confirm that the planning of new amenities such as housing, transport, education, health and welfare, does not take migrants into account. Under the circumstances, it is obvious that the faster the growth of the temporary population, the wider the gap will be between planned provision and eventual users.

Where social services are concerned, the claim of migrants is still not recognized; only permanent residents have the right to subsidized rations and public welfare. Denial of social entitlements means that temporary residents have to be as self-sufficient as possible in obtaining their daily requirements. In Guangzhou and Shenzhen, visitors can easily come across illicit structures or shanty towns built by immigrants from the same province. Such neighbourhoods are usually marked by their decrepit appearance, poor hygiene and lawlessness. It is said that even the police are reluctant to venture into such places. Temporary dwellers have likewise organized makeshift schools for their children, markets, abattoirs and day care. When communal catering becomes difficult, however, they have to turn to commercial provisions and pay market prices for goods and services. It is not uncommon for school and nurseries to charge higher tuition fees and one-off payments to replenish equipment and facilities from nonlocal parents. To the most affluent, this is not a problem, but the majority on low pay or irregular work may not be able to afford basic services for themselves and their families.

Migrants who are able to obtain regular work are more fortunate. Most, however, are engaged as temporary employees and do not enjoy job tenure. Many work under appalling conditions, in unsafe and poor working environments and with no protection against unreasonable working hours. The failure to address welfare needs of workers is often borne out by frequent and serious outbreaks of industrial accidents. In Guangdong, the latest tragedy took the form of a fire in a Shenzhen toy factory on 19 November 1993. In this incident, eighty-four workers died and thirty more were injured. According to newspaper reports, all were guest workers from outside Guangdong.[37] A very sad thing about this fire was that it was almost a repeat experience of what happened in a raincoat factory in Dongguan in 1991, when more than sixty workers burned to death. In both cases, the doors and windows of all workshops and staff dormitories were locked, under the pretext of preventing theft by the workforce. Needless to say, when a fire broke out, there was simply no escape.

It is not difficult to pin down the causes of such debacles. One is employer irresponsibility. Many enterprises where disasters occur are under joint or foreign ownership. The overseas owners concerned are plainly obsessed with maximizing output and cutting costs, to the complete disregard of work safety.

Another factor is the absence of laws and regulations on industrial safety. Some investors actually choose to operate in places without stringent rules so that they can get away with flagrant exploitation of their workers. Besides, employer objections to the setting up of trade unions and the lack of organization among migrant workers also mean that they are at the mercy of capitalists and managers.

Even if there are rules and regulations, however, their implementation cannot be assumed. Official laxity in enforcement is often caused by reluctance to upset employers, especially foreign bosses. Meanwhile, infringements can also be ignored through bribing officials. The Shenzhen factory fire is a good case. According to the investigation report completed by the All-China Federation of Trade Unions, the Hong Kong plant owner had paid HK$3,000 to obtain a fire safety pass without having to make the required installations. After the disaster, the fire department tried to recover the real certificate from the owner and replace it by a false document to cover up its misdeed. Another piece of evidence comes from a survey conducted by the Independent Commission Against Corruption, Hong Kong's anticorruption agency. In July 1993, the commission released the result of a survey of 162 Hong Kong firms which operate factories in mainland China. The respondents (fifty-eight firms) reported that they spent 3–5 percent of their business expenses on buying gifts and building relationships (*guanxi*).[38] My business informants also readily admit to such practices; illicit payment is either demanded by local cadres or offered to them. Often, such payments turn out to be much cheaper than following the rules.

So far, the central and local governments have not found a way to manage the migrant challenge. Existing policies and practices are haphazard, piecemeal and uncoordinated. No central agency exists to plan, administer and supervise work relating to the floating population. In the case of Guangdong, we have seen some valuable attempts to grapple with the problems. However, most measures are reactions to contingencies rather than long-term solutions. What's more, migrants are a very mobile group. What happened to Guangdong is now happening to Shanghai and other places undergoing fast economic growth. Unless the right to free movement is curtailed, people will flock to places where opportunities are more abundant. National policies rather than local ones are imperative in dealing with what is after all a national issue.

The migrant challenge is likely to grow with its numbers. The 1990 census recorded 21.35 million people as having left their permanent residence for more than one year. Another source counted 50 million people who had left their registered place for less than one year. This meant that in the early 1990s, one person out of sixteen was on the move. As far as one can tell, their ranks will sooner well than shrink as the pressure of surplus rural workers increases. Between now and the year 2000, a further 100 million farm workers may become redundant.[39] Indeed, agriculture in China has suffered a deep malaise in the last three years due to insufficient state investment, low farm prices, the worsening prices, shrinking farm acreage and heavy burdens imposed on peasants. These have produced much peasant hardship. Concurrently, the appeal of agriculture as an occupation has been significantly tarnished. In the last two years, the agony facing farmers and agriculture has commanded a good deal of official and academic attention and is well documented. Relating to migration, the implication is obvious. Unless improvements in the rural situation occur, the prospect of a hastened exodus from the countryside will loom larger than ever before.

Even within the urban industrial complex, the spectre of worsening unemployment is becoming more ominous. Currently, it is estimated that between 15 and 50 percent of urban employees are really not needed.[40] As state enterprises join the rush to become financially independent and shed excess staff, many urbanites will be forced to join the job chase. This will inflate the ranks of itinerant labourers.

To conclude, urban migration has many positive outcomes—for the exporting and receiving communities as well as the nation as a whole. That they have been depicted as a threat to urban society reflects the bias of the state which is unwilling to concede to the claims of such citizens and the vested interest of urban residents who fear a dilution of their old privileges. Nevertheless, from the angle of public administration, attention to the negative sides of migration is justified. Public policy is about problem solving. The current record of managing migrants is poor. For Chinese society and the state, shying away from the complex reality of urban migration and the rights of migrants can be very costly. Such a stance will be harder to sustain in the future, for as China goes further down the road to a market society, a free flow of capital, skills and labour is vital. Urban migrants are harbingers of these priceless assets and the sooner their rightful place is reckoned with, the better the chances for national integration and social stability.

NOTES

1. For an official definition of *liudong renkou,* see Zhang Qingwu, "Guanyu Renkou Qianyi Yu Liudong Renkou Gainian Wenti" (Population transference and the concept of the floating population), *Renkou Yanjiu* (Population Research), no. 3 (1988), p. 18. See also Dorothy Solinger, "China's Transients and the State: A Form of Civil Society?" (Hong Kong: Chinese University Press, 1991), p. 10. For definition of *mangliu,* see Lin Weiye, "Gaige Kaifang Yilai Guangdong Wailei Zanzhu Renkou De Xinqingkuang Ji Zhian Guanli Duice" (The new situation related to the non-indigenous temporary resident population and public security administration in Guangdong since the reform and open door), in *Renmin Daxue Fuyin Baokan Ziliao Shuangyuekan (Renkouxue)* (People's University of China Xerox Newspaper and Magazine Materials—Demography Bimonthly), no. 1 (1993), p. 82, see also *Yangcheng Wanbao,* 19 March 1993, p. 1.
2. For a discussion of social entitlements of urban residents, see Flemming Christiansen, "Social Division and Peasant Mobility in Mainland China: The Implications of the Hu-k'ou System," *Issues and Studies,* vol 26, no. 4 (April 1990), p. 23; also see *Xiandairen Bao* (Contemporary People Magazine), 25 April 1989, pp. 92–95. On welfare for

peasants, see W.I. Parish and M.K. Whyte, *Village and Family in Contemporary China* (Chicago: Chicago University Press, 1978), pp. 47–72. See also Vivienne Shue, *The Reach of the State—Sketches of the Chinese Body Politic* (Stanford: Stanford University Press, 1988), pp. 49 and 60.

3. Wen Lang Li, "Migration, Urbanization, and Regional Development: Toward a State Theory of Urban Growth in Mainland China," *Issues and Studies,* vol 28, no. 2 (February 1992), pp. 85–102.

4. Solinger, "China's Transients," p. 9; Judith Banister, "urban-rural Population Projections for China" (Washington, D.C.: U.S. Bureau of the Census, 1986), Center for International Research Staff paper, no. 15 (March 1986), p. 9. See also Jeffrey R. Taylor, "Rural Employment Trends and the Legacy of Surplus Labour, 1978–86," *The China Quarterly,* no. 116 (December 1988), p. 759.

5. Ma Xia and Wang Weizhi, "Zhongguo Chengzhen Renkou Qianyi Yu Chengzhenhua Yanjiu—Zhongguo 74 Chengzhen Renkou Qianyi Diaocha" (Transference of China's urban population and urbanization study—survey on 74 cities and towns in China), *Renkou Yanjiu* (Population Research), no. 2 (1988), p. 2. See also Wang Xiangming, "Renkou Qianyi He Liudong Dui Renkou Chengzhenhua Guocheng de Yingxiang" (The impact of residence transfer and migration flow on the process of urbanization), in Zhongguo Shehui Kexueyuan Renkou Yanjiusuo, ed., *Zhongguo Renkou Qianyi Yu Chengshihua Yanjiu* (Population transference and urbanization research in China) (Beijing: Beijing Jingji Xueyuan Chubanshe, 1988), p. 48.

6. On the floating population in Shanghai, see Chiang Chen-chang, "The Influx of Rural Labour into Mainland China's Major Cities," *Issues and Studies,* vol 25, no. 10 (October 1989), p. 66; see also "Chengshi Liudong Renkou Wenti Tantao" (Exploration on the urban floating population problem), *Shehui Kexue,* no. 2 (1990), p. 74. For Guangzhou migrant figures in 1988, see *Yangcheng Wanbao.* no. 2 (1990), p. 74. For Guangzhou migrant figures in 1988, see *Yangcheng Wanbao,* 9 January 1988, p. 1; see also Zhou Guangfu and Dang Xiaoqing, eds., *Zhongguo Renkou Guoqing* (Situation of the Chinese population) (Beijing: Zhongguo Renkou Chubanshe, 1990), p. 173. On national estimates of the floating population, see Zhang Qingwu, "Guanyu Renkou," p. 18; Zhou and Dang, *Zhongguo Renkou,* p. 172; *Beijing Review,* 20–26 March 1989, p. 7; *Economic Digest,* 9 April 1991, p. 1; and Alan Liu, "Economic Reform, Mobility Strategies and National Integration in China," *Asian Survey,* vol. 31, no. 5 (May 1991), p. 393. On floating populations in big cities, see Chiang, "Influx of Rural Labour"; *The Nineties* (April 1989),p. 55; and *Yangcheng Wanbao,* 11 May 1988, p. 1.

7. On the 1989 migrant wave, see *The Nineties* (April 1989), p. 53; *Nangfang Ribao,* 2 March 1989, p. 1; *Yangcheng Wanbao,* 1 March 1989,p. 1; *Beijing Review,* 20–26 March 1989, p. 7. for subsequent migrant influxes in the spring holidays, see *Yangcheng Wanbao,* 16 February 1990, p. 1; 18 February 1990, p. 1 and 22 February 1991, p. 1. See also *Nanfang Ribao,* 22 February 1991, p. 1; *Ming Pao,* 13 February 1992, p. 1, and 14 February 1992, p. 1; and *Yangcheng Wanbao,* 19 March 1992, p. 1. On the migrant rush to Shanghai in 1993, see *Outlook Weekly,* 22 February 1993, pp. 6–7. According to the rail authorities in Shanghai, there were 620,000 migrant labourers arriving at the city on 1 February 1993 and 640,000 on 2 February 1993. Such numbers exceeded the total labour demand at Pudong district (500,000–600,000) by two fold.

8. Hou Jianzhang, "Meitian 140 Wan—Beijing De Liudong Zanzhu Renkou" (1.4 million a day—Beijing's floating and temporary population), *Chengshi Wenti* (Urban Issues), no. 6 (1992), p. 6; and *Outlook Weekly,* 22 February 1993, p. 6.

9. Li Mengbai and Hu Xin, eds., *Liudong Renkou Dui Dachangshi Fazhan De Yingxiang Ji Duice* (The impact of population mobility on the growth of big cities and policy response) (Beijing: Jingji Ribao Chubanshe, 1991), pp. 63 and 71.

10. Xia Jizhi and Dang Xiaojie, eds. *Zhongguo De Jiuye Yu Shiye* (Employment and unemployment in China) (Beijing: Zhongguo Laodong Chubanshe, 1991), p. 31. See also Zhang Zhiguang, Mu Guangzhong et al., eds. *Chaoyue De Tudi—Ernan Jingji De Zhongguo Renkou Wenti* (Insufficient land—the dual economic dilemma of China's population) (Shenyang: Shenyang Chubanshe, 1989), p. 66; and *Outlook Weekly,* 22 February 1993, p. 3.

11. *Yangcheng Wanbao,* 27 May 1991, p. 1.

12. *Beijing Review,* 20–26 March 1989, p. 7. Various other publications alleged that the floating population were responsible for a major proportion of criminal activities in the country: half of all criminals and crime committed in Guangzhou in 1987 (*Yangcheng Wanbao,* 11 May 1988, p. 1); one third of all criminals (*Bai Shing,* 16 June 1989, p. 46); 31.4 percent of criminals in Shanghai, 57.9 percent of criminals in Guangzhou, 90.0 percent of criminals in Hangzhou, 23.0 percent of criminals in Tianjin, 69.8 percent of criminals in Shenyang and 33.0 percent of criminals in Wuhan (Li and Hu, *Luidong Renkou,* pp. 47–53).

13. A. John Jowett, "Mainland China: A National One-Child Program Does Not Exist" (Part One), *Issues and Studies,* vol. 25, no. 9 (September 1989), pp. 48–70. See also Gui Shixuan, "Qieshi Jiajiang Dui Liuru Renkou De Jihua Shengyu Guanli" (Resolutely strengthen the management of fertility planning on immigrants), *Renkou Dongtai* (Population Dynamics), no. 1 (1992), pp. 9–10; and Tu Qianyu and Cui Sixing, "Liudong Renkou Jihuawai Shengyu De Yuanyin Ji Duice Chutan" (Initial exploration on the reasons for unplanned births among the floating population and policy response), *Renkou Dongtai* (Population Dynamics), no. 4 (1990), p. 28.

14. *Yangcheng Wanbao,* 9 January 1988, p. 1. See also Xiong Yue, "Dui Liudong Renkou Chaosheng Wenti De Fenxi" (Analysis of above-plan births among the floating population), *Renkou Zhuankan* (Special Population Journal), no. 1 (1990), p. 59. See also Zhou and Dang, *Zhongguo Renkou,* pp. 185–86; and Li and Hu, *Luidong Renkou,* pp. 58–60.

15. Linda Wong, "Slighting the Needy? Social Welfare Under Transition," in Joseph Cheng and Maurice Brosseau, eds., *China Review 1993* (Hong Kong: The Chinese University Press, 1993), pp. 23.6–23.7.

16. Lewis Diane, *The Prostitute and Her Clients. Your Pleasure is Her Business* (Springfield: Charles C. Thomas, 1985); D. Kelly Weisberg, *Children of the Night—A Study of Adolescent Prostitution* (Lexington: Lexington Books, 1985); Roberta Perkins, *Working Girls, Their Life and Social Control* (Canberra: Australian Institute of Criminology, 1991).

17. Alan Liu, "Economic Reform," pp. 405–408; *Xiandairen Bao* (Contemporary People Magazine), 25 April 1989, pp. 94–95.

18. Zhang Qingwu, *Huji Shouce* (Household registration handbook) (Beijing: Qunzhong Chubanshe, 1987), p. 32. See also *Zhonghua Renmin Gongheguo Fagui Huibian January–December 1985* (Compendium of the People's Republic of China's laws and regulations) (Beijing: Falu Chubanshe, 1986), pp. 35–38; Ding Shuimu, "Xianxing Huji Zhidu De Gongnang Jiqi Gaige Zouxiang" (The existing household registration system: its functions and direction of reform), *Shehuixue Yanjiu* (Sociological Research) (Beijing), no. 6 (1992), pp. 100–104.

19. For data in 1985 and 1988, see Guangzhou Shizhengfu Bangongshi, "Guangzhoushi Liudong Renkou Wenti Ji Duice Yanjiu" (Study of Guangzhou's floating population problem and policy response), in Bada Chengshi Zhengfu Tiaoyan Jigou Lianhe Ketiju, ed., *Zhongguo Dachengshi Renkou Yu Shehui Fazhan* (Population and social development in Chinese metropolises) (Beijing: Zhongguo Chengshi Jingji Shehui Chubanshe, 1990), pp. 2, 79 and 239. Figures for 1992 were supplied by the Guangzhou Population Census Bureau.

20. *The Nineties,* April 1989, pp. 53–55; *Nanfang Ribao,* 28 February 1989, p. 1.

21. *Yangcheng Wanbao,* 13 February 1992, p. 1; *Nanfang Ribao,* 27 February 1991, p. 1, and 17 February 1991, p. 1.

22. *Zhongguo Laodong Kexue* (China Labour Science), no. 10 (1993), pp. 16–17.

23. Guangzhoushi Liudong Renkou Yanjiu Ketiju, ed., *(Guangzhoushi Liudong Renkou Yanjiu* (Guangzhou city floating population study) (Guangzhou: Zhongshan Daxue Chubanshe, 1991), pp. 26–27 and 144; *Nanfang Ribao,* 21 March 1991, p. 2. See also *Yangcheng Wanbao,* 20 May 1991, p. 3; 30 January 1992, p. 2 and 8 February 1992, p. 2.

24. *Guangzhoushi Liudong Renkou Yanjiu,* p. 114.

25. Lin Weiye, "Gaige Kaifang," p. 82; see also *Yangcheng Wanbao,* 19 March 1992, p. 1.

26. Information obtained from the author's interviews with labour officials in Dongguan, Shunde, Nanhai and Zhongshan in July 1993.

27. *Yangcheng Wanbao,* 12 February 1991, p. 1.

28. *Ibid.,* 15 October 1986, p. 1; 28 February 1989, p. 1; 21 May 1992, p. 1. See also *Guangzhou Nianjian 1987* (Guangzhou Yearbook 1987), p. 638.

29. *Nanfang Ribao,* 28 March 1991, pp. 1, 3; 16 January 1992, p. 1; 4 March 1992, p. 1. See also *Guangzhou Nianjian 1989* (Guangzhou Yearbook 1989), pp. 657–58 and *Zhuhai Nianjian 1990* (Zhuhai Yearbook 1990), pp. 362–63.

30. *Yangcheng Wanbao,* 26 February 1990, p. 1; *Nanfang Ribao,* 28 March 1991, p. 1. See also Guangdongsheng Laodongju Faguichu, ed., *Laodong Fagui Huibian 1992* (Guangdong labour laws and regulations 1992), pp. 270–73.

31. *Yangcheng Wanbao,* 3 March 1992, p. 1; 4 March 1992, p. 1 and 5 March 1992, p. 1. See also Zhao Zhiqiang, "Dui Mingongchao De Renshi Yu Sikao" (Perception and thinking on the migrant labour tide), *Zhongguo Laodong Kexue* (China Labour Science), no. 10 (1993), pp. 16–17.

32. *Yangcheng Wanbao,* 13 October 1987, p. 1; 21 August 1989, p. 1; 20 May 1991, p. 1; 19 January 1992, p. 1 and 25 May 1992, p. 1. See also *Nanfang Ribao,* 18 July 1987, p. 1 and Guangdongsheng Renmin Zhengfu Bangongting, ed., *Guangdongsheng Fagui Guizhang Huibian 1987–1988* (Compendium of Guangdong province laws and regulations 1987–1988), pp. 279–81 and *Bai Shing,* 16 June 1989, p. 47.

33. *Zhonghua Renmin Gongheguo Fagui Huibian 1991* (Compendium of laws and regulations of the People's Republic of China 1991), vol. 4, pp. 114–17. See also Yang Huifu, "Liudong Renkou Jihua Shengyu Guanli Banfa Neirong Jianjie" (Introducing the contents of the floating population birth planning management regulations), *Renkou Dongtai* (Population Dynamics), no. 1 (1992), pp. 4–7.

34. *Yangcheng Wanbao,* 9 May 1987, p. i. See also *Guangdongsheng Fagui,* pp. 325–36.

35. Minzhengbu, ed., *Minzhengbu Dashiji* (Key events in the Ministry of Civil Affairs) (Beijing: Minzhengbu, 1988), p. 734. See also Cecilia Chan, *The Myth of Neighbourhood Mutual Help—The Contemporary Community-based Welfare System in Guangzhou* (Hong Kong: Hong Kong University Pres, 1993), pp. 219–37. According to the *Zhongguo Minzheng Tongji Nianjian 1993* (Chinese civil affairs statistical yearbook 1993), p. 216, the percentage of state civil affairs spending out of the total state budget was as follows:

First FYP period: 1.90%; Second FYP period: 1.41%;

Third FYP period: 1.42%; Fourth FYP period: 1.19%;

Fifth FYP period: 1.62%; Sixth FYP period: 1.65%;

Seventh FYP period: 1.52%; Eighth FYP period: 1.54%;

Average for all periods: 1.56%.

36. *Guangzhoushi Liudong Renkou Yanjiu,* pp. 2, 146–60 and 197.

37. *Ming Pao:* 20 November 1993, p. A2; 21 November 1993, p. A2; 1 January 1994, p. A13. See also *South China Morning Post,* 20 November 1993, p. 1, and *China Times Weekly,* 20–26 March 1994, pp. 8–16.

38. *Ming Pao,* 25 July 1993, p. 2, and *Hong Kong Economic Journal,* 25 July 1993, p. 2.

39. On the total number of migrants, see *Zhongguo Renkoubao,* 27 December 1990, p. 1. According to *Zhongguo Nianjian 1991* (p. 421), the number of floaters in 1990 amounted to 70 million. This figure of 70 million is similar to the sum of people who had left their registered home for over one year and for less than one year in 1990. See also Siu Yat-ming and Li Si-ming, "Population Mobility in the 1980s: China on the Road to An Open Society", in Cheng and Brosseau, *China Review 1993,* p. 19.9. On redundant farm labourers, see Li Chen (ed.), *Jiuye, Gaige, Chulu* (Employment, reform, future prospects) (Beijing: Zhongguo Shehuixue Chubanshe, 1991), p. 251; Ma Chuanyou, "Dui Zhongguo Laodongli Zhuangkuang De Sikao" (Reflections on the labour supply situation in China), in *Renkou Xuekan* (Population Journal), no. 4 (August 1992), p. 22; *Cheng Ming* (June 1992), p. 33; Zhou and Dang, Zhongguo Renkou, p. 126; *Outlook Weekly,* 16 November 1992, pp. 8–9; 8 February 1993, pp. 12–14; 15 February 1993, p. 3; and 22 February 1993, p. 3. See also *Renmin Ribao,* 18 May 1988, p. 1; *Ming Pao,* 20 October 1993, p. A10; and *Asia Week,* 1 March 1992, p. 16.

40. *Ming pao,* 22 February 1992, p. 24; Zhou Tianyong, "Woguo Weilai 20 Nian Laodongli Renkou De Gonggei Taishi" (Trends in our country's supply of productive, population in the next 20 Years), in *Renkou Xuekan* (Population Monthly), no. 2 (1992), pp. 6–11; Li Chen, *Jiuye,* p. 223.

Effects of Institutions and Policies on Rural Population Growth with Application to China

D. Gale Johnson

This article has two main purposes. The first is to show that families' decisions determining fertility are significantly influenced by the institutions and policies that affect their lives and that the appropriate mix of policies and institutions can lead to rapid declines in fertility. The second is to present a set of institutions and policies that would achieve and maintain low levels of fertility in China while permitting families to have the number of children they desire. This approach would overcome an important defect of China's present policies that rely on the allocation of birth quotas. The current emphasis on strict limitations on the number of births a family may have creates tensions between rural people and the government that threaten the long- run viability of the policy.

The article proceed as follows. I first present a framework for understanding the factors that influence family fertility decisions and families' ability to have the number of children that they desire. This is followed by a comparison of the fertility changes over the past four decades in China and in several other developing countries that have achieved similar rapid declines with a mixture of policies and institutions that made it possible for families to have the number of children they desired. I then summarize the evidence on the major factors that influence family fertility decisions in a developing country, discuss the de facto pronatalist policies that exist in China and their probable influence on rural fertility, and suggest an effective alternative to China's current mixture of such pronatalist policies and numerical controls on births. Given the tension the current population policy has created between farm families and the

D. Gale Johnson, population scientist, "Effects of Institutions and Policies on Rural Population Growth with Application to China," *Population and Development Review,* September 1994: 503–531.

government, it is vital that full consideration be given to the combination of policies and institutions that will harmonize the interests of farm people with the government's stated purpose of reducing the rate of population growth. The remainder of the article presents evidence to support the conclusion that, within relatively wide limits, the size of China's population will have little effect on per capita food supplies or real per capita incomes. Consequently it is not essential that the alternative policy result in the same stationary population size as would be achieved by the current mix of policies that influence birth rates. The alternative policy might, in fact, result in a smaller population, though that is not the reason the alternative merits support.

A SIMPLE MODEL OF FERTILITY DETERMINATION

My analysis is derived from the evidence that families are rational in their decisions affecting fertility in the same sense that they are rational in organizing their resources to achieve a maximum level of satisfaction. The performance of China's rural economy after the reforms instituted in 1979 supports the thesis that the assumption of rational behavior is applicable to Chinese rural households. A basic assumption of the rural reforms of the past 15 years was that if rural people were permitted to make their own decisions in a policy framework that provided appropriate incentives, they would allocate their resources in an efficient manner and increase their productivity, output, and incomes. The assumption of rational behavior that guides the decisions of competent individuals and families in using their productive resources has been strongly confirmed by the success of the rural reforms. That same assumption is applied here to family fertility decisions.

Actual fertility is determined by the number of children desired by a family and the cost of achieving the desired number (Becker 1960). The desired number of children is the result of equating the anticipated costs and benefits of an additional child. The desired number of children is determined when the anticipated costs of an additional child equal or exceed the anticipated benefits. The costs of an additional child include the cost of parents' time, the costs of schooling and health care not borne by government, and the costs of food, clothing, and housing. The time cost is a function of the wage rate or education level and of whether the work is in agriculture or paid employment outside of agriculture. The cost to a woman of pregnancy and birth is also involved.

The anticipated benefits to parents of an additional child include several components. One is the earnings of the child or the contribution to household activities through cooking, caring for a sibling, cleaning, gardening, collecting fuel, and animal watching and care. In some settings, if the child is a male, an important benefit is the provision of security of income and care for old age or illness. In some institutional settings, an important benefit may be the income or capital transfers that may result from having an additional child if land in a village is reallocated on the basis of demographic changes in a village. Over and above the pecuniary benefits of an additional child are the consumption or satisfaction benefits obtained.

Once a family reaches an implicit or explicit decision concerning the desired number of children, the cost and availability of means for achieving that number influence actual fertility. The family's ability to have the desired number of children is dependent on fecundity and is affected by the availability, reliability, quality, and cost of contraceptive devices and the willingness and ability to resort to abortion. The degree to which families achieve the desired number of children is influenced by the level of education of the parents, especially of the mother, because increased levels of education improve knowledge about contraception and thus reduce search costs for appropriate and acceptable methods.

This simple model of fertility decisions is useful in understanding the factors that have influenced the rate of fertility decline in developing countries. The model makes clear that China has a number of policies, institutions, and conditions that increase the number of children rural families desire and that have adverse effects on the ability of families to have the desired number of children. It is evident that there are reasons for differences in the number of children desired by rural and urban families and that a national population program should not be concerned primarily with the provision of contraceptive devices and services or with limits on the number of births but should recognize these differences and include measures that minimize their consequences.

RAPID FERTILITY DECLINES IN DEVELOPING COUNTRIES

The rapid decline in fertility in the People's Republic of China over the past quarter century is indisputable. The total fertility rate, which stood at 5.99 in 1965–70, fell by more than half to 2.38 in 1985–90 (Table 1). It now stands at about replacement level (State Family Planning Commission 1994: 3). Table 1 provides data for eight other developing economies that also had rapid declines in fertility. The (unweighted) average total fertility rate for the eight developing economies was 4.70 for 1965–70 and 2.16 for 1985–90. The 1985–90 average was some 10 percent lower than China's but the other developing economies started from a lower base in 1965–70. The percentage declines were nearly the same—60 percent for China and 54 percent for the eight market economies. Two of the latter had slightly larger declines than China—South Korea at 62 percent and Hong Kong at 66 percent, while the decline for Taiwan was nearly the same as for the Mainland. The comparison group is a selected one; there is no claim they represent a random sample of developing countries. They have been selected to illustrate that China's experience over the past

Table 1. Total Fertility Rates for China and Selected Countries, 1950–90

Country	1950–55	1955–60	1960–65	1965–70	1970–75	1975–80	1980–85	1985–90
China	6.24	5.40	5.93	5.9	4.76	2.90	2.52	2.38
South Korea	5.18	6.07	5.40	4.52	4.11	2.80	2.40	1.73
Thailand	6.62	6.42	6.42	6.14	5.01	4.27	2.96	2.57
Sri Lanka	5.74	5.44	5.16	4.68	4.00	3.83	3.25	2.67
Chile	5.10	5.30	5.28	4.44	3.63	2.90	2.80	2.73
Guyana	6.68	6.76	6.15	6.11	4.90	3.94	3.26	2.77
Hong Kong	4.43	4.70	5.30	4.01	2.89	2.31	1.80	1.36
Singapore	6.41	6.00	4.93	3.46	2.63	1.87	1.69	1.69
Taiwan	6.7	6.0	5.1	4.2	3.4	2.7	2.17	1.74
China[a]								
Urban	5.34	5.07	4.36	3.37	2.49	1.51	1.33	na
Rural	6.25	5.49	6.43	6.51	5.24	4.97	2.83	na

na = not available

[a]There are small differences in the estimated total fertility rates in the UN and State Statistical Bureau sources.

Sources United Nations 1993: Table 41: State Statistical Bureau, Department of Population 1989, 1991.

quarter century has not been unique. Except for Singapore none of the countries did more than provide voluntary family planning services: Singapore has used a variety of financial penalties and rewards to obtain adherence to a small-family norm. However, in 1987 Singapore shifted to a policy of encouraging more births and now provides financial incentives to that end.

There is no implication that the policies, institutions, and conditions affecting fertility in China and the other developing economies have been the same or that China would have achieved the same rates of fertility decline without its current population control programs. My purpose is to show that countries other than China that had very low incomes in the 1950s have achieved rapid fertility declines.

WHY FERTILITY HAS DECLINED IN DEVELOPING COUNTRIES

Many studies have assessed the factors associated with changes in birth rates or fertility. Here I summarize some of the more significant findings. In brief, the most important determinants of fertility in developing countries have been shown to be the level of education (especially of women), provisions for old-age security (pensions, asset ownership), urbanization, mortality or life expectancy, the availability of family planning services, and per capita income level or income change. Increased employment of women in the formal urban sector, especially as occurred in China and other socialist countries, has had a significant effect in decreasing fertility through delaying marriage and raising the cost of children (Cheng and Maxim 1992). Since several, if not most, of these variables are interrelated, it is often difficult to isolate the effects of any one. For example, in developing countries the following variables are positively related to one another: women's education, provisions for old-age security, urbanization, life expectancy, and per capita income. In most empirical studies, women's education is shown to have a major effect on fertility—the higher the level of education, the lower is fertility—but when urbanization and per capita gross domestic product (GDP) are also included, the coefficient for women's education may not be significant.

Subbarao and Raney (1995) estimated a fertility model for developing countries that included as explanatory variables female and male secondary school enrollment (percent of population group), GDP per capita, family planning services, urban population, population per physician, and three dummy variables representing regions (Africa, Asia, and Latin America). For the developing countries, holding all other variables constant at their means, a doubling of the percentage of girls enrolled in secondary schools from 19 percent to 38 percent as of 1975 reduced the total fertility rate in 1985 from 5.3 to 3.9. A similar exercise for family planning services indicated that a doubling of those services would have reduced the total fertility rate from 5.5 to 5.0. Increasing female education reduces the fertility rate through two main routes. One is by significantly lowering the desired family size: an increase in the percentage of girls enrolled in secondary school from 20 to 30 percent would reduce desired family size by 0.6. The other is by increasing the use of contraceptives: a similar gain in female enrollment increased contraceptive use from 24 percent to 33 percent. Thus increased education acts to reduce desired family size and to raise the use of methods for reducing actual family size. In the developing countries studied, the effects of female education on fertility were negative until 80 percent of the females were in secondary education.

Jefferson and Petri (1987) estimated a model for developing countries that included expenditures on social security and welfare as an explanatory variable. They found that social security and welfare expenditure per person 65 years and older had a statistically significant negative effect on fertility, as did life expectancy at birth and income growth. Female education did not have a significant coefficient, probably because it is highly correlated with life expectancy and productivity as well as with the provision of social insurance and welfare.

In an analysis of data for urban China, Jefferson (1990) analyzed the effects on fertility of the extensive system of social services, including pensions, provided by all state and most collective enterprises. The urban areas include the rural locations that are part of the urban administrative units; for the 180 urban areas with usable data, 36 percent of the labor force wa engaged in agriculture and rural services. It is reasonable to assume that nearly everyone in this latter group was employed in agriculture. The remainder of the employment was classified by the characteristics of the employer—in industry, whether state-owned, collective-owned, or rural, and in nonindustrial enterprises by a similar classification. Of the total employment, state-owned enterprises accounted for 40 percent, collective-owned 14 percent. State-owned agricultural enterprises in the rural areas accounted for only 2 percent of the total employment.

In addition to the employment variables, the analysis included death rates, the rate of inflation (1980–87), and the amount of housing space. High death rates are associated with high birth rates as expected. Housing space per capita is positively associated with birth rates: when housing space is limited there are fewer children. Families that are classified as independent have the highest birth rates. Significant negative effects on birth rates of the employer-employee relationships were found for rural and state-owned industry. It is not clear what role the pension and retirement provisions of employment in rural industry may have played; the negative effect on the birth rate may reflect the absence of any significant attachment to the land.

A striking result of the analysis was that when the effects of the indicated variables were accounted for, there was no difference in the birth rates of those engaged in agriculture and in all other activities in the urban areas. This result indicates that when the conditions influencing fertility decisions are approximately the same for farm and nonfarm people, the birth rates are very similar. This was true even though the birth rates were for 1987 when there had been some relaxation of the one-child policy for rural areas and the total fertility rate was 18 percent above its 1985 level. This result strongly supports the conclusion that higher birth rates in rural than urban areas are not due to different tastes or preferences but to different objective conditions with respect to education, income security, housing space, and mortality rates. These conditions are largely determined by public policy.

PRONATALIST POLICIES IN RURAL CHINA

China has several policies or conditions that are in effect pronatalist even though it pursues policies designed to limit the growth of population. Some of its pronatalist strategies are similar to those that exist in most other countries—policies that require society to pay a substantial part of the costs of raising and educating a child. These include free or highly subsidized education and medical care. These measures have been long justified because of their externalities—a society and economy gain from increasing the general level of education and health of its members. The effect of education levels on labor productivity is beyond dispute, while such health measures as immunization clearly provide substantial externalities. Such measures are accepted even under conditions where it is agreed they are pronatalist—they encourage population growth, all other things equal, by lowering the costs of a child and increasing the benefits to be derived by the family. But subsidies to education and health care are unlikely to be pronatalist in their total effects.

As noted above, increased education will in time, actually in a relatively short time, reduce fertility through changing preferences and increasing the ability of parents to achieve their desired family size. But would the fertility effect be even ore negative if parents had to bear the full costs of educating their children? Probably not. The total effect of free education on fertility is almost certainly negative because its availability increases the level of education attained and thereby indirectly reduces fertility by more than the provision of free education directly increases the birth rate. So far as I know, there has been no empirical test of this conclusion, but the large effects of rather modest increases in education levels in reducing fertility support the hypothesis. Improvements in health that reduce child and infant mortality also result in lowered fertility and thus may be at least neutral in terns of effects on population growth.

Three socioeconomic policies in rural China induce or result in higher levels of fertility than would exist under alternative policies. Changing the policies could bring the voluntary fertility behavior of Chinese rural families to the levels achieved by the current emphasis on strict limitation of births. The pronatalist policies are: (1) the reallocation of farm land in villages in response to population changes in families; (2) discrimination against rural areas in provision of social security and retirement pensions; and (3) restraints on migration from rural to urban areas.

A condition that has a major impact on rural fertility is discrimination against rural areas in the provision of education and the resulting relatively low level of education, especially for females (World Bank 1985: 16). It may not be appropriate to say that the large difference between educational opportunities in rural and urban areas reflects deliberate policy, but clearly certain policy decisions would increase the levels of education of rural youth.

The introduction of the responsibility systems and the subsequent abolition of the collectives have been cited as a factor in increasing rural birth rates because the control over farm people was greatly diminished. No longer did men and women assemble to receive their work assignments for the day, and little control remained over the allocation of income to a family. In other words, the structure of rewards and punishments for abiding by the family planning policy was changed significantly. It is not clear from the data on fertility whether the gradual introduction of responsibility systems and the elimination of the collectives (essentially complete by the end of 1983) had increased rural fertility. While the rural fertility rate increased by 24 percent from 1980 to 1982 as economic controls over rural people were being reduced, urban fertility also increased by 26 percent in the same period. The subsequent declines in fertility were approximately the same from 1982 to 1984—21 percent in the countryside and 23 percent in the cities. Population policy was undergoing major change at the time; this may account for some of the observed changes.

Given the factors that influence families' decisions about births, the abolition of the collectives may have increased the desired number of children. First, family income variability over time was increased, both in the short and long run. The household income form the collective was the average outcome for a significant number of families and covered production from a relatively large area. However, the significant increase in real incomes that followed the reforms may have offset all or most of the effects of increased income variability on the number of desired children. Second, the existence of the commune system provided a minimal form of old-age support for the elderly who had no children to support them. Third, and most relevant, while some production teams distributed part of the income on a per capita basis and income from the collective presumably was based on work points, in fact household income was determined mainly by the number of able-bodied workers in the household (Selden 1985). Consequently the birth of a child did not result in a significant short-run increase in family income; such an increase did not occur until the child was a teenager and permitted to earn work points.

LAND REALLOCATION WITH DEMOGRAPHIC CHANGES

All this seems to have changed with the rules that have been followed in the allocation of income-earning opportunities—primarily farm land—under the household responsibility systems. While there is some dispute concerning the facts, it appears that many villages—perhaps most—periodically reallocate farm land among the families in a production team on the basis of changes in family size. Thus the birth of a child results in a larger allocation of land for the family while a death results in a smaller allocation. In many, if not most, villages such allocations occur as frequently as every three years even though the national policy is to provide allocations for 15 years or more (Prosterman and Hanstad 1993: 38–39).[1]

The increase in land allocated to a family on the birth of a child represents both an immediate capital transfer and a long-term increase in real income. On the other hand, reducing the land allocation upon a death reduces the capital assets of a family and reduces the amount of potential income for the support of surviving members, especially the elderly. The practice of land reallocation upon a birth increases the desired number of children without regard to sex, and the loss of land upon a death increases the desired number of sons to provide for old-age security for the surviving spouse.

If land is reallocated on the basis of family size, the incentive to have an additional child is likely to be significant. How large it is depends on the value of land or the income stream that would be generated from the additional land. The average amount of cultivated land per capita assigned to farm families in China was 2.11 mu (that is, 0.14 ha) in 1989 (State Statistical Bureau 1990: 340). With land reallocation a child would bring an asset to the family equal to the present value of the income produced by 2.11 mu of land. A number of estimates indicate that the share of land in agriculture's product is at least 0.4 (40 percent) and may be as large as 0.7 (Feder et al. 1992: 16; Fleisher and Liu 1992: 116; Zhao 1993). Let us assume that the marginal or additional product of land is 0.4 of total crop output: this assumes that land contributes nothing to animal husbandry or sideline production. The value of crop output in 1989 was 460 yuan per registered agricultural resident (State Statistical Bureau 1990). If the coefficient of the value of land's marginal product is 0.4 and an additional child is allocated the per capita amount of land, 184 yuan annually would be added to a family's income. The rural household survey indicates that per capita living expenditures of farm families amounted to 535 yuan in 1989.

The land reallocation on the birth of a child may be less than the full per capita share in many if not most villages. The reallocation may be on the order of the amount of land required for the family food supply rather than the total amount of land, which includes land to produce products that are to be marketed or required to meet government marketing quotas. While the value of the benefit may be less than the stream of income from a full per capita share of a village's land, any land reallocation provides a positive benefit from having an additional child.[2]

Where land is reallocated in response to changes in family size, the income due to that reallocation can represent a large percentage of the cost of the child and constitutes a significant incentive to have additional children.[3] If children born outside the birth quota are not registered for a number of years, it is possible that the benefit from an additional child is delayed. There is a need for more accurate determination of actual practice.

In Meitan County, Guizhou Province the periodic reallocation of agricultural land was halted in 1987 in favor of a long-term assignment of specific land plots to households. In addition, the land use rights can be rented or sold and can be used as collateral for a mortgage. The primary reason for halting the reallocation of land was to provide a significant incentive for farmers to invest in land improvement. When land is reallocated periodically, farmers may lose much of the value of any land improvement they make. The authors of the experiment—the Rural Policy Research Department of Guizhou Province—anticipated a decrease in the desire for large families.

Data on birth rates in Meitan County have been made available for 1989, 1990, and 1992 (Gu 1993). While it would be desirable to have data for the years prior to 1987, the comparison of birth rates for Guizhou Province and

Meitan County for recent years strongly supports the conclusion that the assignment of land use rights for long periods and the marketability of those rights have had a major negative effect on birth rates, as the fertility model predicted. The following are the birth rate data (births per thousand population):

Year	Guizhou Province	Meitan County	Meitan birth rate as percent of province birth rate
1989	21.16	17.65	83
1990	23.09	16.05	70
1991	22.42	—	
1992	22.40	14.85	66

The Meitan County birth rate declined from 83 percent of the birth rate in Guizhou Province in 1989 to 66 percent in 1992. To attribute the decline in the birth rate in Meitan County relative to the rest of the province to the county's unique policy on land assignment, one must assume that changes, if any, in other relevant factors, such as the enforcement of the population policy, were similar in both county and province. Gu Xiulin has informed me in private correspondence that she has seen no evidence that the population program followed in Meitan County differs from that of the province generally. Accepting that population program implementation was the same as for the province, the policy change on land reallocation may have resulted in a decline in the birth rate by a fifth. Other factors, such as migration of young people may have had some effect. If reducing population growth is a high-priority national objective, prompt consideration should be given to providing the same land use rights throughout rural China that now exist in Meitan County. Verbal reports indicate that agricultural investment in land improvement by Meitan farmers increased substantially, boding well for future productivity by overcoming one of the few significant shortcomings of the rural reforms initiated in 1979.

In a 1992 survey in Meitan County 50 percent of the respondents indicated that they did not want additional children because they would not receive more land, as they had in the past (Gu 1993). At least for these respondents a prediction of the fertility model is supported.

RESTRAINTS ON RURAL-TO-URBAN MIGRATION

The restraints on the migration of farm people to the cities have increased population growth in China compared to what it would have been had there been freedom of movement. In developing countries the birth rates of urban residents are everywhere lower than for rural residents. This is not because the people are different; rather, the costs and advantages of having children differ because of differences in the economic and social institutions. The net cost of children in cities is much greater than in the country; not only do children in cities cost more to care for, but their contribution to a family's income and security is much smaller. These differences arise from conditions of employment, including prohibitions against child labor as hired workers, and the provision of pensions or other forms of income and old-age security. Urban children require more time in the form of supervision than do rural children, thus increasing costs. Housing space per capita is significantly less in cities than in the country, thus serving to reduce urban birth rates. I am not addressing the issue of whether migration from rural to urban areas should be unrestricted. The point is simply that restricting migration has implications for population growth, and it would seem appropriate for national population policy to recognize such effects.

Some readers might question whether there was significant restraint on rural-to-urban migration in China, given the large floating population—variously estimated at 70 million to 100 million. But the floating population does not represent the normal migration from country to city. It consists primarily of single people, not families, with preponderance of males, according to a 1990 study in Hubei (Gu, Wu, and Zhu). These migrants have few rights in the cities—they have little or no claim on housing, medical care, or education. Consequently relatively few families are found in the floating population. Some families have used membership in the floating population or temporary migration as a means of evading the population controls in their home community.

The Hubei study cited above classified the population, both urban and rural, in the following categories: permanent immigrants, temporary migrants, commuters, and nonmigrants. The temporary migrants were registered in a place other than where they were living. People living in large cities, towns, and rural villages were included in the survey. Temporary migrants accounted for 9 percent of the sample. The authors considered the effect of temporary migration on fertility: "A . . . hypothesis suggested that temporary migrants in urban areas were more likely to have higher fertility rates than nonmigrants in rural China." Their conclusion: "For those aged 20–29, no difference were apparent in the provincial capital between temporary migrants, commuters and non-migrants. The average number of children ever born to these childbearing temporary migrants living in urban areas . . . was 0.64, compared to 1.041 for non-migrants in rural villages. . . . Among women aged 30–34, the fertility rate of temporary migrants was also lower than that of non-migrants in rural villages. Obviously, no evidence could be obtained which shows that temporary mobility has a pro-natalist influence" (Gu, Wu, and Zhu 1990: 95–96).

The Hubei survey confirms that permanent migrants have a somewhat higher rate of fertility than nonmigrants in urban areas but substantially lower fertility than nonmigrants in rural areas. For women aged 30–34 who were permanent migrants to the large cities, the number of children ever born was 1.27 compared to 2.12 for nonmigrant residents of rural villages. Among women aged 30–34 and 35–44 the number of children ever born to women who were permanent migrants in rural villages was the same as that for the nonmigrant rural population (ibid.: 99).

URBAN-RURAL DIFFERENCES IN OLD-AGE SECURITY

A second difference between urban and rural areas that causes the birth rate to be higher in rural areas is the absence for farm people of a formal pension system or other systematic provision for retirement with a reasonable income. Farm people have traditionally provided for old-age security and other exigencies in a number of ways. If there were a complete system of financial markets, financial savings would be one avenue but such opportunities, while increasingly available, remain limited in China. Another form, especially for minimizing the effects of the death of the household head, has been life insurance, which generally does not exist in developing countries. In most developing countries old-age security has been achieved through one or both of two mechanisms: having one or more surviving sons and owning land or other important physical assets. In rural China only one of these avenues exists; farm land cannot be owned and an active and reliable market for the permanent sale of land use rights does not exist. Thus in China the rural family's primary source of old-age security is surviving sons. This role of sons results in higher birth rates in rural than in urban areas. It also represents a significant incentive to evade restraints on the number of children that a family can have, particularly if daughters are the only children in the family.

DISPARITIES IN RURAL-URBAN EDUCATIONAL OPPORTUNITIES

Given the geographic differences in costs of children and in the conditions of employment, we would expect, all other conditions equal, birth rates to be lower in the city than in the country. But all other conditions that affect birth rates are not the same in urban and rural areas and cause differences in birth rates to be greater than can be attributed to costs of children and employment conditions. Nearly everywhere in the world, both currently and over the past century, urban children receive more and better education than rural children. The evidence is clear; additional education has a large effect in reducing birth rates, with the greatest effect due to increasing female education. Consequently, rural birth rates will be significantly greater than urban rates as long as different levels of educational attainment remain. This cause of differences between rural and urban birth rates could be eliminated and will be; it is only a question of how long it will take to make secondary education universal in rural as well as urban areas.

In 1965 the percentage of girls attending secondary school in China (urban and rural combined) may be estimated at 15 to 20 percent in the relevant age group. This figure has since increased to almost 40 percent (38 percent in 1989 according to World Bank 1992). According to results obtained by Subbarao and Raney (1995) this would have reduced the total fertility rate by 1.5 births, or by almost 30 percent; if the percentage of girls in secondary schools increased to 60 percent, the total fertility rate would decline by an additional 0.6 as these women completed their childbearing years. The decline in fertility that can be attributed to an increase in the proportion of females attending secondary school from 20 to 60 percent equals the actual reduction in China's fertility rate between 1973 and 1987. During most of this period policy measures were enforced, varying in intensity over time, to reduce fertility. The actual improvement in female education was only to about 40 percent but the effect of that increase, had it occurred in rural areas, might have accounted for some 70 percent of the actual reduction in the rural fertility rate from 5.01 to 2.94. Those who attribute all or even most of the reduction in fertility in China since the early 1970s to the official population programs do so on very weak evidence.

TWO RELEVANT CASES OF RAPIDLY DECLINING FERTILITY

Since 1950 South Korea and Taiwan have shared a number of attributes. In the present context five are worthy of note. First, both were poor in the mid-1950s, with real per capita incomes significantly below that of China today. Second, they achieved large declines in total fertility rates between 1950 and 1990. South Korea and Taiwan had higher total fertility rates in the late 1950s than did China and lower rates in the late 1980s. third, in both nearly all farmers owned their own land as a result of land reforms in the 1950s. Thus farm families had land and its productivity as an important source of security. Consequently the demand for sons was reduced and the desired family size declined rapidly over time, even while 40 percent or more of the labor force was engaged in agriculture. Fourth, each experienced rapid urbanization; by the mid-1980s each was more than two-thirds urban from less than one-third urban as late as 1965. Finally, each provided family planning services. Taiwan engaged in an extensive educational campaign on the merits of reducing the number of births, but there were no penalties for having a child or rewards for not having one. These experiences indicate that attainable policies and institutions had generated a rapid transition from a high rate of fertility to replacement and then to less than replacement fertility rates. The relevant conditions have been those that were highlighted in the analysis of factors associated with declines in fertility in the empirical studies reviewed above. The experience of these two economies is consistent with and supports the results of the analyses of factors influencing fertility in developing countries.

AN EFFECTIVE ALTERNATIVE TO CHINA'S POPULATION POLICIES

Of course, differences existed between the Chinese economy and the other East Asian economies that had equally rapid or more rapid declines in fertility since the 1950s. Two important differences stand out. One is that for the period since at least 1960 their real per capita incomes have been significantly greater than China's. Another related difference is in urbanization; Hong Kong and Singapore are city states while South Korea and Taiwan reached China's current level of urbanization at least a quarter of a century ago. These two factors undoubtedly made important contributions to the rapid declines in fertility. Consequently if China had followed the same family planning measures as the other four East Asian economies, it would not have realize the same reduction in fertility as was achieved by them or by China. But the higher per capita incomes and greater urbanization of the other East Asian economies were not the only differences that influenced the decline in fertility. Each of the countries included in Table 1 had other policies and institutions that China has not adopted that reduced the desired number of children and thus the fertility rate.

China could have followed policies that would have permitted families to bear the number of children they desired and that would have resulted in large reductions in fertility over the past three decades. Arguably, these policies would have brought fertility to the replacement level in the not too distant future. If (a) farm people had the right to own their land; (b) there had been a modest social security system; (3) there had been a significant increase in rural education, especially of women; and (d) there had been no artificial barrier to a more rapid rate of urbanization, the decline in fertility would not have lagged far behind what actually occurred.

Could these changes in institutions and policies have been made? Where required, could necessary resources have been made available? The answer to both of these questions is yes. Permitting farmers to own their land and more or less freely buy and sell it is a matter of policy and is in no way affected by resource limitations. The real financial costs would have been nil, and there would not have been a significant loss of revenue to the government as a consequence. The avenues that the government now uses to extract revenue from farm people would have existed whether farmers owned their land or not. Establishing delivery quotas and procurement prices below market prices has been the main method used to transfer income out of agriculture; this could have been the practice if farmers owned their land.

A rural pension program is financially attainable if given a reasonably high priority. A pension could have been provided in China to all rural residents 65 years and older in 1989 at a rate equal to 80 percent of the per capita incomes of all rural residents. There were 56 million persons aged 65 years or older living outside cities; the annual cost of the pension would have been 34 billion yuan. This was less than the budgetary cost of the grain price subsidy in 1991, a subsidy that went to urban residents, who on the average had far higher incomes than rural people. True, the direct grain price subsidies have been eliminated, and employers pay their workers per capita income subsidies to approximately cover the increased cost of grain, but a large share of the subsidy cost remains a charge against the government budget.

If farmers were permitted to own their land to rent it or sell it during their retirement if necessary, the pension rate need not be as high as 80 percent of average income to provide a high degree of old-age security. The total cost of a rural pension system could be a third less than indicated above while providing a reasonable level of security. Nor would it be necessary for the government to pay the whole cost; rural families could contribute a modest percentage of their annual incomes, though this would not be fair unless urban families also contributed to their pensions.

The major real cost involved in reducing fertility with a noncoercive population policy would be in expanding the rural educational system. The increased costs should represent an investment in the future productivity of the economy. Unfortunately, the evidence indicates that the rate of economic return to education in China is very low, much below that in other developing countries. Studies undertaken by graduate students at the University of Chicago indicate that a large part of the return to education for farm people in China is not in increasing their productivity in agriculture but in increasing their chances of obtaining a higher paying nonagricultural job (Yang 1993; Zhao 1993). It is reasonable to assume that the low rate of return will not persist as the technological level of productive activities approaches those of developed countries.

ARE THERE SIGNIFICANT RISKS IN THE ALTERNATIVE APPROACH?

Policymakers may respond that an approach that combines appropriate change designed to reduce the desired number of children with the provision of *voluntary* family planning measures might result in a delay of some years in China's maintaining a voluntarily achieved and sustained replacement level of fertility. If there were a delay, the long-run size of the population would be increased. Would there be a substantial risk—a large cost—in terms of the future economic development of the Chinese economy if a larger population were the result of the alternative policy?

Current Policies May Not Be Viable in the Long Run

It is far from certain that the stationary population level that would result from the alternative policies would differ significantly from what present policies will generate. If nothing is done with respect to land allocation and ownership and other measures to provide old-age security, and no special effort is made to increase the education of young rural women, the number of children rural families would voluntarily elect to have will change very slowly over time. Consequently the tensions that still exist in the countryside because of the birth quotas that limit the number of children each family may have are likely to continue indefinitely. In order to prevent social disorder and unrest it may be necessary at times to accept relaxation of the enforcement of current policies. This appears to have been the reason for the relaxation of enforcement of population control in the mid-1980s followed by a significant increase in birth rates from 1986 through 1990. According to official data, birth rates for 1986–89 averaged 20 percent more than the average for 1984–85. A temporary increase in birth rates has a permanent effect on population size even when that increase is followed by a sharp tightening of enforcement as appears to have occurred in late 1991.

Adverse Effects of a Larger Population Are Exaggerated

Since policymakers may be risk averse, one might ask what would be the consequences if China reached a stable population a decade or two later and with 10 percent more people under the alternative policy?[4] A strong case can be made that there would be no significant difference in the welfare of the average Chinese if the population is stabilized at a level that is 10 percent higher. (It should be recognized, of course, that substantial future population growth in China is a virtual certainty under any policy regime that might be contemplated.) Space is limited but let us first consider the case for "less is better"—a smaller population is preferred to a larger—and then turn to the reasons why population size is largely irrelevant to the welfare of that population.

The belief that there are now or will be too many people has an ancient origin. Approximately 18 centuries ago Tertullian wrote: "The greatest evidence of the large numbers of people: we are burdensome to the world, the resources are scarcely adequate to us; our needs straiten us and complaints are everywhere while already nature does not sustain us. Truly, pestilence and hunger and war and flood must be considered as a remedy for nations, like a pruning back of the human race becoming excessive in numbers" (Holland 1993: 329).

Thus Malthus's gloomy conclusion concerning the effect of population growth on per capita food supply was hardly original, yet the model or theory that is now used to support the conclusion of significant negative effects of population growth on real per capita incomes has hardly advanced beyond where he left it. Two reasons have dominated the argument that population growth can have adverse effects. First, important resources are in fixed supply and, second, there are diminishing returns to the application of other resources—labor and capital—to the fixed resources. The fixed resources include land for producing food; minerals; water for human, industrial, and agricultural use; and energy and space for living.

Food Supply and Technological Innovation

A critical question is whether diminishing returns are a serious restraint on maintaining at least constant per capita incomes and food supplies. So far, the empirical record says that diminishing returns have not been such a restraint, but this is not enough to satisfy those who fear the effects of population growth. For most of the nineteenth century and the first half of the twentieth, the world's increased food supply came mostly from expanding the cultivated area. Diminishing returns were not a potential restraint on production expansion since land and labor devoted to crop production increased at more or less the same pace. But the expansion of the cultivated area is now more costly than in the past—there is room, though only with heavy investment, for expanding the cultivated area in Africa and South America (FAO 1993). But for most of the rest of the world, including China, nearly all future growth in crop production must and will come from increasing output per unit of cultivated land.

The world's population has more than doubled between 1950 and 1990 while the cropland area increased by about 20 percent. And almost all of the increase in cropland occurred prior to 1975. Yet per capita food output has continued to increase and the real prices (costs) of food have continued to decline. The law of diminishing returns has not been repealed; it can't be. It remains as true today as it was in 1950 that, other things constant, adding a kilogram of fertilizer to a hectare of land sown to wheat will result in a smaller increase in output than the previous applications of nitrogen. But it also remains true that "other things" are not constant. Through experience and research mankind can now produce two blades of grass or two ears of corn where one grew before. In fact, in some parts of the world, four ears of corn grow where one grew before.

Land has not been a significant restraint on food production in recent years because we have learned how to make resources more productive. This has been true of labor and capital as well as land, and this is why real per capita incomes are now far higher than ever before. If one thinks of the function that relates output of a crop to a range of fertilizer inputs, land held constant, it has been possible to shift that function to the right not once or twice but more or less continuously, year after year for the past five decades. No single discovery has been the source of the yield increases; literally scores of small changes have occurred. When hybrid corn was first introduced in the United States in the mid-1930s, if all other inputs were held constant, yields per unit of land increased 15 percent. Yields were then about 2 tones per hectare, rising to 8.2 tons per hectare in 1992 and averaging 7.4 tons per ha over the four years ending in 1993. Hybrid corn was a necessary but not sufficient condition for the enormous increase in output.

Probably no idea has been more durable and more widely accepted, in spite of its contradiction and repudiation by history, than the conclusion that food production could not keep up with population growth. Those who have accepted this conclusion saw the potential neither for expanding the world's cultivated area nor for increasing yields. Let us consider a brief review of the record since the end of the eighteenth century when Malthus wrote (World Bank 1992; Fogel 1992; Bogue 1969):

- Today only three countries, comprising 1.3 percent of the world's population, have a lower per capita caloric supply of food than France had in the 1780s.
- At the end of the eighteenth century, England's per capita production of calories was 10 percent below India's daily consumption in 1989.
- People in the world's poorest countries now eat as well as or better than people in the world's richest countries two centuries ago.
- The improvements in per capita food supplies occurred while the world's population increased more than sixfold.
- The lowest life expectancy at birth in any country today (42 years) is significantly higher than was the case in France and England at the beginning of the nineteenth century, the two most developed countries at that time.

Rapid Population Growth Is Consistent with Rapid Economic Growth

The period of rapid population growth in the developed countries was from the middle of the eighteenth to the last quarter of the twentieth century. This was also the period of the most rapid economic growth of those countries and the period of great improvement in the standard of living. Life expectancy at birth in Western Europe and the United States was less than 41 years as late as 1840; it is now about 75. In the United States infant mortality was 160 per thousand births in 1900, declining to half that number 20 years later and to less than 10 today.

The rate of population growth in the developing countries from 1750 to 1920, at 0.4 percent annually, was significantly less than in the developed countries, yet this period saw very little improvement in the well-being of their people (Bogue 1969: 49). The growth rate of China's population from 1750 to 1925 is estimated at 0.4 percent annually; clearly slow population growth does not assure improvement in the welfare of a population. Until well into the twentieth century, life expectancy in the developing countries was no more than 25 to 30 years, reaching approximately 40 by 1950. After centuries of stagnation followed by a brief period with modest increase, life expectancy in developing countries has increased rapidly, reaching approximately 62 years by 1990 (World Bank 1992). During the period 1950–90 the developing countries saw unprecedented increases in population. Population growth after 1950 averaged over 2 percent annually, more than double the rate of the developed countries. Yet this was the period of remarkable growth of real income per capita—2.9 percent annually for 1965–85 compared to 2.4 percent for the developed countries (World Bank 1986). Rapid population growth has been and is consistent with rapid economic growth.

Does Population Growth Matter?

The above is a brief summary of the record—the greatest improvements in the living standards and the rapid declines in mortality have been achieved during periods of high rates of population growth. The periods of slow population growth in the world's history were periods of near stagnation and China was no exception.

How can this record be squared with the view that continued population growth is a threat to human welfare? In asking the question I do not imply that rapid population growth has been the cause of the improvements in human welfare. It seems that more probable that if there is a causal relationship, it is from improvements in productivity (real per capita income) to population growth. But it is incumbent on those who act on the conclusion that there are significant negative consequences to population growth to provide evidence that verifies such consequences.

Support for negative consequences cannot be found in cross-country comparisons of the relationship between population growth rates and per capita real income growth rates for either the developing countries alone or for all countries during the past several decades. Table 2 presents regressions of growth rates in per capita gross domestic product (GDP) for three decades for developing countries on lagged population growth, lagged GDP level, and primary school enrollment. In the six regression coefficients of income growth on lagged population growth rate, only one is significantly different from zero at the 10 percent level of significance and that was for the middle-income developing countries during the 1960s. None of the co-efficients of the lagged population variable for the low-income countries was significantly different from zero but all had positive signs, quite the opposite of what those who believe population growth has an adverse effect on income growth would expect. . . .

Table 2. Cross-Country Regressions of Per Capita GDP Growth Rates

	1960–70	1970–80	1980–90
Low-income countries			
Lagged population growth	0.053	0.115	0.319
Primary school enrollment	−0.015	0.025	−0.015
Lagged GDP growth	0.226	−0.221	−0.286
Lagged GDP level	−0.001	−0.003*	−0.00
Dummy: Africa	−0.931	−0.742	−3.371*
$\bar{R}^2$	−0.004	0.163	0.059
η	12	32	33
Middle-income countries			
Lagged population growth	−0.524**	0.319	−0.551
Primary school enrollment	0.017	0.029	0.024
Lagged GDP growth	0.236	0.163	0.320*
Lagged GDP level	−0.005	−0.000	−0.000**
Dummy: Africa	−0.711	−0.241	−0.792
Latin America	−0.859	−0.608	−2.115**
$\bar{R}^2$	0.163	−0.043	0.055
η	32	61	58

Notes: GDP data are from *Quarterly Journal of Economics,* vol. CVII, no. 2; World Bank, *World Development Report,* various years. Lagged population and lagged GDP growth rates are for the prior decade; lagged GDP level is for beginning year of the decade. Africa and Latin America dummies are 1 for country in region, 0 otherwise. Constant terms not presented. Low-income and middle-income as designated by the World Bank.

Sources: Summers and Heston (1991) and World Bank, *World Development Report,* various years.

*Statistically significant at 5 percent level.   **Statistically significant at 10 percent level.

The empirical relationships between population growth and per capita income growth are by themselves insufficient to prove that population has little or no effect on economic growth. Additional evidence and theoretical underpinnings are required. These are available in the report of the Working Group of the US National Research Council (National Research Council 1986). *Population Growth and Economic Development: Policy Questions.* This report systematically addresses the various relationships between population growth and economic growth and, in my opinion, supports the conclusion that population growth has little or no negative effect on economic development. Among its most important findings was that savings rates were independent of population growth and of the age structure (p. 87). This conclusion has been supported by later and independent work by Kelley (1988), who found little evidence that the aggregate savings rate was affected by population growth rates or by the age structure of the population. The substantial importance of savings rates is indicated by the consistently large coefficient for the investment share in GDP in Table 3. If population growth did have a negative effect on the savings rate, it would have an important negative effect on the growth of GDP per capita. The one significant negative effect of population growth was that the quality of schooling, as measured by levels of expenditure per pupil, was adversely affected. Enrollment rates, however, seem not to be negatively related to population growth rates.

To summarize, economic growth rates depend on many variables. China's own experience supports the view that fundamental governmental policies affecting how the economy is organized are the primary determinants of economic growth. The rapid economic growth that has followed the reforms begun in 1979 clearly indicates that for this period population growth could not have had a significant negative effect on China's economic growth. True, the annual rate of population growth after 1978 was 0.63 percentage points lower than in the two decades before, but the difference in growth of per capita consumption was several times greater than the difference in population growth rates.

Let us make the counterfactual assumption that the actual increase in China's population from 1979 through 1991 had been equal to the population growth rate of 1957 to 1978 and that the additional persons contributed nothing to national output. If this were true, the 7.2 percent per capita output growth for 1979–91 was only 0.63 percentage points greater than it would have been with the larger population. Compare this assumed effect to the actual difference in real annual per capita income growth rates of 3.3 percent for 1957–78 and 7.2 percent for 1979–91. For China, as for elsewhere, population growth is at most a minor factor in determining per capita income growth or other measures of economic development.

POPULATION GROWTH AND CHINA'S FOOD SUPPLY

I indicated above how technological change has overcome the restraints imposed by limited land resources and diminishing returns on improving per capita food supplies. But one cannot escape the conclusion that many Chinese, including decisionmakers, remain unconvinced that China has the capacity to provide all or most of the food that will be demanded by a future larger and richer population in spite of the remarkable improvements in the quantity and quality of food made since the inauguration of the rural reforms in 1979. It is difficult to understand the pessimism about the future if the accomplishments of the recent period are understood.

For the first time in its modern history, China has a daily per capita food intake of 2640 kilocalories that is adequate for a healthy labor force capable of working every day without limitations imposed by a lack of energy. This is a 33 percent greater caloric intake than in 1969–71 (FAO 1991). Per capita meat and poultry consumption in 1992 was about three times as much as in 1978 and more than 50 percent greater than in 1985. This large increase in meat and poultry output was achieved while grain stocks grew by more than 150 million tons from 1986 through 1990 and apparently increased somewhat more in the subsequent years (Crook 1993a).

The quantity and variety of fruits and vegetables increased enormously after 1984 in northern Chinese cities. Part of this improvement was due to the introduction of plastic film technology, and this technology (which extends the effective growing period) has a great unrealized potential. Part was due to removing the restraints on the importation of fruits and vegetables in the less well-endowed regions of China from other areas of the country.

As real per capita incomes increase, the demand for animal and poultry products will increase, though not at the 10 percent annual rate of growth of meat and poultry production from 1985 to 1992. If this rate of growth were to continue for a decade, annual per capita meat and poultry consumption would increase to 71 kg, the equivalent of the current consumption level in Western Europe. A significant part of the recent increase in production has come from the realization of output potentials that were suppressed under the commune system. One measure of this is the increase in pork production from 35 kg per hog in the livestock inventory at the beginning of 1980 to 69 kg in 1992. But this source of improved feeding efficiency is far from exhausted; in developed countries pork production per hog in the inventory is almost double the 1992 figure for China.

As striking as the agriculture output growth of the past 15 years has been in China, there remains a significant potential for further expansion. This is true for crop production as well as for livestock production. China now has a level of grain production more than adequate to meet all requirements for direct human consumption, seed, and industrial use, and sufficient for feed for a per capita consumption of meat and poultry that could not have been imagined as recently as 1980. But the present level of grain production does not mean that further significant production growth will not occur. If farmers are provided sufficient incentives, and the buying and selling of grain occurs in a normal market—thus eliminating the disincentive effects of the procurement process as it has functioned in recent years—grain production in the foreseeable future can continue to grow at 2 to 3 percent annually. This is a significantly higher growth rate than is required to reach the year 2000 goal of 500 million tons of grain.

If grain prices are to be held in check, it will be necessary to evolve land policies that permit the gradual enlargement of farms that specialize in grain production. As real wages rise, the costs of grain production will increase unless there is productivity improvement that permits substitution of machinery for labor. Such substitution becomes profitable and consistent with steady or declining real prices of grain only as farm operating units are enlarged.[5]

This process will occur if the market is permitted to function through buying and selling and renting of land or land use rights. Thus the policy change that would permit farm households to obtain old-age security through owning their land or the rights to use the land as an alternative to having sons would also contribute to greater efficiency in grain production.[6] A negative factor for agricultural production is the continuing loss of cropland to the boom in rural housing, industrial development in rural areas, roads, and city expansion. With improved policies, such as zoning and proper pricing of land, the loss of land can be reduced to less than the recent annual rates of about 0.4 percent (Smil 1993). It may be noted that the actual area of cultivated land exceeds the published estimates of the State Statistical Bureau by as much as 40 percent (Crook 1993b: 34). Many factors besides the amount of land affect food output, including research and input and output prices. In any case, China is not living in isolation. It can procure food by exporting nonagricultural products, certainly in amounts equal to the effect of declining land area on farm output.

Chinese farmers will not be called on to increase food production at the same rate as their remarkable achievements of the past 15 years. Even with the high rate of growth in per capita food consumption, over the last few years farmers have been faced with declining real prices for grains. This is a clear indication that supply has not been lagging demand—neither for grain for human consumption nor for all other uses of grain, including grain for the rapidly growing livestock sector.

CONCLUDING COMMENTS

By changing relatively few policies that now encourage high fertility and by significantly increasing education at the primary and secondary levels in rural areas, China would achieve even lower rates of fertility if families were permitted to have the number of children desired and the means were available to them to achieve that objective.

Two important policy changes are now under consideration in China. At the Beijing Conference on China's Reform and Development in December 1993 the theme report proposed that when the existing land contracts run out, the new use contracts be issued for 30 years and that during that period the distribution of land should remain unchanged whether the number of people increased or decreased. A second proposal was that the household registration system "shall be gradually phased out." The purpose of this proposal is to reduce the current isolation of the countryside—to gradually eliminate the separation of urban and rural areas and to bring China's urbanization to a level comparable with other countries with similar per capita incomes. There are indications that steps have been announced to make it much easier to change from a rural to an urban registration (Chen 1994: A19).

A third important proposed policy change was that the rural social security system be strengthened. However, the proposal was "to develop the mutual assistance and cooperations among the farmers within the communities with the support from the State." A subsequent statement by He Guanghui, Vice Minister of the State Commission for Restructuring the Economic System, ruled out a national social security system for rural areas comparable to what is available in urban areas (He 1994: 59). Apparently no major change is contemplated: "The broad number of rural residents should continue to uphold the good traditional practices of looking after the elderly at home and helping their neighbors." Thus, son preference would continue to be a major factor of fertility decisions of rural families. At the 1994 session of the United Nations Population Commission, the Chinese representative, Mme. Pen Yu, stated that the rural social security network "with its expenses shared by the government, local communities and individuals, [has] been developed and [has] now covered 31.5 percent of the nation's rural areas, reducing the people's desire for more children." She recognized that "economic development, improvement of women's status and promotion of social welfare services are part of the major causes for the decline of population birth rate . . . in China, especially in her east provinces in recent years" (Peng 1994: 490). It is highly probable, however, that the social security network, which she did not describe, is limited primarily to the higher-income rural communities and is not generally available in the rural areas of China with the highest birth rates.

A fourth policy change—perhaps the most important one—namely, significantly increasing the eduction of rural youth, especially girls, received no mention in the report of the conference organizers nor do there appear to be any major policy changes under consideration that would allocate more funds from the central budget to support rural education.

The two policy changes now under consideration—modification of the barriers to migration, and long-term land use rights not subject to reallocation due to population change—if implemented are important steps that will improve the circumstances of rural life, reduce desired fertility in rural areas, and further reduce the national fertility rate as migrants quickly adopt the fertility patterns found in urban areas. These are positive steps that will reduce the tension between rural families and the government. But a further substantial voluntary reduction in rural fertility will require improving educational opportunities for rural youth and providing alternatives to sons in achieving old-age security. A further reform of the land system that would permit the ownership, sale, and renting of farm land would go far toward providing such security.

My final point is this. The appropriate national population policy is to provide families with the means to have the number of children they desire combined with the adoption of policies and institutions that are known to influence fertility desires in the direction of achieving a total fertility rate voluntarily sustained at the replacement level. This is clearly not an argument for rapid population growth. It is an argument that any country that is concerned about the growth and size of its population should review and modify its current policies and institutions that have significant pronatalist effects rather than resort to penalties and coercive measures to influence fertility decisions. To do so would not only help a country to achieve its population goals but would contribute both to improving the productivity of its human and physical resources and to increasing real per capita incomes. It is an argument based on the assumption that if people are given the appropriate incentives, their personal decisions will be in the interest of all.

NOTES

1. There is contradictory evidence on how prevalent land reallocation is. Prosterman and Hanstad (1993) report a study by the former Research Center for Rural Development of the State Council that found that in 280 villages surveyed, land readjustments due to demographic change occurred in 65.2 percent. However, in a survey of approximately 800 households in four counties in 1987 and 1988 Feder et al. (1992) reported that in three of the counties only 17 to 24 percent of the farmers thought there was a likelihood of contract disruption during the period of their contract while in one county 75 percent feared such disruption (p. 7).

2. In rural areas fines of varying amounts are imposed when a child is born outside the birth quotas. These fines negate a part of the benefit of land reallocation on the birth of a child. But the existence of the fines in no way contradicts the fact that land reallocation is a pronatalist policy and that if this policy were abandoned, a is now under consideration, there would be a reduction in the number of children desired by rural families. The fines offset part of the pronatalist effect of the land reallocation, just as the whole structure of the population policy—birth quotas enforced by an array of penalties of which the fines are one—serves to reduce the effects on birth rates of the array of pronatalists rural policies and institutions. It is not claimed that the existing population programs have no effect on birth rates. The argument is that a significant though unknown part of the restraining effects of the birth quotas is necessary to offset the effects of various pronatalist policies on the desired number of children.

3. It was estimated in the early 1980s that it cost 2,200 yuan for a child to be reared to age 16 (Qian 1983). Assuming that rural prices increased by 75 percent by 1989, the cost of a child became 3,850 yuan; the undiscounted annual cost per year for a child would be 240 yuan. This is less than a third more than the increase in family income due to the reallocation of land; it would take a very modest contribution of the child to the family's income in the teenage years to fully cover the child's cost.

4. Space does not permit considering the environmental consequences of population and economic growth in China. I have dealt with some of these effects elsewhere though not with the global warming issue that now seems to dominate so much of the environmental literature. While I agree with at least some of the skeptics that the warnings of global warming and the adverse consequences that are projected are based on weak foundations (Smil 1993: 131–136), this is not the reason for excluding the issue. My reason is that the alternative population policy that I am proposing here would result in a stationary Chinese population little or no larger than a continuation of the present

set of policies and institutions. The alternative population policy is not one of encouraging unrestricted population growth. Quite the contrary, it includes measures designed to change the desired number of children. The current mix of policies is analogous to two mules hitched to different ends of a wagon and pulling against each other. China now has policies with pronatalist effects that it tries to offset by rationing the number of births. It is not obvious that this mix of contradictions can persist indefinitely.

5. China should avoid the mistakes made in the land and farm policies of Japan and Taiwan. The land reform policies adopted in those economies in the 1950s included stringent controls over the buying, selling, and renting of land, and in spite of some reform efforts most of the restraints exist today. A major effect of these policies has been to prevent enlargement o the cultivated area as required by the rise in the real earnings of labor. The result has been that the costs of producing land-intensive farm products, such as grain, have risen in real terms in Japan though much less so in Taiwan. While in international markets grain prices have declined since the 1950s, grain prices in Japan have increased sharply due to the high costs of producing grain on farms of one hectare. By permitting and supporting the consolidation of fields and joint farm work, Taiwan has overcome most of the adverse effects of the small size of farms.

6. If the expansion in farm size is achieved through the market, specialized grain farms will emerge and meet the demand for grain while employing significantly less labor than is now the case. The labor shifted out of grain production would go to nonagricultural sectors. The decline in the share of farm employment will have a permanent effect in reducing fertility. The increase in China's national income due to the transfer of labor from low to high productivity employments will provide the capacity to purchase grain in world markets in case of natural disasters and thus enhance the government's ability to assure its citizens adequate food at all times.

Editor's Note: The original article was edited for publication here.